STUDY GUIDE

PARKIN

MICROECONOMICS

SECOND EDITION

STUDY GUIDE

PARKIN

MICROECONOMICS

SECOND EDITION

DAVID E. SPENCER

Brigham Young University

ADDISON-WESLEY PUBLISHING COMPANY

Reading, Massachusetts • Menlo Park, California • New York
Don Mills, Ontario • Wokingham, England • Amsterdam • Bonn
Sydney • Singapore • Tokyo • Madrid • San Juan • Milan • Paris

Reproduced by Addison-Wesley from camera-ready copy supplied
by the author.

Copyright © 1993 by Addison-Wesley Publishing Company, Inc.

ISBN 0-201-54666-3
1 2 3 4 5 6 7 8 9 10-BA-9695949392

CONTENTS

GUIDE TO SECOND EDITION CONTENTS: ECONOMICS, MICROECONOMICS, MACROECONOMICS

PREFACE:
TO THE STUDENT

My objective in preparing this *Study Guide* to accompany *Microeconomics, Second Edition,* by Michael Parkin is to help you master course material in order to do well on examinations. If that objective is realized, you will not only achieve a higher grade in the course but you will develop a deeper understanding of economics and the many economic issues that play such an important role in all our lives.

A study guide, however, is not a substitute for the text. Before you approach a chapter in the *Study Guide*, you should carefully read the corresponding chapter in the text. The major purpose of this *Study Guide*, then, is to *reinforce* and *deepen* your understanding of economics, not to initiate that understanding. I have tried to keep that purpose sharply in focus as I have prepared each chapter. Each chapter of the *Study Guide* contains two parts. The first part contains four sections intended to enhance your individual study effectiveness while the second part consists of several self-test sections followed by answers to all the self-test questions. Let's take a look at the basic content of each chapter by discussing each of these sections.

CHAPTER CONTENTS

Chapter in Perspective: As students proceed from chapter to chapter through the text, they frequently get bogged down in the detail and lose sight of the broader picture. The purpose of this first section of each *Study Guide* chapter is to put each chapter of the text into perspective by indicating how it relates to preceding and following chapters and by highlighting some of the central issues that are examined.

Learning Objectives: This section simply repeats the learning objectives from the text. As you work through each chapter of the *Study Guide*, it would be a good idea to ask yourself if you have achieved each of these objectives.

Helpful Hints: When you encounter difficulty in mastering concepts or techniques, you will not be alone. Many students find certain concepts difficult and often make the same kinds of mistakes. A major purpose of this section is to help students avoid these common errors. An additional purpose is to highlight or supplement the text's discussion of key concepts.

Key Figures and Tables: Each chapter of the text contains numerous figures and tables but not all are equally important. Some are designated as "key" figures or tables and identified in the textbook by a diamond-shaped icon. In this section each of these is discussed to help you focus your study on the most important diagrams.

Self-Test: Along with the Helpful Hints, this will be the most useful section of the *Study Guide*. The questions are designed to give you practice and to test the skills and techniques you must master to do well on exams. The Self-Test section contains five parts (listed below) and is followed by an Answer section.

Concept Review: This section contains simple "recall" questions designed to check your knowledge of the basic terminology and fundamental concepts of each chapter. These questions should build your confidence. This part is not a test of deep understanding, or mastery of analytical skills.

True or False: These questions test your basic knowledge of chapter concepts as well as your ability to apply these concepts. These are the first questions to challenge your understanding to see if you can identify mistakes in statements using basic concepts.

Multiple Choice: These more difficult questions test your analytical ability by asking you to apply concepts to new situations, to manipulate information, and to solve numerical and graphical problems. Since most examinations will consist mainly—if not exclusively—of multiple choice questions, these questions will provide useful practice.

Short Answer: Each chapter contains several short answer questions that ask about basic concepts and can generally be answered in a few sentences or a paragraph. Avoid the tendency simply to read the questions and think you know the answer. Writing down brief responses or answering the questions out loud in a study group will prove to be very beneficial.

Problems: The best way to learn economics is to do problems. Thus each self-test concludes with a collection of several numerical or graphical problems. In most chapters, this section will be the most challenging part of the Self-Test. It is also likely to be the most helpful in deepening your understanding of the chapter material. The problems are designed to teach as much as to test. They are purposely arranged so as to lead you through the problem-solving analysis in a gradual and sequential fashion, from easier to more difficult parts.

Answers: The Self-Test is followed by a section that contains the answers to all Self-Test items. I recommend that you complete the entire Self-Test before looking at the answers. Then, when you find a difference between your answer and the correct answer, return to the text chapter to correct or extend your understanding.

SOME FRIENDLY ADVICE

The best way to ensure a good grade in your economics course is to develop a thorough understanding of economics, and that will require effort. There is no effective method short of that. With that in mind, let me offer some advice on how to develop such an understanding and how this study guide can help.

1. *Read the chapter in the text first.* Make a commitment to yourself at the beginning of the course that you will read the relevant chapter *before* your instructor lectures on it. You may be amazed at how your instructor's ability to teach improves if you come to class prepared. In this initial reading, note the concepts and issues that seem more difficult but don't concentrate on these yet. Your purpose at this point is to get a general understanding of the concepts and issues.

2. *Read the first four sections of the study guide chapter.* Study both the Helpful Hints and Key Figures and Tables sections especially carefully. They are intended first to help you identify which ideas and concepts are relatively more important and then to help you extend and deepen your understanding of them. Hopefully, some of the difficulties you noted in your first reading of the textbook chapter will be overcome by this process.

3. *Keep a good set of lecture notes.* Good lecture notes are vital for focusing your study. Your instructor will only lecture on a subset of topics from the textbook and those topics should usually be given priority when studying for exams.

4. *Return to the text.* After your instructor's lecture, read the chapter again, but this time for mastery of the detail. Use a pencil and paper to make notes and to work through the analysis of the text, especially when graphs are involved. By the end of this experience

you should have a thorough understanding of the material and be ready to test yourself.

5. *Complete the Self-Test sections of the study guide.* To test your understanding and to identify areas of weakness, complete the Concept Review, True or False, Multiple Choice, Short Answer, and Problem sections of the Self-Test. I recommend using a pencil to write your answers in the *Study Guide*. This will allow you to erase your mistakes and have neat, completed pages from which to study. I also recommend writing the answers to the Multiple Choice questions on a separate sheet of paper so that these questions can be freshly reviewed later.

Avoid the mistake of thinking that because your test will only contain multiple choice questions, you will not benefit greatly from completing the Short Answer and Problem sections. Indeed, these may be the most instructive exercises.

As you respond to the Short Answer questions, you will learn more if you will take the time *actually to write* brief responses rather than simply saying to yourself: "I know the answer to that one." The act of physically writing answers will reveal weaknesses of which you are yet unaware. This is at least as true for working through the Problems section. The problems are generally sequential and intended to guide you step-by-step through some important aspect of economic analysis. In many cases, your deepest learning will take place as you work these problems.

Once you have tested your understanding and identified areas where that understanding might be weak, you should review the relevant parts of the textbook chapter.

6. *Use your instructor and/or teaching assistants.* When you have questions about any concept, ask someone who can give you appropriate help. Depending on the arrangements at your university, your instructor or the teaching assistants assigned to your class are anxious to

respond to your questions and, indeed, expect you to ask them.

7. *Carefully prepare for each exam.* If you have followed the previous six suggestions, you are an unusually wise student and your preparation for exams will be much less frustrating than for many of your colleagues. In preparation for an exam, review your lecture notes as well as each chapter in the text paying special attention to the Review sections and to each Chapter Summary. For each chapter, take another look at the Helpful Hints and Key Figures and Tables sections of the *Study Guide*. Also, quickly review the sections of the Self-Test, *except* the Multiple Choice section. If you used paper and pencil as you previously worked through the Short Answer and Problems sections, your review will likely proceed more quickly. Then, as a final preparation, complete the Multiple Choice section of the study guide again. This time, however, be sure not only to know why the correct choice is correct, but also to see if you *know why each incorrect choice is incorrect*. If you can do this, you will be very well prepared.

If available, working old exams your instructor has given in previous years is an excellent additional preparation. In addition to providing useful practice, old exams give you a feel for the style of question your instructor may ask. Remember, though, that old exams are a useful study aid only if you use them to *understand* the reasoning behind each question. Do not try to memorize answers in the hope that your instructor will ask the same question again.

8. *Form a study group.* A very useful way to motivate your study and to learn economics is to discuss the things you are learning with other students. As you discuss concepts and issues *aloud*, your understanding will deepen and your areas of weakness will become apparent. When you answer a question in your head only, you often skip steps in the chain of reasoning without realizing it. When you are forced to explain your reasoning out loud,

gaps and mistakes quickly appear, and you (and your fellow group members) can readily correct your reasoning.

As you effectively use the textbook and study guide together, you will not only be well prepared for tests, but, more important in the long run, you will have developed analytical skills and powers of reasoning that will benefit you throughout your life.

DO YOUR HAVE ANY FRIENDLY ADVICE FOR ME?

I have attempted to make this *Study Guide* as clear and as useful as possible, and to avoid errors. No doubt, I have not been entirely successful. This study guide has been carefully checked for errors but, most likely some were not detected. If you discover errors or have other suggestions for improving the *Study Guide*, please let me know. Send your correspondence to

> Professor David E. Spencer
> Department of Economics
> Brigham Young University
> Provo, UT 84602

ACKNOWLEDGMENTS

One cannot teach bright and motivated economics students without learning much from them about how to do a better job. Thus, I am grateful to the many students I have had the privilege of knowing. I would also like to express appreciation to Barbara Rifkind, Marjorie Williams, Cindy Johnson, Kari Heen, Amy Willcutt, and Sarah Hallet Corey at Addison-Wesley Publishing Co. Above all, I am grateful to my wife, Jan, whose love and support, both direct and indirect, continue to be invaluable.

Provo, Utah   D.E.S.

1 WHAT IS ECONOMICS?

CHAPTER IN PERSPECTIVE

This first chapter introduces the *subject* of economics by briefly discussing what kinds of questions economics tries to answer and why these questions are interesting and important. The fundamental economic problem is scarcity. Because wants exceed the resources available to satisfy them, we cannot have everything we want and must make choices. This problem leads to economizing behavior — choosing the best or optimal use of the resources available. Economics, as a subject, is the study of how we use limited resources to try to satisfy unlimited wants.

This chapter also introduces the *method* of economics: how economists use economic theory and models to answer economic questions and to analyze and understand how people and economic systems cope with the fundamental problem of scarcity.

LEARNING OBJECTIVES

After studying this chapter, you will be able to:

- State the kinds of questions that economics tries to answer

- Explain why all economic questions and economic activity arise from scarcity

- Explain why scarcity forces people to make choices

- Define opportunity cost

- Describe the function and the working parts of an economy

- Distinguish between positive and normative statements

- Explain what is meant by an economic theory and how economic theories are developed by building and testing economic models

HELPFUL HINTS

1. The definition of economics (the study of how people use limited resources to satisfy unlimited wants) leads us directly to three important economic concepts—choice, opportunity cost, and competition. Since wants exceed resources, we cannot have everything we want and therefore must make *choices* among alternatives. In making a choice we forgo alternatives that we might have chosen and the *opportunity cost* of any choice is the value of the best forgone alternative. The fact that wants exceed resources also means that wants and individuals must *compete* against each other for the scarce resources.

2. Another fundamental point of this chapter is that economics is a science. It is important to understand that, like other sciences, economics seeks to enlarge our understanding of the world by constructing, examining, and testing *economic models*. Such models are highly simplified representations of the real world. Rather than making models less useful, this simplicity actually enhances their usefulness. By selectively abstracting from the less relevant complexity of the real world, economic models allow us to focus more clearly on those factors that are most important for the question under investigation.

Models are frequently compared to maps, which are useful because they "abstract from" real world detail. A map does not indicate every feature of the landscape (e.g., trees, streetlamps, etc.) but rather offers a simplified view, which is carefully selected according to the purpose of the map.

3. The most important purpose for studying economics is not to learn *what* to think about economics but *how* to think about economics. The "what" — the facts and descriptions of the economy — can always be found in books. The principal value of a course in economics is the ability to think critically about economic problems and to understand how the economy works. This comes through the mastery of economic theory and model-building.

KEY FIGURE

Figure 1.1 A Picture of the Economy
This figure illustrates the flow of goods and services as well as flows of money in the economy. There are three decision-making sectors (households, firms, and governments) and two groups of markets (goods markets and factor markets). Households supply factors of production to firms through factor markets for which they receive payment of wages, interest, rent, and profits. Firms supply goods and services to households through goods markets for which they receive money payments. Governments collect taxes from both households and firms and supply goods and services to both in addition to other benefits (transfer payments) to households and subsidies to firms.

SELF-TEST

CONCEPT REVIEW

1. The fundamental and pervasive fact that gives rise to economic problems is _____. This simply means that human wants _____ the resources available to satisfy them. The inescapable consequence is that people must make_____.

2. When we choose an action, the value of the best forgone alternative is the _____ cost of that action.

3. The process of evaluating the costs and benefits of our choices in order to do the

best we can with limited resources is
called _____.

4. An economy is a mechanism that determines _____ is produced,
_____ it is produced, and
_____ _____ it is pro-
duced.

5. The three groups of decision makers in
the economy are _____,
_____, and _____.

6. Factors of production are classified under
three general headings. The physical and
mental resources of human beings are
called _____, natural resources
are called _____, and manufactured goods used in production (e.g.,
machines and factories) are called
_____.

7. While all economies must have some way
of coordinating choices, there are two fundamental mechanisms. The _____
mechanism relies on the authority of some
kindof central planning, while the
_____ mechanism relies on the
adjustment of _____ in economic
markets. A(n) _____ economy
has elements of both of these fundamental
mechanisms.

8. An economy that is economically linked
with other economies in the world is
called _____.

9. Statements about what *is* are called

_____ statements, while those
about what *ought* to be are called
_____ statements.

10. The branch of economics that studies the
choices of individual households and
firms is called _____, while the
branch which studies behavior of the
economy as a whole is called
_____.

TRUE OR FALSE

____ 1. Scarcity is a problem only for capitalist (market) economies.

____ 2. Economics is the study of how to use
unlimited resources to satisfy limited
wants.

____ 3. Scarcity can be eliminated through
cooperation.

____ 4. The notion of opportunity cost is
illustrated by the fact that because
Fred studied for his economics exam
last night he was unable to see a
movie with his friends.

____ 5. Competition is a contest for command over scarce resources.

____ 6. The opportunity cost of any action is
the cost of all forgone alternatives.

____ 7. To economists, capital is the money
used by businesses to buy assets.

____ 8. The pair of scissors a barber uses to
cut hair is an example of capital as a
factor of production.

____ 9. In an economy in which economic
activity is coordinated by a command

mechanism, the decisions of *what*, *how*, and *for whom* are the result of price adjustment.

____10. A mixed economy is one in which there is both internal and international trade.

____11. The U.S. is a pure market economy.

____12. In economics, a closed economy is one in which there is very limited economic freedom.

____13. The U.S. is an open economy.

____14. Careful and systematic observation and measurement are basic components of any science.

____15. Economics is not a science since it deals with the study of willful human beings and not inanimate objects in nature.

____16. "An increase in the income tax rate will cause total tax revenue to fall." This is an example of a positive statement.

____17. Science is silent on positive questions.

____18. A positive statement is about what *is*, while a normative statement is about what *will be*.

____19. One of the key assumptions of an economic model is that people make choices which they expect to make them as well-off as possible.

____20. Economic models are of very limited value in helping us understand the real world because they abstract from the complexity of the real world.

____21. Models are complete descriptions of reality.

____22. Microeconomic is concerned with the economy as a whole.

____23. Macroeconomics includes the study of the causes of inflation.

____24. Testing an economic model requires comparing its predictions against real world events.

____25. When the predictions of a model conflict with the relevant facts, a theory must be discarded or modified.

MULTIPLE CHOICE

1. The fact that human wants cannot be fully satisfied with available resources is called the problem of
   a. opportunity costs.
   b. scarcity.
   c. normative economics.
   d. what to produce.

2. The problem of scarcity
   a. exists only in economies which rely on the market mechanism.
   b. exists only in economies which rely on the command mechanism.
   c. exists in all economies.
   d. means that at least some prices are too high.

3. When the government chooses to use resources to build a dam, those resources are no longer available to build a highway. This illustrates the concept of
   a. microeconomics.
   b. macroeconomics.
   c. opportunity cost.
   d. optimizing.

4. Sally has the chance to either attend an economics lecture or play tennis. If she chooses to attend the lecture, the value of playing tennis is
    a. equal to the value of the lecture.
    b. greater than the value of the lecture.
    c. not comparable to the value of the lecture.
    d. the opportunity cost of attending the lecture.

5. The opportunity cost of getting a $10 haircut is
    a. the customer's best alternative use of the $10.
    b. the customer's best alternative use of the time it takes to get a haircut.
    c. the customer's best alternative use of both the $10 and the time it takes to get a haircut.
    d. the value of $10 to the barber.

6. *All* decision makers in an economy
    a. coordinate choices between groups.
    b. supply factors of production.
    c. make choices.
    d. produce goods or services.

7. Which of the following is an example of capital as a factor of production?
    a. Money held by General Motors
    b. A General Motors bond
    c. An automobile factory owned by General Motors
    d. All of the above

8. All of the following are factors of production *except*
    a. government.
    b. natural resources.
    c. land.
    d. labor.

9. A closed economy is one that
    a. has strict government control of production.
    b. has no economic links with other economies
    c. maintains strict control of its borders.
    d. is characterized by a dominant agricultural sector.

10. The U.S. economy is best described as a
    a. closed economy.
    b. market economy.
    c. command economy.
    d. mixed economy.

11. A normative statement is one about
    a. what is usually the case.
    b. the assumptions of an economic model.
    c. what ought to be.
    d. what is.

12. "The rich face higher income tax rates than the poor" is an example of
    a. a normative statement.
    b. a positive statement.
    c. a negative statement.
    d. a theoretical statement.

13. An economic model is tested by
    a. examining the realism of its assumptions.
    b. comparing its predictions with the facts.
    c. the Testing Committee of the American Economic Association.
    d. the detail of its descriptions.

14. Which of the following is NOT a key assumption of an economic model?
    a. People have preferences.
    b. People economize.
    c. People are constrained by a given technology and a fixed amount of resources.
    d. People's choices are not coordinated.

15. When economists say that people are rational, it means they
    a. do not make errors of judgment.
    b. make the best decision from their perspective.
    c. act on complete information.
    d. will not later regret any decision made now.

16. The branch of economics that studies the decisions of individual households and firms is called
    a. microeconomics.
    b. macroeconomics.
    c. positive economics.
    d. normative economics.

17. All of the following are microeconomic issues EXCEPT
    a. wages and earnings.
    b. distribution of wealth.
    c. production.
    d. unemployment.

18. Which of the following would NOT be considered a macroeconomic topic?
    a. The reasons for a decline in the price of orange juice
    b. The cause of recessions
    c. The effect of the government budget deficit on inflation
    d. The determination of aggregate income

SHORT ANSWER

1. What is meant by scarcity?

2. Why does the existence of scarcity mean that we must make choices?

3. Why will cooperation not eliminate scarcity?

4. What is meant by opportunity cost? What is the opportunity cost of spending two hours studying for an economics exam?

5. Sarah takes five courses each school term. She is considering taking economics as her fifth course this term. If she decides to do so, what is the opportunity cost of taking the economics course?

6. What are the three broad classifications of factors of production? Give two examples of each.

7. Why is the U.S. economy considered to be mixed?

8. Is the following statement normative or positive? *Why?* "All college students should take an economics course."

9. How are economic models tested?

PROBLEMS

1. It takes one hour to travel from Boston to New York by airplane and five hours by train. Further, suppose that air fare is $100 and train fare is $60. Which mode of transportation has the lower opportunity cost for the following people?
    a) A person who can earn $5 an hour
    b) A person who can earn $10 an hour
    c) A person who can earn $12 an hour

2. Suppose the government builds and staffs a hospital in order to provide "free" medical care.
    a) What is the opportunity cost of the free medical care?
    b) Is it free from the perspective of society as a whole?

3. Indicate whether each of the following statements is positive or normative. If it is normative (positive), rewrite it so that it becomes positive (normative).
    a) "The government ought to reduce the size of the deficit in order to lower interest rates."

b) "Government imposition of a tax on tobacco products will reduce their consumption."

4. Suppose we examine a model of plant growth which predicts that, given the amount of water and sunlight, the application of fertilizer stimulates plant growth. How might you test the model?

ANSWERS

CONCEPT REVIEW

1. scarcity; exceed; choices
2. opportunity
3. optimizing
4. what; how; for whom
5. households; firms; governments
6. labor; land; capital
7. command; market; prices; mixed
8. open
9. positive; normative
10. microeconomics; macroeconomics

TRUE OR FALSE

1. F	6. F	11. F	16. T	21. F
2. T	7. F	12. F	17. F	22. F
3. F	8. T	13. T	18. T	23. T
4. T	9. F	14. T	19. F	24. T
5. T	10. F	15. F	20. F	25. T

MULTIPLE CHOICE

1. b	5. c	9. b	13. b	17. d
2. c	6. c	10. d	14. d	18. a
3. c	7. c	11. c	15. b	
4. d	8. a	12. b	16. a	

SHORT ANSWER

1. Scarcity is the universal condition that human wants always exceed the resources available to satisfy them.

2. The fact that goods and services are scarce means that individuals cannot have all of everything they want. It is therefore necessary to choose among alternatives.

3. Scarcity is a problem of essentially infinite wants and limited resources. While cooperation is one way to organize our activity as we confront the problem of scarcity, it cannot eliminate it and therefore cannot eliminate economic problems.

4. Opportunity cost is the best forgone alternative (opportunity). The opportunity cost of spending two hours studying for an economics exam is the best alternative activity you would have chosen. This, obviously, will be different for different individuals. It might be attending the opera, watching TV, or sleeping.

5. The opportunity cost of choosing the economics course is the course Sarah would have chosen otherwise. If her *next* best choice is a sociology course, then that would be the opportunity cost.

6. *Labor*: the effort and skill of a carpenter, the ability of an actor.
    Land: trees, water.
    Capital: a tractor, a factory building.

7. The U. S. economy is a mixed economy because it relies on both the market and command mechanisms. Most coordination is carried out through the market mechanism, but there are many economic decisions which are either made by or regulated by the government.

8. The given statement, however wise, is normative because it is about what ought to (should) be rather than what is.

9. Economic models are tested by comparing the model's predictions with the facts of the real world. If the predictions of the model are in conflict with those facts, the model is rejected, otherwise we do not reject the model.

PROBLEMS

1. The point here is to recognize that the opportunity cost of travel includes the best alternative value of travel time as well as the train or air fare.
   a) Thus, if the opportunity cost of the time spent traveling is the $5 an hour that could have been earned (but wasn't), the opportunity cost of train travel (in dollars) is the $60 train fare plus the $25 ($5 an hour times five hours) in forgone income for a total of $85. In this case the opportunity cost of air travel is the $100 air fare plus $5 in forgone income, for a total of $105. Therefore, for a person whose best alternative use of time is to earn $5 an hour, the opportunity cost of traveling by train is less than the opportunity cost of traveling by air.
   b) For a person who can earn $10 an hour, the opportunity cost of train travel will be $110 ($60 fare plus $50 in forgone earnings) and the opportunity cost of air travel is $110 ($100 fare plus $10 in foregone earnings). In this case the opportunity costs are the same.
   c) For a person who could have earned $12 an hour the opportunity cost of train travel ($120) exceeds the opportunity cost of air travel ($112).

2. a) Even though medical care may be offered without charge ("free"), there are still opportunity costs. The oppor-tunity cost of providing such health care is the best alternative use of the resources used in the construction of the hospital and the best alternative use of the resources (including human re-sources) used in the operation of the hospital.
   b) These resources are no longer available for other activities and therefore repre-sent a cost to society.

3. a) The given statement is normative. The following is positive:
   "If the government reduces the size of the deficit, interest rates will fall."
   b) The given statement is positive. The following is normative:
   "The government ought to impose a tax on tobacco products."

4. The prediction of the model can be tested by conducting the following experiment and carefully observing the outcome. Select a number of plots of ground of the same size which have similar characteris-tics and will be subject to the same amount of water and sunlight. Plant equal quantities of seeds in all the plots. In some of the plots apply no fertilizer and in some of the plots apply (perhaps varying amounts of) fertilizer. When the plants have grown, measure the growth of the plants and compare the growth mea-sures of the fertilized plots and the unfer-tilized plots. If plant growth is *not* greater in fertilized plots, we discard the theory (model).

2 MAKING AND USING GRAPHS

CHAPTER IN PERSPECTIVE

As a science, economics is characterized by systematic observation and measurement as well as the development of economic theory. In both of these components of economic science the use of graphs plays an important role.

Economic theory describes relationships among economic variables and graphs offer a very convenient way to represent such relationships. Indeed, the use of graphs allows us to economize in the sense that we are able to obtain much information with little effort. Graphs give a "picture" of the behavior of measured economic variables. Representing data graphically can be extremely useful for quickly conveying information about general characteristics of economic behavior.

As we will see in the next few chapters, graphical analysis of economic relationships is especially helpful when we are interested in discovering the theoretical consequences of a change in economic circumstances. Given the pervasive use of graphs in economics, this chapter reviews all the concepts and techniques you will need to construct and use graphs in this course.

LEARNING OBJECTIVES

After studying this chapter, you will be able to:

- Make and interpret a time-series graph and a scatter diagram

- Distinguish among linear and nonlinear relationships and relationships that have a maximum and a minimum

- Define and calculate the slope of a line

- Graph relationships among more than two variables

HELPFUL HINTS

1. The chapters of the text discuss numerous relationships among economic variables. Almost invariably these relationships will be represented and analyzed graphically. Thus an early, complete understanding of graphs will greatly facilitate mastery of the economic analysis of later chapters. Avoid the common mistake of assuming that a superficial understanding of graphs will be sufficient.

2. If your experience with graphical analysis is limited, this chapter will be crucial to your ability to readily understand later economic analysis. You will likely find significant rewards in occasionally returning to this chapter for review. If you are experienced in the construction and use of graphs, the chapter may be "old hat." Even in this case, the chapter should be skimmed and the Self-Test in this *Study Guide* completed. The main point is that you should be thoroughly familiar with the basic concepts and techniques of this chapter.

3. Slope is a *linear* concept since it is a property of a straight line. For this reason, the slope is constant along a straight line but is different at different points on a curved (nonlinear) line. When we are interested in the slope of a curved line, we actually calculate the slope of a straight line. The text presents two ways of choosing such a straight line and thus two alternative ways of calculating the slope of a curved line: (1) slope across an arc, and (2) slope at a point. The first of these calculates the slope of the *straight line* formed by the arc between two points on the curved line. The second calculates the slope of the *straight line* that just touches (is tangent to) the curve at a point.

4. Pay particular attention to graphing relationships among more than two variables.

KEY FIGURES

Figure 2.8 Positive Relationships

Variables that move up and down together are positively related. Three different positive relationships are illustrated in this figure. In each case, as the variable measured on the horizontal axis increases, the variable measured on the vertical axis also increases. Part (a) illustrates a positive linear relationship while parts (b) and (c) illustrate positive relationships that are not linear.

Figure 2.9 Negative Relationships

This figure is a companion to Fig. 2.8 and illustrates negative relationships. Variables that move in opposite directions are negatively related. Three different negative relationships are illustrated in this figure. In each case, as the variable measured on the horizontal axis increases, the variable measured on the vertical axis decreases. Part (a) illustrates a negative linear relationship, while parts (b) and (c) illustrate negative relationships that are not linear.

Figure 2.10 Maximum and Minimum Points

The relationship in part (a) reaches a maximum. As the variable measured on the horizontal axis increases, the value of the variable measured on the vertical axis increases, reaches a maximum at point *a* and then decreases. Similarly, the relationship in part (b) reaches a minimum at point *b*.

Figure 2.11 Variables with No Relationship

If there is no relationship between two variables, changes in one will have no effect on the other. The two parts of this figure illustrate how we can represent such a lack of relationship. Part (a) illustrates the fact that changes in the variable measured on the horizontal axis leave the variable measured on the vertical axis unchanged. Part (b) illustrates that changes in the variable measured on the vertical axis leave the variable measured on the horizontal axis unchanged.

Figure 2.12 The Slope of a Straight Line

The slope of a straight line tells us how much and in what direction the variable on the vertical axis changes when the variable on the horizontal axis changes. The slope is computed by dividing the change in y (the *rise*) by the change in x (the *run*). When both x and y move in the same direction, as in part (a), the slope is positive and when x and y move in opposite directions, as in part (b), the slope is negative.

Figure 2.13 The Slope of a Curve

Slope is a linear concept, so even when we measure the slope of a curve we do so by calculating the slope of a straight line. This figure illustrates the two ways of choosing a straight line to do this. Part (a) calculates the slope of the straight line that just touches (is tangent to) the curve at a point. Part (b) calculates the slope of the straight line formed by the arc between two points on the curved line.

Figure 2.14 Graphing a Relationship Among Three Variables

When graphing a relationship among three variables, we can reduce the problem to graphing the relationship between two variables by holding one of the variables constant and graphing the relationship between the other two. This is illustrated in this figure using as an example the relationship among ice cream consumption, the price of a scoop of ice cream, and air temperature. Part (a) shows the negative relationship between ice cream consumption and the price of a scoop of ice cream if the air temperature is held constant (at 70^0 F and also at 90^0 F). Part (b) shows the positive relationship between ice cream consumption and air temperature if the price of a scoop of ice cream is held constant. Finally, part (c) shows the positive relationship between the air temperature and the price of a scoop of ice cream if the consumption of ice cream is held constant.

CONCEPT REVIEW

1. A graph that measures an economic variable on the vertical axis and time on the horizontal axis is called a(n) _____-_____ graph.

2. The tendency for a variable to rise or fall over time is called the _____ of the variable.

3. Suppose the value of one economic variable is measured on the x-axis and the value of a second is measured on the y-axis. A diagram that plots the value of one variable corresponding to the value of the other is called a(n) _____ diagram.

4. If two variables tend to move up or down together they exhibit a(n) _____ relationship. Such a relationship is represented graphically by a line that slopes _____ (to the right).

5. Two variables that move in opposite directions exhibit a(n) _____ relationship. Such a relationship is represented graphically by a line that slopes _____ (to the right).

6. Suppose variables A and B are unrelated. If we measure A on the y-axis and B on the x-axis, the graph of A as we increase B will be a(n) _____ line.

7. The slope of a line is calculated as the change in the value of the variable measured on the _____ axis divided by the change in the value of the variable measured on the _____ axis.

8. A straight line exhibits _____ slope at all points.

9. To graph a relationship among more than two variables we simply graph the relationship between _____ variables, holding all others constant.

TRUE OR FALSE

____ 1. A time-series graph measures time on the horizontal axis.

____ 2. A time-series graph gives information about the level of the relevant economic variable, as well as information about changes and the speed of those changes.

____ 3. A graph that omits the origin will always be misleading.

____ 4. A two-variable time-series graph can help us see if the two variables tend to move together over time.

____ 5. A one-dimensional graph that represents measured rainfall along a horizontal line is an example of a scatter diagram.

____ 6. If the graph of the relationship between two variables slopes upward (to the right) the variables move up and down together.

____ 7. If variable a rises when variable b falls and falls when b rises, then the relationship between a and b is negative.

____ 8. If the relationship between y (measured along the vertical axis) and x (measured along the horizontal axis) is such that y reaches a maximum as x increases, then the relationship must be negative before and positive after the maximum.

____ 9. If the value of y (measured along the vertical axis) doesn't change as we increase x (measured along the horizontal axis), the graph of the relationship between x and y is horizontal.

____10. The graph of the "relationship" between two variables that are in fact unrelated will be either horizontal or vertical.

____11. The slope of a straight line is calculated by dividing the change in the value of the variable measured on the horizontal axis by the change in the value of the variable measured on the vertical axis.

____12. The slope of a curved line is not constant.

____13. If we want to graph the relationship among three variables, we must hold two of them constant as we represent the third.

____14. Refer to Fig. 2.1. The value of y increased between 1970 and 1971.

Figure 2.1

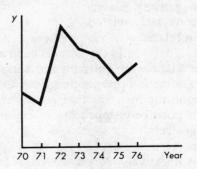

15. Refer to Fig. 2.1. The value of y increased much more rapidly between 1971 and 1972 than between 1975 and 1976.

16. Figure 2.1 is a scatter diagram.

17. In Fig. 2.2, the relationship between y and x is first negative, reaches a minimum, and then becomes positive as x increases.

Figure 2.2

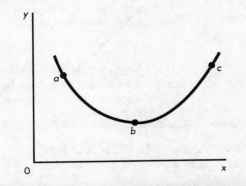

18. In Fig. 2.2, the slope of the curve is increasing as we move from point b to point c.

19. In Fig. 2.2, the slope of the curve is approaching zero as we move from point a to point b.

20. In Fig. 2.2, the value of x is a minimum at point b.

21. For a point on a two-variable graph, the length of the line running from the point to the vertical axis is the y-coordinate.

22. The slope of a line can be described as "rise over run."

23. For a straight line, if a small change in y is associated with a large change in x, the slope is large.

MULTIPLE CHOICE

1. The behavior of a single economic variable over time is best illustrated by a
a. one-variable graph.
b. two-variable graph.
c. time-series graph.
d. scatter diagram.

2. Figure 2.3 is a
a. one-variable time-series graph.
b. two-variable time-series graph.
c. scatter diagram.
d. both b and c.

3. The dotted line in Fig. 2.3 represents variable y. Which of the following statements best describes the relationship between x and y in Fig. 2.3?
a. x and y tend to move in opposite directions over time.
b. x and y tend to move together over time.
c. x tends to move in the same direction as y, but one year later.
d. y tends to move in the same direction as x, but one year later.

Figure 2.3

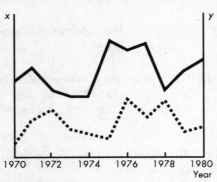

1970   1972   1974   1976   1978   1980
                                    Year

4. The data in Table 2.1 could <u>NOT</u> be represented by
    a. two one-variable time-series graphs.
    b. one two-variable time-series graph.
    c. a three-variable time-series graph.
    d. a scatter diagram.

Table 2.1

Year	x	y
1980	6.2	143
1981	5.7	156
1982	5.3	162

5. From the information in Table 2.1, it appears that
    a. x and y tend to exhibit a negative relationship.
    b. x and y tend to exhibit a positive relationship.
    c. there is no relationship between x and y.
    d. there is first a negative and then a positive relationship between x and y.

6. If variable, x and y move up and down together, they are said to be
    a. positively related.
    b. negatively related.
    c. conversely related.
    d. unrelated.

7. The relationship between two variables that move in opposite directions is shown graphically by a line that
    a. is positively sloped.
    b. is steep.
    c. is relatively flat.
    d. is negatively sloped.

8. What is the slope of the line in Fig. 2.4?
    a. 1
    b. -1
    c. -5
    d. -1/5

Figure 2.4

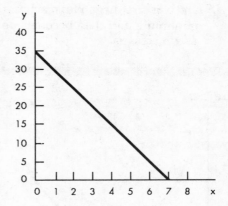

9. Refer to Fig. 2.4. When x is zero, y
    a. is zero.
    b. is 35.
    c. is 7.
    d. cannot be determined from the graph.

10. In Fig. 2.5 the relationship between x and y is
   a. positive with slope decreasing as x increases.
   b. negative with slope decreasing as x increases.
   c. negative with slope increasing as x increases.
   d. positive with slope increasing as x increases.

Figure 2.5

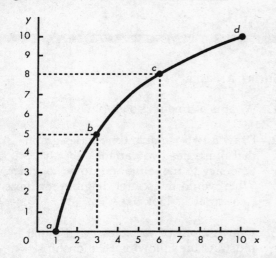

11. In Fig. 2.5, the slope across the arc between b and c is
   a. 1/2.
   b. 2/3.
   c. 1.
   d. 2.

12. In Fig. 2.5, consider the slopes of the arc between a and b and the arc between b and c. The slope at point b is difficult to determine exactly, but it must be
   a. greater than 5/2.
   b. about 5/2.
   c. between 5/2 and 1.
   d. less than 1.

13. If the price of an umbrella is low and the number of rainy days per month is large, more umbrellas will be sold each month. On the other hand, if the price of an umbrella is high and there are few rainy days per month, fewer umbrellas will be sold each month. On the basis of this information, which of the following statements is true?
   a. The number of umbrellas sold and the price of an umbrella are positively related, holding the number of rainy days constant.
   b. The number of umbrellas sold and the price of an umbrella are negatively related, holding the number of rainy days constant.
   c. The number of rainy days and the number of umbrellas sold are negatively related, holding the price of an umbrella constant.
   d. The number of rainy days and the price of an umbrella are negatively related, holding the number of umbrellas sold constant.

14. Given the data in Table 2.2, holding income constant, the graph relating the price of strawberries (vertical axis) to the purchase of strawberries (horizontal axis)
   a. is a vertical line.
   b. is a horizontal line.
   c. is a positively-sloped line.
   d. is a negatively-sloped line.

15. Consider the data in Table 2.2. Suppose family income decreases from $400 to $300 per week. Then the graph relating the price of strawberries (vertical axis) to the number of boxes of strawberries purchased (horizontal axis) will
   a. no longer exist.
   b. become positively sloped.
   c. shift to the right.
   d. shift to the left.

Table 2.2

Weekly family income (dollars)	Price per box strrawberries (dollars)	Number of boxes purchased per week
300	1.00	5
300	1.25	3
300	1.50	2
400	1.00	7
400	1.25	5
400	1.50	4

Figure 2.6

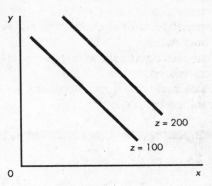

16. Given the data in Table 2.2, holding price constant, the graph relating family income (vertical axis) to the purchase of strawberries
    a. will be a positively sloped line.
    b. will be a negatively sloped line.
    c. reaches a maximum.
    d. cannot be drawn if we hold price constant.

17. In Fig. 2.6, x is
    a. positively related to y and negatively related to z.
    b. positively related to both y and z.
    c. negatively related to y and positively related to z.
    d. negatively related to both y and z.

SHORT ANSWER

1. What is a time-series graph?

2. Draw a two-variable time-series graph that illustrates two variables that have a tendency to move up and down together. What would the scatter diagram for these two variables look like?

3. Draw graphs of variables x and y that illustrate the following relationships.
   a) x and y move up and down together
   b) x and y move in opposite directions
   c) as x increases y reaches a maximum
   d) as x increases y reaches a minimum
   e) x and y move in opposite directions, but as x increases y decreases by larger and larger increments for each unit increase in x
   f) y is independent of the value of x
   g) x is independent of the value of y

4. What does it mean to say that the slope of a line is -2/3?

5. Explain how we measure the slope of a curved line
   a) at a point.

b) across an arc.

6. How do we graph a relationship among more than two variables (using a two-dimensional graph)?

7. Draw a curve that is positively sloped but starts out relatively flat, becomes steeper, and then gets flatter again as the variable measured on the horizontal axis increases.

PROBLEMS

1. Consider the data given in Table 2.3.
   a) Draw a time-series graph for the interest rate.
   b) Draw a two-variable time-series graph for both the inflation rate and the interest rate.
   c) Draw a scatter diagram for the inflation rate (horizontal axis) and the interest rate.
   d) Would you describe the general relationship between the inflation rate and the interest rate as positive, negative, or none?

2. Compute the slope of the lines in Fig. 2.7 (a) and (b).

3. Draw a straight line
   a) with slope = -10 and passing through the point given by x-coordinate = 2 and y-coordinate = 80.
   b) with slope = 2 along which $y = 10$ when $x = 6$.

4. Using the graph in Fig. 2.8, compute the slope
   a) across the arc between points a and b.
   b) at point b.
   c) at point c, and explain your answer.

Table 2.3

Year	Inflation rate (percent)	Interest rate (percent)
1970	5.4	6.4
1971	3.2	4.3
1972	3.4	4.1
1973	8.3	7.0
1974	11.8	7.9
1975	6.7	5.8
1976	4.9	5.0
1977	6.5	5.3
1978	8.6	7.2
1979	12.3	10.0

Figure 2.7 (a)

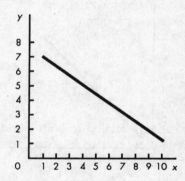

5 In Table 2.4, x represents the number of umbrellas sold per month, y represents the price of an umbrella, and z represents the average number of rainy days per month.
   a) On the same diagram, graph the relationship between x (horizontal axis) and y (vertical axis) when $z = 4$, when $z = 5$, and when $z = 6$. Suppose that, on average, it rains six days per month. This implies a certain average relationship between monthly umbrella sales

and umbrella price. Suppose that the "greenhouse effect" reduces the average monthly rainfall to four days per month. What happens to the graph of the relationship between umbrella sales and umbrella prices?

b) On a diagram, graph the relationship between x (horizontal axis) and z (vertical axis) when $y = \$10$ and when $y = \$12$. Is the relationship between x (horizontal axis) and z (vertical axis) positive or negative?

c) On a diagram, graph the relationship between y (horizontal axis) and z (vertical axis) when $x = 120$ and when $x = 140$. Is the relationship between y and z positive or negative?

Figure 2.8

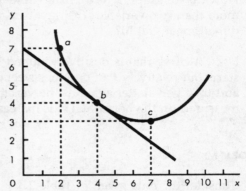

Figure 2.7 (b)

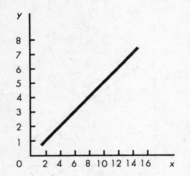

Table 2.4

Umbrellas sold per month (x)	Price per umbrella (y)	Average number of rainy days per month (z)
120	$10	4
140	$10	5
160	$10	6
100	$12	4
120	$12	5
140	$12	6
80	$14	4
100	$14	5
120	$14	6

ANSWERS

CONCEPT REVIEW

1. time-series
2. trend
3. scatter
4. positive; upward
5. negative; downward
6. horizontal
7. vertical (y); horizontal (x)
8. constant
9. two

TRUE OR FALSE

1. T	6. T	11. F	16. F	21. F
2. T	7. T	12. T	17. T	22. T
3. F	8. F	13. F	18. T	23. F
4. T	9. T	14. F	19. T	
5. F	10. T	15. T	20. F	

MULTIPLE CHOICE

1. c	5. a	9. b	13. b	17. c
2. b	6. a	10. a	14. d	
3. d	7. d	11. c	15. d	
4. c	8. c	12. c	16. a	

SHORT ANSWER

1. A time-series graph is a graph that plots the value of the variable of interest on the vertical axis against time on the horizontal axis.

2. Figure 2.9 (a) illustrates a two-variable time-series graph of two variables with a tendency to move up and down together, while Fig. 2.9 (b) illustrates a scatter diagram for such variables.

3. Figures 2.10 (a)—(g) illustrate the desired graphs.

Figure 2.9

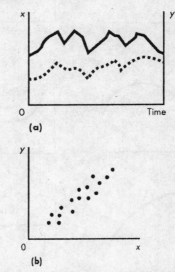

4. The negative sign in the slope of -2/3 means that there is a negative relationship between the two variables. The value of 2/3 means that when the variable measured on the vertical axis decreases by 2 units the *rise* or Δy), the variable measured on the horizontal axis increases by 3 units (the *run* or Δx).

5. In both cases we actually measure the slope of a straight line.
a) The slope at a point is measured by calculating the slope of the straight line that is   tangent to (just touches) the curved line at the point.
b) The slope across an arc is measure by calculating the slope of the straight line that forms the arc.

Figure 2.10

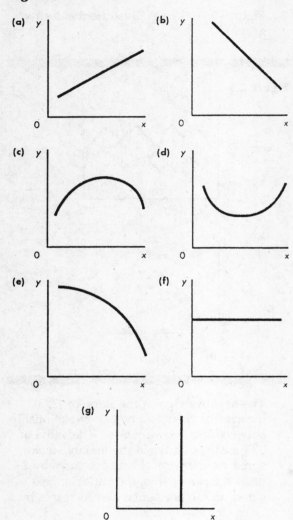

6. To graph a relationship among more than two variables we hold all the variables but two constant and graph the relationship between the remaining two. Thus we can graph the relationship between any pair of variables of interest, given the constant values of the other variables.

7. Figure 2.11 illustrates such a curve.

PROBLEMS

1. a) A time-series graph for the interest rate is given in Fig. 2.12 (a).
   b) Figure 2.12 (b) is a two-variable time-series graph for both the inflation rate and the interest rate.
   c) The scatter diagram for the inflation rate and the interest rate is given in Fig. 2.12 (c).

Figure 2.11

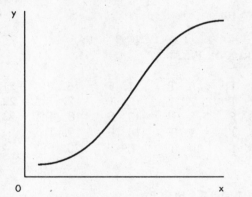

d) From the graphs in Fig. 2.12 (b) and (c), we see that the relationship between the inflation rate and the interest rate is generally positive.

Figure 2.12 (a)

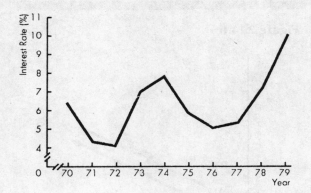

Figure 2.12 (b)

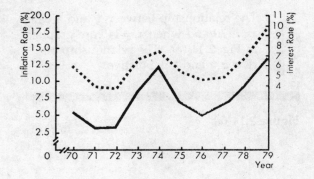

Figure 2.12 (c)

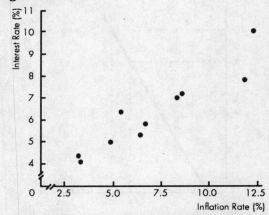

Figure 2.13 (a)

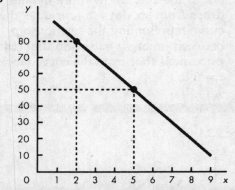

2. The slope of the line in Fig. 2.7 (a) is -2/3 and the slope of the line in Fig. 2.7 (b) is 2.

3. a) The requested straight line is graphed in Fig. 2.13 (a).
   b) The requested straight line is graphed in Fig. 2.13 (b).

4. a) The slope across the arc between points *a* and *b* is -3/2.
   b) The slope at point *b* is -3/4.
   c) The slope at point *c* is 0 since it is a minimum point. At a minimum point the slope changes from negative to positive; that is, it is 0.

Figure 2.13 (b)

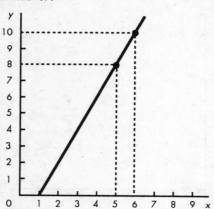

graphed in Fig. 2.14 (b). The relationship between x and z is positive.

Figure 2.14 (b)

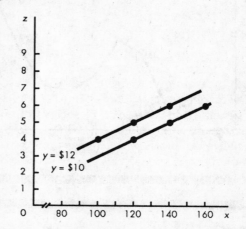

5. a) The relationships between x and y for z = 4, 5, and 6 are graphed in Fig. 2.14 (a). If the average monthly rainfall drops from six days to four days the curve representing the relationship between umbrella sales and umbrella prices will shift from the curve labeled $z = 6$ to $z = 4$.

c) The relationship between y and z when $x = 120$ and when $x = 140$ are graphed in Fig. 2.14 (c). The relationship between y and z is positive.

Figure 2.14 (a)

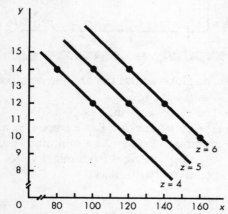

Figure 2.14 (c)

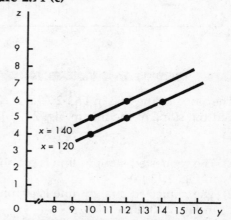

(b)   The relationships between x and z when y is \$10 and when y is \$12 are

3 PRODUCTION, SPECIALIZATION, AND EXCHANGE

CHAPTER IN PERSPECTIVE

In the first chapter we learned that the existence of scarcity is the fundamental and pervasive social problem giving rise to economic activity. Because all individuals and all economies are faced with scarce resources, choices must be made, each of which has an opportunity cost. Economies that are generally considered to be successful in coping with the problem of scarcity are characterized by a broad array of goods and services produced by a highly specialized labor force. Since workers specialize as producers but consume a variety of goods and services, exchange is a necessary complement to specialization.

This chapter explains why specialization and exchange are the natural consequences of attempts to get the most from scarce resources (i.e., to optimize). It also discusses the critical role of opportunity cost in explaining why individuals and countries specialize in the production of goods and services and why tremendous gains occur from specialization and exchange.

LEARNING OBJECTIVES

After studying this chapter, you will be able to:

- **Define the production possibility frontier**

- **Calculate opportunity cost**

- **Explain why economic growth and technical change do not provide free gifts**

- **Explain comparative advantage**

- **Explain why people specialize and how they gain from trade**

- **Explain why property rights and money have evolved**

HELPFUL HINTS

1. This chapter reviews the absolutely critical concept of *opportunity cost*, which was introduced in the first chapter. It is important to recognize that the opportunity cost of an activity is *not* the *time* the activity requires but the *best alternative activity* which could have been pursued in that period of time. What matters for economic decisions is the opportunity cost of an activity, not how long it takes. Thus, when we are given information about the time involved in an activity, it is very useful to immediately make a simple opportunity cost table by asking what else could have been done.

2. A very helpful formula for opportunity cost, which works well in solving problems, especially problems that involve moving up or down a production possibility frontier is:

$$Opportunity\ cost = \frac{Give\ up}{Get}$$

Opportunity cost equals the quantity of goods you must give up divided by the quantity of goods you will get. To illustrate, look again at three possibilities on Jane's production possibility frontier in Fig. 3.1 in the text.

Possibility	Corn (pounds per month)	Cloth (yards per month)
a	20	0
b	18	1
c	15	2

First consider an example of moving down the production possibility frontier. In moving from *a* to *b*, what is the opportunity cost of an additional yard of cloth? Jane must *give up* 2 pounds of corn (20 - 18) to *get* 1 yard of cloth (1 - 0). Substituting into the formula, the opportunity cost is:

$$\frac{2\ pounds\ corn}{1\ yard\ cloth} = \frac{2\ pounds\ corn}{per\ yard\ of\ cloth}$$

Next, consider an example of moving up the production possibility frontier. In moving from *b* to *a*, what is the opportunity cost of an additional pound of corn? Jane must *give up* 1 yard of cloth (1 - 0) to *get* 2 pounds of corn (20 - 18). Substituting into the formula, the opportunity cost is:

$$\frac{1\ yard\ cloth}{2\ pounds\ corn} = \frac{1/2\ yard\ cloth}{per\ pound\ of\ corn}$$

Opportunity cost is always measured in the units of the *forgone good*.

3. A production possibility frontier represents the boundary between attainable and unattainable levels of production for a fixed quantity of resources and a given state of technology. It indicates the best that can be done with existing resources and technology. Thus, the production possibility frontier will shift out if the quantity of resources increases (e.g., an increase in the stock of capital goods) even if the ability to use those resources does not change. The production possibility curve will also shift out if there is an increase in the ability to produce (i.e., a technological improvement) with no change in resources.

4. The text defines absolute advantage as a situation where one person has greater productivity than another in the production of all goods. We can also define *absolute advantage in the production of one good*. In comparing the productivity of two persons, this narrower concept of absolute advantage can be defined either in terms of greater output of the good per unit of inputs, or fewer inputs per unit of output.

It is useful to understand these definitions of absolute advantage only to demonstrate that absolute advantage has *no role* in explaining specialization and trade. The gains from trade depend only on differing comparative advantages. An individual has a comparative advantage in producing a good if he can produce it at lower opportunity cost than others.

5. One of the principle goals of this chapter is to develop a deeper appreciation of the gains (in terms of standard of living) that result from trade and institutional arrangements which enhance trade. The following thought experiments may be useful in this context. Each of them asks you to imagine how things would be different without some of the attributes of our current economic system.

   a) How would your standard of living be different if there were no specialization and trade (i.e., if everyone were required to be self-sufficient)? Think of all the goods and services you now use on a regular basis (e.g., television, stereo equipment, automobiles, toothpaste, nail polish, etc.). How many of these would you not have or find it necessary to consume in lesser quantity and quality?

   b) Suppose we allow specialization and exchange but have no clearly defined property rights. How would your life be different from the situation above and from what it is now?

   c) Now suppose we have property rights as at present in the U. S. but that there is no money. Exchange must be conducted by barter. How would your life be different?

6. This chapter gives us our first opportunity to develop and use an economic model. It is valuable to think about the nature of that model in the context of the general discussion about such models in Chapter 1. The model developed in the chapter is a representation of the production possibilities in the two-person and two-good world of Jane and Joe. We note that the model abstracts greatly from the complexity of the real world in which there are billions of people and innumerable different kinds of goods and services. The model allows us to explain a number of phenomena that we observe in the world (e.g., specialization and exchange). The model also has some implications or predictions (e.g., countries that devote a larger proportion of their resources to capital accumulation will have more rapidly expanding production possibilities). The model can be subjected to "test" by comparing these predictions to the facts we observe in the real world.

KEY FIGURES

Figure 3.1 Jane's Production Possibility Frontier

A production possibility frontier gives the boundary between attainable and unattainable level of production for a fixed quantity of resources and a given state of technology. This figure illustrates the concept by constructing the production possibility frontier for Jane, who produces corn and cloth. Each point on the frontier shows the most cloth she is able to produce given that she is producing a particular quantity of corn. Points beyond the frontier are unattainable. Points inside the production possibility frontier are attainable but inferior to points on the production possibility frontier.

Figure 3.2 Jane's Opportunity Costs of Corn and Cloth

This figure uses information from Fig. 3.1 to calculate opportunity costs as we move along the production possibility frontier. Part (a) simply displays the increasing opportunity cost of cloth. Part (b) relates that increasing opportunity cost to movement down the frontier from points a to f as we increase the production of cloth. In moving from a to b, we give up 2 pounds of corn to get 1 yard of cloth; the opportunity cost of the first yard of cloth is 2 pounds of corn. Similar calculations show increasing opportunity cost as we increase cloth production of cloth.

Figure 3.3 Economic Growth on Jane's Island

If resources are used to produce capital goods (e.g., tools), productive capacity will increase. This is represented by an outward shift of the production possibility frontier. The greater the proportion of resources used to produce capital goods, the faster the production possibility frontier will shift out. This figure illustrates this concept using the example of Jane's production of corn and cloth. Jane can choose to use all resources to produce corn and cloth (point *e*). In this case, her production possibility frontier remains in its initial position, since Jane's ability to produce will not change. If, however, Jane decides to reduce her current production of corn and cloth in order to produce tools (e.g., point *d*) her future productive ability will increase, and so her production possibility frontier will shift out. This figure clearly illustrates the opportunity cost of increasing future production possibilities by producing tools: forgone current production (consumption) of corn and cloth.

SELF-TEST

CONCEPT REVIEW

1. The process of converting resources into goods and services is called __production__.

2. We divide production resources into three classes. Resources such as iron ore and running rivers are examples of __land__, the skill of a computer programmer and the physical strength of a bricklayer are examples of __labor__, and a shoe factory and an olive pitting machine are examples of __capital__ resources.

3. The graphical representation of the boundary between attainable and unattainable production levels is called the __Production possibility frontier__.

4. The __opportunity cost__ of a choice is the value of the best forgone alternative choice.

5. Two key activities that can shift the production possibility frontier out are __technological__ progress and __capital__ accumulation.

6. The opportunity cost of producing capital goods now in order to expand future production is forgone current __consumption__ goods.

7. If Martha can produce salad forks at a lower opportunity cost than Jill, we say that Martha has a(n) __comparative__ advantage in the production of salad forks.

8. The economic system that permits private individuals to own the capital resources used in production is called __private enterprise__.

9. A system in which goods are traded directly for goods is known as __barter__.

10. In order for exchange to take place in such a system there must be a double __coincidence__ of wants.

11. __Money__ is defined as a medium of exchange.

TRUE OR FALSE

Figure 3.1

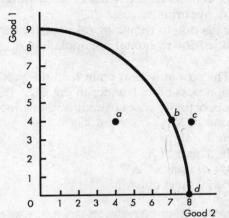

Refer to the production possibility frontier in Fig. 3.1 for questions 1-4.

F 1. At point *b*, 7 units of good 1 and 4 units of good 2 are produced.

F 2. Point *a* is not attainable.

T 3. The opportunity cost of increasing the production of good 2 from 7 to 8 units is 4 units of good 1.

T 4. Point *c* is not attainable.

F 5. The bowedout shape of a production possibility frontier reflects decreasing opportunity cost as we increase the production of either good.

T 6. The production possibility frontier will shift out if there is a technological improvement.

T 7. Reducing the current production of consumption goods in order to produce more capital goods will shift the production possibility frontier out in the future.

F 8. Bill has a comparative advantage in producing good *a* if he can do it faster than Joe.

T 9. Consider an economy with two goods, X and Y, and two producers, Bill and Joe. If Bill has a comparative advantage in the production of X, then Joe must have a comparative advantage in the production of Y.

T 10. Any time two individuals have different opportunity costs they can both gain from specialization and trade.

F 11. The incentives for specialization and exchange do not depend on property rights but only on differing opportunity costs.

F 12. Any system that uses capital in production is a capitalist system.

T 13. With specialization and trade, a country can consume at a point outside its production possibility frontier.

F 14. With specialization and trade, a country can produce at a point outside its production possibility frontier.

F 15. The principle of comparative advantage helps us understand why the existence of cheap foreign labor means that sooner or later no one in other countries will buy U.S.-produced goods.

F 16. A monetary exchange system requires a double coincidence of wants.

Use the following information to answer questions 17-20. In one hour, Jack can produce either four pails of water *or* eight candlesticks, while Jill can produce either 10 pails of water or 10 candlesticks.

T 17. The opportunity cost of one pail of water for Jill is one candlestick.

T 18. Jack has a comparative advantage in the production of candlesticks.

T 19. Jill has an absolute advantage in the production of both pails of water and candlesticks.

T 20. Both Jack and Jill could be made better off if Jack specialized in candlesticks and Jill specialized in pails of water and they engaged in exchange.

MULTIPLE CHOICE

1. Which of the following is <u>NOT</u> an example of a capital resource?
   a. A hydroelectric dam
   b. A dentist's drill
   c. A shovel
   d. A lawyer's knowledge of the law

2. If Harold can increase production of good x without decreasing the production of any other good, then Harold
   a. is producing on his production possibility frontier.
   b. is producing outside his production possibility frontier.
   c. is producing inside his production possibility frontier.
   d. must prefer good x to any other good.

3. The bowedout shape of a production possibility frontier
   a. reflects the existence of increasing opportunity cost.
   b. reflects the existence of decreasing opportunity cost.
   c. is due to technological improvement.
   d. is due to capital accumulation.

4. The economy is at point b on the production possibility frontier in Fig. 3.2. The opportunity cost of producing one more unit of X is
   a. 1 unit of Y.
   b. 1 unit of X.
   c. 20 units of Y.
   d. 20 units of X.

Figure 3.2

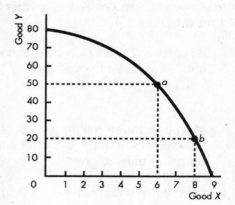

5. The economy is at point b on the production possibility frontier in Fig. 3.2. The opportunity cost of increasing the production of Y to 50 units is
   a. 6 units of X
   b. 2 units of X
   c. 8 units of Y
   d. 30 units of Y

6. Because productive resources are scarce, we must give up some of one good in order to acquire more of another. This is the essence of the concept of
a. specialization.
b. monetary exchange.
c. comparative advantage.
d. opportunity cost.

7. A production possibility frontier will shift *outward* if
a. there is a technological improvement.
b. there is an increase in the stock of capital.
c. there is an increase in the labor force.
d. all of the above.

8. The opportunity cost of pushing the production possibility frontier outward is
a. the value of the increase in new capital resources required.
b. the value of the increase in technological improvement required.
c. the value of the reduction in current consumption required.
d. the amount by which the production possibility frontier shifts.

9. In general, the higher the proportion of resources devoted to technological research in an economy,
a. the greater will be current consumption.
b. the faster the production possibility frontier will shift outward.
c. the faster the production possibility frontier will shift inward.
d. the closer it will come to having a comparative advantage in the production of all goods.

10. Refer to Table 3.1. The opportunity cost of increasing the production of X from 4 to 8 units is
a. 4 units of X.
b. 4 units of Y.
c. 8 units of Y.
d. 28 units of Y.

Table 3.1 Points on the Production Possibility Frontier for Goods X and Y

Point	Production of X	Production of Y
a	0	40
b	4	36
c	8	28
d	12	16
e	16	0

11. The diagram of the PPF corresponding to the data in Table 3.1 would be
a. negatively sloped and linear.
b. negatively sloped and bowed in.
c. negatively sloped and bowed out.
d. positively sloped for X and negatively sloped for Y.

12. From the data in Table 3.1, the production of 10 units of X and 28 units of Y is
a. impossible given the available resources.
b. possible but leaves some resources less than fully utilized.
c. on the PPF between points c and d.
d. We cannot infer whether it is possible or not from the table.

13. Mexico and Canada each produce both oil and apples using only labor. A barrel of oil can be produced with four hours of labor in Mexico and eight hours of labor in Canada. A bushel of apples can be produced with eight hours of labor in Mexico and 12 hours of labor in Canada. Canada has
    a. an absolute advantage in oil production.
    b. an absolute advantage in apple production.
    c. a comparative advantage in oil production.
    d. a comparative advantage in apple production.

14. There are two goods: X and Y. If the opportunity cost of producing good X is lower for Pam than for Gino, then we know that
    a. Pam has an absolute advantage in the production of X.
    b. Gino has an absolute advantage in the production of Y.
    c. Pam has a comparative advantage in the production of
    d. Gino has a comparative advantage in the production of X.

Fact 3.1

In an eight-hour day, Andy can produce either 24 loaves of bread or eight pounds of ubtter. In an eight-hour day, Bob can produce either eight loaves of bread or eight pounds of butter.

---

15. Refer to Fact 3.1. Which of the following statements is true?
    a. Andy has an absolute advantage in butter production.
    b. Bob has an absolute advantage in butter production.
    c. Andy has a comparative advantage in butter production.
    d. Bob has a comparative advantage in butter production.

16. Refer to Fact 3.1. Andy and Bob
    a. can gain from exchange if Andy specializes in butter production and Bob specializes in bread production.
    b. can gain from exchange if Andy specializes in bread production and Bob specializes in butter production.
    c. cannot gain from exchange because Bob does not have any comparative advantage.
    d. can exchange, but only Bob will be able to gain.

17. If individuals a and b can both produce only goods x and y and a does NOT have a comparative advantage in the production of either x or y, then we know that
    a. b has an absolute advantage in the production of x and y.
    b. a and b have the same opportunity cost for x and for y.
    c. b has a comparative advantage in the production of both x and y.
    d. the gains from trade will be large but only in one direction.

18. Which of the following would NOT limit private property rights?
    a. High market prices
    b. Export restrictions
    c. Laws prohibiting slavery
    d. Income taxes

19. Anything that is generally acceptable in exchange for goods and services is
    a. a medium of exchange.
    b. private property.
    c. a barter good.
    d. called an exchange resource.

20. Which of the following is an advantage of a monetary exchange system over barter?
    a. A monetary exchange system eliminates the basis for comparative advantage.
    b. Only in a monetary exchange system can gains from trade be realized.
    c. In a monetary system exchange does not require a double coincidence of wants.
    d. A monetary exchange system does not require a medium of exchange.

SHORT ANSWER

1. Explain why points *on* the production possibility frontier are best. What do points inside or outside this frontier mean?

2. Why is a production possibility frontier negatively sloped? Why is it bowed out?

3. What factors can shift the production possibility frontier outward? Inward?

4. Lawyers earn $100/hour while secretaries earn $10/hour. Use the concepts of absolute and comparative advantage to explain why a lawyer, who is a better typist than her secretary, will still *specialize* in doing only legal work and will *trade* with the secretary for typing services.

5. What would be the cost to the U.S. of increasing the production of capital goods? What would the benefits be?

6. What is meant by comparative advantage?

7. Consider an economy with two individuals (*A* and *B*) producing two goods (*X* and *Y*). If we determine that *A* has a comparative advantage in the production of *X*, explain why we know that *B* must have a comparative advantage in the production of *Y*. [Hint: If the opportunity cost of producing one unit of *X* is two units of *Y*, then the opportunity cost of producing one unit of *Y* must be 1/2 units of *X*; that is, since there are only two goods, the opportunity cost of producing one is the reciprocal of the opportunity cost of producing the other. Do you understand why?]

8. Explain why individuals can gain from specialization and trade.

9. Explain how taxes *modify* property rights. If a society must pay for its judicial system and police protection, explain how taxes *enhance* property rights.

10. Explain, using a specific example of exchange, why a monetary exchange system is more efficient than barter.

PROBLEMS

1. Suppose that an economy with unchanged capital goods (no toolmaking) has the production possibility frontier shown in Table 3.2.

Table 3.2 Production Possibilities

Possibility	Units of butter	Units of guns
a	200	0
b	180	60
c	160	100
d	100	160
e	40	200
f	0	220

a) On graph paper, plot these possibilities, label the points, and draw the production possibility frontier. (Put guns on the horizontal axis.)
b) If the economy moves from possibility *c* to possibility *d*, the opportunity cost *per unit of guns* will be how many units of butter?
c) If the economy moves from possibility *d* to possibility *e*, the opportunity cost *per unit of guns* will be how many units of butter?
d) In general terms, what happens to the opportunity cost of guns as the output of guns increases?
e) In general terms, what happens to the opportunity cost of butter as the output of butter increases?
f) Given the production possibility frontier you have plotted, is a combination of 140 units of butter and 130 units of guns per week attainable? Would you regard this combination as an efficient one? Explain.
g) Repeat the question asked in part f) for a combination of 70 units of butter and 170 units of guns.
h) If the following events occur (consider each a separate event, unaccompanied by any other), what would happen to the production possibility frontier?
   i) A new, easily exploited, energy source is discovered.
   ii) A large number of skilled workers immigrate into the country.
   iii) The output of butter is increased.

iv) A new invention increases output per person in the butter industry but not in the guns industry.
v) A new law is passed compelling workers, who could previously work as long as they wanted, to retire at age 60.

2. Draw a linear (straight-line) production possibility frontier and a bowedout production possibility frontier. Demonstrate that the linear frontier reflects constant opportunity cost while the bowedout frontier reflects increasing opportunity cost.

3. Suppose that the country of Quark has historically devoted 10 percent of its resources to the production of new capital goods. Use production possibility frontier diagrams to compare the consequences (i.e., costs and benefits) of each of the following.
a) Quark continues to devote 10 percent of its resources to the production of capital goods.
b) Quark begins now to permanently devote 20 percent of its resources to the production of capital goods.

4. Tove and Ron are the only two remaining inhabitants of the planet Melmac. They spend their 30-hour days producing widgets and woggles, the only two goods needed for happiness on Melmac. It takes Tove one hour to produce a widget and two hours to produce a woggle while Ron takes three hours to produce a widget and three hours to produce a woggle.
a. For a 30-hour day, draw an individual production possibility frontier for Tove and for Ron.
b. What does the shape of the production possibility frontiers tell us about opportunity costs?
c. Assume initially that Tove and Ron are each self-sufficient. Explain what the

individual consumption possibilities
are for Tove and for Ron.

d. Who has an absolute advantage in the
production of widgets? Of woggles?

e. Who has a comparative advantage in
the production of widgets? Of
woggles?

f. Suppose Tove and Ron each specialize
in producing only the good in which
she/he has a comparative advantage
(one spends 30 hours producing
widgets, the other spends 30 hours
producing woggles). What will be the
total production of widgets and
woggles?

g. Now, suppose Tove and Ron exchange
seven widgets for five woggles. On
your production possibility frontier
diagrams, plot the new point of Tove's
consumption; of Ron's consumption.
Explain how these points illustrate the
gains from trade.

ANSWERS

CONCEPT REVIEW

1. production

2. land; labor; capital

3. production possibility frontier

4. opportunity cost

5. technological; capital

6. consumption

7. comparative

8. capitalism

9. barter

10. coincidence

11. money

TRUE OR FALSE

1. F	5. F	9. T	13. T	17. T
2. F	6. T	10. T	14. F	18. T
3. T	7. T	11. F	15. F	19. T
4. T	8. F	12. F	16. F	20. T

MULTIPLE CHOICE

1. d	5. b	9. b	13. d	17. b
2. c	6. d	10. c	14. c	18. a
3. a	7. d	11. c	15. d	19. a
4. c	8. c	12. a	16. b	20. c

SHORT ANSWER

1. Points outside the production possibility
frontier are unattainable and thus
irrelevant. Points inside the frontier mean
that some resources are not fully utilized.
Points on the frontier are best because
they represent more of both goods than
points inside the frontier.

2. The negative slope of the production
possibility frontier reflects opportunity
cost: in order to have more of one good
some of the other must be forgone. It is
bowed out because of increasing
opportunity cost.

3. The production possibility frontier will
shift outward if the quantity of resources
available (e.g., the stock of capital goods)
increases or if there is a technological
improvement. A loss of resources (e.g.,
during a war) or any other event that
reduces ability to produce (e.g., bad
weather) will shift the frontier inward.

4. The lawyer has an absolute advantage in
producing both legal and typing services
relative to the secretary. Nevertheless, she
has a comparative advantage in legal
services, and the secretary has a
comparative advantage in typing. To

demonstrate these comparative advantages we can construct a table of opportunity costs. (See Table 3.3.)

Consider first the lawyer's opportunity costs. The lawyer's best forgone alternative to providing one hour of legal services is the $100 she could earn by providing another hour of legal services. If she provides one hour of typing, she is also forgoing $100 (one hour) of legal services. What would the secretary have to forgo to provide one hour of legal services? He would have to spend three years in law school, forgoing three years of income in addition to the tuition he must pay. His opportunity cost is a very large number, certainly greater than $100. If he provides one hour of typing, his best forgone alternative is the $10 he could have earned at another secretarial job. Thus Table 3.3 shows that the lawyer has a lower opportunity cost (comparative advantage) of providing legal services, and the secretary has a lower opportunity cost (comparative advantage) of providing typing services. It is on the basis of comparative advantage (not absolute advantage) that the trade will take place from which both parties gain.

Table 3.3 Opportunity Cost of One   Additional Hour ($)

	Legal Services	Typing
Lawyer	100	100
Secretary	100	10

5. The cost to the U.S. of increasing the production of capital goods would be the consumption goods that must be forgone when resources are switched from the production of consumer goods to capital goods. The benefit is faster growth of the production possibility frontier and therefore greater *future* consumption.

6. A person has a comparative advantage in the production of a good if his or her opportunity cost of producing the good is lower than the opportunity cost of anyone else.

7. In the simple two-person two-good model used in this chapter, the opportunity cost of producing one good is the amount of the other good that must be forgone if the first is produced. If individual a's opportunity cost of producing good x is less than individual b's opportunity cost, then we know that the reciprocals of these costs have the opposite relationship; that is, the reciprocal of a's opportunity cost of producing good x is greater than the reciprocal of b's opportunity cost of producing x. By the hint, this means that a's opportunity cost of producing y is greater than b's opportunity cost of producing y.

8. If each individual specializes in the good for which he or she has the lowest opportunity cost (i.e., a comparative advantage), then more of each good can be produced and this increase in output will be divided by exchange.

9. Taxes limit property rights directly by eliminating individual control over property which passes to the government in the form of tax payments. Without income taxes, for example, each individual would have property rights over their entire income. With income taxes, however, the individual retains property rights only over the part that remains after taxes are paid. Taxes enhance property rights by paying for the institutional enforcement necessary for an effective system of property rights. In this sense, taxes are a prerequisite for property rights.

10. The principle reason for the efficiency of a monetary exchange system relative to barter is that the monetary system does not require a double coincidence of wants to complete a successful exchange. For example, suppose you specialize in the production of apples but like to eat bananas. In a barter economy, you would likely not be able to complete an exchange with the first person you found who had bananas to trade. It would be necessary for that person to also want to trade the bananas for apples and not for carrots or some other good. In a monetary economy, you would always be able to make a successful exchange with the first person you found with bananas to trade since he or she would be willing to accept money in exchange. Similarly, in a money exchange system, you would be able to sell your apples for money to the first person you found who wanted apples (even if that person did not have bananas to sell).

PROBLEMS

1. a) The graph of the production possibility frontier is given in Fig. 3.3.
   b) In moving from c to d, in order to gain 60 units of guns, we must give up 160 - 100 = 60 units of butter. The opportunity cost per unit of guns is:

$$\frac{60 \; units \; butter}{60 \; units \; guns} = \frac{1 \; unit \; of \; butter}{per \; unit \; of \; guns}$$

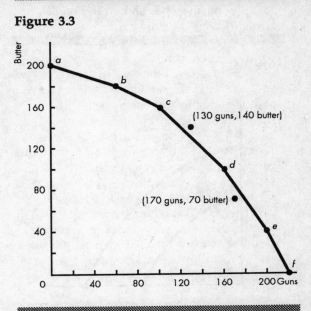

Figure 3.3

c) In moving from d to e, in order to gain 40 units of guns, we must give up 100 - 40 = 60 units of butter. The opportunity cost per unit of guns is:

$$\frac{60 \; units \; butter}{40 \; units \; guns} = \frac{1.5 \; units \; of \; butter}{per \; unit \; of \; guns}$$

d) The opportunity cost of producing more guns increases as the output of guns increases.
e) Likewise, the opportunity cost of producing more butter increases as the output of butter increases.
f) This combination is outside the frontier and, therefore, is not attainable. Since the economy cannot produce this combination, the question of efficiency is irrelevant.
g) This combination is inside the frontier and is attainable. It is inefficient because the economy could produce more of either or both goods.
h) i.) Assuming that both goods require energy for their production, the

entire frontier shifts out to the
northeast as shown in Fig. 3.4.

Figure 3.4

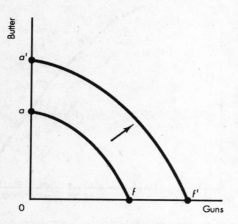

ii.) Assuming that both goods use
skilled labor in their production,
the entire frontier shifts out to the
northeast. See Fig. 3.4.
iii.) The frontier does not shift. An
increase in the output of butter
implies a movement *along* the
frontier to the left, not a shift of
the frontier itself.
iv.) The new invention implies that
for every level of output of guns,
the economy can now produce
more butter. The frontier swings
to the right, but remains anchored
at point *f* as shown in Fig. 3.5.

Figure 3.5

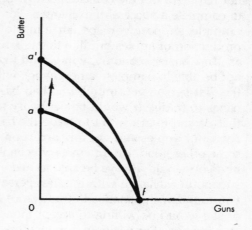

2. Parts (a) and (b) of Fig. 3.6 straight-line
and bowedout production possibility
frontiers respectively.

Figure 3.6

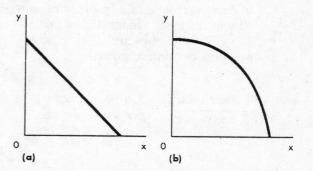

The fact that the slope of a straight line is
constant implies that the amount of one
good that must be given up in order to
obtain one more unit of the other is constant. In the case of a bowedout curve,

however, we see that the slope is becoming steeper as x increases which indicates that more of good y must be given up for each additional unit of x. Thus the bowed out production possibility frontier reflects increasing opportunity cost.

3. a) The situation for Quark is depicted by Fig. 3.7. Suppose Quark starts on production possibility frontier 1. If it continues to devote only 10 percent of its resources to the production of new capital goods, then it is choosing to produce at a point like a. This will shift the frontier out in the next period but only to the curve labeled 2 where, presumably, Quark will choose to produce at point b.

Figure 3.7

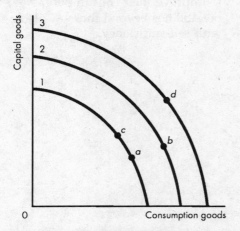

b) Starting from the same initial production possibility frontier, if Quark now decides to increase the resources devoted to the production of new capital to 20 percent, it will be choosing to produce at a point like c. In this case, next period's frontier will shift further — to curve 3 and a point like d, for example.

Thus, in comparing points a and c, we find the following costs and benefits: point a has the benefit of greater present consumption but at a cost of lower future consumption; point c has the cost of lower present consumption, but with the benefit of greater future consumption.

4. a) The individual production possibility frontiers for Tove and Ron are given by Fig. 3.8 (a) and (b) respectively.

Figure 3.8 (a)

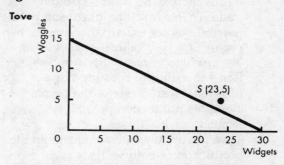

Figure 3.8 (b)

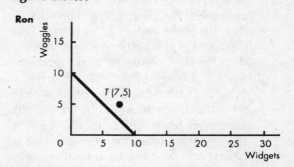

b) The linear shape of the production possibility frontiers tells us that opportunity costs are constant along each frontier.

These linear production possibility frontiers with constant opportunity costs abstract from the complexity of the real world. The world generally has increasing opportunity costs, but that fact is not essential for understanding the gains from trade, which is the objective of this problem. Making the model more complex by including increasing opportunity costs would not change our results, but it would make it more difficult to see them.

c) Individuals are self-sufficient if they consume only what they produce. This means there is no trade. Without trade, Tove's (maximum) consumption possibilities are exactly the same as her production possibilities—points along her production possibility frontier. Ron's (maximum) consumption possibilities are likewise the points along his production possibility frontier.

d) Tove has an absolute advantage in the production of both widgets and woggles. Her absolute advantage can be defined either in terms of greater output per unit of inputs or fewer inputs per unit of output. A comparison of the production possibility frontiers in Fig. 3.8 shows that, for given inputs of 30 hours, Tove produces a greater output of widgets than Ron (30 versus 10) and a greater output of woggles that Ron (15 versus 10). The statement of the problem tells us equivalently that per unit of output, Tove uses fewer inputs that Ron for both widgets (one hour versus three hours) and woggles (two hours versus three hours). Since Tove has greater productivity than Ron in the production of all goods (widgets and woggles), we say that, overall, she has an absolute advantage.

e) Tove has a comparative advantage in the production of widgets, since she can produce them at lower opportunity cost that Ron (1/2 woggle versus 1 woggle). On the other hand, Ron has a comparative advantage in the production of woggles since he can produce them at a lower opportunity cost than Tove (1 widget versus 2 widgets).

f) Tove will produce widgets and Ron will produce woggles, yielding a total production between them of 30 widgets and 10 woggles.

g) After the exchange, Tove will have 23 widgets and 5 woggles (point *S*). Ron will have 7 widgets and 5 woggles (point *T*). These new post-trade consumption possibility points lie outside Tove's and Ron's respective pre-trade consumption (and production) possibilities. Hence, trade has yielded gains that allow the traders to improve their consumption possibilities beyond those available with self-sufficiency.

4 DEMAND AND SUPPLY

CHAPTER IN PERSPECTIVE

George Bernard Shaw, the renowned Irish playwright, is reported to have said that one could make a parrot into an economist by teaching it to say "demand and supply." While no parrot has (yet) won the Nobel Prize in economics, Shaw's quip does point out the central role of the concepts of demand and supply in economic thinking. This chapter introduces these basic ideas, which will show up again and again in future chapters.

The previous chapter emphasized the tremendous economic benefits that result from specialization and exchange. Most formal exchange takes place in "markets" at prices determined by the interaction of buyers (demanders) and sellers (suppliers) in those markets. There are markets for goods (like wheat or textbooks), for services (like haircuts or tattoos), for financial assets (like IBM stock, or U.S. dollars, or government bonds). Demand and supply are very powerful tools that economists use to explain how much will be traded and at what price. Careful use of these tools will allow us to explain a wide array of economic phenomena and even predict changes in prices and quantities traded.

Given that demand and supply are so fundamental to economic analysis, extra time and effort spent to truly master the concepts discussed in this chapter will pay large dividends during the rest of the course.

LEARNING OBJECTIVES

After studying this chapter, you will be able to:

- Construct a demand schedule and a demand curve

- Construct a supply schedule and a supply curve

- Explain how prices are determined

- Explain how quantities bought and sold are determined

- Explain why some prices rise, some fall, and some fluctuate

- Make predictions about price changes using the demand and supply model

39

HELPFUL HINTS

1. It is important that you have a complete understanding of everything in this chapter. *Avoid the tendency to memorize*; learn for understanding. The more you can rely on logical analysis, the deeper your understanding will be. Once again, the tools discussed in this chapter will be used again and again in many different forms throughout the text. Demand and supply are two of the most important economic tools you will learn about in the course.

2. When you are first learning about demand and supply it is useful to *think in terms of examples* to help build an intuitive understanding. Have some favorite examples in the back of your mind. For example, if the situation calls for the analysis of complementary goods, you may want to think about hamburgers and french fries; if the situation calls for analysis of substitute goods, you may want to think of hamburgers and hot dogs. This will help reduce the "abstractness" of the economic theory.

3. The statement that "price is determined by demand and supply" is a shorthand way of saying that price is determined by all of the factors affecting demand (prices of related goods, income, population, expected future prices, preferences) and all of the factors affecting supply (prices of factors of production, prices of related goods, expected future prices, the number of suppliers, technology). The benefit of using demand and supply *curves* is that they allow us to systematically sort out the influences on price of each of these separate factors. Changes in the factors affecting demand will shift the demand curve and move us up or down the supply curve. Changes in the factors affecting supply will shift the supply curve and move us up and down the given demand curve.

Any demand and supply problem requires you to sort out these influences carefully. In so doing, *always draw a graph*, even if it is just a small graph in the margin. Graphical representation is a very efficient way to "see" what happens. You can avoid many mistakes by using graphs effectively. As you become comfortable with graphs, you will find that they are effective and powerful tools for systematically organizing your thinking.

Also, when you do draw a graph, be sure to *label the axes*. As the course progresses, you will encounter many graphs with different variables on the axes. It is very easy to become confused if you do not develop the habit of labelling the axes.

4. A very common mistake among students is a failure to *correctly distinguish between a shift in a curve and a movement along a curve*. This distinction applies both to demand and supply curves. Many questions in the Self-Test are designed to test your understanding of this distinction, and you can be sure that you instructor will test you carefully on this. The distinction between *shift in* versus *movements along* a curve is crucial for systematic thinking about the factors influencing demand and supply and for understanding the determination of equilibrium price and quantity traded.

Consider the example of the demand curve. The quantity of a good demanded depends on its own price, the prices of related goods, income, expected future price, population, and preferences. The term *demand* refers to the relationship between the price of a good and the quantity demanded, holding constant all of the other factors on which the quantity demanded depends. This demand relationship is represented graphically by the demand curve. Thus, the effect of a change in price on quantity demanded is already reflected in the slope of the demand curve; that is, the effect of a change in the price of the good itself is given by a movement along the demand curve. This is referred to as a *change in quantity demanded*.

On the other hand, if one of the other factors affecting the quantity demanded changes, the demand curve itself will shift; that is, the quantity demanded at each price will change. This shift of the demand curve is referred to as a *change in demand*. The critical thing to remember is that a change in the price of a good will not shift the demand curve, it will only cause a movement along the demand curve. Similarly, it is just as important to distinguish between shifts in the supply curve and movements along the supply curve.

To confirm your understanding, consider the effect of an increase in household income on the market for compact discs (CDs). (Draw a graph!) First note that an increase in income affects the demand for CDs and not supply. Next we want to determine whether the increase in income causes a shift in the demand curve or a movement along the demand curve. We ask: Will the increase in income increase the quantity of CDs demanded *even if the price of CDs does not change*? Since the answer to this question is yes, we know that the demand curve will shift to the right. Note further that the increase in the demand for CDs will cause the equilibrium price to rise. This price increase will be indicated by a movement along the supply curve (an increase in the quantity supplied) and will *not* shift the supply curve itself.

Remember: It is shifts in demand and supply curves that cause the market price to change, not changes in the price that cause demand and supply curves to shift.

5. Once we understand supply and demand analysis, we can *predict* how certain events, such as an increase in income or a technological change, will affect market price. More frequently, however, we observe changes in prices that have already taken place. Then our objective is to use supply and demand analysis to *explain* these observed price changes.

For example, suppose we observe an increase in the price of grapes. We know that this could be the result of either an increase in the demand for grapes or a decrease in supply. If, however, we know that vineyards in California suffered an infestation of grape-consuming insects, we conclude that the price increase is due to a decrease in supply. Suppose that we do not know about the insects, but we do observe a decrease in the quantity of grapes traded. This information also leads us to conclude that the price increase is not the result of an increase in demand but due to a decrease in supply.

KEY FIGURES AND TABLES

Figure 4.1 The Demand Schedule and the Demand Curve

While the content of this figure corresponds specifically to the tapes example developed by Parkin in Chapter 4, it is important to recognize that the principles illustrated are general. There are two ways to represent the relationship between the price of a good or service and the quantity demanded: the demand schedule and the demand curve. A demand schedule is a table that lists the quantities consumers demand at each price, if everything else remains constant. For example, if the price of a tape is $4, consumers would be willing to buy 3 million tapes per week, assuming that other things (like income and the price of a Walkman) remain unchanged. The law of demand is reflected by the fact that as the price of a tape increases, *ceteris paribus*, the quantity of tapes that consumers would be willing to buy decreases.

A demand curve is the graphical representation of the relationship between the quantity demanded of a good and its price, holding constant all other influences on consumers' planned purchases. Price appears on the vertical axis and quantity demanded on the horizontal axis. The demand curve in this figure tells us how many tapes consumers will be willing to buy in a week at each price, other things held constant. An equivalent interpretation of the demand curve is that it gives the highest price that consumers are willing to pay for the last unit purchased. For example, the highest price that consumers will pay for the 3 millionth tape is $4. The law of demand is reflected in the negative slope of the demand curve.

Figure 4.3 A Change in Demand Versus a Change in the Quantity Demanded

The principal purpose of this figure is to help us learn to distinguish between a change in demand (represented by a shift in the demand curve) and a change in the quantity demanded (represented by a movement along a given demand curve). As indicated above in Helpful Hint 4, failure to make the correct distinction will lead to incorrect conclusions. Remember that a change in the price of a good or service implies that the quantity demanded changes. Since this is exactly the relationship captured in the demand curve, the change in quantity demanded is represented by a movement along the curve. If there is a change in any of the other factors affecting the willingness of consumers to buy at a given price, then we say there is a change in demand which is represented by a shift in the demand curve itself.

Figure 4.4 The Supply Schedule and the Supply Curve

The purpose of this figure parallels that of Fig. 4.1. Just as there are two useful ways to represent the demand relationship, there are two ways to represent the relationship between the price of a good or service and the quantity supplied. A supply schedule is a table that lists the quantities that producers will plan to sell at each price, if everything else remains constant. For example, if the price of a tape is $4, producers will plan to sell 5 million tapes per week, assuming that other things (like the technology used to

produce tapes) remain unchanged. The law of supply is reflected by the fact that the quantity supplied increases as the price increases (*ceteris paribus*).

A supply curve is the graphical representation of the relationship between the quantity of a good supplied and its price, holding constant all other influences on producers' planned sales. The supply curve in this figure tells us how many tapes producers will be willing to sell per week at each price, other things held constant. Another interpretation of the supply curve is that it tells us the lowest price that will induce producers to offer a given quantity for sale. For example, the lowest price that will induce producers to offer 5 million tapes for sale per week is $4. The law of supply is reflected in the positive slope of the supply curve.

Figure 4.6 A Change in Supply Versus a Change in the Quantity Supplied

This figure helps us learn to distinguish between a change in supply (represented by a shift in the supply curve) and a change in the quantity supplied (represented by a movement along a given supply curve). Remember that a change in the price of a good or service implies that the quantity supplied changes. Since this is the relationship represented by the supply curve, the change in quantity supplied is represented by a movement along the supply curve. If there is a change in any other factor affecting the willingness of producers to offer a given quantity for sale at a given price, then we say there is a change in supply which is represented by a shift in the supply curve itself.

Figure 4.7 Equilibrium

In this figure, the demand and supply curves are combined in the same graph in order to examine the price and quantity traded that leaves both buyers and sellers satisfied. Equilibrium price is defined as that price at which the quantity demanded is equal to the quantity supplied. The equilibrium price ($3 in the example) can be identified using either the table or the diagram. The idea of equilibrium as a point of rest is also illustrated. Note that when the price is below the equilibrium price there is a shortage which will cause the price to rise toward equilibrium. When the price is above the equilibrium price, there is a surplus which will cause the price to fall toward equilibrium. Only at the equilibrium price will there be no tendency for the price to change.

Table 4.1 The Demand for Tapes

This table specifies the law of demand: the quantity demanded increases when the price of the good or service falls and decreases when the price rises. These changes are represented by movements along the demand curve. The factors that cause changes in demand are also listed. Changes in these factors will cause the demand curve to shift. Note that the table assumes that tapes are a normal good since a rise in income will cause the demand for tapes to increase. If the good in question is inferior, a rise in income will cause demand to decrease whereas a fall in income will cause demand to increase. As implied by the name, most goods and services are normal.

Table 4.2 The Supply of Tapes

In parallel to Table 4.1, this table specifies the law of supply: The quantity supplied increases as the price rises and decrease as the price falls. These changes are represented by movements along the supply curve. The table also lists the factors that cause changes in supply. Changes in these factors will cause the supply curve to shift.

CONCEPT REVIEW

1. The _____ _____ of a good or service is the amount that consumers are willing and able to purchase at a particular price.

2. The law of demand states that, other things being equal, the higher the _____ of a good, the _____ is the quantity demanded.

3. A demand _____ is a list of the quantities of a good demanded at different _____.

4. A demand curve illustrates the _____ price that consumers are willing to pay for the last unit of a good purchased.

5. The entire relationship between the quantity of a good demanded and its _____ is referred to as demand.

6. The demand curve for most goods will shift to the right if income _____, or if the price of a substitute _____, or if the price of a complement _____, or if the size of the population _____.

7. A good is said to be _____ if the demand for it increases as income increases and _____ if demand decreases as income increases.

8. A decrease in the price of a good will cause an increase in the _____

_____ ; that is represented by a downward _____ _____ the demand curve.

9. The amount of a good or service that producers plan to sell at a particular price is called the _____ _____ .

10. The law of supply states that the higher the _____ of a good, the _____ is the quantity supplied.

11. A supply curve shows the quantity supplied at each given _____ .

12. A decrease in supply is represented by a shift to the _____ in the supply curve.

13. The supply curve will shift to the right if the price of a complement in production _____ , or if the price of a substitute in production _____ , or if there is a technological _____ , or if the price of a productive resource _____ .

14. An increase in the price of a good will cause an increase in the _____ _____ ; that is represented by a (an) _____ movement along the supply curve.

15. The price at which the quantity demanded equals the quantity supplied is called the _____ price.

16. If the price is above equilibrium, a (an) _____ will exist, causing the price to _____ .

17. When demand increases, the equilibrium price will _____ and the quantity traded will _____ .

18. When supply increases, the equilibrium price will _____ and the quantity traded will _____ .

19. If demand increases and supply increases, then we know that the quantity traded must _____ ; but equilibrium price may increase, decrease, or remain unchanged.

TRUE OR FALSE

___ 1. If the quantity of a good demanded exceeds the quantity available, then the quantity traded will be less than the quantity demanded.

___ 2. The law of demand tells us that as the price of a good rises the demand decreases.

___ 3. The law of demand tells us that as the price of a good rises the quantity demanded decreases.

___ 4. The negative slope of a demand curve is a result of the law of demand.

___ 5. An increase in the price of apples will shift the demand curve for apples to the left.

___ 6. Hamburgers and french fries are complements. If Burger Doodle reduces the price of french fries, the demand for hamburgers will increase.

____ 7. If an increase in income causes a decrease in the demand for turnips, then turnips are inferior goods.

____ 8. A demand curve shows the least that consumers are willing to pay for the last unit.

____ 9. A demand curve is a graphical representation of the relationship between the price of a good and quantity demanded given the level of income, prices of other goods, population, and tastes.

____ 10. The law of supply implies that a supply curve will have a negative slope.

____ 11. A cost-reducing technological improvement will shift a supply curve to the right.

____ 12. If we observe a doubling of the price of mozzarella cheese (an ingredient in any pizza), we will expect the supply curve for pizza to shift to the left.

____ 13. When a cow is slaughtered for beef, its hide becomes available to make leather. Thus, beef and leather are substitutes in production.

____ 14. If the price of beef rises, we would expect to see an increase in the supply of leather and in the quantity of beef supplied.

____ 15. If the current price is such that the quantity demanded exceeds the quantity supplied, the price will tend to rise.

____ 16. If demand increases, we would predict an increase in equilibrium price and a decrease in quantity traded.

____ 17. If potatoes are inferior goods, we would expect a rise in income to result in a fall in the price of potatoes.

____ 18. A change in demand will cause equilibrium price and quantity traded to move in opposite directions.

____ 19. A decrease in the supply of a good will result in a decrease in both the equilibrium price and the quantity traded.

____ 20. Suppose there is a significant decline in the price of iron ore (used in making steel). We would predict that the equilibrium price of steel will fall and the quantity traded will increase.

____ 21. Suppose the demand for personal computers increased while the cost of producing them decreased. With this information, we can predict that the quantity of personal computers traded will increase but the price could rise or fall.

____ 22. An increase in the price of avocados and a decrease in the quantity traded is consistent with a decrease in the supply of avocados.

____ 23. When the actual price is above the equilibrium price, a shortage occurs.

MULTIPLE CHOICE

1. If an increase in the price of good *a* causes the demand curve for good *b* to shift to the left, then
   a. *a* and *b* are substitutes in consumption.
   b. *a* and *b* are complements in consumption.
   c. *b* must be an inferior good.
   d. *a* must be a normal good.

2. The law of demand implies that, other things being equal,
   a. as the price of lobsters rises, the quantity of lobsters demanded will increase.
   b. as the price of lobsters rises, the quantity of lobsters demanded will decrease.
   c. as income increases, the quantity of lobsters demanded will increase.
   d. as the demand for lobsters increases, the price will rise.

3. Which of the following would lead to an increase in the demand for hamburgers?
   a. A new fad hamburger diet.
   b. A decrease in population size.
   c. An increase in the price of french fries, a complement.
   d. A decrease in consumer income.

4. Which of the following is NOT one of the "other things" held constant along a demand curve?
   a. Income
   b. Prices of other goods
   c. The price of the good itself
   d. Tastes

5. Good *a* is a normal good if
   a. an increase in the price of a complement causes the demand for *a* to decrease.
   b. an increase in income causes the demand for *a* to increase.
   c. an increase in the price of a substitute causes the demand for *a* to increase.
   d. it satisfies the law of demand.

6. If turnips are an inferior good, then, *ceteris paribus*, an increase in income will cause
   a. a decrease in the demand for turnips.
   b. an increase in the demand for turnips.
   c. a decrease in the supply of turnips.
   d. an increase in the supply of turnips.

7. A decrease in quantity demanded is represented by
   a. a rightward shift of the demand curve.
   b. a leftward shift of the demand curve.
   c. a movement upward and to the left along the demand curve.
   d. a movement downward and to the right along the demand curve.

8. The price of a good will tend to rise if
   a. there is a surplus at the current price.
   b. the current price is above equilibrium.
   c. the quantity demanded exceeds the quantity supplied at the current price.
   d. income decreases.

9. The fact that a decline in the price of a good causes producers to reduce the quantity of the good they plan to produce illustrates
   a. the law of supply.
   b. the law of demand.
   c. a change in supply.
   d. the nature of an inferior good.

10. Which of the following would <u>NOT</u> shift the supply curve of good x to the right?
   a. A reduction in the price of resources used in producing x
   b. An improvement in technology affecting the production of x
   c. An increase in the price of y, a complement in the production of x
   d. An increase in the price of x

11. A decrease in quantity supplied is represented by
   a. a movement down the supply curve.
   b. a movement up the supply curve.
   c. a rightward shift in the supply curve.
   d. a leftward shift in the supply curve.

12. Which of the following will shift the supply curve for good x to the left?
   a. A decrease in the wages of workers employed to produce x
   b. An increase in the cost of machinery used to produce x
   c. A technological improvement in the production of x
   d. A situation where quantity demanded exceeds quantity supplied

13. If a producer can use its resources to produce either good a or good b, then a and b are
   a. substitutes in production.
   b. complements in production.
   c. substitutes in consumption.
   d. complements in consumption.

14. If the market for good a is in equilibrium, then
   a. the scarcity of good a is eliminated.
   b. producers would like to sell more at the current price.
   c. consumers would like to buy more at the current price.
   d. there will be no surplus.

15. A shortage
   a. will exist if the price is above equilibrium.
   b. is the amount by which quantity demanded exceeds quantity supplied.
   c. is the amount by which quantity traded exceeds quantity supplied.
   d. is the amount by which quantity demanded exceeds the equilibrium quantity.

16. Which of the following correctly describes how price adjustment eliminates a shortage?
   a. As the price rises, the quantity demanded decreases while the quantity supplied increases.
   b. As the price rises, the quantity demanded increases while the quantity supplied decreases.
   c. As the price falls, the quantity demanded decreases while the quantity supplied increases.
   d. As the price falls, the quantity demanded increases while the quantity supplied decreases.

17. A surplus can be eliminated by
   a. increasing supply.
   b. government raising the price.
   c. decreasing the quantity demanded.
   d. allowing the price to fall.

18. Suppose we observe an increase in the price of oranges. Which of the following is <u>NOT</u> a possible cause?
   a. A decrease in the price of apples, a substitute
   b. A scientific discovery that oranges will cure the common cold
   c. An increase in income
   d. A freeze in Florida

19. If *a* is a normal good and consumer income rises, the demand for *a* will
    a. increase, and thus the price and quantity traded will increase.
    b. increase, and thus the price will rise but quantity will decrease.
    c. decrease, and thus the price and quantity traded will decrease.
    d. decrease, and thus the price will fall but the quantity traded will increase.

20. If *a* and *b* are complementary goods (in consumption) and the cost of a resource used in the production of *a* decreases, then
    a. the price of *b* will fall but the price of *a* will rise.
    b. the price of *b* will rise but the price of *a* will fall.
    c. the price of both *a* and *b* will rise.
    d. the price of both *a* and *b* will fall.

21. If both demand and supply increase, what will be the effect on the equilibrium price and quantity traded?
    a. Both the price and quantity traded will increase.
    b. Price will fall but the quantity traded will increase.
    c. Quantity traded will increase but the equilibrium price could either rise or fall.
    d. Price will increase but the quantity traded could either increase or decrease.

22. Which of the following will definitely cause an increase in the equilibrium price?
    a. An increase in both demand and supply
    b. A decrease in both demand and supply
    c. An increase in demand combined with a decrease in supply
    d. A decrease in demand combined with an increase in supply

23. Farm land can be used to produce either cattle or corn. If the demand for cattle increases, then
    a. demand for corn will increase.
    b. supply of corn will increase.
    c. demand for corn will decrease.
    d. supply of corn will decrease.

SHORT ANSWER

1. Explain the difference between wants and demands.

2. List three events that would likely cause an increase in the demand for peanut butter. What effect would such an increase in demand have on the price of peanut butter and the quantity traded?

3. Suppose we observe that the consumption of peanut butter increases at the same time as its price rises. What must have happened in the market for peanut butter? Is the observation consistent with the law of demand?

4. Explain how a fall in price eliminates a surplus.

5. The price of personal computers has continued to fall even in the face of increasing demand. Explain.

6. A tax on crude oil would raise the cost of the primary resource used in the production of gasoline. A proponent of such a tax has claimed that it will not raise the price of gasoline using the following argument: While the price of gasoline may rise initially, that price increase will cause the demand for gasoline to decrease which will push the price back down. What is wrong with this argument?

PROBLEMS

1. Table 4.1 gives the demand and supply
    schedules for cases of grape jelly.
    a) In the graph provided by Fig. 4.1 (or a
       similar graph you construct yourself),
       graphically represent the demand and
       supply curves for grape jelly. Be sure
       to properly label the axes. Label the
       demand and supply curves D_0 and S_0
       respectively.
    b) What are the equilibrium price and
       quantity traded in the grape jelly
       market? In your diagram, label the
       equilibrium point a.
    c) Is there a surplus or shortage at a price
       of $40? How much?

Table 4.1

Price per case of grape jelly (dollars)	Quantity of jelly demanded (cases per week)	Quantity of jelly supplied (cases per week)
70	20	140
60	60	120
50	100	100
40	140	80
30	180	60

Figure 4.1

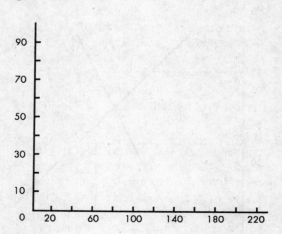

2. Suppose income increases sufficiently that
    the demand for grape jelly increases by 60
    cases per week at every price.
    a) Constrct a table (price, quantity
       demanded) giving the new demand
       schedule.
    b) Draw the new demand curve and label
       it D_1.
    c) Label the new equilibrium point b.
       What are the new equilibrium price
       and quantity traded?

3. Figure 4.2 is a graphical representation of
    the market for potatoes.
    a) What is the quantity of potatoes
       demanded at a price of $130 per ton?
       What is the quantity supplied at that
       price?
    b) What is the quantity of potatoes
       demanded at a price of $70 per ton?
       What is the quantity supplied at that
       price?
    c) What are equilibrium price and
       quantity traded?

Figure 4.2

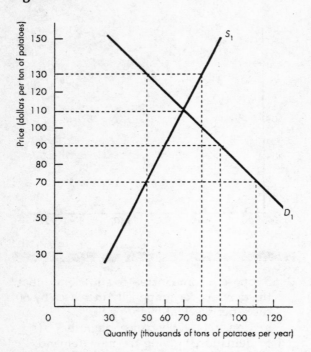

4. Now suppose that a new genetically improved strain of potatoes is developed which reduces the cost of producing any given quantity of potatoes. As a result, the supply of potatoes increases: at every price, the quantity supplied increases by 30,000 tons per year.
    a) Draw this new supply curve in Fig. 4.2. What are quantity demanded and quantity supplied at $110 per ton?
    b) What are the new equilibrium price and quantity traded?

5. Suppose further that new scientific studies demonstrate that french fries cure the common cold. As a result, the demand for potatoes increases at every price, the quantity demanded increases by 30,000 tons per year. Draw the new demand curve in Fig. 4.2. What are the resulting equilibrium price and quantity traded?

6. Soft drink makers use large quantities of sweeteners in the production of soft drinks. Both sugar and corn syrup make excellent sweeteners for this purpose. Historically, soft drink makers have used sugar, but several years ago the price of sugar rose significantly. As a consequence, soft drink manufacturers switched to the use of corn syrup. Think about the effects in the market for corn syrup as well as the market for soft drinks.
    a) Graphically show the effects in the market for corn syrup resulting from an increase in the price of sugar. What curve will shift? Why? What will happen to equilibrium price and quantity traded?
    b) Graphically show the effects in the market for soft drinks resulting from an increase in the price of sweeteners. What curve will shift? Why? What will happen to equilibrium price and quantity traded?

CONCEPT REVIEW

1. quantity demanded
2. price; lower
3. schedule; prices
4. highest
5. price
6. increases; increases; decreases; increases
7. normal; inferior
8. quantity demanded; movement along
9. quantity supplied
10. price; higher

11. price

12. left

13. increases; decreases; improvement; decreases

14. quantity supplied; upward

15. equilibrium

16. surplus; fall

17. increase; increase

18. decrease; increase

19. increase

TRUE OR FALSE

1. T	6. T	11. T	16. F	21. T
2. F	7. T	12. T	17. T	22. T
3. T	8. F	13. F	18. F	23. F
4. T	9. T	14. T	19. F	
5. F	10. F	15. T	20. T	

MULTIPLE CHOICE

1. b	6. a	11. a	16. a	21. c
2. b	7. c	12. b	17. d	22. c
3. a	8. c	13. a	18. a	23. d
4. c	9. a	14. d	19. a	
5. b	10. d	15. b	20. b	

SHORT ANSWER

1. Wants reflect our unlimited desires for goods and services without regard to our ability or willingness to make the sacrifices necessary to obtain them. The existence of scarcity means that many of those wants will not be satisfied. On the other hand, demands refer to plans to buy and therefore reflect decisions about which wants to satisfy.

2. Any three events that are consistent with the following will increase the demand for peanut butter.
   a) An increase in the price of a substitute for peanut butter (perhaps sliced ham)
   b) A decrease in the price of a complement (perhaps bread)
   c) An increase in consumer income (assuming that peanut butter is a normal good)
   d) An increase in population size
   e) The price of peanut butter is expected to rise in the future (perhaps due to bad weather in Georgia).
   f) A change in tastes that now makes peanut butter more desirable
   Any of these will increase the demand for peanut butter and will thus cause the price of peanut butter to rise and the quantity of peanut butter traded to increase.

3. The observation that the consumption of peanut butter increases at the same time as the price of peanut butter rises is entirely consistent with the law of demand (i.e., a negatively sloped demand curve). It simply reflects that the demand for peanut butter has increased (the demand has shifted to the right).

4. The existence of a surplus means that, at the current price, the quantity supplied is greater than the quantity demanded. Thus, to eliminate the surplus, either the quantity demanded must increase or the quantity supplied must decrease (or both). As the price falls, we get exactly the necessary results (due to the laws of demand and supply): the quantity demanded increases and the quantity supplied decreases.

5. Due to the tremendous pace of technological advance, not only has the demand for personal computers been increasing, but the supply has been

increasing as well. Indeed, supply has been increasing much more rapidly than demand, which has resulted in falling prices. Thus, *much* (but not all) of the increase in sales of personal computers reflects a movement along a demand curve rather that a shift in demand.

6. This argument confuses a movement along an unchanging demand curve with a shift in the demand curve. The proper analysis is the following. The increase in the tax on crude oil will increase the cost of the primary resource used in production of gasoline and thus shift the supply curve for gasoline to the left. This will cause the equilibrium price of gasoline to increase and thus the *quantity of gasoline demanded* will decrease -- demand itself will not decrease (i.e., the demand curve will not shift). The decrease in supply causes a movement along an unchanged demand curve.

PROBLEMS

1. a) Figure 4.1 Solution graphically illustrates the demand and supply curves for the grape jelly market. They are labeled D_0 and S_0 respectively. Note the labeling of the axes.
   b) The equilibrium is given at the intersection of the demand and supply curves (labeled point a). The equilibrium price is $50 per case and the equilibrium quantity traded is 100 cases per week.
   c) At a price of $40 there is a shortage of 60 cases per week.

Figure 4.1 Solution

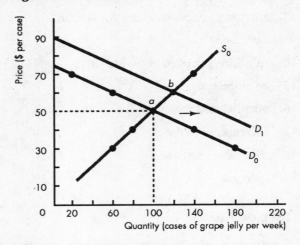

2. a) The new demand schedule is given in Table 4.3. The (unchanged) supply schedule is also included.

Table 4.3 Demand and Supply Schedules for Grape Jelly per Week

Price (per case)	Quantity Demanded (cases)	Quantity Supplied (cases)
$30	240	60
$40	200	80
$50	160	100
$60	120	120
$70	80	140

   b) The new demand curve is labeled D_1 in Fig. 4.1 Solution above.
   c) The new equilibrium is labeled point b. The new equilibrium price is $60 per case and the quantity traded is 120 cases of grape jelly per week.

3. See Fig. 4.2 Solution.

Figure 4.2 Solution

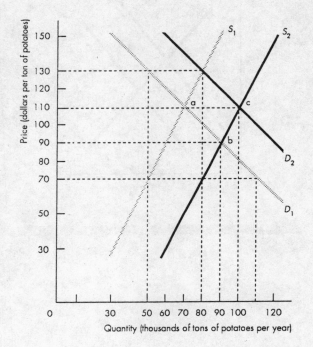

Quantity (thousands of tons of potatoes per year)

a) At a price of $130 per ton, 50,000 tons of potatoes are demanded and 80,000 tons of potatoes are supplied. Thus, at this price we observe a surplus of 30,000 tons.

b) At a price of $70 per ton, 110,000 tons of potatoes are demanded and 50,000 tons of potatoes are supplied. Thus, at this price there is a shortage of 60,000 tons.

c) The equilibrium price is $110 and the equilibrium quantity traded is 70,000 tons of potatoes per year. The equilibrium is indicated as point *a* in Fig. 4.2 Solution.

4. a) The technological advance shifts the supply curve to the right. The new supply curve is given by S_2 in the figure. After the shift, $110 is no longer the equilibrium price, since at that price, the quantity demanded remains at 70,000 tons while the quantity supplied has increased to 100,000 tons. A surplus of 30,000 tons is the result.

    b) The new equilibrium price is $90 and the new equilibrium quantity traded is 90,000 tons per year. This new equilibrium is labeled point *b* in the figure.

5. The change in tastes shifts the demand curve to the right, to D_2. The new equilibrium is labeled point *c* in the figure and corresponds to a price of $110 and quantity traded of 100,000 tons of potatoes per year.

6. a) The effect on the market for corn syrup is illustrated in Fig. 4.3. The demand curve for corn syrup will shift from D_1 to D_2 due to an increase in the price of a substitute, sugar. This will cause both price and quantity traded to increase as the market achieves a new equilibrium.

Figure 4.3

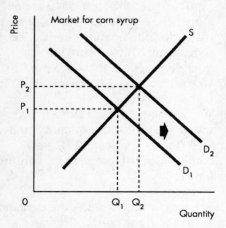

Figure 4.4

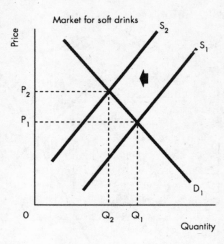

b) Figure 4.4 illustrates the effect on the market for soft drinks. The supply curve for soft drinks will shift to the left, from S_1 to S_2, because of the increase in the cost of resources (sugar or corn syrup) used in the production of soft drinks. In this market, the price of soft drinks will rise and the quantity traded will decline.

5 ELASTICITY

CHAPTER IN PERSPECTIVE

The analysis in Chapter 4 showed how changes in demand and supply can explain the *direction* of changes in quantity and price. If , for example, the supply of a good falls, its quantity demanded falls and its price rises -- but, how much? In this chapter, we learn to calculate the *magnitude* of these changes -- for example, by *how much* does the quantity demanded fall?

The key concept for calculating the magnitude of such changes is *elasticity*. Elasticity is a measure of the *responsiveness* of quantity demanded or supplied to changes in other key economic variables. Using different applications of elasticity, we learn to calculate how much quantity demanded will respond to changes in price, income, or changes in the prices of substitutes or complements, and by how much quantity supplied will respond to a change in price. The concept of elasticity is very useful. It can help a company decide whether lowering the price of its product will increase or decrease total revenue from sales. It can also help a government policymaker estimate how much revenue a sales tax will raise.

LEARNING OBJECTIVES

After studying this chapter, you will be able to:

- Define and calculate the price elasticity of demand

- Explain what determines the elasticity of demand

- Distinguish between short-run demand and long-run demand

- Use elasticity to determine whether a price change will increase or decrease revenue

- Define and calculate other elasticities of demand

- Define and calculate the elasticity of supply

- Distinguish between momentary supply, long-run supply, and short-run supply

HELPFUL HINTS

1. Once again: *Avoid the tendency just to mem orize formulas.* Once you develop a thorough understanding of the elasticity concepts introduced in the chapter, you will find that recalling the formulas becomes almost natural.

2. Use Table 5.6 in the chapter as a convenient review device.

3. There are many elasticity formulas in this chapter, but they are all based on the same simple intuitive principle -- *responsiveness.* All of the demand and supply elasticity formulas measure the *responsiveness* (sensitivity) of *quantity* (demanded or supplied) to changes in something else. Thus percentage change in quantity is always in the numerator of the relevant formula. As you come to understand how quantity responds to changes in price, income, and prices of related goods, you will be able to work out each elasticity formula, even if you have temporarily forgotten it.

4. The law of demand assures us that price and quantity demanded always move in opposite directions along any demand curve. Thus, the formula for the *price* elasticity of demand will always yield a negative number. Because our main interest is in the *magnitude* of the response of quantity demanded to a change in price, for convenience, we define the **elasticity of demand** as the absolute value of the *price* elasticity of demand. The complete formula for calculating the elasticity of demand between two points on the demand curve as shown in Table 5.1 is:

$$\eta = \left| \frac{\% \, \Delta \, QuantityDemanded}{\% \, \Delta \, Price} \right|$$

$$= \left| \left(\frac{\Delta Q}{Q_{AVE}} \right) \Big/ \left(\frac{\Delta P}{P_{AVE}} \right) \right|$$

5. Remember that elasticity is *not* the same as slope, although they are related. Indeed, along a straight-line demand curve the slope is constant, but the elasticity varies from infinity to zero as we move down the demand curve. At the midpoint of a linear demand curve, the price elasticity is equal to 1.

6. An important practical use of the concept of elasticity of demand is that it allows us to predict the *effect on total revenue* of a change in price. The law of demand tells us that price and quantity move in opposite directions along any demand curve. For example, an *increase* in price will cause a *decrease* in quantity demanded. Since total revenue is price times quantity, the increase in price will tend to increase total revenue, while the decrease in quantity demanded will decrease total revenue. The net effect depends on which of these individual effects is larger. If the percentage increase in price is greater than the percentage decrease in quantity demanded, the price effect will dominate and total revenue will increase. However, saying that the percentage change in price is greater than the percentage change in quantity demanded is exactly the same as saying that demand is inelastic. Thus we see that there is a precise connection between the elasticity of demand and the effect of an increase in price on total revenue. You should work through this same logic for elastic demand as well. The main point to understand is that if demand is inelastic the direction of the price change will dominate (i.e., the net effect on total revenue will be positive if the price change is positive), but if demand

is elastic, the direction of the change in quantity will dominate.

7. Two other important elasticity concepts are the income elasticity of demand and the cross elasticity of demand .

Income Elasticity of Demand:

$$\eta_Y = \frac{\% \Delta\, QuantityDemanded}{\% \Delta\, Income}$$

$$= \left(\frac{\Delta Q}{Q_{AVE}}\right) \Big/ \left(\frac{\Delta Y}{Y_{AVE}}\right)$$

Cross Elasticity of Demand:

$$\eta_X = \frac{\% \Delta\, Quantity\ Demanded\ of\ Good\ A}{\% \Delta\, Price\ of\ Good\ B}$$

$$= \left(\frac{\Delta Q^A}{Q^A_{AVE}}\right) \Big/ \left(\frac{\Delta P^B}{P^B_{AVE}}\right)$$

Notice that these two elasticity formulas do *not* have absolute value signs and can take on either positive or negative values. While any elasticity measures responsiveness, in these cases, both the magnitude *and the direction* of the response are important. In the case of income elasticity of demand, the response of quantity demanded to an increase in income will be positive for a normal good and negative for an inferior good. In the case of cross elasticity of demand, the response of the quantity demanded of good A to an increase in the price of good B will be positive if the goods are substitutes and negative if the goods are complements.

KEY FIGURES AND TABLES

Figure 5.2 Calculating the Elasticity of Demand

This figure illustrates how to calculate the elasticity of demand (η) between two points on a demand curve. The elasticity of demand is calculated as the percentage change in quantity demanded divided by the percentage change in price. The *percentage change* in quantity demanded is the *change* in quantity demanded divided by the *average* quantity. Similarly, the percentage change in price is the change in price divided by the average price. Thus, we measure the elasticity of demand midway between the old and new price-quantity points on the demand curve.

Figure 5.3 Elasticity Along a Straight-Line Demand Curve

While the slope of a straight-line demand curve is constant, the elasticity varies systematically as we move along a straight-line demand curve. The elasticity decreases as the price of the good falls and the quantity demanded rises. At the midpoint of a straight-line demand curve, elasticity is 1 (demand is unit elastic). In the price range above the midpoint, demand is elastic, and in the price range below the midpoint, demand is inelastic.

Figure 5.4 Demand Curves with Constant Elasticity

This figure illustrates three demand curves with constant price elasticity. The first, part (a), is a vertical demand curve which has 0 elasticity since any price change will have no effect on quantity demanded. The demand curve in part (b) has constant unitary elasticity. The horizontal demand curve in part (c) is infinitely elastic (the measure of elasticity is infinite).

Figure 5.5 Income Elasticity of Demand

The three graphs in this figure illustrate relationships between *income* (measured

on the horizontal axis) and quantity demanded (measured on the vertical axis). Part (a)
shows a relationship in which the quantity
demanded increases as income increases, but
the quantity demanded increases by a greater
percentage than income. Thus the income
elasticity is greater than 1. In part (b) quantity demanded and income again increase together but the percentage change in quantity
demanded is less than the percentage change
in income. The first part of the relationship in
part (c) is similar to that of part (b). However, as income continues to increase, eventually
the quantity demanded reaches a maximum
and thereafter decreases. At the point of
maximum quantity demand, the income elasticity is zero and it is negative for higher levels of income.

Table 5.1 Calculating the Elasticity of Demand

The price elasticity of demand is defined as the percentage change in the quantity
demanded divided by the percentage change
in the price. This table illustrates the procedure for calculating the price elasticity of
demand. The top part of the table shows the
calculation of the percentage change in price
and the bottom part shows the calculation of
the percentage change in quantity demanded.

Table 5.6 A Compact Glossary of Elasticities of Demand

Three kinds of elasticities of demand
are presented in this chapter of the text: price
elasticities, income elasticities, and cross elasticities of demand. The purpose of this table
is to summarize the economic meaning of
these measures as they assume values in alternative ranges. This table should serve as an
excellent study device.

SELF-TEST

CONCEPT REVIEW

1. A units-free measure of the responsiveness of quantity demanded to price changes is given by the _____ _____ of demand.

2. The (price) elasticity of demand is calculated as the percentage change in the _____ _____ divided by
the percentage change in the _____.

3. If the elasticity of demand is between zero
and one, demand is said to be _____; if it is greater than one,
demand is said to be _____; if it
is equal to one, demand is said to be _____ _____.

4. A good that has many good substitutes is
likely to have demand that is _____. If only a small proportion
of income is spent on a good, its demand
will likely be _____.

5. As time passes after a change in the price
of a good, demand will tend to become
more _____.

6. If demand is elastic, an increase in the
price implies that revenue (expenditures)
will _____.

7. A measure of the responsiveness of the
quantity demanded of a good to changes
in income is given by the _____ _____ of demand.

8. The income elasticity of demand is calculated as the percentage change in the _____ _____ divided by the percentage change in _____.

9. The income elasticity is _____ for inferior goods.

10. The responsiveness of the quantity demanded of one good to a change in the price of a complement or substitute is given by the _____ _____ of demand.

11. The cross elasticity of demand with respect to the price of a substitute is _____. The cross elasticity of demand with respect to the price of a complement is _____.

12. The elasticity of supply is a measure of the responsiveness of the _____ _____ to changes in _____.

13. To illustrate the initial change in quantity supplied induced by a sudden change in price we use the _____ supply curve. To illustrate the response of quantity supplied after all technologically possible long-run adjustments in the production process have been made we use the _____-_____ supply curve.

14. The long-run supply curve will generally be more _____ than a short-run supply curve, which will be more _____ than the momentary supply curve.

TRUE OR FALSE

____ 1. The elasticity of demand measures how responsive prices are to changes in demand.

____ 2. A horizontal demand curve is perfectly inelastic.

____ 3. An increase in supply will increase revenue (expenditure) if demand is elastic.

____ 4. Elasticity of demand is constant along a linear demand curve.

____ 5. The demand for gasoline is likely to become more inelastic with the passage of time after a price increase.

____ 6. If an increase in the price of a good from $7 to $9 causes quantity demanded to decrease from 8500 units to 7500 units, the elasticity of demand is .5.

____ 7. If a 10 percent decrease in the price of automobiles results in a 10 percent increase in quantity demanded, demand is unit elastic.

____ 8. The more readily available substitutes are for a good, the more inelastic will be its demand.

____ 9. If total revenue falls following a reduction in price, demand must be inelastic.

____10. If you like Pepsi Cola and Coca-Cola about the same, your demand for Pepsi is likely to be elastic.

____11. If your expenditures on toothpaste are a small proportion of your total income, your demand for toothpaste is likely to be inelastic.

____12. The income elasticity of demand is the percentage change in quantity demanded divided by the percentage change in income.

____13. If the income elasticity of the demand for turnips is positive, then turnips are an inferior good.

____14. The effect of the change in the price of one good on the quantity demanded of another good is measured by the cross elasticity of demand.

____15. We would expect the cross elasticity of demand between hamburgers and hot dogs to be negative.

____16. If a 10 percent increase in the price of good *a* causes a six percent increase in the quantity of good *b* demanded, then *a* and *b* must be complements.

____17. If goods *a* and *b* are substitutes, then an increase in the demand for *a* will lead to an increase in the equilibrium price of *b*.

____18. Supply elasticity is a measure of the responsiveness of the quantity of a good supplied to changes in income.

____19. If a three percent decrease in price induces a nine percent decrease in quantity supplied, then the supply curve is elastic.

____20. Supply will generally be more inelastic in the long run than in the short run.

____21. If an increase in price from $9 to $11 causes an increase in quantity supplied from 19,500 units to 20,500 units, the elasticity of supply is .25.

____22. A vertical aggregate supply curve exhibits a supply elasticity of zero.

____23. If a decrease in supply causes revenue to decrease, then demand must be inelastic.

____24. For a linear demand curve, demand is more elastic at higher price ranges than at lower price ranges.

____25. If a 10 percent increase in the price of good *a* causes a six percent increase in the quantity of good *b* demanded, the cross elasticity of demand between *a* and *b* is .6.

____26. If a 12 percent increase in income causes a nine percent increase in quantity demanded, the income elasticity of demand is 1.33.

____27. If a price cut leaves revenue unchanged then the demand curve is unit elastic.

____28. If a nine percent increase in price leads to a five percent decrease in quantity demanded, total revenue has decreased.

MULTIPLE CHOICE

1. The price elasticity of demand is calculated as
   a. the change in quantity demanded divided by the change in price.
   b. the change in price divided by the change in quantity demanded.
   c. the percentage change in quantity demanded divided by the percentage change in price.
   d. the percentage change in price divided by the percentage change in quantity demanded.

2. If a small (percentage) drop in the price of a good causes a large (percentage) increase in quantity demanded,
   a. demand is inelastic.
   b. demand is elastic.
   c. demand is unit elastic.
   d. the price elasticity of demand is close to zero.

3. If a five percent increase in price causes a six percent decrease in quantity demanded, demand is
   a. elastic.
   b. inelastic.
   c. unit elastic.
   d. income inelastic.

4. If a five percent decrease in price causes a six percent increase in quantity demanded, the price elasticity of demand is
   a. .30.
   b. .6.
   c. 1.2.
   d. 3.0.

5. The quantity of apples demanded has fallen by eight percent in the face of an eight percent increase. The demand for apples is apparently
   a. elastic.
   b. inelastic.
   c. unit elastic.
   d. upward sloping.

6. A vertical demand curve
   a. is unit elastic.
   b. is perfectly elastic.
   c. is likely to arise in the long run.
   d. has price elasticity of zero.

7. Suppose a rise in the price of a good from $5.50 to $6.50 causes a decrease in quantity demanded from 12,500 to 11,500 units. In this range of the demand curve, the price elasticity of demand is
   a. 1.0.
   b. 2.0.
   c. .5.
   d. 20.

8. For which of the following will demand be the most elastic?
   a. Milk
   b. Happy Cow brand milk
   c. Happy Cow brand milk at Ralph's Grocery Store
   d. Each of the above will exhibit the same demand elasticity.

9. A good will have more inelastic demand
   a. the higher its price.
   b. the larger the percentage of income spent on it.
   c. the longer the time elapsed.
   d. if it has no close substitutes.

10. A given percentage increase in the price of a good is likely to cause a larger percentage decline in quantity demanded
   a. the shorter the passage of time.
   b. the larger the proportion of income spent on it.
   c. the harder it is to obtain good substitutes.
   d. the more elastic is supply.

11. If a four percent rise in the price of peanut butter causes the total revenue from peanut butter sales to fall by eight percent, then demand for peanut butter
   a. must be elastic in the relevant price range.
   b. must be inelastic in the relevant price range.
   c. must be unit elastic in the relevant price range.
   d. has elasticity equal to .5 in the relevant price range.

12. If the oil minister of the country of Saudi Petrolia claims that an increase in the supply of OPEC oil will increase total oil sales revenue, then he must believe the demand for oil to be
   a. income inelastic.
   b. income elastic.
   c. price elastic.
   d. price inelastic.

13. If the Jets decrease ticket prices and find that total revenue does not change, then the price elasticity of demand for tickets is
   a. zero.
   b. greater than zero but less than one.
   c. equal to one.
   d. greater than one.

14. If a large percentage increase in income results in a small percentage decrease in quantity demanded at the current price, then
   a. demand must be elastic.
   b. demand must be inelastic.
   c. the good in question is normal.
   d. the good in question is inferior.

15. If a 10 percent increase in income causes a five percent increase in quantity demanded (at a constant price), what is the income elasticity of demand?
   a. .5
   b. -.5
   c. 2.0
   d. -2.0

16. Fred's income has just risen from $950 per week to $1050 per week. As a result, he decides to double the number of movies he attends each week. Fred's demand for movies
   a. is price elastic.
   b. is price inelastic.
   c. is income elastic.
   d. is income inelastic.

17. The cross elasticity of demand is a measure of
   a. the responsiveness of the quantity of one good demanded to changes in the price of another.
   b. the responsiveness of the quantity of a good demanded to changes in its price.
   c. the responsiveness of the elasticity of demand for one good to changes in the elasticity of demand for another good.
   d. the responsiveness of the elasticity of demand for one good to changes in income.

18. If goods *a* and *b* are substitutes, then
   a. the cross elasticity of demand between *a* and *b* is zero.
   b. the cross elasticity of demand between *a* and *b* is negative.
   c. the cross elasticity of demand between *a* and *b* is positive.
   d. their income elasticities of demand are both negative.

19. Suppose the cross elasticity of demand between peanut butter and jelly is negative, then
   a. an increase in the price of peanut butter will cause an increase in the equilibrium price of jelly.
   b. an increase in the price of peanut butter will cause a decrease in the equilibrium price of jelly.
   c. an increase in the price of peanut butter will have no effect on the equilibrium price of jelly.
   d. peanut butter and jelly are substitutes.

20. Suppose that a decrease in the price of *a* from $10.50 to $9.50 causes an increase in the quantity of *b* demanded (at the current price of *b*) from 7960 units to 8040 units. The cross elasticity of demand between *a* and *b* is
   a. -.01.
   b. -.1.
   c. .01.
   d. .1.

21. The elasticity of supply is calculated by
   a. dividing the percentage change in quantity supplied by the percentage change in price.
   b. multiplying the percentage change in quantity supplied by the percentage change in price.
   c. dividing the percentage change in price by the percentage change in quantity supplied.
   d. dividing the change in quantity supplied by the change in price.

22. Supply is inelastic if
   a. a small percentage change in price causes a large percentage change in quantity supplied.
   b. a large percentage change in price causes a small percentage change in quantity supplied.
   c. the good in question is normal.
   d. the good in question is inferior.

23. A rise in the price of good A from $7 to $9 results in an increase in quantity supplied from 4500 to 5500 units. Then the elasticity of supply is
   a. .625.
   b. .8.
   c. 1.0.
   d. 1.25.

24. The magnitude of *both* the elasticity of demand and the elasticity of supply depend on
   a. the ease of substitution between goods.
   b. the proportion of income spent on a good.
   c. the time elapsed since the price change.
   d. the technological conditions of production.

25. The long-run supply curve is likely to be
   a. more elastic than momentary supply but less elastic than short-run supply.
   b. less elastic than momentary supply but more elastic than short-run supply.
   c. less elastic than both momentary and short-run supply curves.
   d. more elastic than both momentary and short-run supply curves.

SHORT ANSWER

1. Why is elasticity superior to slope as a measure of the sensitivity of quantity demanded to changes in price?

2. In each of the following, compare the price elasticity of demand for each pair of goods and explain why the demand for one of the goods is more elastic than demand for the other.

   a) IBM personal computers before the development of other "clone" personal computers versus IBM personal computers after the production of such clones

   b) Television sets versus matches

   c) Electricity just after an increase in its price versus electricity two years after the price increase

   d) Aspirin versus Bayer-brand aspirin

3. Why does demand tend to be more elastic in the long run?

4. Why does supply tend to be more elastic in the long run?

5. Explain why knowing that demand is elastic tells us that a decrease in price will cause an increase in total revenue.

6. Why is the income elasticity of demand negative for an inferior good?

7. What is meant by the cross elasticity of demand? Why is the cross elasticity of demand positive between goods that are substitutes?

8. A freeze in Florida will have a larger effect on the price of oranges the more inelastic the demand for oranges. Explain.

PROBLEMS

1. a) Given the demand curve in Fig. 5.1, complete the second and third columns of Table 5.1 for η (the price elasticity of demand) and ΔTR (the change in total revenue) as the price falls from the

higher price to the lower price. Describe the relationship between elasticity and change in total revenue as price falls (moving down the demand curve).

Figure 5.1

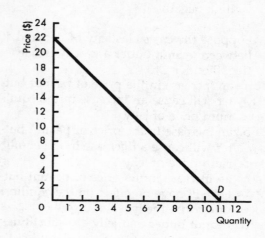

Table 5.1

ΔP($)	η	ΔTR($)	η′	ΔTR′($)
16 − 14				
14 − 12				
12 − 10				
10 − 8				
8 − 6				

b) Suppose income, which initially was $10,000, increases to $14,000, causing an increase in demand: at every price, quantity demanded increases by 2 units. Draw the new demand curve in and label it D′. Use this new demand curve to complete the last two columns of Table 5.1 for η′ (the new price elasticity of demand) and $\Delta TR'$ (the new change in revenue).

c) Explain (in words) why D' is more inelastic than D over any price range.

d) Calculate the income elasticity of demand, assuming the price remains constant at $12. Is this a normal or inferior good? Explain why you could have answered the question even without calculating the income elasticity of demand.

2. Which demand curve in Fig. 5.2 (D_1 or D_2) is more elastic in the price range P_1 to P_2? Explain why.

Figure 5.2

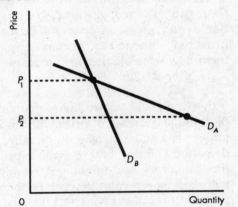

3. Table 5.2 gives the demand schedules for good A when the price of good B (P_B) is $8 and when the price of good B is $12. Complete the last column of Table 5.2 by computing η_x, the cross elasticity of demand between goods A and B for each of the three prices of A. Are A and B complements or substitutes?

Table 5.2 Demand Schedules for Good A

	$P_B = \$8$	$P_B = \$12$	
P_A	Q_A	Q'_A	η_x
8	2,000	4.000	
7	4.000	6.000	
6	6.000	8.000	

ANSWERS

CONCEPT REVIEW

1. price elasticity
2. quantity demanded; price
3. inelastic; elastic; unit elastic
4. elastic; inelastic
5. elastic
6. decrease
7. income elasticity
8. quantity demanded; income
9. negative
10. cross elasticity
11. positive; negative
12. quantity supplied; price
13. momentary; long-run
14. elastic; elastic

TRUE AND FALSE

1.	T	7.	T	13.	F	19.	T	25.	T
2.	F	8.	F	14.	T	20.	F	26.	T
3.	T	9.	T	15.	F	21.	T	27.	T
4.	F	10.	T	16.	F	22.	T	28.	F
5.	F	11.	T	17.	T	23.	F		
6.	T	12.	T	18.	F	24.	T		

MULTIPLE CHOICE

1.	c	6.	d	11.	a	16.	c	21.	a
2.	b	7.	c	12.	c	17.	a	22.	b
3.	a	8.	c	13.	c	18.	c	23.	b
4.	c	9.	d	14.	d	19.	b	24.	c
5.	c	10.	b	15.	a	20.	b	25.	d

SHORT ANSWER

1. The slope of a demand curve tells us how much quantity demanded changes when price changes, but its numerical value depends on the units we use to measure price and quantity and will change if our unit of measure is changed even though demand is unchanged. For example, if we change our unit of measure for quantity from tons to pounds, the new slope of the (same) demand curve will be 2000 times the old slope. On the other hand, elasticity gives a *units-free* measure of the responsiveness of quantity demanded to price changes.

2. a) The demand for IBM personal computers will be more elastic after the production of clone personal computers since there would then be more readily available substitutes.
   b) The demand for television sets will be more elastic since they will generally take a larger proportion of consumer income.
   c) The demand for electricity after the passage of two years will be more elastic since consumers will have more time to find substitutes for electricity (e.g., a gas stove).
   d) The demand for Bayer aspirin is more elastic. There are far more substitutes for Bayer aspirin (e.g., other brands of aspirin) than there are for aspirin in general.

3. Demand is more responsive to price changes (more elastic) in the long run because more substitutes become available to consumers. Not only are new goods invented but consumers also learn about and begin to use new substitutes.

4. Supply is more elastic in the long run because the passage of time allows producers to find better (more efficient) ways of producing that are not available in the short run. The responsiveness of production to an increase in price will increase as firms have time to discover and implement new technologies or to increase the scale of operation.

5. If demand is elastic, we know that any percentage decrease in price will cause a larger percentage increase in quantity demanded. Since total revenue is price times quantity, and quantity demanded increases by a greater percentage than price decreases, the net effect on total revenue must be an increase.

6. In Chapter 4 an inferior good was defined as any good for which demand decreases as income increases. For an inferior good, if we have a *positive* change in income the change in quantity demanded must be *negative*. Thus the income elasticity will be negative.

7. The cross elasticity of demand is a units-free measure of the responsiveness of the quantity of one good demanded when the price of another changes. It is the ratio of

the percentage change in the quantity of a good demanded to the percentage change in the price of the other good. Two goods are substitutes if an increase in the price of one increases the demand for the other. In this case both the change in price and the change in quantity demanded have the same sign and so the cross elasticity of demand between the goods is positive.

8. A freeze in Florida will cause the supply curve for oranges to shift to the left by some amount. This will cause the price of oranges to rise, but the percentage effect on price depends on the elasticity of demand. If demand is inelastic we know that relatively large percentage increases in price are associated with any given percentage decreases in quantity demanded. Thus the more inelastic the demand for oranges the larger will be the effect on price of a change in quantity. Figure 5.3 illustrates the point. In the diagram, the initial supply of oranges is given by S. We have drawn two possible demand curves: D_e, which is elastic and D_i, which is relatively inelastic. The freeze in Florida will cause the supply curve for oranges to shift to S'. It is clear from the diagram that the price increase will be much greater for D_i, the inelastic demand.

Figure 5.3

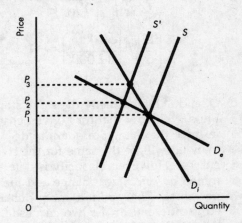

PROBLEMS

1. a) The second and third columns of Table 5.1 have been completed below in Table 5.1 Solution. These columns show that as price falls, total revenue increases when demand is elastic; total revenue falls when demand is inelastic.

Table 5.1 Solution

$\Delta P(\$)$	η	$\Delta TR(\$)$	η'	$\Delta TR'(\$)$
16 − 14	2.14	8	1.36	4
14 − 12	1.44	4	1.00	0
12 − 10	1.00	0	0.73	-4
10 − 8	0.69	-4	0.53	-8
8 − 6	0.47	-8	0.37	-12

b) The new demand curve is labeled D' in the Fig. 5.1 Solution below. The last two columns of Table 5.3 have been completed on the basis of the new demand curve.

$$\eta_Y = \left(\frac{\Delta Q}{Q_{AVE}}\right) / \left(\frac{\Delta Y}{Y_{AVE}}\right)$$

$$= \left(\frac{2}{6}\right) / \left(\frac{4,000}{12,000}\right) = +1$$

c) D' and D have exactly the same slope. Thus, we know that for a given change in price the change in quantity demanded will be the same for the two curves. However, elasticity is determined by *percentage* change and the percentage change in quantity demanded is different for the two curves (although the percentage change in price will be the same). For a given percentage change in price, the percentage change in quantity demanded will always be less for D'. For example, as the price increases from \$14 to \$16 (a 13 percent increase), the quantity demanded decreases from 6000 to 5000 units along D' but from 4000 to 3000 along D. The percentage change in quantity demanded is only 18 percent along D' and 29 percent along D. Since the percentage change in price is the same for both curves, D' is more inelastic than D.

d) Income increases from \$10,000 to \$14,000. At a constant price of \$12, the increase in income, which shifts out the demand curve to D', increases the quantity consumers will demand from 5 units to 7 units. Substituting these numbers into the formula for income elasticity of demand yields:

The income elasticity of demand is a positive number, since both ΔQ and ΔY are positive. Therefore, this is a normal good. We already knew that from the information in part (b), which stated that the demand curve shifted to the

right with and increase in income. If this were an inferior good, the increase in income would have shifted the demand curve to the left, and the income elasticity of demand would have been negative.

Figure 5.1 Solution

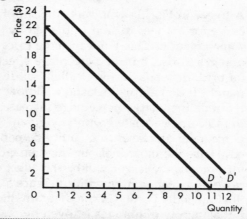

2. D_A is more elastic than D_B. To see why, look at the formula for the elasticity of demand:

$$\eta = \left| \frac{\% \, \Delta \, QuantityDemanded}{\% \, \Delta \, Price} \right|$$

$$= \left| \left(\frac{\Delta Q}{Q_{AVE}}\right) / \left(\frac{\Delta P}{P_{AVE}}\right) \right|$$

The percentage change in price is the same for the two demand curves. But the percentage change in quantity is greater for D_A as illustrated in Figure 5.2 Solution. At P_1, the initial quantity demanded is the same for both demand curves (Q_1). With the fall in price to P_2, the increase in quantity demanded is greater for D_A (to Q_{2A})

than for D_B (to Q_{2B}). Therefore, D_A is more elastic than D_B.

3. The cross elasticities of demand between A and B have been computed and reported in the last column of Table 5.2 Solution below. Since the cross elasticities are positive we know that A and B are substitutes.

Figure 5.2 Solution

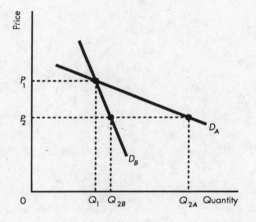

Table 5.2 Solution   Demand Schedules for Good A

	$P_B = \$8$	$P_B = \$12$	
P_A	Q_A	Q_A'	η_x
8	2,000	4.000	1.67
7	4.000	6.000	1.00
6	6.000	8.000	0.71

6 MARKETS IN ACTION

CHAPTER IN PERSPECTIVE

In the two previous chapters we learned how markets respond to the forces of demand and supply. This chapter uses the theory of demand and supply to examine the behavior of price and quantity traded in markets that are subject to outside influences. It begins by analyzing the effects of government regulation of prices. In an attempt to control price fluctuations resulting from shifts in demand or supply, governments sometimes introduce price ceilings (for example, rent controls) and price floors (for example, minimum wages). When prices are not allowed to adjust to restore equilibrium between buyers and sellers, what happens? This is the first major question addressed in this chapter. We find that when legal prices cannot adjust to changes in demand and supply, the adjustment instead takes the form of costly search activity, black markets, or unemployment.

This chapter also uses the theory of demand and supply to examine the effect of a sales tax or the prohibition of a good on the price and quantity of the good traded. Finally, the chapter uses the theory to explain the wide fluctuations in farm revenue and how farm revenue is affected by inventory speculation and government programs.

LEARNING OBJECTIVES

After studying this chapter, you will be able to:

- Explain the short-run and long-run effects of a change in supply on price and the quantity traded

- Explain the short-run and long-run effects of a change in demand on price and the quantity traded

- Explain the effects of price controls

- Explain why price controls can lead to black markets

- Explain how sales taxes affect prices

- Explain how the prohibition of a good affects its price and quantity consumed

- Explain why farm prices and revenues fluctuate

Explain how inventories and speculation limit price fluctuations

HELPFUL HINTS

1. In the real world we frequently observe market intervention by governments in the form of price constraints of one form or another. It is thus important to study the effects of such intervention in its own right. Another significant benefit of exploring the effects of government intervention, however, is a clearer and deeper understanding of how markets work when the government does *not* inhibit their natural operation.

Whenever something happens to disturb an equilibrium in a n unregulated (free) market, the desires of buyers and sellers are brought back into balance by price movements. If prices are controlled by government regulation, however, the price mechanism can no longer serve this purpose. Thus, *balance* must be restored in some other way. In the case of price ceilings, black markets are likely to arise. If black markets cannot develop because of strict enforcement of the price ceiling, then demanders will be forced to bear the costs of increased search activity, waiting in line, or something else.

2. This chapter focuses on government price constraints in two specific markets: rental housing and labor. It is important to realize that the principles that come to bear in those two examples can be generalized to other markets.

a) In *any* market with a legal price ceiling set below the market-clearing price, we will observe excess quantity demanded, because the price cannot increase to eliminate it. As a consequence, the value of the last unit of the good available will exceed the controlled price, and therefore, demanders are willing to engage in costly activities up to the value of that last unit (e.g., search activity, waiting lines, and black market activity) in order to obtain the good. Further-

more, if the price is allowed to increase in response to a decrease in supply or an increase in demand, there are incentive effects on suppliers to produce more and demanders to purchase less (i.e., movements along the supply and demand curves). Indeed it is the response to these incentives that restores equilibrium in markets with freely adjusting prices. If, however, the price cannot adjust, these price-induced incentive effects do not have a chance to operate. Specifically, in the case of rent ceilings, we see that the inability of rents (price) to rise (after an earthquake, for example) means that: (1) there is no inducement to use the current stock of housing more intensively in the short run, and (2) there is no incentive to construct new housing in the long run.

b) Similarly, the effects on *any* market in which a minimum price (price floor) is set above the market-clearing (equilibrium) price will be similar to those discussed in the text for the labor market under a minimum wage.

3. As we learned in Chapter 4, the supply curve gives the minimum amount a supplier must receive in order to be willing to offer any given quantity for sale. The imposition of a sales tax raises that minimum price by the amount of the tax. Thus, the after-tax supply curve lies above the before-tax supply curve by the amount of the tax. For a positively sloped supply curve, this implies that the after-tax equilibrium price will rise by *less* than the amount of the tax as long as demand is not perfectly inelastic.

4. Even markets for goods which have been legally prohibited by the government are subject to the laws of supply and demand. If the government enforces the prohibition by punishing sellers, the cost of selling the good

increases and, accordingly, the after-prohibition supply curve will lie above the before-prohibition supply curve by the amount of that additional cost. The effect is essentially the same as imposing a sales tax on a legally consumed good. If the penalty for violating the prohibition is imposed on the buyer, the demand for the good decreases because the willingness to pay for the good decreases.

5. In a market in which inventories are held, price fluctuations will be smaller. The reason is that if the current price of a good deviates from its expected future price, there is a potential for profits to be made by "buying low and selling high." For example, if the current price falls below the expected future price, there will be an incentive to buy at the current low price and sell later at the higher expected future price. Attempts to do so will drive the current price up until the profit opportunity is eliminated. Thus, (ignoring storage costs) the current price is always equal to the expected future price; that is, the supply curve becomes perfectly elastic at the expected price.

KEY FIGURES AND TABLES

Figure 6.1 The San Francisco Housing Market in 1906

In 1906, San Francisco was hit by a devastating earthquake that destroyed more than half the existing housing. This figure illustrates the response of the unregulated housing market in San Francisco. Part (a) of the figure gives the equilibrium situation before the earthquake. The short-run response of the market is illustrated in part (b). After the earthquake, the short-run supply of housing decreases and the short-run supply curve shifts from SS to SS_A. At the old equilibrium rent of $110 per month, there is a large shortage of housing, which drives rent up to the new equilibrium level of $120 per month. As the rent rises the shortage is eliminated because existing housing is used more intensive-

ly (reflected in the movements along the D and SS_A curves). The increase in rent to $120 also provides a profit incentive to build more housing units. Since the current rent of $120 is higher than the long-run supply price of housing, new units will be built. This shifts the SS_A curve to the right until the rent has fallen back to $110 per month, as indicated in part (c).

Figure 6.2 A Rent Ceiling

This figure illustrates what would have happened in the San Francisco housing market after the 1906 earthquake if a rent ceiling of $110 per month had been imposed. Since rent could not rise to clear the market, there would be no incentive to use existing housing more intensively or to construct additional housing in the long run. This means that the quantity of housing units supplied would remain at 44,000. At this level the value of the last unit of housing is $130 per month. The difference between this value and the rent ceiling of $110 will be "spent" by individuals in the form of search time or other transactions costs.

Figure 6.3 A Market for Unskilled Labor

This figure illustrates the consequences of a decrease in the demand for labor in an unregulated market for unskilled labor. Part (a) illustrates the market in an initial equilibrium at a wage rate of $4 per hour and employment of 30 million hours of labor per year. Then a labor-saving machine is invented which shifts the demand for labor curve to the left; from D to D_A in part (b). If the wage rate is allowed to adjust freely, it will fall to $3 per hour and employment will fall to 20 million hours in the short run. At the lower wage, some workers have the incentive to leave the unskilled labor market to seek training that qualifies them for higher paying jobs. This causes the short-run supply curve of labor to shift to the left; from SS to SS_A in part (c). As a result, the wage rate begins to rise and, as illustrated here, eventually returns to $4 an hour, while employment falls to 10 million hours per year.

Figure 6.4 The Minimum Wage and Unemployment

As in Fig. 6.3, here we examine the consequences of a decrease in the demand for unskilled labor, but now we impose a minimum wage of $4 per hour. In this case, the wage rate is not able to fall to $3 per hour to clear the market. Instead, the wage rate will remain at $4 per hour and employment will fall to 10 million hours. We note that the quantity of labor supplied at $4 per hour is 30 million hours, but the quantity of labor demanded is only 10 million hours. Thus, 20 million hours of labor per year is unemployed as a result of the minimum wage.

Figure 6.5 A Sales Tax

The effect of a sales tax on market price and quantity traded is illustrated in this figure. The pre-tax demand and supply curves for CD players are given by D and S respectively, the price is $100 per player and 5000 CD players a week are traded. Then a sales tax of $10 per CD player is imposed which increases the minimum price that suppliers are willing to accept. This is reflected in the new supply curve, $S + Tax$, which has shifted up by the amount of the tax per CD player. The after-tax equilibrium price is $105 and 4000 CD players a week are traded. Notice that the equilibrium price has risen by only $5 per unit even though the sales tax is $10. The figure also illustrates the tax revenue ($40,000 per week) which is the tax per unit ($10) times the number of units sold each week (4000).

Figure 6.8 The Market for a Prohibited Good

This figure illustrates the effects of prohibiting a good. Without prohibition, the demand and supply curves for drugs are given by D and S respectively and the market is in equilibrium at point c. Once the good is prohibited there is a penalty for violating the prohibition. The penalty is the cost of breaking the law (CBL). If the penalty is imposed on the seller of drugs, the cost of selling drugs

rises by CBL and the supply curve shifts up to $S + CBL$ (i.e., supply decreases). The new equilibrium is at point a at a higher price but a lower quantity traded. If, on the other hand, the penalty for violating the prohibition is imposed on the buyer, the willingness to pay falls by CBL and the demand curve shifts down to $D + CBL$ (i.e., demand decreases). The new equilibrium is at point b with a lower price and lower quantity traded. If penalties are imposed equally on both sellers and buyers, the new equilibrium is at point d and price remains unchanged while quantity traded decreases by a large amount.

SELF-TEST

CONCEPT REVIEW

1. In an unregulated housing market, a sudden decrease in the supply of housing would cause rent to _____ in the short run and thus create an incentive for the construction of new housing to _____ in the long run.

2. A(n) _____ _____ is a regulation making it illegal to charge a rent higher than a specified level.

3. If a price ceiling is below the market clearing price, an excess quantity _____ of the relevant good (e.g., rental housing) will exist. In such a situation two mechanisms will tend to arise in order to achieve equilibrium. We will observe an increase in _____ activity as demanders spend more time tryingto find a seller. In addition, illegal

markets, called _____ markets, may arise in order to satisfy demand.

4. The invention of a new labor-saving technology will cause the demand curve for unskilled labor to shift to the _____. If the labor market is unregulated the wage rate will _____.

5. Unemployment will be created if a legal minimum wage is established that is _____ the market clearing wage rate.

6. When a sales tax is imposed on a good, the _____ curve shifts up by the amount of the _____. The more elastic the demand, the _____ the price increase resulting from the tax.

7. If the supply curve is perfectly elastic, a sales tax will be paid by the _____. If the demand curve is perfectly elastic, a sales tax will be paid by the _____.

8. If trading in a good is prohibited and the penalty for violating the prohibition falls on sellers, the cost of selling the good _____, and the _____ curve shifts up. If the penalty for violating the prohibition falls on buyers, willingness to pay for the good _____ to pay for the good _____ and the _____ curve shifts down.

9. Goods that can be stored (held as inventories) will exhibit _____ price fluctuations in the face of demand and supply fluctuations than goods that cannot be stored.

TRUE OR FALSE

____ 1. In an unregulated housing market, higher rents will quickly result in an increase in the quantity of housing supplied.

____ 2. In an unregulated housing market, higher rents will create an incentive to increase construction of new housing.

____ 3. In a housing market with rent ceilings, there will be a strong incentive to construct new housing.

____ 4. In a housing market with rent ceilings, there will be greater incentive for landlords to take care of apartments they rent than in an unregulated housing market.

____ 5. A black market will exist only if there is a price ceiling set below the market-clearing price.

____ 6. Search activity will tend to be greater in unregulated markets than in markets with price ceilings.

____ 7. The black market price of a good is usually below the regulated price.

____ 8. An increase in the minimum wage will reduce the number of workers employed.

____9. If the legal minimum wage is set below the market-clearing wage, the actual wage rate will be the legal minimum.

____10. In an unregulated labor market a decline in the demand for labor causes the wage rate to increase.

____11. If the wage rate for unskilled workers falls due to the invention of a labor-saving technology, many workers will now have an incentive to obtain training for higher paid jobs.

____12. The impact of minimum wage laws on unemployment among young workers tends to be about the same as it is for older workers.

____13. The more elastic the supply of a good, the larger is the portion of a sales tax paid by the buyer.

____14. The more elastic the demand for a good, the larger is the portion of a sales tax paid by the buyer.

____15. The price of good A will rise by the full amount of a sales tax on A if the supply curve is perfectly elastic.

____16. If consumption of a good is prohibited and the penalty for violating the prohibition is imposed on the buyer, price will rise and quantity traded will decrease.

____17. Taxing a good at a sufficiently high rate can achieve the same consumption level as prohibition.

____18. If no inventories are held, a poor wheat harvest will decrease farm revenue.

____19. Suppose the supply curve for corn fluctuates widely but that the demand curve is stable. The price of corn will fluctuate more if demand is elastic rather than inelastic.

____20. Buying goods to be put into inventory is equivalent to decreasing supply.

____21. By stabilizing prices, inventory speculation will stabilize farm revenue.

____22. Farm stabilization programs that set price floors usually create shortages.

MULTIPLE CHOICE

1. The short-run supply curve for rental housing will be positively sloped because
    a. the supply of housing is fixed in the short run.
    b. the current stock of buildings will be used more intensively for housing if rent rises.
    c. the cost of constructing new buildings increases as the number of buildings in existence increases.
    d. the cost of constructing a new building is about the same regardless of the number of buildings already in existence.

2. Rent ceilings imposed by governments
    a. keep rental prices below prices that would exist in an unregulated market.
    b. keep rental prices above prices that would exist in an unregulated market.
    c. keep rental prices equal to prices that would exist in an unregulated market.
    d. increase the stock of rental housing.

3. Which of the following is <u>NOT</u> a likely outcome of rent ceilings?
   a. A black market for rent-controlled housing
   b. Long waiting lists of potential renters of rent-controlled housing
   c. A short-run shortage of housing
   d. Black market prices below the rent ceiling prices

4. In an unregulated market which of the following is <u>NOT</u> a likely result of an earthquake that suddenly destroys a large proportion of the stock of housing?
   a. Higher rental prices
   b. A shortage of rental housing
   c. More basement apartments offered for rent
   d. More families sharing living quarters

5. Which of the following is <u>NOT</u> true?
   a. In the long run, the stock of available housing will be greater in an unregulated market than in a market with rent ceilings.
   b. In the short run, the quantity of rental housing supplied will be greater in an unregulated market than in a market with rent ceilings.
   c. Search activity costs will be lower in a housing market with rent ceilings than in an unregulated market.
   d. Rent ceilings will likely lead to a black market.

6. Refer to Fig. 6.1. What is the level of unemployment (in millions of hours) if the minimum wage is set at $3 per hour?
   a. 40
   b. 30
   c. 20
   d. 0

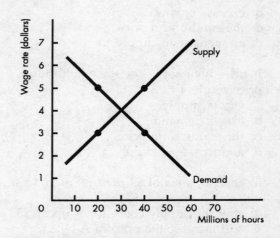

Figure 6.1

7. Refer to Fig. 6.1. What is the level of unemployment (in millions of hours) if the minimum wage is set at $5 per hour?
   a. 40
   b. 30
   c. 20
   d. 0

8. Which of the following types of labor would be most significantly affected by an increase in the legal minimum wage?
   a. Professional athletes
   b. Young, unskilled labor
   c. Skilled union workers
   d. College professors

9. Which of the following would <u>NOT</u> be considered a search activity?
   a. Time spent moving from one job to another
   b. Time spent looking for a new job
   c. Reading a consumer magazine for information as you shop for a new stereo
   d. Time spent looking for the best price for a chair

10. A price ceiling set below the equilibrium price will result in
    a. excess supply.
    b. excess demand.
    c. the equilibrium price.
    d. an increase in supply.

11. A price floor set below the equilibrium price results in
    a. excess supply.
    b. excess demand.
    c. the equilibrium price.
    d. an increase in supply.

12. In general, a tax of $3 per unit of good A will
    a. shift the supply curve for A up by $3 and increase the price of A by $3.
    b. shift the supply curve for A up by $3 and increase the price of A by less than $3.
    c. shift the supply curve for A up by more than $3 and increase the price of A by $3.
    d. shift the supply curve for A up by less than $3 and increase the price of A by less than $3.

13. Figure 6.2 gives the demand and supply for imported cheese. Suppose that the government imposes a $3 tax per pound of imported cheese. What will happen to the price?
    a. It will increase by $3 to $7.
    b. It will increase by $3 to $6.
    c. It will increase by $2 to $6.
    d. It will increase by $2 to $5.

Figure 6.2

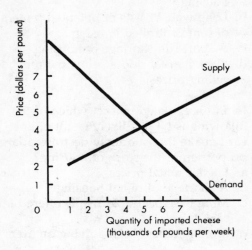

14. Consider again the $3 per pound tax discussed in the previous question. How is the burden of the tax shared between consumers and producers?
    a. The entire $3 is borne by consumers in the form of a higher price.
    b. The entire $3 is borne by producers in the form of lower sales.
    c. $2 is borne by producers in the form of lower receipts per unit and $1 is borne by consumers in the form of a higher price.
    d. $2 is borne by consumers in the form of a higher price and $1 is borne by producers in the form of lower receipts per unit.

15. A sales tax will be paid in full by the seller if
    a. demand is inelastic.
    b. supply is elastic.
    c. supply is perfectly elastic.
    d. supply is perfectly inelastic.

16. In Fig. 6.3, D and S indicate the demand and supply curves for good A in an unregulated market.   Suppose good A is prohibited and that the penalty for violating the prohibition (CBL - cost of breaking the law) is imposed on the buyer. Which point represents the outcome?
    a. a
    b. b
    c. c
    d. d

Figure 6.3

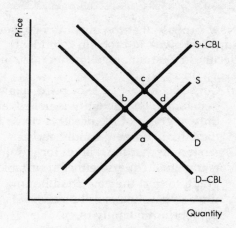

17. The existence of inventories will generally
    a. reduce price fluctuation but increase the fluctuation in quantity traded.
    b. reduce price fluctuation and reduce the fluctuation in quantity traded.
    c. increase price fluctuation and increase the fluctuation in quantity traded.
    d. increase price fluctuation but reduce the fluctuation in quantity traded.

18. If inventory speculation stabilizes wheat prices, a poor wheat harvest will
    a. increase farm revenue while a bumper crop will decrease farm revenue.
    b. decrease farm revenue while a bumper crop will increase farm revenue.
    c. increase farm revenue as will a bumper crop.
    d. decrease farm revenue as will a bumper crop.

SHORT ANSWER

1. Suppose there is a significant reduction in the supply of gasoline. Explain how an unregulated market adjusts. What is it that induces consumers to willingly reduce their consumption of gasoline?

2. Suppose a landlord owns two similar apartments in neighboring communities, one of which has rent ceilings while the other is unregulated. Why is the landlord likely to take better care of the apartment in the community with an unregulated housing market?

3. Why would no black market arise if a legal price is set above the actual market-clearing price?

4. What are the effects of a minimum wage that is set above the market-clearing wage rate for unskilled labor?

5. Why do the employment effects of an increase in the minimum wage tend to be greater on younger workers?

6. Explain how a sales tax on a good affects the supply of and demand for the good. Under what circumstances will the full sales tax be paid by the buyer?

7. Consider the market for a good that has just been prohibited. Explain why the

price declines and quantity traded declines when the penalty for violating the prohibition falls on the buyer.

8. If there are no crop inventories, why does farm revenue increase when there is a poor harvest?

9. Suppose the supply of a good that can be stored is subject to unpredictable fluctuations. Explain how inventories help reduce the variability of the price of the good.

10. If inventory speculation takes place, why does farm revenue decrease when there is a poor harvest?

PROBLEMS

1. Suppose that the market for rental housing is initially in (long-run) equilibrium. Use graphs to answer the following.
   a) Explain how an unregulated market for rental housing would adjust if there is a sudden significant increase in demand. What will happen to rent and the quantity of units rented in the short run? What will happen in the long run? Be sure to discuss the effect on incentives (in both the short run and the long run) as the market determined price (rent) changes.
   b) Now explain how the market would adjust to the increase in demand if rent ceilings are established at the level of initial equilibrium rent. What has happened to supplier incentives in this case?

2. Consider information about the demand for and supply of gasoline given in Table 6.1. What is the equilibrium price of gasoline and the equilibrium quantity of gasoline traded?

Table 6.1

Price (dollars per gallon)	Quantity demanded	Quantity supplied
	(millions of gallons per day)	
1.40	8	24
1.30	10	22
1.20	12	20
1.10	14	18
1.00	16	16
.90	18	14
.80	20	12
.70	22	10

3. Now suppose that the quantity of gasoline supplied given in Problem 2 suddenly declines by 8 million gallons per day at every price.
   a) Construct a new table of price, quantity demanded, and quantity supplied, and draw a graph of the demand curve and the initial and new supply curves.
   b) Assuming that the market for gasoline is unregulated, use either your table or graph to find the new equilibrium price of gasoline and the new equilibrium quantity of gasoline traded?
   c) How has the increase in price affected the behavior of demanders? The behavior of suppliers?

4. Suppose that the government imposes a price ceiling of $1.00 on a gallon of gasoline at the same time as the decrease in supply reported in Problem 3.
   a) What is the quantity of gasoline demanded?
   b) What is the quantity of gasoline supplied?
   c) What is the quantity of gasoline actually sold?
   d) What is the excess quantity of gasoline demanded?

e) What is the highest price demanders are willing to pay for the last gallon of gasoline available?

f) Consider someone who values gasoline as in (e). How long would such a person be willing to sit in line to buy 10 gallons of gasoline if his/her best alternative was to work at a wage rate of $8 per hour?

5. Return to the demand for and supply of gasoline given in Table 6.1. Now suppose that the government imposes a sales tax on gasoline of $.40 a gallon.

a) Table 6.2 gives the new (partial) after-tax demand and supply schedules. Complete the table.

b) Draw a graph of the gasoline market illustrating the effect of the sales tax.

c) What is the after-tax equilibrium price. What is the after-tax equilibrium quantity traded.

d) How much tax revenue does the government collect?

e) How is the burden of the $.40 tax divided between buyers and sellers?

Table 6.2

Price (dollars per gallon)	Quantity demanded	Quantity supplied
	(millions of gallons per day)	
1.40		
1.30		
1.20		
1.10		

6. The market for wheat is illustrated in Fig. 6.4. The demand curve for wheat is given by D.

a) Suppose there is a normal wheat harvest and the momentary supply curve is given by MS_0. What is the equilibrium price of wheat? What is

total farm revenue?

b) Suppose now that there is a poor harvest and the momentary supply curve is given by MS_1. Assuming that wheat inventories are <u>not</u> held, what is the equilibrium price of wheat? What is total farm revenue?

c) Consider the case of a poor harvest once again but now assume that wheat inventories are held and that the expected future price of wheat is $2 per bushel. Wheat is sold from inventories whenever the current price exceeds the expected future price and is purchased to be stored if the current price is less than the expected future price. What is the equilibrium price now? What is total farm revenue?

Figure 6.4

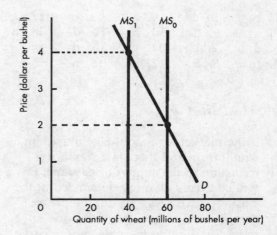

ANSWERS

CONCEPT REVIEW

1. increase; increase

2. rent ceiling

3. demanded; search; black

4. left; fall

5. above

6. supply; tax; smaller

7. buyer; seller

8. increase; supply; decrease; demand

9. smaller

TRUE OR FALSE

1. T	6. F	11. T	16. F	21. F
2. T	7. F	12. F	17. T	22. F
3. F	8. T	13. T	18. F	
4. F	9. F	14. F	19. F	
5. T	10. F	15. T	20. T	

MULTIPLE CHOICE

1. b	5. c	9. a	13. c	17. a
2. a	6. d	10. b	14. d	18. b
3. d	7. c	11. c	15. d	
4. b	8. b	12. b	16. a	

SHORT ANSWER

1. If the market for gasoline is initially in equilibrium and there is a significant reduction in the supply of gasoline, there will be excess quantity demanded at the existing price. As a result, the price of gasoline will rise, which will cause movements along the new supply curve and the demand curve. As the price rises there will be a price induced increase in quantity supplied and a price induced decrease in quantity demanded. The price will continue to rise until the excess quantity demanded is eliminated. Note that it is the price increase that causes consumers to reduce their desired consumption of gasoline.

2. Since the landlord cannot increase the rent on the apartment subject to rent ceilings and because there is likely a waiting list for people to get into it (reflecting the excess quantity demanded), there is little incentive for him/her to spend time and effort caring for it. We would expect to see the apartment in the unregulated community to be better cared for.

3. No black market would arise in this case because the ceiling price would not be effective. If the price ceiling is set above the market-clearing (equilibrium) price, the price will be the market-clearing price.

4. A minimum wage that is set above the market clearing wage rate for unskilled labor will result in unemployment among unskilled workers; that is, excess quantity of unskilled workers supplied.

5. Minimum wage laws tend to have a greater impact on younger workers because they are more likely to be unskilled and thus face a market-clearing wage lower than the legal minimum. This is part of the explanation for the fact that the unemployment rate among the young is more than twice the average rate.

6. A sales tax raises the minimum price suppliers are willing to accept for each quantity sold. This effectively shifts the supply curve up by the amount of the tax. In the text, this new curve was denoted *S + Tax*. The demand curve is unaffected by the sales tax. The full sales tax will be paid by the buyer if either demand is perfectly inelastic or supply is perfectly elastic.

7. When the penalty for violation of a prohibition is imposed on the buyer, the maximum price the buyer is willing to pay for the each quantity of the good declines: the demand curve shift down by

the cost of breaking the law. In the text, this new demand curve was labelled $D - CBL$. The decline in demand will result in a reduction in both price and quantity traded.

8. When there is a poor harvest, the supply of farm products declines and price rises. Since the demand for most farm products is inelastic, the increase in price implies an increase in farm revenue as we learned in Chapter 5.

9. Inventories are held to exploit any potential profit opportunities by selling goods from inventories if the current price is higher than the expected future price or buying goods to be added to inventories if the current price is below the expected future price. Selling if the price is above or buying if the price is below the expected future price means that the price will not deviate very far from the expected future price. Thus inventories help to reduce price fluctuations.

10. Since inventory speculation stabilizes prices, a poor harvest will result in a smaller quantity sold but no change in price. Thus, farm revenue falls since revenue is price times quantity.

PROBLEMS

1. a) Figure 6.5 corresponds to an unregulated market for rental housing. The initial demand, short-run supply, and long-run supply curves are D_0, SS_0, and LS, respectively. The market is initially in long-run equilibrium at point a corresponding to rent given by R_0 and number of units rented given by Q_0. Now demand increases to D_1 creating excess quantity demanded of $Q_2 - Q_0$. In the short run, in an unregulated market, rent will rise to R_1

to clear the market and the equilibrium quantity of housing rented is Q_1 (point b). Note that as the rent rises, the quantity of rental housing supplied increases as the existing stock of housing is used more intensively. Also the quantity of housing demanded decreases. Together, these eliminate the excess quantity demanded. The higher rent also provides an incentive to construct new housing in the long run. This is illustrated by the shift in the supply curve from SS_0 to SS_1. Finally, a new long-run equilibrium is achieved at point c, with rent restored to is original level and the number of units rented equal to Q_2.

Figure 6.5

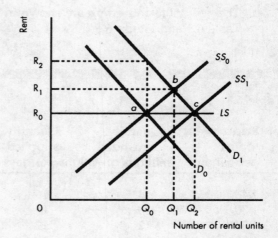

b) We now use the graph above to discuss the behavior of a market with a rent ceiling set at R_0. Again we start in the same long-run equilibrium at point a. Once again we observe an increase in demand from D_0 to D_1. In this case, however, the rent cannot rise to restore equilibrium. There will be no incentive to use the existing stock of housing more intensively in the short run or to construct new housing in the long run. The quantity of rental housing supplied will remain at Q_0. Since the last unit of rental housing is valued at R_2 but rent is fixed at R_0, demanders of rental housing will be willing to bear additional costs up to $R_2 - R_0$ (in the form of additional search activity or illegal payments) in order to obtain rental housing.

2. The equilibrium price of gasoline is $1.00 per gallon since, at that price, the quantity of gasoline demanded is equal to the quantity supplied (16 million gallons per day). The equilibrium quantity of gasoline traded is 16 million gallons of gasoline per day.

3. a) The new table and graph are shown in Table 6.3 and Figure 6.6.

Figure 6.6

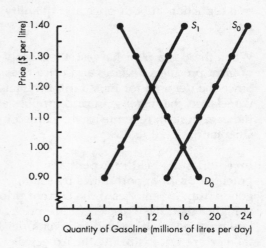

Table 6.3

Price (dollars per gallon)	Quantity demanded (millions of gallons per day)	Quantity supplied (millions of gallons per day)
1.40	8	16
1.30	10	14
1.20	12	12
1.10	14	10
1.00	16	8
.90	18	6
.80	20	4
.70	22	2

b) The new equilibrium price is $1.20 per gallon since, at that price, the quantity of gasoline demanded equals the new quantity supplied (12 millon gallons per day). The new equilibrium quantity traded is 12 million gallons of gasoline per day.

c) The increase in the price has caused the quantity of gasoline demanded to decrease by 4 million gallons per day (from 16 to 12 million) and the quantity of gasoline supplied to increase by 4 million gallons per day (from 8 to 12 million).

4. a) At the ceiling price of $1.00, the quantity demanded is 16 million gallons per day.

b) The quantity of gasoline supplied is 8 million gallons of gasoline per day.

c) The quantity of gasoline actually sold is equal to 8 million gallons per day.

d) The excess quantity of gasoline demanded is 8 million gallons per day.

e) The highest price consumers are willing to pay for the last unit of gasoline supplied (8 million gallons per day) is $1.40.

f) The regulated pump price of gasoline is $1.00 a gallon but the value of the last unit is $1.40 a gallon so the consumer in question would be willing to bear costs in the amount of $4.00 above the actual price of gasoline to obtain 10 gallons. If his or her best alternative is to earn $8.00 an hour, he or she would be willing to spend up to a half hour sitting in line to buy the 10 gallons.

5. a) Table 6.2 is completed as Table 6.2 Solution.

Table 6.2 Solution

Price (dollars per gallon)	Quantity demanded (millions of gallons per day)	Quantity supplied
1.40	8	16
1.30	10	14
1.20	12	12
1.10	14	10

b) The effects of the $.40 a gallon sales tax on gasoline are illustrated in Fig. 6.6. Notice that the after-tax supply curve, S_1, lies above the before-tax supply curve, S_0, by the amount of the tax.

c) The new equilibrium occurs at the intersection of the demand curve, D_0, and the after-tax supply curve, S_1. The after-tax equilibrium price is $1.20 a gallon and the after-tax equilibrium quantity traded is 12 million gallons per day.

d) A $.40 tax on 12 million gallons per day yields government tax revenue of $4.8 million dollars per day.

e) The after-tax price of $1.20 is $.20 above the before-tax price of $1.00.

Therefore, gasoline buyers bear $.20 of the $.40 per gallon tax. The remaining $.20 is borne by gasoline sellers since, after the tax, the price they receive is $.80.

6. a) The equilibrium price of wheat, $2 per bushel, is given by the intersection of the demand curve, D, and the normal momentary supply curve, MS_0. Total farm revenue is the price of $2 per bushel times the 60 million bushels of wheat sold: $120 million per year.

b) If there is a poor harvest and the momentary supply curve is given by MS_1, the equilibrium price of wheat is $4 a bushel. The sale of 40 million bushels at a price of $4 a bushel gives total farm revenue of $160 million per year.

c) If wheat is sold out of inventories whenever the price of wheat exceeds its expected price of $2 a bushel and wheat is purchased to add to inventories whenever the price of wheat falls below $2 a bushel, the equilibrium price of wheat will stabilize at $2 a bushel. (Recall Short Answer Question 9.) Only 40 million bushels of wheat are produced in a poor harvest year. Since, with inventory speculation, the price is $2 a bushel, total farm revenue is only $80 million.

7 UTILITY AND DEMAND

CHAPTER IN PERSPECTIVE

The fundamental economic concept of demand was introduced in Chapter 4. There we *assumed* that as the price of a good rises, the quantity of it demanded will decline. Assuming the law of demand allowed us to draw a number of useful conclusions and make predictions about the behavior of prices and quantity traded. But because demand is such an important concept, our confidence in these results would be enhanced if it were not necessary to assume the law of demand—if the law of demand could be derived as a prediction of a more fundamental theory. This is the major task of this chapter. Not only is the law of demand derived as a prediction of the marginal utility theory, but other results that had previously been assumed also turn out to be predictions.

This chapter and the next greatly deepen our understanding of the forces underlying the law of demand and associated concepts. It is difficult to overestimate the intellectual achievement of marginal utility theory in the development of modern economic thought.

LEARNING OBJECTIVES

After studying this chapter, you will be able to:

- Explain the connection between individual demand and market demand

- Define utility and marginal utility

- Explain the marginal utility theory of consumer choice

- Use the marginal utility theory to predict the effects of changing prices

- Use the marginal utility theory to predict the effects of changing income

- Define and calculate consumer surplus

- Explain the paradox of value

HELPFUL HINTS

1. The concept of utility is an extremely useful abstract device which allows us to think more clearly about consumer choice. Do not become confused by the fact that the units used to measure utility are arbitrary. The only thing that is important for marginal utility theory is that an individual is able to judge whether the additional satisfaction per dollar spent on good X is greater or less than the additional satisfaction per dollar spend on Y. If it is greater, then the decision is to consume an additional unit of X. How much greater is irrelevant, and perhaps meaningless, for the decision.

2. The marginal utility per dollar spent on good X can be written as MU_X / P_X where MU_X is the marginal utility of the last unit of X consumed and P_X is the price of a unit of good X. The consumer equilibrium (utility maximizing) condition for goods X and Y can thus be written:

(a) $$\frac{MU_X}{P_X} = \frac{MU_Y}{P_Y}$$

This implies that, in consumer equilibrium, the ratio of marginal utilities will equal the ratio of prices of the two goods; that is,

$$\frac{MU_X}{MU_Y} = \frac{P_X}{P_Y}$$

This result is sometimes useful.

3. If an individual is not in consumer equilibrium, then equation (a) above is not satisfied. For example, consider spending all of one's income on a consumption plan for which:

$$\frac{MU_X}{P_X} > \frac{MU_Y}{P_Y}$$

or equivalently,

$$\frac{MU_X}{MU_Y} > \frac{P_X}{P_Y}$$

Since P_X and P_Y are given, this means that MU_X is "too large" and MU_Y is "too small." Utility can be increased by increasing consumption of X (and thereby decreasing MU_X due to the principle of diminishing marginal utility) and decreasing consumption of Y (and thereby increasing MU_Y due to diminishing marginal utility).

4. Table 7.6 in the text is a good review device.

KEY FIGURES AND TABLE

Figure 7.1 Individual and Market Demand Curves

The market demand curve is obtained by adding the quantities demanded at each price by each individual. This figure illustrates this in a market with two individuals. At each price, quantity demanded in the market is equal to the quantity demanded by Lisa plus the quantity demanded by Chuck. This is illustrated graphically and in a table.

Figure 7.2 Consumption Possibilities

Consumption choices are constrained by income and the prices of goods available. This figure illustrates these consumption possibilities for Lisa. Lisa's income is $30 a month which she allocates between consumption of movies and soda. The table and graph illustrate the possible ways of allocating her income between these goods when the price of a movie is $6 and the price of a six-pack of soda is $3. The line in the graph reflects the boundary between affordable and unaffordable combinations of goods.

Figure 7.3 Total Utility and Marginal Utility

This figure shows (a) the total utility Lisa derives from consumption of movies as well as (b) the marginal (additional) utility resulting from each additional movie. The table shows that, as Lisa watches additional movies, her total utility increases but the marginal utility resulting from each additional movie is less than the marginal utility of the previous movie. For example, the additional satisfaction (marginal utility) from watching the sixth movie in a month is 21 units while the marginal utility from watching the seventh movie is 18 units. Because of diminishing marginal utility, as Lisa watches additional movies, her total utility increases but at a diminishing rate. The graph in part (a) illustrates the increase in total utility as monthly movie consumption increases while the graph in part (b) illustrates the decline in marginal utility as movie consumption increases.

Figure 7.4 Equalizing Marginal Utility per Dollar Spent

This figure plots the marginal utility per dollar associated with each of the possible consumption bundles given Lisa's income and the prices of movies and soda. It is important to recognize that it is these possible combinations of goods, from a to b, that are measured on the horizontal axis. For example, consumption possibility b corresponds to 1 movie and 8 six-packs of soda. If Lisa consumes possibility b, she obtains 8.33 units of utility from the last dollar spent on movies and 5.67 units of utility from the last dollar spent on soda. Since the marginal utility from the last dollar spent on movies is greater than the marginal utility of the last dollar spent on soda, Lisa can increase her utility by increasing her consumption of movies and decreasing her consumption of soda. Lisa's utility is a maximum when she consumes possibility c (2 movies and 6 six-packs of soda) where the marginal utility per dollar spent on movies and soda is equal (6.33).

Figure 7.5 A Fall in the Price of Movies

This figure illustrates the impact of a decrease in the price of movies on Lisa's demand in two different markets. In the movie market (part (a)), the fall in price causes a movement down *along* her demand curve, increasing her *quantity demanded* of movies. In the soda market (part (b)), because soda and movies are considered to be substitutes, the fall in the price of movies causes a leftward *shift* in her demand curve for soda, decreasing Lisa's *demand* for soda.

Figure 7.6 An Rise in the Price of Soda

This figure illustrates the impact of an increase in the price of soda on Lisa's demand in two different markets. In the soda market (part (a)), the increase in price causes a movement up *along* her demand curve, decreasing her *quantity demanded* of soda. In the movie market (part (b)), because soda and movies are considered to be substitutes, the rise in the price of soda causes a rightward *shift* in her demand curve for movies, increasing Lisa's *demand* for movies.

Figure 7.7 Consumer Surplus

Consumer surplus is the difference between the most a person is willing to pay for a good (its value to that person) and its price (the amount actually paid). This figure illustrates the calculation of consumer surplus by examining Lisa's demand for movies. We note that if the price of a movie is $3, Lisa will see 5 movies per month. While the value of the fifth movie is $3 to Lisa, the values of the first through fourth movies are higher. Thus Lisa enjoys some consumer surplus. The value of the first movie is $7, but since the ticket price is $3, Lisa receives consumer surplus of $4 on it. Similarly, she receives $3 on the second, $2 on the third, and $1 on the fourth movie. Thus, her total consumer surplus is the sum of these: $10.

Table 7.7 Marginal Utility Theory
   This table summarizes the assumptions, implications, and predictions of marginal utility theory. We note particularly that the first prediction is the law of demand.

SELF-TEST

CONCEPT REVIEW

1. The _____ demand curve is the sum of the quantities demanded by each individual at each _____.

2. The benefit or satisfaction a person receives from the consumption of a good or a service is called _____.

3. As consumption increases utility _____.

4. The additional utility a person receives from consuming one more unit of a good is called _____ _____.

5. As consumption increases marginal utility _____. This is called the principle of _____ marginal utility.

6. We assume that a household will choose quantities to consume so as to _____ utility subject to its income and the prices it faces.

7. The marginal utility per dollar spent is the marginal utility of the last unit of a good consumed divided by its _____.

8. Utility will be maximized if the marginal utility per dollar spent is _____ for all goods.

9. Marginal utility theory predicts that if the price of one good rises, _____ of it will be consumed and _____ of other goods will be consumed.

10. "When the price of a good rises, the quantity demanded falls" is an assumption of the consumer demand model of Chapter 4 but is a(n) _____ of the marginal utility theory.

11. Marginal utility theory predicts that the higher is household income, the _____ is the quantity consumed of all normal goods.

12. The difference between the value of a good and its price is called _____ _____.

TRUE OR FALSE

_____ 1. Market demand is the sum of all individual demands.

_____ 2. Marginal utility theory was invented by Adam Smith.

_____ 3. The units with which we measure utility are arbitrarily chosen.

_____ 4. The utility of a good is a measure of how useful it is in production.

_____ 5. The additional utility from consuming one more unit of a good is called marginal utility.

____ 6. The principle of diminishing marginal utility means that as consumption of a good increases, total utility declines.

____ 7. The marginal utility theory assumes that as consumption increases, total utility declines while marginal utility increases.

____ 8. A consumer equilibrium exists when a consumer has allocated his/her income in a way that maximizes total utility.

____ 9. Economists assume that households try to maximize their marginal utility.

____ 10. A household will be maximizing utility if the marginal utility per dollar spent is equal for all goods and all its income is spent.

____ 11. When the price of good X rises, the marginal utility from the consumption of X decreases.

____ 12. When the price of good X rises, the marginal utility per dollar spent decreases.

____ 13. If the marginal utility per dollar spent on good X exceeds the marginal utility per dollar spent on good Y; consumers can increase their utility by increasing consumption of X and decreasing consumption of Y.

____ 14. Marginal utility theory predicts that the higher the price of turnips the lower the quantity of turnips demanded.

____ 15. Marginal utility theory predicts that if the price of a good falls, consumption of substitute goods will rise.

____ 16. The price of good X is $2. The total utility of consuming 7 units of X is 76 while the total utility of consuming 8 units is 80. The marginal utility per dollar spent on X is 2 if 8 units are consumed.

____ 17. "The quantity demanded of normal goods increases as income increases" is a prediction of the marginal utility theory.

____ 18. Utility cannot be observed or measured.

____ 19. The fact that utility cannot be observed or measured makes the marginal utility theory essentially useless.

____ 20. Marginal utility theory does NOT make predictions about the thought processes of consumers.

____ 21. Marginal utility theory does make predictions about the actions of consumers.

____ 22. The value of a good is always the price of the good.

____ 23. The principle of diminishing marginal utility assures that consumers will always make some consumer surplus.

____ 24. Consumer surplus is the difference between the value of a good and its price.

____ 25. The fact that water is essential to life but has a low price while diamonds are quite inessential but are very expensive contradicts the marginal utility theory.

MULTIPLE CHOICE

1. Market demand is
   a. the sum of prices demanded by individuals at each quantity.
   b. the sum of the quantities demanded by each individual at each price.
   c. the sum of both prices and quantities demanded by all individuals.
   d. the total amount demanded by the largest buyer at each price.

2. As consumption of a good increases,
   a. total utility increases.
   b. total utility decreases.
   c. total utility remains unchanged.
   d. marginal utility increases.

3. The fact that the fourth slice of pizza did not generate as much satisfaction as the third slice is an example of
   a. consumer surplus.
   b. diminishing total utility.
   c. diminishing marginal utility.
   d. the paradox of value.

4. The benefit or satisfaction that a person receives from the consumption of goods and services is called
   a. marginal utility.
   b. utility.
   c. consumer demand.
   d. consumer equilibrium.

5. If the price of good X increases,
   a. the marginal utility from the consumption of X increases.
   b. the total utility from the consumption of X increases.
   c. the marginal utility per dollar spent on X increases.
   d. the consumption of X decreases.

6. The value for b in Table 7.1 should be
   a. 38.
   b. 48.
   c. 53.
   d. 63.

Table 7.1

Quantity	Utility	Marginal utility
0	0	0
1	20	20
2	a	18
3	b	15
4	63	c

7. The value for c in Table 7.1 should be
   a. 10.
   b. 13.
   c. 15.
   d. 22.

8. If a consumer is in equilibrium, then
   a. utility is maximized given the consumer's income and the prices of goods.
   b. marginal utility is maximized given the consumer's income and the prices of goods.
   c. marginal utility per dollar spent is maximized given the consumer's income and the prices of goods.
   d. the marginal utility of the last unit of each good will be the same.

9. If Ms. Petersen is maximizing her utility in the consumption of goods *A* and *B*, which of the following statements must be true?

a. $M_A = M_B$

b. $\dfrac{M_A}{P_A} = \dfrac{M_B}{P_B}$

c. $\dfrac{M_A}{P_B} = \dfrac{M_B}{P_A}$

d. $TU_A = TU_B$

10. Sam consumes apples and bananas and is in consumer equilibrium. The marginal utility of the last apple is 10 and the marginal utility of the last banana is 5. If the price of an apple is $.50, we know that the price of a banana must be
a. $.10.
b. $.25.
c. $.50.
d. $1.00.

11. Suppose that Arnie spends his entire income of $10 on law books and silk ties. Law books cost $2 and silk ties cost $4. The marginal utility of each good is shown in Table 7.2. If Arnie is maximizing his utility, how many silk ties does he buy?
a. 1
b. 2
c. 3
d. 4

Table 7.2

| Quantity | Marginal utility | |
	Law books	Silk ties
1	12	16
2	10	12
3	8	8
4	6	4

12. Which of the following is NOT an *assumption* of marginal utility theory?
a. Consumers derive utility from consuming goods.
b. Marginal utility is positive.
c. Utility is maximized when the marginal utility per dollar spent is equal for all goods.
d. As consumption of a good increases, the marginal utility declines.

13. Which of the following is NOT a *prediction* of marginal utility theory?
a. Other things being equal, the higher the price of a good, the lower is the quantity demanded.
b. Other things being equal, the higher the price of a good, the higher is the consumption of substitutes for that good.
c. The law of demand.
d. Decreasing marginal utility.

14. The "inventor" of marginal utility theory is
a. Adam Smith.
b. Michael Edgeworth.
c. Alfred Marshall.
d. Milton Friedman.

15. If a consumption plan that spends all of income has marginal utility per dollar spent on X of 4 and marginal utility per dollar spent on Y of 2, we know that
    a. utility can be increased by increasing the consumption of X and decreasing the consumption of Y.
    b. utility can be increased by decreasing the consumption of X and increasing the consumption of Y.
    c. the price of Y must be twice the price of X.
    d. utility is maximized.

16. Refer to Table 7.3. If the price of X is $2 per unit and the price of Y is $1 per unit, the first $4 of income should be used to purchase
    a. 2 units of good X.
    b. 2 units of good Y and 1 unit of X.
    c. 4 units of good Y.
    d. Cannot be determined from the table.

Table 7.3

| Quantity | Total utility | |
	Good X	Good Y
1	20	14
2	32	24
3	42	32
4	48	37
5	52	40
6	54	42
7	55	43

17. Refer to Table 7.3. If the price of X is $2 per unit, and the price of Y is $1 per unit, and income is $13, then utility is maximized with consumption of
    a. 6 units of X and 1 unit of Y.
    b. 5 units of X and 3 units of Y.
    c. 4 units of X and 5 units of Y.
    d. 3 units of X and 7 units of Y.

18. Suppose that Madonna spends her entire income of $6 on purple nail polish and leather outfits. Nail polish costs $1/unit and outfits cost $2/unit. The marginal utility of each good is shown in Table 7.4. If Madonna is maximizing her utility, what is her *total* utility?
    a. 19
    b. 28
    c. 38
    d. 42

Table 7.4

| | Marginal utility | |
Quantity	Nail polish	Outfits
1	8	16
2	6	12
3	4	10
4	3	6

19. Chuck and Barry have identical preferences but Chuck has a much higher income. If each is maximizing his utility, then
    a. they will have equal total utilities.
    b. Chuck will have lower total utility than Barry.
    c. Chuck will have lower marginal utility than Barry for most goods.
    d. Chuck will have higher marginal utility than Barry for most goods.

20. Squid costs $2 per pound and octopus costs $1 per pound. Jacques buys only octopus and gets 10 units of utility of satisfaction from the last pound he buys. Assuming that Jacques has maximized his utility, his marginal utility from the first pound of squid must be
   a. more than 10 units.
   b. less than 10 units.
   c. more than 20 units.
   d. less than 20 units.

21. The value of a good is defined as
   a. the price paid by an individual.
   b. the average price paid by individuals in a market.
   c. the cost of producing the good.
   d. the highest price an individual is willing to pay.

22. The difference between the value of a good and its price is known as
   a. excess demand.
   b. consumer surplus.
   c. consumer excess.
   d. marginal utility.

23. One criticism of marginal utility theory is that people do not really complete the calculations necessary to maximize utility. Choose the best rebuttal to this criticism.
   a. The usefulness of a theory depends upon the accuracy of its predictions.
   b. The usefulness of a theory depends upon the accuracy of its assumptions.
   c. The usefulness of marginal utility theory depends upon the measurability of the utility function.
   d. People actually do compute the conditions for consumer equilibrium.

24. The demand schedule for audio tapes is shown in Table 7.5. If the actual price is $7, what is total consumer surplus?
   a. 0
   b. $3
   c. $6
   d. $12

Table 7.5 Demand Schedule for Audio Tapes

Price (per tape)	Quantity demanded
$10	1
$ 9	2
$ 8	3
$ 7	4
$ 6	5

25. The high price of diamonds relative to the price of water reflects the fact that at typical levels of consumption
   a. the total utility of water is much lower than the total utility of diamonds.
   b. the marginal utility of water is high.
   c. the demand for diamonds is upward sloping.
   d. the marginal utility of diamonds is high.

SHORT ANSWER

1. How do we obtain the market demand curve from individual demands?

2. What is meant by utility. Can it be measured?

3. What is meant by marginal utility?

4. What is the principle of diminishing marginal utility?

5. What is the condition for utility maximization?

6. Consider the following information relevant to a consumer who is trying to allocate her income between goods X and Y so as to maximize utility. The price of X is $2 and the price of Y is $1 per unit. When income is spent the marginal utility of the last unit of X is 20 and the marginal utility of the last unit of Y is 16.
   a) Why is the consumer not in equilibrium?
   b) To increase utility, which good should this consumer consume more of and which less?

7. Explain why the consumer equilibrium condition and the principle of diminishing marginal utility imply the law of demand.

8. What is meant by consumer surplus?

9. How can marginal utility theory be useful even though utility cannot be measured?

10. How does marginal utility theory resolve the diamonds/water paradox of value?

PROBLEMS

1. Table 7.6 gives the demand schedules for broccoli for three individuals: Tom, Jana, and Ted.
   a) Calculate the market demand schedule.
   b) On a single diagram, draw the individual demand curves for Tom, Jana, and Ted, as well as the market demand curve.

Table 7.6 Individual Demand for Broccoli

Price (per pound)	Quantity demanded (pounds per week)		
	Tom	Jana	Ted
$0.50	10	4	10
$0.75	9	2	7
$1.00	8	0	4
$1.25	7	0	1

2. Tables 7.7 and 7.8 give the utility from the consumption of popcorn and candy bars by Amy during a week. Complete the tables.

Table 7.7 Amy's Utility from Popcorn

Bags of popcorn	Total utility	Marginal utility
1	20	
2	36	
3	50	
4		12
5	72	
6	80	
7	86	

Table 7.8 Amy's Utility from Candy Bars

Number of candy bars	Total utility	Marginal utility
1	14	
2	26	
3		10
4	44	
5	51	
6	57	
7	61	

3. Suppose the price of a bag of popcorn is $1 and the price of a candy bar is $.50. Given the information in Tables 7.7 and 7.8, complete Table 7.9 where MU/P means marginal utility divided by the price, which is equivalent to marginal utility per dollar spent.

Table 7.9

Bags of popcorn	MU/P	Number of candy bars	MU/P
1		1	
2		2	
3		3	
4		4	
5		5	

4. If the prices for popcorn and candy bars are as given in Problem 3,
   a) how should Amy spend her first dollar of weekly allowance? Why?
   b) how should she spend her second dollar of weekly allowance? Why?

5. Amy's weekly allowance is $4. Answer the following if she spends her entire allowance on popcorn and candy.
   a) How much popcorn and how many candy bars will Amy consume each week if she maximizes her utility?
   b) Show that the utility maximum condition is satisfied.
   c) What is total utility?
   d) Show that the consumption of slightly different quantities (still satisfying Amy's budget constraint) will result in a lower level of total utility.

6. Suppose that Amy's preferences remain as they were in Problem 2, but the price of a candy bar doubles to $1.
   a) Construct a new table (similar to Table 7.7 in problem 2) of MU/P for popcorn and candy bars.
   b) Amy's allowance continues to be $4. After the price change, how much popcorn and how many candy bars will she consume each week?
   c) Are popcorn and candy bars substitutes or complements for Amy? Why?
   d) Based on the information you have obtained, draw Amy's demand curve for candy bars.
   e) Suppose that both bags of popcorn and candy bars continue to sell for $1 each, but now, Amy's allowance increases to $6 per week.
     i) How many candy bars and bags of popcorn will Amy choose to consume per week under the new situation?
     ii) Are popcorn and candy bars normal goods? Why or why not?

7. Amy's friend Bonnie also likes popcorn and candy bars (indeed, her preferences are the same as Amy's). Her weekly allowance is $6, the same as Amy's new allowance. Suppose that the utility Bonnie derives from popcorn and candy bar consumption is exactly twice the utility de-

---

rived by Amy. Thus a table of Bonnie's utility can be obtained from Tables 7.7 and 7.8 by multiplying each of the numbers in the utility columns by 2. If candy bars and bags of popcorn continue to sell for $1 each,

a) How many candy bars and bags of popcorn will Bonnie choose to consume in a week?

b) How does this compare with Amy's consumption? What does this illustrate?

8. Andy's weekly demand for pizza is given in Table 7.10. If the price of a pizza is $9, what is Andy's consumer surplus on
   a) the first pizza he buys?
   b) the second pizza he buys?
   c) the total number of pizzas he buys at that price?

Table 7.10 Demand Schedule for Pizza

Price (per pizza)	Quantity demanded
$15	1
$12	2
$10	3
$ 9	4
$ 8	5

ANSWERS

CONCEPT REVIEW

1. market; price
2. utility
3. increases
4. marginal utility
5. decreases; diminishing
6. maximize
7. price
8. equal
9. less; more
10. prediction
11. greater
12. consumer surplus

TRUE OR FALSE

1. T	6. F	11. F	16. T	21. T
2. F	7. F	12. T	17. T	22. F
3. T	8. T	13. T	18. T	23. T
4. F	9. F	14. T	19. F	24. T
5. T	10. T	15. F	20. T	25. F

MULTIPLE CHOICE

1. b	6. c	11. a	16. b	21. d
2. a	7. a	12. c	17. c	22. b
3. c	8. a	13. d	18. a	23. a
4. b	9. b	14. c	19. c	24. c
5. d	10. b	15. a	20. d	25. d

SHORT ANSWER

1. The market demand curve is obtained as the sum of the quantity demanded for each individual at each price.

2. Utility is defined as the benefit or satisfaction that an individual obtains from consuming a good or a service. Utility cannot be measured.

3. Marginal utility is the additional utility derived from the last unit of a good or service consumed.

4. The principle of diminishing marginal utility says that as consumption of a good increases marginal utility declines.

5. Utility is a maximum when income is spent and the marginal utility per dollar spent is the same for all goods.

6. a) This consumer is not in equilibrium because the marginal utility per dollar spent is not the same for goods X and Y. The marginal utility per dollar spent on X is $MU_X/P_X = 20/2 = 10$, which is less than the marginal utility per dollar spent on Y: $MU_Y/P_Y = 16$.

   b) To equate the marginal utilities per dollar spent (and thus increase utility), this consumer should increase consumption of Y and decrease consumption of X. The principle of diminishing marginal utility implies that this will decrease the marginal utility of Y and increase the marginal utility of X.

7. Suppose we observe an individual in consumer equilibrium consuming X_0 units of good X and Y_0 units of good Y with the prices of X and Y given by P_X and P_Y respectively. This means that at consumption levels X_0 and Y_0, the marginal utility per dollar spent on X equals the marginal utility per dollar spent on Y. Now let the price of X increase to P_X'. This increase implies that the marginal utility per dollar spent on X declines and thus is now less than the marginal utility per dollar spent on Y. Thus, to restore equilibrium, our consumer must increase the marginal utility of X and decrease the marginal utility of Y. From the principle of diminishing marginal utility we know that the only way to do this is to decrease the consumption of X and increase the consumption of Y. This demonstrates the law of demand since an increase in the price of X has been shown to require a decrease

in the consumption of X to restore consumer equilibrium.

8. Consumer surplus is the difference between the value of a good (the most that a person would be willing to pay for it) and the price of the good.

9. The fact that utility cannot be measured does not hinder us from deriving the law of demand and other useful results from marginal utility theory. All that is necessary are the assumptions that people derive utility (satisfaction) from the consumption of goods and services, that utility increases when people consume more, and that the principle of diminishing marginal utility holds. None of these require an ability to measure utility.

10. The paradox of value is resolved by recognizing that while the total utility from consumption of water is large, the marginal utility from the last unit of water is small. Likewise, the total utility from the consumption of diamonds is small, but the marginal utility of the last unit of diamonds is large. If consumers are in equilibrium, then the requirement that the marginal utility per dollar spent be the same for water and diamonds means that the price of water must be low and the price of diamonds must be high.

PROBLEMS

1. a) The market demand schedule in Table 7.11 is obtained by adding the quantities demanded by Tom, Jana, and Ted at each price.

Table 7.11   Market Demand Schedule for Broccoli

Price (per pound)	Quantity demanded (pounds per week)
$0.50	24
$0.75	18
$1.00	12
$1.25	8

b) Figure 7.1 illustrates the individual demand curves for Ton, Jana, and Ted, as well as the market demand curve.

Figure 7.1

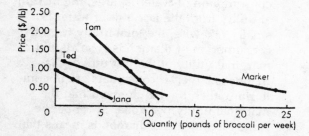

2. The completed table appears as Table 7.7 Solution and Table 7.8 Solution.

Table 7.7 Solution

Bags of popcorn	Total utility	Marginal utility
1	20	20
2	36	16
3	50	14
4	62	12
5	72	10
6	80	8
7	86	6

Table 7.8 Solution

Number of candy bars	Total utility	Marginal utility
1	14	14
2	26	12
3	36	10
4	44	8
5	51	7
6	57	6
7	61	4

3. The completed table is given in Table 7.9 Solution.

Table 7.9 Solution

Bags of popcorn	MU/P	Number of candy bars	MU/P
1	20	1	28
2	16	2	24
3	14	3	20
4	12	4	16
5	10	5	14
6	8	6	12

4. a) To obtain the most utility, the first dollar should be used to buy 2 candy bars, since the marginal utility per dollar spent on candy bars (24) exceeds the marginal utility per dollar spent on popcorn (20). We can confirm that this is the better choice by observing that total utility is greater after spending the first dollar on candy bars (26) than it would have been if the first dollar had been spent on popcorn (20).

   b) The second dollar should be spent on popcorn and the argument is similar. The marginal utility per dollar spent on popcorn (20) exceeds the marginal utility per dollar spent on candy bars (16). Similarly, total utility is 46 if the second dollar is spent on popcorn but only 44 if spent on candy bars.

5. a) She will consume 2 bags of popcorn and 4 candy bars, since all her income is spent and the utility maximum condition is satisfied.

   b) The utility maximum condition is satisfied since the marginal utility per dollar spent is the same for popcorn and candy bars (16).

   c) Total utility is the utility from the consumption of 2 bags of popcorn (36) plus the utility from the consumption of 4 candy bars (44): 80.

   d) Consider 3 bags of popcorn and 2 candy bars: total utility is 76. Consider 1 bag of popcorn and 6 candy bars: total utility is 77. In both cases total utility is less than 80, the total utility from the consumption of 2 bags of popcorn and 4 candy bars.

6. a) Table 7.12 gives the new table.

Table 7.12

Bags of popcorn	MU/P	Number of candy bars	MU/P
1	20	1	14
2	16	2	12
3	14	3	10
4	12	4	8
5	10	5	7
6	8	6	6

   b) Amy will consume 3 bags of popcorn and 1 candy bar. She spends all of her income ($4) and the marginal utility per dollar spend is the same for popcorn and candy bars (14).

   c) Popcorn and candy bars are substitutes for Amy, since an increase in the price of a candy bar causes an increase in the demand for popcorn.

   d) Amy's demand curve for candy bars is given in Fig. 7.2. Two points on the demand curve have been identified: when the price of a candy bar is $1, 1 candy bar will be demanded, and when the price is $0.50, 4 candy bars will be demanded. The demand curve is a line through these two points.

   e) i) Now, Amy will choose to consume 4 bags of popcorn and 2 candy bars (instead of 3 bags of popcorn and 1 candy bar). Amy spends all of her income ($6) and the marginal utility per dollar spent is the same for popcorn and candy bars (12).

ii) Popcorn and candy bars are both normal goods for Amy since the increase in income (allowance) leads to increases in the demand for both goods.

Figure 7.2 Amy's Demand Curve for Candy Bars

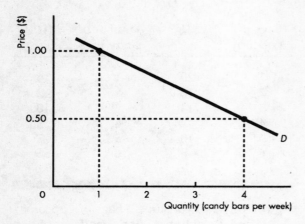

7. a) Bonnie will choose to consume 4 bags of popcorn and 2 candy bars.

   b) This is exactly the same consumption chosen by Amy even though Bonnie's utility is twice as high. This illustrates the fact that the units with which we measure utility make no difference.

8. a) The most Andy would be willing to pay for the first pizza is $15, but the price is only $9. Therefore, his consumer surplus is $6, ($15 - $9).

   b) Andy's consumer surplus on the second pizza is the difference between the most he would be willing to pay ($12) and the price ($9). His consumer surplus is $3.

   c) At a price of $9, Andy will buy 4 pizzas. He will receive consumer surplus on the first three pizzas in the amount of $6, $3, and $1, respectively. Thus, his total consumer surplus is $10.

8 POSSIBILITIES, PREFERENCES, AND CHOICES

CHAPTER IN PERSPECTIVE

This chapter provides an alternative analysis of consumer choice and the law of demand that complements the marginal utility analysis of Chapter 7. Here the analysis uses a model of consumer behavior based on a budget equation which represents *possible choices* given a consumer's income and an indifference curve representation of *preferences*.

The model developed in this chapter allows more systematic analysis of what happens to quantity demanded when the price of a good changes and when income changes, as well as more insight into the distinction between normal and inferior goods. Compared with the marginal utility analysis, the budget equation/indifference curve model has the advantage that it does not depend on the abstract notion of utility.

LEARNING OBJECTIVES

After studying this chapter, you will be able to:

- Calculate and graph a household's budget line

- Work out how the budget line changes when prices and income change

- Make a map of preferences using indifference curves

- Calculate a household's optimal consumption plan

- Predict the effects of price and income changes on the pattern of consumption

- Explain why the workweek gets shorter as wages rise

- Explain how budget lines and indifference curves can be used to understand all household choices

HELPFUL HINTS

1. Although the analysis in this chapter may seem narrow and restrictive at first, it is helpful to maintain a broad view of the issues under investigation. From the most general economic perspective, the consumer problem is to do the best one can given the constraints he/she faces. These constraints, which limit the range of possible choices, depend on income and the prices of goods and are represented graphically by the *budget line*. Doing the best one can means finding the *most preferred* outcome consistent with those constraints. In this chapter, preferences are represented graphically by *indifference curves*. Thus, as represented graphically, the consumer problem is to find the highest indifference curve attainable given the budget line. To make graphical analysis feasible, we restrict ourselves to choices between only two goods, but the same principles apply in the real world where the array of choices is much broader.

2. The marginal rate of substitution (*MRS*) is the rate at which a consumer gives up good Y (measured on the vertical axis) for an additional unit of good X (measured on the horizontal axis) and still remains indifferent. The *MRS* equals the magnitude of the slope of the indifference curve, $\Delta Q_Y / \Delta Q_X$

Because indifference curves are bowed towards the origin, the magnitude of the slope and hence the *MRS* diminishes as we move down the indifference curve. The diminishing *MRS* means that the consumer is willing to give up less of good Y for each additional unit of good X. As the consumer moves down an indifference curve and, thus, decreasing consumption of Y and increasing consumption of good X,, the consumer is coming to value good Y more and value good X less. This is a reflection of the principle of diminishing marginal utility discussed in Chapter 7.

3. Understanding the distinction between the income and substitution effects of a change in the price of a good is sometimes a challenge for students. Consider a decrease in the price of good A. This has two effects which will influence the consumption of A. First, the decrease in the price of A will reduce the relative price of A and, second, it will increase real income. The substitution effect is the answer to the following question: How much would the consumption of A change as a result of the relative price decline if we also (hypothetically) reduce income by enough to leave the consumer indifferent between the new and original situations? The income effect is the answer to this question: How much more would the consumption of A change if we (hypothetically) restore the consumer's real income but leave relative prices at the new level?

KEY FIGURES AND TABLES

Figure 8.1 The Budget Line
Household consumption is limited by the level of household income and the prices of goods and services. A budget line graphically represents those limits to consumption choices. This figure illustrates a budget line faced by Lisa who has a monthly income of $30 to be allocated between two goods: movies and soda. The price of a movie is $6 and the price of a six-pack of soda is $3. The table indicates six possible allocations of Lisa's income, given these prices. The budget line simply represents these points graphically. To locate the budget line, it is sufficient to find the end points by asking how many six-packs of soda could be purchased if all income is spent on soda and how many movies could be seen if all income is spent on movies.

Figure 8.3 Mapping Preferences
An indifference curve shows all the combinations of two goods among which an individual is indifferent. An indifference curve is thus a boundary between combinations of the two goods that are preferred to any combina-

tion on the indifference curve and combinations that are inferior and so not preferred. An indifference curve for Lisa is illustrated in this figure. We start with Lisa consuming 2 movies and 6 six-packs per month, point *c* in part (a), and ask what other combinations of movies and soda would leave Lisa just as well off. Since Lisa prefers more movies and soda to less, the indifference curve must be negatively sloped. If we *reduce* her consumption of soda we must *increase* her consumption of movies in order to leave her just as well off. This is illustrated by part (b) of the figure, since the indifference curve cannot pass through any part of the spaces labeled "Preferred" or "Not preferred." The indifference curve represented in part (c) gives the combinations of movies and sodas consumed among which Lisa is indifferent; each combination leaves her just as well off as point *c*. All combinations of soda and movies represented by points above the indifference curve are preferred to point *c* and all combinations represented by points below the indifference curve are inferior to point *c*.

Figure 8.4 A Preference Map

A preference map is a series of indifference curves for the same individual. This figure illustrates three indifference curves in Lisa's preference map. Along each indifference curve, Lisa is indifferent among the alternative consumption combinations; each would make her equally happy. However, higher indifference curves represent more preferred points. For example, all the movie and soda consumption combinations represented by points on the indifference curve labeled I_1 are preferred to those represented by points on the curve labeled I_0. Points on a higher indifference curve are preferred to points on a lower indifference curve.

Figure 8.7 The Best Affordable Point

The budget line indicates the limits to consumption; i.e., it indicates what is affordable. Higher indifference curves indicate more

preferred consumption points; that is, better consumption points. The objective of a consumer is to obtain the best (most preferred) affordable consumption point possible. Graphically, this means that a consumer will choose the consumption point that is on the budget line and also on the highest indifference curve possible. In this figure, this occurs at consumption point *c*. This is the best affordable consumption point because all other affordable points (i.e., all other points on the budget line) correspond to lower indifference curves. In addition, all points on higher indifference curves are not affordable.

Table 8.1 Calculating the Budget Equation

This table derives the equation of Lisa's budget line, given her income and the prices of movies and soda. The procedure for deriving any budget line is similar. In the first part of the table, symbols are defined (on the left) and the specific values for income and prices are given corresponding to the example in the text (on the right). The second part of the table gives the general expression of the budget equation. It simply says that the amount spent on soda ($P_s Q_s$) plus the amount spent on movies ($P_m Q_m$) is equal to income (y). In the third part of the table, we proceed to solve this equation for the quantity of soda (Q_s). That solution is given in the fourth part of the table as the budget line equation.

SELF-TEST

CONCEPT REVIEW

1. A _____ line describes the maximum amounts of consumption a household can undertake given its income and the prices of the goods it buys.

2. Real income is income expressed in units of _____.

3. The price of one good divided by the price of another is called a(n) _____ price.

4. If the quantity of good A consumed is measured on the horizontal axis and the quantity of good B consumed is measured on the vertical axis, an increase in the price of good A will make the budget line _____. An increase in income will shift the budget line _____.

5. A(n) _____ curve shows all combinations of goods that would leave a consumer indifferent.

6. Suppose we measure good A on the horizontal axis and good B on the vertical axis. The rate at which a person would give up good B to obtain more of good A is called the _____ rate of _____. As the consumer increases consumption of good A (and decreases consumption of good B so as to remain indifferent), this rate _____.

7. The indifference curve for perfect complements will be _____.

8. The best affordable consumption point will be on both the _____ line and highest attainable _____ curve.

9. If the price of good A rises, the _____ effect will always imply that less of A will be consumed, while the _____ effect reinforces this only if A is a normal good.

10. If a decrease in income causes an increase in the consumption of good B, then B is a(n) _____ good.

11. As the wage rate rises, the substitution effect encourages _____ leisure and the income effect encourages _____ leisure.

TRUE OR FALSE

____ 1. At any point on the budget line, all income is spent.

____ 2. The graph of a budget line will be bowed toward the origin.

____ 3. An increase in the price of the good measured on the horizontal axis will make the budget line flatter.

____ 4. Other things remaining unchanged, an increase in the price of goods means that real income falls.

____ 5. The slope of the budget line depends on income while its position depends on the relative price of the goods.

____ 6. An increase in income will cause an inward parallel shift of the budget line.

____ 7. Preferences depend on income and the prices of goods.

____ 8. We assume that more of any good is preferred to less of the good.

_____ 9. An indifference curve shows all combinations of two goods which the consumer can afford.

_____10. It is logically possible for indifference curves to intersect each other.

_____11. Higher indifference curves mean higher levels of satisfaction.

_____12. The principle of the diminishing marginal rate of substitution explains why indifference curves are bowed toward the origin.

_____13. The magnitude of the slope of an indifference curve is equal to the marginal rate of substitution.

_____14. Perfect substitutes will have L-shaped indifference curves.

_____15. At the best affordable consumption point, the slope of the budget line is equal to the slope of the indifference curve.

_____16. At the best affordable consumption point of movies and pop, the marginal rate of substitution equals the ratio of the price of movies to the price of pop.

_____17. For normal goods, a fall in the relative price of a good leads to increased consumption of that good.

_____18. When the relative price of a good falls, the substitution effect leads to less consumption of the good if it is inferior.

_____19. An assumption of our model of consumer choice is that households cannot influence the prices of goods.

_____20. The law of demand is implied by our model of consumer choice.

_____21. The *theory* of consumer choice says that people actually compute marginal rates of substitution and set them equal to relative prices in order to make spending decisions.

_____22. The model of consumer choice *cannot* be used to analyze household choices between how much of income to spend on current consumption and how much to save.

MULTIPLE CHOICE

1. Which of the following statements best describes a consumer's budget line?
   a. The amount of each good a consumer can purchase
   b. The limits to a consumer's consumption choices
   c. The desired level of consumption for the consumer
   d. The consumption choices made by a consumer

2. The budget line depends on
   a. income.
   b. prices.
   c. income and prices.
   d. preferences.

3. Let I = income, Q_X = quantity of good X, and Q_Y = quantity of good Y, P_X = price of good X and P_Y = price of good Y. The budget equation is given by
   a. $I = P_X Q_X + P_Y Q_Y$
   b. $I = Q_X + P_Y Q_Y / P_X$
   c. $Q_X = I + (P_X/P_Y)Q_Y$
   d. $Q_X = Q_Y + (P_X/P_Y)I$

4. If the price of the good measured on the vertical axis increases, the budget line will
   a. become steeper.
   b. become flatter.
   c. shift inward but parallel to the original budget line.
   d. shift outward but parallel to the original budget line.

5. If income increases, the budget line will
   a. become steeper.
   b. become flatter.
   c. shift inward but parallel to the original budget line.
   d. shift outward but parallel to the original budget line.

6. Bill consumes apples and bananas. Suppose Bill's income doubles and the prices of apples and bananas also double. Bill's budget line will
   a. remain unchanged.
   b. shift out but not change slope.
   c. shift out and become steeper.
   d. shift out and become flatter.

7. Which of the following statements is <u>NOT</u> true?
   a. Indifference curves are negatively sloped.
   b. A preference map consists of a series of nonintersecting indifference curves.
   c. Indifference curves are bowed out from the origin.
   d. The slope of an indifference curve is given by the marginal rate of substitution.

8. Figure 8.1 gives three indifference curves for Brenda. Which of the following is <u>NOT</u> true.
   a. Brenda would be equally happy consuming at either point b or point c.
   b. Brenda prefers consuming at point b to consuming at point a.
   c. Brenda prefers consumption at point d to consumption at either point b or point c.
   d. The marginal rate of substitution is higher at point c than at point b.

Figure 8.1

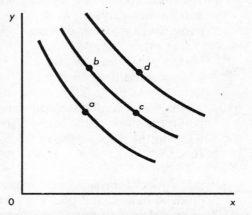

9. Suppose good X is measured on the horizontal axis and good Y on the vertical axis. The marginal rate of substitution is best defined as
   a. the relative price of X in terms of good Y.
   b. the relative price of Y in terms of good X.
   c. the rate at which a consumer will give up good Y in order to obtain more of X and remain indifferent.
   d. the rate at which a consumer will give up good X in order to obtain more of Y and remain indifferent.

10. In general, as a consumer moves along an indifference curve, increasing consumption of good X (measured on the horizontal axis),
    a. more of Y must be given up for each additional unit of Y.
    b. less of Y must be given up for each additional unit of X.
    c. the relative price of Y increases.
    d. the relative price of Y decreases.

11. If two goods are perfect substitutes, then their
    a. indifference curves are positively-sloped straight lines.
    b. indifference curves are negatively-sloped straight lines.
    c. indifference curves are L-shaped.
    d. marginal rate of substitution is zero.

12. Which of the following statements is NOT a characteristic of the best affordable consumption point?
    a. The point is on the budget line.
    b. The income effect is equal to the substitution effect.
    c. The marginal rate of substitution between the two goods is equal to their relative price.
    d. The highest affordable indifference curve has the same slope as the budget line.

13. Consider the budget line and indifference curve in Figure 8.2. If the price of good X is $1, then the price of good Y is
    a. $.75.
    b. $1.
    c. $1.25.
    d. $2.

Figure 8.2

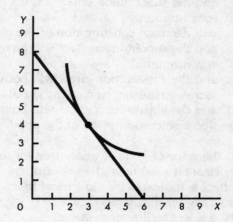

14. Consider the budget line and indifference curve in Figure 8.2. At the best affordable point, the marginal rate of substitution is
    a. 1/2.
    b. 2.
    c. 4/3.
    d. 3/4.

15. When the price of a good changes, we call the change in consumption that leaves the consumer indifferent, the
    a. utility effect.
    b. substitution effect.
    c. income effect.
    d. price effect.

16. If the price of a normal good rises, the income effect
    a. will increase consumption of the good and the substitution effect will decrease consumption.
    b. will decrease consumption of the good and the substitution effect will increase consumption.
    c. and the substitution effect will both increase consumption of the good.
    d. and the substitution effect will both decrease consumption of the good.

17. If the price of good X (measured on the horizontal axis) falls, the substitution effect is indicated by movement to
    a. a higher indifference curve.
    b. a lower indifference curve.
    c. a flatter part of the same indifference curve.
    d. a steeper part of the same indifference curve.

18. Which of the following is <u>NOT</u> an assumption of the indifference curve model of consumer behavior?
    a. Consumers cannot influence the price of goods.
    b. Consumers compute marginal rates of substitution.
    c. A consumer has a given level of income to allocate among various goods.
    d. A consumer chooses the most preferred affordable combination of goods.

19. The initial budget line labelled RS in Fig. 8.3 would shift to RT as a result of
    a. An increase in the price of good X.
    b. A decrease in the price of good X.
    c. An increase in the price of good Y.
    d. A decrease in the price of good Y.

Figure 8.3

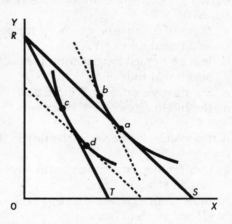

20. When the initial budget line labelled RS in Fig. 8.3 shifts to RT, the substitution effect is illustrated by the move from point
    a. a to d.
    b. a to b.
    c. d to c.
    d. a to c.

21. When the initial budget line labelled RS in Fig. 8.3 shifts to RT, the income effect is illustrated by the move from point
    a. a to b.
    b. b to d.
    c. b to c.
    d. d to a.

22. Over the last 100 years, the quantity of labor supplied has fallen as wages have increased. This indicates that, as the wages have increased, the income effect
   a. and the substitution effect have both operated to discourage leisure.
   b. and the substitution effect have both operated to encourage leisure.
   c. discouraging leisure has been dominated by the substitution effect encouraging leisure.
   d. encouraging leisure has dominated the substitution effect discouraging leisure.

SHORT ANSWER

1. Explain how to find the vertical and horizontal intercepts of the budget line.

2. Using your explanation in Question 1, explain why the budget line will be flatter if the price of the good measured on the vertical axis increases.

3. Using your explanation in Question 1, explain what happens to the budget line when income increases.

4. Bob's income is $1000 per week. What happens to his *real* income if the price of goods rises? Explain.

5. Why is an indifference curve negatively sloped?

6. What is the marginal rate of substitution?

7. Why will the marginal rate of substitution between the two goods be equal to the relative price of the goods at the best affordable consumption point?

8. Suppose the price of a normal good falls. Without the use of graphs, distinguish between the income and substitution effects of this price decline.

PROBLEMS

1. Jan and Dan both like bread and peanut butter and have the same income. Since they each face the same prices, they have identical budget lines. Currently, Jan and Dan consume exactly the same quantities of bread and peanut butter; that is, they have the same best affordable consumption point. Jan, however, views bread and peanut butter as close (though not perfect) substitutes, while Dan considers bread and peanut butter to be quite (but not perfectly) complementary.
   a) In the same diagram, draw the budget line and relevant indifference curves for Jan and Dan. (Measure the quantity of bread on the horizontal axis.)
   b) Now, suppose the price of bread declines. Graphically represent the substitution effects for Jan and Dan. For whom is the substitution effect greater?

2. Figure 8.4 illustrates several indifference curves for Sharon who consumes goods X and Y. Initially the price of one unit of X is $2, the price of a unit of Y is $1, and Sharon's income is $12. Use the diagram to respond to the following.
   a) How much of X and Y will Sharon initially consume at her best affordable point?
   b) Suppose the price of X falls to $1.
      (i) What will be the new quantities of X and Y consumed?
      (ii) What is the substitution effect on the consumption of X?
      (iii) What is the income effect on the consumption of X?
   c) The price of X continues to be $1 but Sharon's income now increases to $14. How much of X and Y will now be consumed?
   d) On a separate graph, plot two points on Sharon's demand curve for X and draw her straight line demand curve.

Figure 8.4

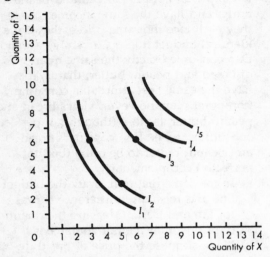

3. Ms. Muffet consumes both curds and whey. The initial price of curds is $1 per unit and the price of whey is $1.50 per unit. Ms. Muffet's initial income is $12.
    a) What is the relative price of curds?
    b) Derive Ms. Muffer's budget equation and draw her budget line in a graph. (Measure curds on the horizontal axis.)
    c) On your graph, draw an indifference curve so that the best affordable point corresponds to 6 units of curds and 4 units of whey.
    d) What is the marginal rate of substitution of curds for whey at this point.
    e) Show that any other point on the budget line is inferior.

4. Given the initial situation described in Problem 3, suppose Ms. Muffet's income now increases.
    a) Illustrate graphically, how the consumption of curds and whey are affected if both goods are normal. (Numerical answers are not necessary. Just show whether consumption increases or decreases.)

    b) Draw a graph showing the effect of an increase in Ms. Muffet's income if whey is an inferior good.

5. Return to the *initial* circumstances described in problem 3. Now, suppose the price of curds doubles to $2 a unit while the price of whey remains at $1.50 per unit and income remains at $12.
    a) Draw the new budget line.
    b) Why is the initial best affordable point (label it point *r*) no longer the best affordable point?
    c) Using your graph, show the new best affordable point and label it *t*. What has happened to the consumption of curds?
    d) Decompose the effect on the consumption of curds into the substitution effect and the income effect. In your graph, indicate the substitution effect as movement from point *r* to point *s* (which you must locate) and indicate the income effect as movement from point *s* to point *t*.

6. What happens to the consumption of goods X and Y when the price of X, the price of Y, and income all increase by 10 percent? Explain.

CONCEPT REVIEW

1. budget

2. goods

3. relative

4. steeper; out

5. indifference

6. marginal; substitution; diminishes

7. L-shaped

8. budget; indifference

9. substitution; income

10. inferior

11. less; more

TRUE OR FALSE

1. T	6. F	11. T	16. T	21. F
2. F	7. F	12. T	17. T	22. F
3. F	8. T	13. T	18. F	
4. T	9. F	14. F	19. T	
5. F	10. F	15. T	10. T	

MULTIPLE CHOICE

1. b	6. a	11. c	16. d	21. c
2. c	7. c	12. b	17. c	22. d
3. a	8. d	13. a	18. b	
4. b	9. c	14. c	19. a	
5. d	10. b	15. b	20. b	

SHORT ANSWER

1. Let the quantity of good X be represented on the horizontal axis and the quantity of good Y be represented on the vertical axis. The horizontal intercept of the budget line is simply the amount of X that could be purchased if zero units of good Y are purchased; that is, if the household's entire income is spent on X. This is obtained by dividing total income by the price of X. Similarly, the vertical intercept is obtained by dividing total income by the price of Y.

2. If the price of good Y increases, it means that the quantity of Y that can be purchased if all of income is spent on Y must be less. Thus the vertical intercept of the budget line will be less. Since the horizontal intercept remains unchanged (i.e.,

income and the price of X have not changed) the budget line must be flatter.

3. When income increases but the prices of goods X and Y remain unchanged, more of each good can now be purchased in the case that all of income is spent on it. This means that both the horizontal and vertical intercepts will increase and thus the budget line will shift out. Since the increase in the horizontal intercept will be inversely proportional to the price of X and the increase in the vertical intercept will be inversely proportional to price of Y, the new budget line will be parallel to the original budget line.

4. Real income is income expressed in units of goods; that is, expressed in terms of how many goods it will buy. If income remains at $1000 while the prices of goods rise, real income must fall since the $1000 will now be able to purchase fewer goods.

5. An indifference curve tells us how much the consumption of one good must change as the consumption of another good decreases in order to leave the consumer indifferent (no better or worse off). It is negatively sloped because the goods we measure on the axes are both desirable. This means that as we *decrease* the consumption of one good, in order to not be made worse off, consumption of the other good must *increase*. This implies a negative slope.

6. The marginal rate of substitution is the rate at which a consumer would be willing to give up one good in order to obtain more of another good and still remain indifferent.

7. The marginal rate of substitution between any two goods is given by the (negative of the) slope of the indifference curve while the relative price of the goods is given by

the (negative of the) slope of the budget line. Since these slopes are equal at the best affordable consumption point, the marginal rate of substitution is equal to the relative price of the goods.

8. A decrease in the price of a good will affect the consumption of the good through two channels. First, we note that, if all other prices remain constant, when the price of one good falls, real income increases. The substitution effect is the increase in consumption of the good resulting from the fall in its relative price accompanied by a (hypothetical) reduction in real income which leaves the consumer indifferent between the new and initial situations. The income effect of a normal good is the further increase in consumption of the good when we (hypothetically) restore the consumer's real income but leave relative prices unchanged at the new level.

PROBLEMS

1. a) Initially, Jan and Dan are at point c on the budget line labeled AB in Fig. 8.5. Jan's indifference curve is illustrated by I_J. Note that her indifference curve is close to a straight line reflecting the fact that bread and peanut butter are close substitutes. On the other hand, since Dan considers bread and peanut butter to be complementary, his indifference curve, I_D, is more tightly curved.

   b) If the price of bread declines, the budget line will become flatter; for example, the line labeled AD in Fig. 8.5. In order to measure the substitution effect we find the point on the original indifference curve that has the same slope as the new budget line. Since Dan's indifference curve is more sharply curved, it becomes flatter quite

rapidly as we move away from point c. Thus the substitution effect is quite small: from c to point e. Since Jan's indifference curve is almost a straight line, the substitution effect must be much larger: from c to point f.

2. a) In order to find Sharon's best affordable point, we draw the budget line in Fig. 8.4 Solution. The initial budget line corresponds to the line labeled AB and thus Sharon's best affordable point will be at point c on indifference curve I_2. Thus Sharon will consume 3 units of X and 6 units of Y.

   b) If the price of X falls to $1, the budget line becomes AD.

Figure 8.5

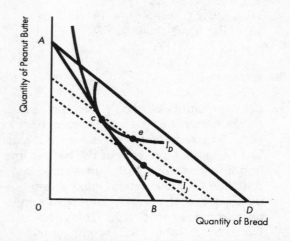

(i) Now Sharon's best affordable point is given by e on indifference curve I_3. This corresponds to consumption of 6 units of X and 6 units of Y.

(ii) To measure the substitution effect, first find the point on the initial indifference curve with the same slope as the new budget line.

This is point f. The substitution effect of the decrease in the price of X is the movement from initial point c to point, which is an increase in the quantity of consumed of two units (from 3 units to 5 units).

(iii) The income effect of the price decline is the movement from point f to point e, which is an increase in the quantity of X consumed of one unit (from 5 units to 6 units).

c) When income increases to $14 the budget line shifts out to the line labeled GH. This allows Sharon to achieve her best affordable point at j, which corresponds to 7 units of X and 7 units of Y consumed.

Figure 8.4 Solution

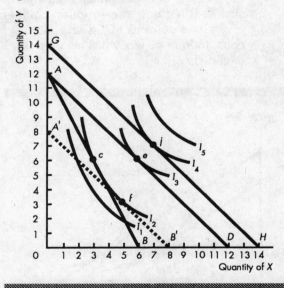

d) From parts (a) and (b) above we learn that, holding income constant at $12 and the price of Y constant at $1, when the price of X is $2, Sharon wants to purchase 3 units of X and when the

price of X is $1, Sharon wants to purchase 6 units of X. This gives us two points on Sharon's demand curve for X, which are labeled a and b in Figure 8.6. Drawing a line passing through these points allows us to obtain her straight line demand curve, labeled D in the diagram.

Figure 8.6

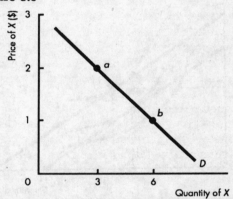

3. a) The relative price of curds is the price of curds divided by the price of whey:

$$\frac{\$1}{\$1.50} = \frac{2}{3}$$

b) Let P_c = the price of curds, P_w = the price of whey, Q_c = quantity of curds, Q_w = quantity of whey, and y = income. The budget equation, in general form, is

$$Q_w = \frac{y}{P_w} - \frac{P_c}{P_w} Q_c$$

Since $P_c = \$1$, $P_w = \$1.50$, and $y = \$12$, Ms. Muffet's budget equation is specifically given by

$$Q_w = 8 - 2/3 \, Q_c$$

The graph of this budget equation, the budget line, is given by the line labeled *AB* in Fig. 8.7.

Figure 8.7

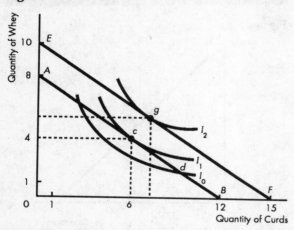

Quantity of Curds

c) If the best affordable point corresponds to 6 units of curds and 4 units of whey, then the relevant indifference curve must be tangent to (just touches) the budget line *AB* at *c*; for example, indifference curve I_1.

d) The marginal rate of substitution is given by the slope of the indifference curve at point *c*. We do not know the slope of the indifference curve directly but we can easily compute the slope of the budget line. Since, at point *c*, the indifference curve and the budget line have the same slope, we can obtain the marginal rate of substitution of curds for whey. Since the slope of the budget line is - 2/3, the marginal rate of substitution is 2/3; that is, Ms. Muffet is willing to give up 2 units of whey in order to receive 3 additional units of curds and still remain indifferent.

e) Since indifference curves cannot intersect each other and since indifference curve I_1 lies everywhere above the budget line (except at point *c*), we know that every other point on the budget line is on a lower indifference curve. For example, point *d* lies on indifference curve I_0. Thus every other point on the budget line is inferior to point *c*.

4. a) An increase in income will cause a parallel outward shift of the budget line; for example, to *EF* in Fig. 8.7. If both curds and whey are normal goods, Ms. Muffet will move to a point like *g* at which the consumption of both goods has increased.

b) If whey is an inferior good, then its consumption will fall as income rises. This is illustrated in Fig. 8.8. Once again the budget line shifts from *AB* to *EF*, but Ms. Muffet's preferences are such that her new consumption point is given by a point like *G'* where the consumption of whey has actually declined.

Figure 8.8

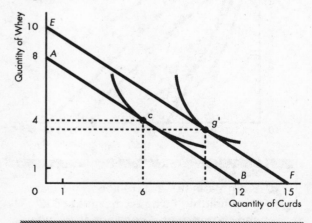

Quantity of Curds

5. a) Ms. Muffet's initial budget line is given
        by *AB* and the initial best affordable
        point by *r* in Fig. 8.9. Note that point *r*
        in Fig. 8.9 is the same as point *c* in
        Fig. 8.7. The new budget line follow-
        ing an increase in the price of curds to
        $2 (income remains at $12) is represent-
        ed by *AH*.

Figure 8.9

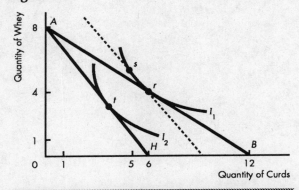

    b) After the price increase, point *r* is no
        longer the best affordable point since it
        is no longer even affordable.
    c) The new best affordable point (labeled
        t in Fig. 8.9) indicates a decrease in the
        consumption of curds.

    d) The substitution effect of the increase
        in the price of curds is indicated by the
        movement from *r* to *s* in Fig. 8.9. This
        gives the effect of the change in relative
        prices while keeping Ms. Muffet on the
        same indifference curve. The income
        effect is indicated by movement from *s*
        to *t*.

6. If income and the prices of goods all in-
    crease by the same percentage, real in-
    come will remain unchanged and thus the
    budget line will not change. So, if income
    increases by 10 percent and the prices of
    goods *X* and *Y* also increase by 10 per-
    cent, the individual will not be able to buy
    any more goods and services than before.
    Since preferences are also unaffected, the
    consumption of *X* and *Y* will remain un-
    changed.

9 ORGANIZING PRODUCTION

CHAPTER IN PERSPECTIVE

In the first chapter of the text, economics was introduced as the science of choice; choice made necessary by the existence of scarcity. Chapters 7 and 8 examined consumer choice and the principles underlying demand. With this chapter, we begin our analysis of firm choice and the principles underlying supply. The analysis here focuses on key differences that exist in how firms organize production.

The first difference relates to types of firms. While there are common characteristics shared by all firms, there are different forms of business organization, each with advantages and disadvantages. The second difference relates to types of business finance. Concepts you read about every day in the business press — bonds, stocks, present value, price-earnings ratios — are examined, as well as a difference between the accountant's and economist's concepts of cost that depends crucially on opportunity cost. The third difference relates to the concepts of technological versus economic efficiency and the concepts of firm versus market coordination. The efficiency of firms (as an institution) make them a primary coordination mechanism through which market economies tackle the problem of scarcity.

LEARNING OBJECTIVES

After studying this chapter, you will be able to:

- Explain what a firm is, and describe the economic problems that *all* firms face

- Describe and distinguish between different forms of business organization

- Explain how firms raise the money to finance their operations

- Calculate and distinguish between a firm's historical costs and opportunity costs

- Define technological efficiency and economic efficiency and distinguish between them

- Explain why firms solve some economic problems and markets solve others

119

HELPFUL HINTS

1. The principal purpose of this chapter is to develop a fundamental understanding of why firms exist. Since it is obvious they do exist, it might seem better to simply begin with that fact and turn immediately to a study of their behavior. Taking firms for granted, however, would eliminate an opportunity to acquire significant insights. As you consider the operation of firms in this and the next several chapters, ask yourself what it is that firms do and what are the alternative mechanisms for doing it. The example in the text of getting a car repaired is a good place to start.

2. In spite of the somewhat abstract central purpose of the chapter, we are also presented with a number of facts. Some of these consist mainly of institutional knowledge like the three main forms of business organization or the three types of stock. You will need to learn these facts, although common experience is likely to have made you aware of many of them.

3. The chapter defines several important economic concepts.

   a) The concept of present value is fundamental in thinking about the value today of an investment or of future amounts of money. The intuition behind present value is that a dollar today is worth more than a dollar in the future because today's dollar can be invested to earn interest. To calculate the value *today* of a sum of money that will be paid in the future, we must discount that future sum to compensate for the forgone interest. The *present value* of a future sum is the amount that, if invested today, will grow as large as that future sum, taking into account the interest that it will earn.

   b) In this chapter, we again meet our old friend opportunity cost. Here we look at the cost firms face with special emphasis on the differences between historical cost measures used by accountants and opportunity cost measures used by economists. Historical cost includes only explicit, out-of-pocket costs. Opportunity cost, which is the concept of cost relevant for economic decisions, includes *explicit costs and imputed costs*. Important examples of imputed costs include the owner's/investor's forgone interest, forgone rent, and forgone income. These differences in cost measures between accountants and economists lead to differences in profit measures as well.

   c) It is important to carefully distinguish between technological efficiency and economic efficiency. Once again, the difference is critical since economic decisions will be made only on the basis of economic efficiency. Technological efficiency is an engineering concept and occurs when it is not possible to increase output without increasing inputs. There is no consideration of input costs. Economic efficiency occurs when the *cost* of producing a given output is at a minimum. All technologically efficient productions methods are not economically efficient but all economically efficient methods are also technologically efficient.

KEY FIGURES AND TABLES

Figure 9.1 The Relative Importance of the Three Main Types of Firms
The three main types of firms are proprietorships, partnerships, and corporations. From part (a) of this figure we learn that while most businesses (about three fourths) are organized as propieterships, most business revenue (about 90 percent) is accounted for by corporations. This is because most proprietorships tend to be small while most large firms are corporations. Part (b) indicates that the relative importance of the main types of firms (measured by total revenue) varies across industries. We see that almost all of the manufacturing industry's revenue is produced by

corporations while about 40 percent of the revenue in agriculture, forestry, and fishing is generated by proprietorships.

Table 9.1 The Pros and Cons of Different Types of Firms

There are three main types of business organization: proprietorship, partnership, and corporation. This table presents some of the characteristics of these types of firms in the form of lists of advantages and disadvantages of each.

Table 9.3 Rocky's Mountain Bikes Revenue, Costs and Profit Statement

It is important to recognize that accounting costs and economic (opportunity) costs are not always the same thing. As a result, accounting profit and economic profit will not always be the same. This table illustrates the differences using the example of Rocky's Mountain Bikes. In this revenue, cost, and profit statement, there are three differences to note. These are discussed in the "Notes" at the bottom of the table.

Table 9.4 Four Ways of Making 10 TV Sets a Day

There are generally many methods available to produce a given quantity of a particular good, each of them using a different combination of inputs. This figure illustrates four combinations of labor (measured on the horizontal axis) and capital (measured on the vertical axis) that can be used to produce ten TV sets a day. Method *a* uses only one unit of labor and 1000 units of capital while method *d* uses 1000 units of labor and only one unit of capital. It is easy to see that method *c* is technically inefficient since the same quantity of TVs can be produced with less capital but the same amount of labor as method *b*.

CONCEPT REVIEW

1. An institution that organizes resources it has purchased or hired to produce and sell goods and services is called a(n) _____.

2. There are three main forms of business organization. The two simpler forms are a(n) _____ (which has a single owner) and a(n) _____. In these two forms owners face _____ liability. The third more complicated form is a(n) _____ in which owners face_____ liability.

3. Business corporations can raise money by selling _____ which are legal obligations to pay specified amounts at specified future dates. Corporations can also raise money by issuing shares of _____.

4. A dollar today is worth _____ than a dollar in the future.   Considering the fact that money can be invested to earn interest, the value today of a promise to receive some amount of money in the future is called the _____ value of that future money.

5. The conversion of a future sum of money to its present value is called _____.

6. The _____ - _____ ratio is given by the current price of a stock divided by the current profit per shares.

7. In assessing costs, accountants measure _____ cost, which values resources at the prices originally paid for them. Economists measure _____ cost.

8. The change in the market price of a durable input over a given period is called economic _____.

9. _____ efficiency is achieved when the cost of producing a given output is as low as possible. _____ efficiency is achieved when no more output can be produced without increasing inputs.

10. Firms coordinate economic activity when they can do so more efficiently than _____.

11. The costs associated with finding a buyer, reaching agreement about exchange, and ensuring the fulfillment of the agreement are _____ costs.

12. _____ of _____ exist when the cost of producing a unit of output falls as we produce more.

13. _____ production occurs when a number of workers each perform specialized tasks in the production process.

TRUE OR FALSE

____ 1. A firm purchases or hires factors of production and organizes production of goods and services.

____ 2. A firm's residual claimant is the last individual or institution to loan money to the firm.

____ 3. A partnership has joint unlimited liability.

____ 4. The residual claimants of a corporation are its bond holders.

____ 5. The income of a proprietorship is taxed twice; once as income to the firm and once as income to the owner.

____ 6. The perpetual "life" of a corporation is an advantage over other forms of business organization when it comes to raising large sums of money.

____ 7. If the interest rate is 10 percent a year, then the present value of $100 in one year is $110.

____ 8. The present value of a sequence of future money payments is the sum of the present values of the payments in each year.

____ 9. An owner of preferred stock has voting rights at stockholders' meetings.

____10. The stake an owner has in a business is called equity.

____11. In general, the price of a share of stock is the present value of its expected future dividends.

____12. Historical cost is more likely to be the same as opportunity costs when firms use their own funds rather than borrowing.

____13. In general, opportunity cost will be greater than historical cost.

____14. When a firm produces using a machine it owns, its opportunity cost is lower than if it had rented the machine.

____15. The opportunity cost of using inventories is the current replacement cost.

____16. A production process that is technologically efficient may become technologically inefficient if the relative prices of inputs changes.

____17. A production process that is economically efficient may become economically inefficient if the relative prices of inputs change.

____18. Firms will coordinate economic activity in situations where there are economies of team production.

____19. Markets will coordinate economic activity in situations where there are economies of scale.

____20. The higher the interest rate, the greater is the present value of a given future sum of money.

MULTIPLE CHOICE

1. Which of the following statements is NOT true of firms?
   a. Firms are like markets since they are another institution for coordinating economic activity.
   b. Firms organize factors of production in order to produce goods and services.
   c. Firms sell goods and services.
   d. Efficient firms can eliminate scarcity.

2. A firm having two or more owners with joint unlimited liability is a
   a. proprietorship.
   b. partnership.
   c. conglomerate.
   d. corporation.

3. Which of the following types of firms issues shares of stock?
   a. Proprietorship
   b. Partnership
   c. Corporation
   d. Not-for-profit

4. Which of the following is the residual claimant of a corporation?
   a. Stockholders
   b. Bondholders
   c. Banks and other creditors
   d. Government taxing agencies

5. Which of the following is a *disadvantage* of a corporation relative to a proprietorship or partnership?
   a. Owners have unlimited liability
   b. Profits are taxed as corporate profits and as dividend income to stockholders
   c. It is difficult to raise money
   d. Perpetual life

6. Most firms are
   a. proprietorships.
   b. partnerships.
   c. corporations.
   d. not-for-profit firms.

7. The owner's stake in a business is called
   a. net worth.
   b. redemption value.
   c. total liabilities.
   d. equity capital.

8. A bond
   a. represents a right to share in the profits of a corporation.
   b. allows the holder to vote for corporate directors.
   c. is a promise by a corporation to pay given amounts of money on specified future dates.
   d. cannot be issued by a corporation.

9. The present value of a future payment of money will be higher
   a. the higher the interest rate or the further in the future the payment.
   b. the lower the interest rate or the further in the future the payment.
   c. the higher the interest rate or the nearer the date of the future payment.
   d. the lower the interest rate or the nearer the date of the future payment.

10. If the rate of interest is 10 percent per year, the present value of $100 in one year is
    a. $90.91.
    b. $95.45.
    c. $100.00.
    d. $110.00.

11. If the interest rate is 10 percent per year, the present value of $100 in *two* years is
    a. $80.00.
    b. $82.64.
    c. $90.91.
    d. $120.00.

12. If the present value of $500 in one year is $463, the interest rate is
    a. 5 percent per year.
    b. 8 percent per year.
    c. 10 percent per year.
    d. 12 percent per year.

13. Which of the following gives the holder the right to vote at stockholders' meetings?
    a. Corporate bonds
    b. Convertible stock
    c. Preferred stock
    d. Common stock

14. XYZ Corporation is expected to pay a dividend of $5 a share every year into the indefinite future. If the interest rate is 5 percent per year, the market price of a share of XYZ stock will be
    a. $4.76.
    b. $50.
    c. $100.
    d. $1000.

15. Historical cost calculates the value of resources
    a. at the original purchase price.
    b. at the current market price.
    c. as the value of the best foregone alternative.
    d. as the value of all foregone alternatives.

16. The construction cost of a particular building is $100,000. The conventional depreciation allowance is 5 percent per year. At the end of the first year the market value of the building is $80,000. For the first year, the depreciation cost would be
    a. $20,000 to an accountant or an economist.
    b. $5,000 to an accountant or an economist.
    c. $5,000 to an accountant but $20,000 to an economist.
    d. $20,000 to an account but $5,000 to an economist.

17. John operates a business and pays himself a salary of $20,000 per year. He was offered a job that paid $30,000 per year. The opportunity cost of John's time in the business is
    a. $10,000.
    b. $20,000.
    c. $30,000.
    d. $50,000.

18. In general, historical costs include
    a. implicit costs only.
    b. explicit costs only.
    c. both implicit and explicit costs.
    d. both implicit and imputed costs.

19. The rate of interest is 10 percent per year. If you invest $50,000 of your own money in a business and earn *accounting* profits of $20,000 after one year, what are your *economic* profits?
    a. $2,000
    b. $5,000
    c. $15,000
    d. $20,000

20. Which of the following statements is *true*?
    a. All technologically efficient methods are also economically efficient.
    b. All economically efficient methods are also technologically efficient.
    c. Technological efficiency changes with changes in relative input prices.
    d. Technologically efficient firms will be more likely to survive than economically efficient firms.

21. Which of the following is <u>NOT</u> a reason for firms frequently being more efficient than the market as a coordinator of economic activity?
    a. Firms have lower transactions costs.
    b. Firms have higher monitoring costs.
    c. Firms have economies of scale.
    d. Firms have economies of team production.

22. Economies of scale exist when
    a. the cost of finding a trading partner is low.
    b. a firm's decision to hire additional inputs does not result in an increase in the price of inputs.
    c. the cost of producing a unit of output falls as the output rate increases.
    d. the firm is too large and too diversified.

SHORT ANSWER

1. What are the three main forms of business organization and what are the principal advantages and disadvantages of each?

2. What does unlimited liability mean?

3. Give the meaning of present value by explaining (in words) why $110 in one year has a present value of $100 if the interest rate is 10 percent per year.

4. What are the three types of corporate stock and what are the principal characteristics of each?

5. What determines the price of a share of stock?

6. Why do stock prices tend to rise when the interest rate falls?

7. Compare the historical cost and opportunity cost approaches in each of the following cases:
   a) Depreciation cost.
   b) The firm borrows money to finance its operation.
   c) The firm uses its own funds rather than borrowing.

8. Distinguish between technological efficiency and economic efficiency.

9. Markets and firms are alternative ways of coordinating economic activity that arise because of scarcity. Why is it that *both* firms and markets exist?

PROBLEMS

1. Complete Table 9.1 by computing the present value of each of three future payment sequences, first assuming the interest rate to be 10 percent per year ($r = .1$) and then assuming the interest rate to be 5 percent per year ($r = .05$). The three future payment sequences are given by:
   A: $100 in one year
   B: $100 in two years
   C: A 2 year $1000 bond with a coupon payment of $100 per year (i.e., the bondholder will receive a $100 coupon payment at the end of one year and again at the end of two years). At the end of two years the bondholder will also receive $1000 (the face value of the bond).

Table 9.1

Future payment sequence	Present value ($)	
	$r = 0.1$	$r = 0.05$
A		
B		
C		

2. Bonds A and B are described as follows
   A: pays $220 in 2 years.
   B: pays $110 in 1 year and $110 in 2 years.
   For which of these bonds would you be willing to pay more? Why? [*Hint*: You do not need to know the interest rate to answer this question. Think of the $220 payment of bond *A* as two $110 payments, each paid after two years.]

3. A share of stock in the PDQ Corporation is expected to pay a dividend of $10 per share per year forever. What is the value of a share of stock in the PDQ Corporation if the rate of interest is 10 percent per year?

4. Frank was a bricklayer, but a year ago, he decided to start his own business as a doll furniture manufacturer. Frank has two sisters: Angela is an accountant and Edith is an economist. (Both sisters are good with numbers, but Edith doesn't have enough personality to be an accountant.) Each of the sisters computes Frank's cost and profit for the first year using the following information:

   (1) Frank took no income from the firm. He has a standing offer to return to work as a bricklayer for $30,000 a year.

(2) Frank rents the machinery he uses from an equipment rental firm. His annual rent is $9,000.

(3) Frank owns the garage in which he produces but could rent it out at $3,000 per year.

(4) To start the business, Frank used $10,000 of his own money and borrowed another $30,000 at the market rate of interest of 10 percent per year.

(5) Frank hires one employee at an annual salary of $20,000.

(6) The cost of materials during the first year is $40,000.

(7) End of year inventory is zero.

(8) Frank's revenue for his first year is $100,000.
   a) Set up a table indicating how Angela and Edith would compute Frank's cost. What is Frank's cost as computed by Angela? By Edith?
   b) What is Frank's profit (or loss) as computed by Angela? By Edith?

5. Your roommate has said that it is always more efficient to produce wheat using machinery than using only labor. Consider the following situation. There are two technologically efficient ways to produce one ton of wheat.

Method 1   Requires 20 machine hours plus 20 human hours.

Method 2   Requires 100 human hours.

Suppose that country A has a highly developed industrial economy, while country B is less developed. In country A the price of an hour of human labor (the wage

rate) is $8, while the hourly wage rate in country B is $4. The price of a machine hour is $20 in both countries. Which method is economically efficient in country A? in country B? Explain.

6. Consider countries A and B described in problem 5.
   a) What wage rate in country B would make the two processes equally efficient in country B?
   b) At what price of a machine hour will the two processes be equally efficient in country A?

ANSWERS

CONCEPT REVIEW

1. firm
2. proprietorship; partnership; unlimited; corporation; limited
3. bonds; stock
4. more; present
5. discounting
6. price; earnings
7. historical; opportunity
8. depreciation
9. Economic; Technological
10. markets
11. transactions
12. Economies; scale
13. Team

TRUE OR FALSE

1. T	5. F	9. F	13. T	17. T
2. F	6. T	10. T	14. F	18. T
3. T	7. F	11. T	15. T	19. F
4. F	8. T	12. F	16. F	20. F

MULTIPLE CHOICE

1. d	6. a	11. b	16. c	21. b
2. b	7. d	12. b	17. c	22. c
3. c	8. c	13. d	18. b	
4. a	9. d	14. c	19. c	
5. b	10. a	15. a	20. b	

SHORT ANSWER

1. See Table 9.1 in the text.

2. Unlimited liability means that the owner(s) of the firm have a legal responsibility for all their debts up to their personal wealth.

3. The present value of $110 in one year is the amount which, invested today at the market rate of interest, would grow to be $110 in one year. Since the interest rate is 10 percent, $100 invested today at 10 percent would grow to be $110 in one year. Thus, $100 is the present value of $110 in one year.

4. a) *Common stock* gives its owner the right to vote at stockholders' meetings, but the size of the dividend (if any) will vary depending on the vote of the directors of the corporation. Generally, the size of the dividend will rise and fall with the size of profits.
   b) An owner of *preferred stock* has no voting rights but will receive a specified fixed dividend regardless of the size of profit.

   c) *Convertible stock* is like a bond in the sense that it carries no voting rights and pays a fixed dividend (coupon payment). The difference is that the owner has the option of converting it into a specified number of shares of common stock.

5. A share of stock is a claim to future sums of money in the form of dividends. Thus the price (market value) of a share of stock is the present value of the future dividends it is expected to pay.

6. When the interest rate falls, the present value of fixed future amounts of money will rise. Since (as indicated in the answer to Question 5) the price of a share of stock is the present value of expected future dividends, that present value will decline as the interest rate rises (holding the amounts of expected future dividends constant).

7. a) From the historical cost approach, depreciation cost is computed as a prespecified percentage of the original purchase price of the capital good, with no reference to current market value. The opportunity cost approach measures depreciation cost as the actual change in the market value of the capital good over the period in question.
   b) If a firm borrows money, the historical and opportunity cost approaches will be the same; both will include the explicit interest payments.
   c) If a firm uses its own funds rather than borrowing, the historical and opportunity cost approaches will again differ. The historical cost will be zero since there are no explicit interest payments. The opportunity cost approach recognizes that those funds could have been loaned out and thus the (imputed) interest income foregone is the opportunity cost.

8. A method is technologically efficient if it is not possible to increase output without increasing inputs. A method is economically efficient if the cost of producing a given level of output is as low as possible. Technological efficiency is independent of prices, while economic efficiency depends on the prices of inputs. An economically efficient method of production is always technologically efficient, but a technologically efficient method is not necessarily economically efficient.

9. As we saw in the text example, car repair can be coordinated by the market or by a firm. The institution (market or firm) which actually coordinates in any given case will be the one which is more efficient. In cases where there are significant transaction costs, economies of scale, or economies of team production, firms are likely to be more efficient, and we will see firms dominate the coordination of economic activity. But the efficiency of firms is limited and there are many circumstances in which we observe market coordination of economic activity because it is more efficient.

PROBLEMS

1. The completed table is shown here as Table 9.1 Solution. While each answer is a straightforward application of the present value formula, details for computing the present value of future payment sequence C when $r = .05$ will be reviewed here. Payment sequence C is best thought of as a two part promise: (1) $100 in one year, and (2) $1100 in two years. The present value is then the sum of the present values of the two parts. The present value of (1) is $100/1.05 = $95.24, and the present value of (2) is $1100/(1.05)^2 = $997.73. Therefore the present value of the 2-year

bond is the sum: $95.24 + $997.73 = $1092.97.

Table 9.1 Solution

Future Payment	Present Value ($)	
Sequence	r = 0.1	r = 0.05
A	$ 90.91	$ 95.24
B	82.64	90.70
C	1000.00	1092.97

2. A bondholder would be willing to pay more for bond B than bond A because bond B has a higher present value. While both bonds pay the same total dollar amount over two years, bond B pays half of that amount after only one year. A holder of bond A, however, must wait two years for the full amount. This is shown in the following expression comparing the present values of bond A (PV_A) and bond B (PV_B).

If we think of the $220 payment of bond A as two $110 payments, each paid after two years, each payment is discounted by (divided by) $(1 + r)^2$. The second $110 payment of bond B is also paid after two years and is also discounted by $(1 + r)^2$. So one $110 payment from bond A and one $110 payment from bond B have equal present values. But the first $110 payment of Bond B is paid after one year and is therefore only discounted by $(1 + r)$, which is a smaller number than the discount factor $(1 + r)^2$, and this applies to the other $110 payment of bond A. Since this discount factor is in the denominator of the present value formula, the smaller denominator for the bond B calculation means a higher present value than for the bond A calculation. This result is shown in the following expression comparing the present values of bond A (PV_A) and bond B (PV_B).

$$PV_B = \frac{110}{1 + r} + \frac{110}{(1 + r)^2}$$

is greater than

$$PV_A = \frac{110}{(1 + r)^2} + \frac{110}{(1 + r)^2} = \frac{220}{(1 + r)^2}$$

3. The value of a share of PDQ stock is the present value of the expected future dividends. The present value of $10 per year forever is the amount which, if invested today at the market rate of interest, would yield $10 per year forever. Given that the market rate of interest is 10 percent per year, $100 invested today would pay $10 per year. So the present value of the expected future dividends (thus the value of the stock) is $100.

4. a) Table 9.2 gives the cost as computed by Angela and Edith. The item numbers correspond to the item numbers in the problem.

Table 9.3

Item number	Angela's accounting computation (historical cost)	Edith's economic computation (opportunity cost)
(1)	$ 0	$30,000
(2)	9,000	9,000
(3)	0	3,000
(4)	3,000	4,000
(5)	20,000	20,000
(6)	40,000	40,000
(7)	0	0

b) Revenue is $100,000. Angela's accounting computation of profit uses this formula:

Accounting profit = Revenues - Historical cost
= $100,000 - $72,000
= $28,000

Edith's economic computation of profit uses the formula:

Economic profit = Revenues - Opportunity cost
= $100,00 - $106,000
= -$6,000 (an economic loss)

5. Both production methods are technologically efficient. To find the economically efficient production method we want to know which of the methods has the lower cost of producing a ton of wheat. In country A, the price of an hour of labor is $8 and the price of a machine hour is $20. Thus, the cost of producing a ton of wheat is $560 using method 1 and $800 using method 2. Therefore method 1 is economically efficient for country A.

The price of an hour of labor is $4 in country B and thus it will face different costs of producing a ton of wheat. Under method 1, cost will be $480 but under method 2 which uses only labor, cost will be $400. So method 2 is economically efficient for country B.

The reason for this difference is that economic efficiency means producing at lowest cost. If the relative prices of inputs is different in two countries, there will be differences in the relative costs of producing using alternative methods. Therefore your roommate is (once again) wrong.

6. a) If the wage rate in country B were to increase to $5 an hour, then production of a ton of wheat would be $500 under either method. Of course, if the wage rate is above $5 an hour, method 1 becomes economically efficient in both

countries. To obtain the desired wage rate we express the cost under method 1 (C_1) and the cost under method 2 (C_2) as follows:

$$C_1 = 20P_m + 20P_h$$
$$C_2 = 100P_h$$

where P_m is the price of a machine hour and P_h is the price of a human hour (the wage rate). We are given that $P_m = \$20$ and asked to find the value of P_h that makes the two methods equally efficient; i.e., the value of P_h that makes $C_1 = C_2$. Thus we solve the following equation for P_h:

$$20P_m + 20P_h = 100P_h$$
$$20 \cdot \$20 + 20P_h = 100P_h$$
$$\$400 = 80P_h$$
$$\$5 = P_h$$

b) If the price of a machine hour is \$32, production of a ton of wheat would be \$800 under either method in country A. This question asks: Given the wage rate of \$8 (P_h) in country A, what value of P_m makes $C_1 = C_2$? Thus we solve the following equation for P_m:

$$20P_m + 20P_h = 100P_h$$
$$20P_m + 20 \cdot \$8 = 100 \cdot \$8$$
$$20P_m = \$640$$
$$P_m = \$32$$

10 OUTPUT AND COSTS

CHAPTER IN PERSPECTIVE

In a modern market economy, goods and services are produced primarily by firms. In Chapter 9 it was claimed that firms exist because they provide economically efficient ways of organizing factors of production in order to produce and sell goods and services. Economic efficiency means producing at the least possible cost. In this chapter we begin to understand the production and cost constraints that firms face, and thus, how efficiency is pursued.

What kinds of costs do firms face? How do these costs change as a firm's planning horizon changes? How will a firm, motivated by the desire to maximize profit, decide how much to produce? When will such a firm hire more labor? When will it increase its plant size? This chapter begins to answer these questions, which are of fundamental importance in exploring the nature of cost and supply.

LEARNING OBJECTIVES

After studying this chapter, you will be able to:

- **Explain the objective of a firm**

- **Explain what limits a firm's profitability**

- **Explain the relationship between a firm's output and its costs**

- **Derive a firm's short-run cost curves**

- **Explain how cost changes when a firm's plant size changes**

- **Derive a firm's long-run average cost curve**

- **Explain why some firms operate with excess capacity and others overutilize their plants**

HELPFUL HINTS

1. This chapter introduces many new concepts and graphs and may at first appear overwhelming. Don't get lost among the trees and lose sight of the forest. There is a simple and fundamental relationship between production functions and cost functions.

    The chapter begins with the short-run production function and the concepts of total product, marginal product, and average product. This is followed by the short-run cost function and the concepts of total cost, marginal cost, average variable cost, and average total cost.

    All of these seemingly disparate concepts are related to the law of diminishing returns. The law states that as a firm uses additional units of a variable input, while holding constant the quantity of fixed inputs, the marginal product of the variable input will eventually diminish. This law explains why the marginal product and average product curves eventually fall, and why the total product curve becomes flatter. When productivity falls, costs increase, and the law explains the eventual upward slope of the marginal cost curve. The marginal cost curve, in turn, explains the U-shape of the average variable cost and average total cost curves. When the marginal cost curve is below the average variable (or total) cost curve, the average variable (or total) cost curve is falling. When marginal cost is above the average variable (or total) cost curve, the average variable (or total) cost curve is rising. The marginal cost curve intersects the average variable (or total) cost curve at the minimum point on the average variable (or total) cost curve.

    Use the law of diminishing returns as the key to understanding the relationships between the many short-run concepts and graphs in the chapter. But all concepts and graphs are not equally important. Pay most attention to the unit cost concepts and graphs

— especially marginal cost, average variable cost, and average total cost — because these will be used the most in later chapters to analyze the behavior of firms. Be sure to thoroughly understand text Figure 10.4(b). It is the most important figure in the entire chapter.

2. You will probably draw the unit cost graph with the marginal cost, average variable cost, and average total cost curves at least one hundred times in this course. Here are some hints on drawing the graph quickly and easily.

    a) Be sure to label the axes; quantity of output (Q) on the horizontal axis and cost on the vertical axis.

    b) Draw an upward-sloping marginal cost curve, as shown here in Fig. 10.1. The marginal cost curve can have a small downward-sloping section at first, but this is not important for subsequent analysis. Draw a shallow U-shaped curve whose minimum point passes through your second point. Finally label the curves.

    c) Any time a test question (including those in the Self-Test) asks about these curves, *draw a graph* before you answer.

3. Be sure to understand how economists use the terms *short run* and *long run*. These terms do not refer to any notion of calendar time. They are better thought of as planning horizons. The short run is a planning horizon short enough that while some inputs are variable, at least one input cannot be varied but is fixed. The long run refers to a planning horizon that is long enough that all inputs can be varied.

Figure 10.1

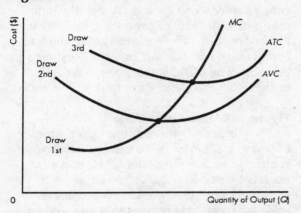

4. The later sections of the chapter explain the long-run production function and cost function when plant size is variable. While diminishing returns was the key for understanding short-run costs, the concept of returns to scale is the key for understanding long-run costs. Returns to scale are the increase in output relative to the increase in inputs when *all inputs* are increased by the same percentage. Returns to scale can be increasing, constant, or decreasing, and correspond to the downward-sloping, horizontal and upward-sloping sections of the long-run average cost curve.

KEY FIGURES AND TABLE

Figure 10.2 Total Product and Marginal Product

This figure illustrates how to calculate marginal product from total product. Marginal product of labor is the increase in total product resulting from the use of an additional unit of labor. The table calculates the marginal product of labor directly as the change in total product as additional units of labor are used. Part (a) illustrates the total product curve and indicates the addition to total product associated with each additional unit of

labor. Notice that the slope of the total product curve, $\Delta TP/\Delta L$, is equal to the marginal product. Thus, if you know the total product curve, you can always derive the marginal product curve.

When graphing the marginal product curve, as in part (b), notice that marginal product is plotted *midway* between the corresponding units of labor, emphasizing that marginal product is the result of *changing* inputs. For example, the marginal product of changing from 0 to 1 workers is 4 sweaters, and the value 4 is plotted midway between 0 and 1 workers.

Figure 10.3 Total Product, Marginal Product, and Average Product

This figure uses the same data as Fig. 10.2. Here the table computes the average product of labor by dividing output by the quantity of labor. As shown in part (a), average product can be measured by the slope of a straight line from the origin to a point on the total product curve. As the quantity of labor increases, we notice that the slope of the line from the origin to the corresponding point on the total product curve first increases, reaches a maximum, and then decreases.

Part (b) simply represents the average product graphically. The concept of average product does not involve any idea of changing inputs, it measures the average product of *fixed* number of units of labor. Hence, values for average product are plotted directly above the corresponding units of labor. For example, the average product of 3 workers is 4.33 sweaters and the value 4.33 is plotted directly above 3 workers. Notice the relationship between the average product and marginal product curves. The marginal product curve is above the average product curve when average product is increasing and below the average product curve when average product is decreasing. The marginal product curve intersects the average product curve when average product is a maximum.

Figure 10.4 Short-Run Costs

In the short run, total cost (*TC*) is divided into total fixed cost (*TFC*) and total variable cost (*TVC*). The left half of the table in this figure gives these costs for Swanky, Inc. Part (a) of the figure illustrates the total cost, total fixed cost, and total variable cost curves. Since *TC* = *TFC* + *TVC*, the vertical distance the *TC* and *TVC* curves is equal to *TFC*, which by definition is constant (fixed).

The graph in part (b) is one of the most important graphs in all of microeconomics, and you must understand it thoroughly. The curves for average total cost (*ATC*), average variable cost (*AVC*), and average fixed cost (*AFC*) are derived by taking the values for *TC*, *TVC*, and *TFC* and dividing them by quantity of output. Since these are average values for a fixed quantity of output, they are plotted directly above the corresponding units of output. On the other hand, marginal cost (*MC*) is the *change* in total cost (or, equivalently, total variable cost) resulting from a one unit increase in output. It is plotted in the graph in part (b) *midway* between the corresponding units of output. The *ATC* and *AVC* curves are both U-shaped. The *MC* curve is also U-shaped and intersects the *ATC* and *AVC* curves at their minimum points. The less important *AFC* curve falls continuously as output increases. See *Helpful Hint 2* for tips on how to draw these crucially important curves.

Figure 10.8 Short-Run and Long-Run Costs

In the short run, the quantity of capital is fixed while in the long-run all inputs are variable. This figure illustrates the relationship between short-run and long-run costs for Swanky, Inc. Four different plants are considered: one for each of one through four units of capital (knitting machines). Given a choice of plant, Swanky, Inc. is then in the short run. For example, if Swanky chooses to buy 2 knitting machines, it has chosen to operate plant b in the short run and thus faces average total cost curve given by *ATC*$_b$ in the

graph in part (a). The costs for each plant are given in the table and the corresponding *ATC* curves are illustrated in part (a). In the long run, Swanky's will choose the plant which minimizes the *ATC* of producing the desired level of output. The construction of the long-run average cost (*LRAC*) curve is illustrated in part (b). The *LRAC* traces the lowest *ATC* possible for each level of output.

Figure 10.9 Returns to Scale

This figure illustrates ranges over which Swanky, Inc. *LRAC* curve exhibits alternative returns to scale. When the *LRAC* curve is negatively sloped (e.g., up to output of 15 sweaters per day), there are economies of scale (or increasing returns to scale). When the *LRAC* curve is positively sloped (e.g., output levels above 15 sweaters per day), there are diseconomies of scale (or decreasing returns to scale).

Table 10.2 A Compact Glossary on Product

Numerous new total and unit product and cost concepts are introduced in this chapter. This table conveniently brings together those having to do with *product*. It includes the term, the symbol used, the equation form of the definition, and a verbal definition. This table should provide a useful study tool.

Table 10.3 A Compact Glossary on Cost

This table is a companion to Table 10.2. It brings the various new total and unit *cost* concepts introduced in this chapter together in a convenient summary form. It includes the term, the symbol used, the equation form of the definition, and a verbal definition. You must know and *understand* all of the equations in this table.

SELF-TEST

CONCEPT REVIEW

1. The profits of a firm are limited by two types of constraints: _____ constraints, which are conditions under which the firm can buy its inputs and sell its output, and _____ constraints, which limit the feasible ways in which inputs can be converted into output.

2. A production process that uses large amounts of capital relative to labor is called a(n) _____ - _____ technique while a/an _____ - _____ technique uses a large amount of labor relative to capital.

3. The term economists use for a period of time in which the quantities of some inputs are fixed while others can be varied is the _____ - _____.
   The period of time in which all inputs are variable is the _____ - _____.

4. The total product curve is a graph of the maximum output attainable at each level of a _____ input, given the amount of fixed inputs. The change in total product resulting from a one-unit increase in labor input, holding the quantity of capital constant, is called the _____ _____ of labor.
   The average product of labor is _____

_____ divided by the units of _____.

5. If marginal product is greater than average product, then average product must be _____. Marginal product is _____ _____ average product when average product reaches a maximum.

6. The shape of the marginal product curve can be described as follows: it first _____, reaches a _____ and then _____ as labor inputs increase.

7. Increasing marginal returns occur when the marginal product of an additional worker is _____ than the marginal product of the previous workers. As more of a variable input is used, holding other inputs fixed, the marginal product of the variable input begins to decline. This is a statement of the law of _____ _____.

8. $TC = TFC +$ _____.

9. Marginal cost is the increase in total cost resulting from a one-unit increase in _____.

10. If the average variable cost curve is decreasing, then the marginal cost curve must be _____ than average variable cost.

11. The output at which a plant's average total cost is a minimum is called the _____ of the plant.

12. If output increases by 20 percent when all inputs are increased by 10 percent, the production process is said to display _____ _____ to _____.

13. If a firm is experiencing constant returns to scale, a 10 percent increase in inputs will result in a _____ percent _____ in output. When the long-run average cost curve falls, there are _____ returns to scale.

14. A technological advance will tend to _____ product curves and _____ cost curves.

TRUE OR FALSE

____ 1. Limitations on the feasible ways in which inputs can be converted into outputs is an example of market constraints on the profits a firm can make.

____ 2. All economically efficient production methods are also technologically efficient.

____ 3. The short run is a time period in which there is at least one fixed input and at least one variable input.

____ 4. All inputs are fixed in the long run.

____ 5. Marginal product is given by the slope of the total product curve.

____ 6. Given a fixed quantity of capital, if 2 additional laborers produce 15 additional units of output, the marginal product of labor is 15 units of output.

____ 7. Average product can be measured as the slope of a line drawn from the origin to a point on the total product curve.

____ 8. The average product curve cuts the marginal product curve from above at the maximum point on the marginal product curve.

____ 9. The law of diminishing returns implies that eventually the marginal product curve will be negatively sloped as the variable input increases.

____10. The law of diminishing returns implies that we will not observe a range of increasing marginal returns.

____11. Average total cost, average variable cost, and average fixed cost are all U-shaped.

____12. Average variable cost reaches its minimum at the same level of output at which average product is a maximum.

____13. In the real world, marginal cost curves are rarely upward sloping.

____14. A firm producing on the downward sloping part of its average total cost curve is said to have excess capacity.

____15. By capacity, economists mean the physical limits of production.

_____16. If average total cost is greater than marginal cost, then average total cost must be increasing.

_____17. No part of any short-run average total cost curve can lie below the long-run average cost curve.

_____18. Increasing returns to scale means that the long-run average cost curve is negatively sloped.

_____19. If a 20 percent increase in variable inputs yields a 20 percent increase in output, then there are constant returns to scale.

_____20. In the long run the total cost and (total) variable cost curves are the same.

_____21. If the price of inputs falls, the average variable cost and average total cost curves will shift up.

_____22. A firm facing highly variable demand for its output would want to increase plant size only if it was persistently operating on the upward-sloping part of its short-run average total cost curve.

MULTIPLE CHOICE

1. In economics, the short run is a time period
   a. of one year or less.
   b. in which all inputs are variable.
   c. in which all inputs are fixed.
   d. in which there is at least one fixed input and at least one variable input.

2. A profit maximizing firm is constrained by all of the following EXCEPT limited
   a. demand for a product.
   b. input supplies.
   c. number of technologically efficient production methods.
   d. competition from other firms.

3. The total product represents the
   a. sum of the average and marginal product curves.
   b. maximum output attainable for each quantity of a variable input at each price of the variable input.
   c. maximum output attainable for each quantity of a variable input given the amount of other inputs.
   d. total output divided by the quantity of the fixed input.

4. The change in total product resulting from a one-unit increase in a variable input is called
   a. average product.
   b. marginal product.
   c. average variable product.
   d. total product.

5. The average product of labor can be measured as the
   a. slope of a straight line from the origin to a point on the total product curve.
   b. slope of the total product curve.
   c. slope of the marginal product curve.
   d. change in output divided by the change in labor input.

6. When the marginal product of labor is less than the average product of labor,
   a. the average product of labor is increasing.
   b. the marginal product of labor is increasing.
   c. the total product curve is negatively sloped.
   d. the firm is experiencing diminishing returns.

7. According to the law of diminishing returns,
   i) marginal productivity eventually rises.
   ii) marginal productivity eventually falls.
   iii) marginal cost eventually rises.
   iv) marginal cost eventually falls.
   a. i) and iii) are true.
   b. i) and iv) are true.
   c. ii) and iii) are true.
   d. ii) and iv) are true.

8. The vertical distance between the *TC* and *TVC* curves is
   a. decreasing as output increases.
   b. equal to *AFC*.
   c. equal to *TFC*.
   d. equal to *MC*.

9. The marginal cost (*MC*) curve intersects the
   a. *ATC*, *AVC*, and *AFC* curves at their minimum points.
   b. *ATC* and *AFC* curves at their minimum points.
   c. *AVC* and *AFC* curves at their minimum points.
   d. *ATC* and *AVC* curves at their minimum points.

10. Total cost is $20 at 4 units of output and $36 at 6 units of output. Between 4 and 6 units of output, marginal cost
   a. is less than average total cost.
   b. is equal to average total cost.
   c. is equal to average variable cost.
   d. is greater than average total cost.

11. A firm's fixed costs are $100. If total costs are $200 for one unit of output and $310 for two units, what is the marginal cost of the second unit?
   a. $100
   b. $110
   c. $200
   d. $210

12. In the long run,
   a. only the scale of plant is fixed.
   b. all inputs are variable.
   c. all inputs are fixed.
   d. a firm must experience decreasing returns to scale.

13. The problem of a firm in the long run is to
   a. derive the long-run average cost curve.
   b. choose the scale of plant that has minimum average cost of producing the desired level of output.
   c. choose the amount of labor that has minimum average cost of producing the desired level of output, given the scale of plant.
   d. produce the largest amount of output possible.

14. When a firm is producing at capacity, it is
   a. maximizing profit.
   b. producing at its physical limits.
   c. producing at the level of output at which marginal cost equals average total cost.
   d. producing on the upward sloping part of its long-run average cost curve.

15. If all inputs are increased by 10 percent and output increases by less than 10 percent, it must be the case that
   a. marginal total cost is decreasing.
   b. the *LRAC* curve is negatively sloped.
   c. there are increasing returns to scale.
   d. there are decreasing returns to scale.

16. The reason for upward sloping marginal cost curves is the law of
   a. diminishing returns.
   b. diminishing marginal utility.
   c. increasing returns to scale.
   d. production.

17. Constant returns to scale means that, as all inputs are increased,
    a. total output remains unchanged.
    b. long-run average cost remains unchanged.
    c. long-run average cost rises at the same rate as inputs.
    d. marginal product is increasing.

18. The long-run average cost curve
    a. is the short-run average total cost curve with the lowest cost.
    b. will shift up when fixed costs increase.
    c. traces out the minimum points on all the short-run average total cost curves for each scale of plant.
    d. traces out the minimum short-run average total cost for each output.

19. A technological advance will shift
    i) *TP, AP,* and *MP* curves up.
    ii) *TP, AP,* and *MP* curves down.
    iii) *TC, ATC,* and *MC* curves up.
    iv) *TC, ATC,* and *MC* curves down.
    a. i) and iii) are true.
    b. i) and iv) are true.
    c. ii) and iii) are true.
    d. ii) and iv) are true.

20. A firm will want to increase its scale of plant if
    a. it is persistently producing on the upward-sloping part of its short-run average total cost curve.
    b. it is persistently producing on the downward-sloping part of its short-run average total cost curve.
    c. it is producing below capacity.
    d. marginal cost is below average total cost.

21. The average variable cost curve will shift up if
    a. there is an increase in fixed costs.
    b. there is a technological advance.
    c. the price of a variable input increases.
    d. the price of output increases.

22. A rise in the price of a fixed input will cause a firm's
    a. average variable cost curve to shift up.
    b. average total cost curve to shift up.
    c. average total cost curve to shift down.
    d. marginal cost curve to shift up.

SHORT ANSWER

1. What market constraints does a firm face on its ability to make profits?

2. What is the difference between the short run and the long run?

3. Why does a steeper slope of the total product curve imply a higher level of the marginal product curve?

4. Why is it the case that the marginal product curve must intersect the average product curve at its maximum point?

5. What is the difference, if any, between diminishing returns and decreasing returns to scale?

6. How is the long-run average cost curve obtained and how does it differ from Jacob Viner's mistaken conception of it?

7. Why does increasing returns to scale imply a negatively sloped long-run average cost curve?

PROBLEMS

1. Table 10.1 gives the total monthly output of golf carts attainable for varying amounts of labor for a given scale of plant.
   a) Complete the table for the marginal product and average product of labor.
   b) Draw a graph of the total product curve (*TP*).
   c) Draw a graph of marginal product (*MP*) and average product (*AP*).

Table 10.1 Monthly Production of Golf Carts

Labor (workers per month)	Output (units per month)	Marginal product	Average product
0	0		
1	1		
2	3		
3	6		
4	12		
5	17		
6	20		
7	22		
8	23		

2. Now let's examine the short-run costs of golf cart production. The first two columns of Table 10.1 are reproduced in the first two columns of Table 10.2 on the next page. The cost of 1 laborer (the only variable input) is $2,000 a month. Total fixed cost is $2,000 per month.
   a) Given this information, complete Table 10.2 by computing total fixed cost (*TFC*), total variable cost (*TVC*), total cost (*TC*), marginal cost (*MC*), average fixed cost (*AFC*), average variable cost (*AVC*), and average total cost (*ATC*). Your completed table should look like the table in text Figure 10.4, with marginal cost entered *midway* between the rows.
   b) Label the axes and draw the *TC*, *TVC*, and *TFC* curves on a single graph.
   c) Label the axes and draw the *MC*, *ATC*, *AVC*, and *AFC* curves on a single graph. Be sure to plot *MC midway* between corresponding units of output.
   d) Now suppose that the price of a laborer increases tp $2,500 per month. Construct a table for the new *MC* and *ATC* curves (output, *MC*, *ATC*). Label the area and draw a graph of the new *MC* and *ATC* curves. What is the effect of the increase in the price of the variable input on these curves?

3. Return to the original price of labor of $2,000 per month. Now suppose that we double the quantity of fixed inputs. This increases the monthly output of golf carts for each quantity of labor as indicated in Table 10.3.

Table 10.3 New Monthly Production of Golf Carts

Laborers (per month)	Output (units per month)
0	0
1	1
2	4
3	10
4	19
5	26
6	31
7	34
8	36

   a) Construct a table for the new *MC* and *ATC* curves (output, *MC*, *ATC*). Label

Table 10.2 Short-run costs (Monthly)

Laborers (per month)	Output (units per month)	TFC ($)	TVC ($)	TC ($)	MC ($)	AFC ($)	AVC ($)	ATC ($)
0	0	2,000						
1	1							
2	3							
3	6							
4	12							
5	17							
6	20							
7	22							
8	23							

the axes and draw a graph of the new *MC* and *ATC* curves.

b) What is the effect on these curves compared to the original *MC* and *ATC* curves in Problem 2(c) of an increase in "plant size?" Are the economies of scale?

c) Draw the long-run average cost (LRAC) curve is these are the only two plant sizes available.

4. Figure 10.2 gives a sequence of short-run *ATC* curves numbered 1 through 7 corresponding to seven different plant sizes.

a) Draw the long-run average cost curve on Fig. 10.2.

b) If the desired level of output is 100 units per day, what is the best plant size? (Give the number of the associated short-run *ATC* curve).

c) If the desired level of output is 200 units per day, what is the best plant size?

Figure 10.2

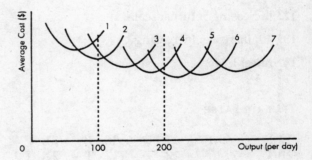

ANSWERS

CONCEPT REVIEW

1. market; technological
2. capital-intensive; labor-intensive
3. short-run; long-run
4. variable; marginal product; total product (output); labor
5. rising; equal to
6. increases; maximum; decreases
7. greater; diminishing returns
8. *TVC*
9. output
10. less
11. capacity
12. increasing returns; scale
13. 10; increase; increasing
14. raise; lower

TRUE OR FALSE

1. F	6. F	11. F	16. F	21. F
2. T	7. T	12. T	17. T	22. T
3. T	8. F	13. F	18. T	
4. F	9. T	14. T	19. F	
5. T	10. F	15. F	20. T	

MULTIPLE CHOICE

1. d	6. d	11. b	16. a	21. c
2. d	7. c	12. b	17. b	22. b
3. c	8. c	13. b	18. a	
4. b	9. d	14. c	19. b	
5. a	10. d	15. d	20. a	

SHORT ANSWER

1. Every firm is constrained by the supply of inputs it uses and by the demand for the output it produces. Because of the law of supply, firms, in general, can obtain more inputs only if they are willing to pay more for them. On the other hand, given the law of demand, firms, in general, can sell more of their output only if they are willing to drop the price.

2. The short run is a period of time short enough that, while some inputs are variable, at least one is fixed. The long run is a period of time long enough that all inputs are variable.

3. Marginal product is equal to the slope of the total product curve since it is defined as the change in total product resulting from an increase in the variable input. Since a steeper slope means a larger slope, it also means a higher marginal product.

4. Since the average product curve first rises and then falls, it is sufficient to show that when average product is rising, marginal product must be greater than average product, and that when average product is falling, marginal product must be lower than average product. If this is the case, then the marginal product curve intersects the average product curve at its maximum point. In order for average product to increase, it must have been *pulled up* by a larger increase in product from the last unit of input; that is, the marginal product is higher than average product. Similarly, when average product is falling, it must be that it has been *pulled down* by a lower marginal product. When average product is at its maximum, it is neither rising nor falling, so marginal product cannot be higher or lower than average product. Therefore, the marginal product must be equal to average product.

5. The law of diminishing returns states that as a firm uses additional units of a variable input, *while holding constant the quantity of fixed inputs* the marginal product of the variable input will eventually diminish. Decreasing returns to scale occur when a firm increases *all of its inputs by an equal percentage*, and this results in a lower percentage increase in output. Diminishing (marginal) returns is a short-run concept since there must be a fixed input. Decreasing returns to scale is a long-run concept since all inputs must be variable.

6. Any given level of output can be produced using alternative scales of plant, but for each level of output, one scale of plant will result in the lowest value of short-run average total cost. The scale of plant can be varied in the long run, and the long-run average cost curve traces out the lowest short-run average total cost at each level of output. Jacob Viner's mistaken conception of the long-run average cost curve was that (a) it must pass through the *minimum point* of each of the short-run average cost curves (which is incorrect) and, (b) it must not be above any short-run cost curve at any point (which is correct). The mistake is that these two properties cannot be satisfied simultaneously. Indeed, the long-run average cost curve does *not* pass through the minimum point of each of the short-run average cost curves.

7. Increasing returns to scale means that as we increase the number of inputs (scale of plant) the percentage increase in output will be greater than the percentage increase in inputs. Average cost is the product of the price of inputs and the quantity of inputs all divided by the level of output.

$$AC = \frac{\textit{price of inputs} \times \textit{quantity of inputs}}{\textit{quantity of output}}$$

Therefore, as the scale of plant increases, both the numerator and denominator of *AC* increase. If the percentage increase in the numerator is less than the percentage increase in the denominator, then *AC* declines as the scale of plant increases (i.e., the long-run average cost curve is negatively sloped). That this is the case follows from the definition of increasing returns to scale and the fact that we are assuming the price of inputs to be constant.

8. Jacob Viner's famous mistake was giving his draftsman impossible instructions for constructing the long-run average cost curves from a sequence of short-run average costs curves. He told him to draw the long-run average cost curve so that it had both of the following properties:
   a) It must pass through the minimum point of each of the short-run average cost curves.
   b) It must not be above any short-run cost curve at any point. The problem, as we have seen clearly in the text, is that these two properties cannot be satisfied simultaneously. Indeed, the long-run average cost curve does not pass through the minimum point of each of the short-run average cost curves.

PROBLEMS

1. a) Completed Table 10.1 is shown here as Table 10.1 Solution.
   b) Figure 10.3 gives the graph of the total product curve.
   c) Figure 10.4 gives the graphs of marginal product and average product.

2. a) Completed Table 10.2 is given here as Table 10.2 Solution on the next page.
   b) The *TC*, *TVC*, and *TFC* curves are graphed in Fig. 10.5.
   c) The *MC*, *ATC*, *AVC*, and *AFC* curves are graphed in Fig. 10.6.

Table 10.1 Solution: Monthly Golf Cart Production

Laborers (per month)	Output (units per month)	Marginal Product	Average Product
0	0		0
		...1	
1	1		1.00
		...2	
2	3		1.50
		...3	
3	6		2.00
		...6	
4	12		3.00
		...5	
5	17		3.40
		...3	
6	20		3.33
		...2	
7	22		3.14
		...1	
8	23		2.88

Figure 10.3

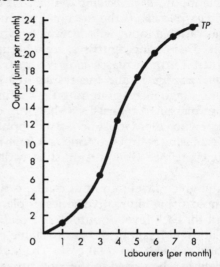

Figure 10.4

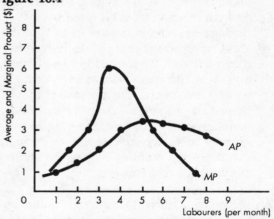

Figure 10.5

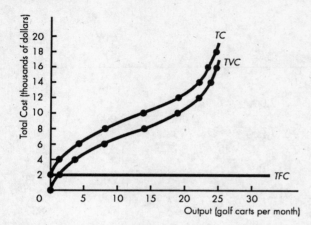

3. a) The new *MC* and *ATC* curves are given
       in Fig. 10.8. The new curves are la-
       beled MC_3 and ATC_3. The original
       curves, MC_1 and ATC_1, are indicated
       for reference.
    b) The curves have shifted (generally)
       down and to the right as a result of
       increasing plant size. There are econo-
       mies of scale (increasing returns to
       scale) up to the level of output at
       which MC_3 intersects ATC_3 (approxi-
       mately 32 units).
    c) The long-run average cost curve is
       indicated in Fig. 10.8 by the heavy line
       tracing out the lowest short-run aver-
       age total cost of producing each level
       of output. In this example, that hap-
       pens to correspond entirely to ATC_3.

Figure 10.6

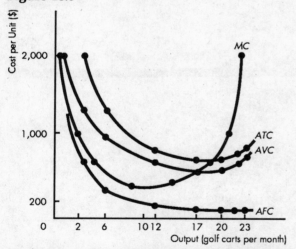

  d) The new *MC* and *ATC* curves (and the
     associated table) are given in Fig. 10.7.
     The original curves, MC_1 and ATC_1 are
     indicated for reference. The new
     curves are labelled MC_2 and ATC_2.
     Both curves have shifted up as a result
     of an increase in the price of labor.

Table 10.2 Solution: Short-run Costs (Monthly)

Laborers (per month)	Output (units per month)	TFC ($)	TVC ($)	TC ($)	MC ($)	AFC ($)	AVC ($)	ATC ($)
0	0	2,000	0	2,000		--	--	--
					 2,000			
1	1	2,000	2,000	4,000		2,000	2,000	4,000
					 1,000			
2	3	2,000	4,000	6,000		667	1,333	2,000
					 667			
3	6	2,000	6,000	8,000		333	1,000	1,333
					 333			
4	12	2,000	8,000	10,000		167	667	833
					 400			
5	17	2,000	10,000	12,000		118	588	706
					 667			
6	20	2,000	12,000	14,000		100	600	700
					 1,000			
7	22	2,000	14,000	16,000		91	636	72
					 2,000			
8	23	2,000	16,000	18,000		87	696	783

4. a) The long-run average cost curve is
       indicated in Fig. 10.2 Solution by the
       heavy line tracing out the lowest short-
       run average total cost of producing
       each level of output.
    b) If the desired level of output is 100
       units, the best plant size is the one
       associated with short-run average total
       cost curve 2.
    c) If the desired level of output is 200
       units, the best plant size is the one
       associated with short-run average total
       cost curve 5.

Figure 10.7

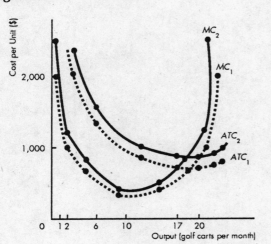

Output	MC($)	ATC($)
0		0
	 2,500	
1		4,500
	 1,250	
3		2,333
	 833	
6		1,583
	 417	
12		1,000
	 500	
17		853
	 833	
20		850
	 1,250	
22		866
	 2,500	
23		957

Figure 10.8

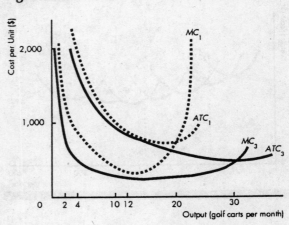

Output	MC($)	ATC($)
0		0
	 2,000	
1		6,000
	 667	
4		2,000
	 333	
10		1,000
	 222	
19		632
	 286	
26		538
	 400	
31		516
	 667	
34		529

Figure 10.2 Solution

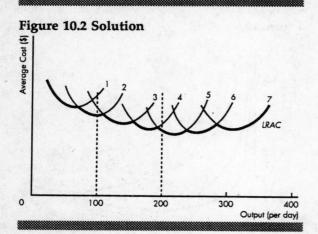

11 COMPETITION

CHAPTER IN PERSPECTIVE

This chapter combines the cost information of Chapters 9 and 10 with new revenue information in order to analyze the profit-maximization decision of firms in a perfectly competitive market. The analysis includes derivations of both the individual firm supply curve and the industry supply curve. While we have previously simply assumed that supply curves are upward sloping, this chapter derives upward-sloping supply curves as a prediction of the theory of perfect competition. The theory also allows us to make precise predictions about the behavior of firms and their responses to changes in market conditions. Although perfect competition does not occur frequently in the real world, the theory allows us to isolate the effects of competitive forces, which are at work in *all* markets, even in those that do not match the assumptions of the theory of perfect competition.

LEARNING OBJECTIVES

After studying this chapter, you will be able to:

- Define perfect competition

- Explain why a perfectly competitive firm cannot influence the market price

- Explain how a competitive industry's output changes when price changes

- Explain why firms sometimes shut down temporarily and lay off workers

- Explain why firms enter and leave an industry

- Predict the effects on an industry and on a typical firm of a change in demand and of a technological advance

- Explain why farmers have had such a bad time in recent years

- Explain why perfect competition is efficient

HELPFUL HINTS

1. Although perfectly competitive markets are quite rare in the real world, there are three important reasons to develop a thorough understanding of their behavior.

First, many markets quite closely approximate perfectly competitive markets. Thus, the analysis developed in this chapter gives direct and useful insights into the behavior of these markets.

Second, the theory of perfect competition allows us to isolate the effects of competitive forces, which are at work in *all* markets, even those that do not match all the assumptions of perfect competition.

Third, the perfectly competitive model serves as a useful benchmark against which to evaluate relative allocative efficiency.

2. A perfectly competitive firm is a price taker; it will always sell at the market price which it cannot influence. Thus, the only variable that is under the control of the firm is output. The problem faced by the perfectly competitive firm is then quite straightforward: choose the output that maximizes profit.

3. Students should understand *why* profit is maximized when marginal revenue equals marginal cost ($MR = MC$). This is a general condition which, as we will see in subsequent chapters, applies to other market structures such as monopoly and monopolistic competition. Since for the perfectly competitive firm, marginal revenue is equal to price, this profit-maximizing condition takes a particular form; choose the level of output at which price is equal to marginal cost ($P = MC$).

4. Although the objective of a firm is to maximize profit, that profit may be negative; that is, it may be a loss. If the market price is less than minimum average total cost (the breakeven point), the firm will experience a loss. In this case, the firm's problem is to minimize its loss and one option it faces is to shut down; that is, to produce nothing. If a firm chooses to shut down, its loss will be equal to total fixed cost. As long as the price is above minimum average variable cost (the shutdown point), however, a firm will decide to produce since it will be covering total variable cost and part of total fixed cost. Thus its loss will be less if it produces (at the output where $P = MC$). On the other hand, if the price is less than minimum average variable cost, a firm that produces output will not even be able to cover total variable cost and so its loss will exceed total fixed cost. Thus, when the price is less than average variable cost, the firm will choose to minimize its loss by shutting down.

5. In the short run, a firm is constrained to its current scale of plant. This means not only that the firm is unable to choose a larger scale of plant in the short run, but also that the firm is unable to go out of business (avoid fixed costs) in the short run. In the long run, however, a firm can choose any scale of plant, including going out of business. Furthermore, in the long run, a new firm can choose to enter the industry.

6. In the long run, fixed costs disappear and the firm can switch between industries and change scale of plant without cost. Economic profits serve as the signal for the movement or reallocation of firm resources until long-run equilibrium is achieved. Firms will enter industries in which there are positive economic profits and leave industries with negative economic profits (losses). Only if economic profits are zero will the industry be at rest with no tendency for firms to enter or exit.

The fact that there are no restrictions on entry into the industry is what assures that economic profits will be zero and that firms will be producing at the minimum of their long-run average cost curves in long-run equilibrium.

7. In long-run equilibrium, three conditions are satisfied for each firm in the industry.
   a) $MR (= P) = MC$. This implies that profits are maximized for each firm.
   b) $P = ATC$. This implies that economic profits are zero for each firm.
   c) MC = minimum $LRAC$. This implies that production takes place at the point of minimum long-run average cost.

KEY FIGURES AND TABLES

Figure 11.2 Total Revenue, Total Cost, and Profit

Profit is defined as total revenue minus total cost. In part (a) of this figure, total revenue and total cost are both illustrated. Profit is the vertical distance between them; a positive profit when total revenue lies above total cost and a loss when total revenue lies below total cost. This difference is plotted against output as the profit curve in the graph in part (b). It is easy to see that, in the example, profit is a maximum when 9 sweaters are produced.

Figure 11.3 Marginal Revenue, Marginal Cost, and Profit-Maximizing Output

This figure illustrates the alternative profit maximizing condition: marginal revenue equals marginal cost. Producing and selling one more unit of a good (sweaters in the example) adds both to revenue and to cost. If the addition to revenue (marginal revenue) is greater than the addition to cost (marginal cost), then profit will increase and so the additional unit should be produced.

If, on the other hand, marginal revenue is less than marginal cost, profit will decrease and so the additional unit should not be produced. Since marginal revenue declines with output and marginal cost rises with output, these rules lead to the conclusion that a profit-maximizing firm should produce each unit up to the point at which marginal revenue equals marginal cost.

This is illustrated here using a table and the corresponding graph in the context of the example of Swanky, Inc. We see that producing each of the first through ninth sweaters adds to profit ($MR > MC$) but that the tenth sweater decreases profit ($MR < MC$). Since, for a perfectly competitive firm, $MR = P$, the profit maximizing condition is $P = MC$.

Figure 11.5 Swanky's Supply Curve

The construction of the supply curve of a perfectly competitive firm is demonstrated here. In the context of the firm's cost and revenue curves, part (a) derives Swanky's supply curve by asking: How much will Swanky, a profit-maximizing firm, produce at given prices? This, of course is exactly what is reflected by a supply curve.

Since the profit maximizing condition is $P = MC$, Swanky's supply curve is the same as its marginal cost curve as long as the price is above minimum average variable cost.   For any price below minimum average variable cost, Swanky will minimize its losses by shutting don and producing nothing. As a result, the firm's supply curve becomes vertical at zero output for prices below minimum average variable cost.

When drawing graphs we usually ignore this vertical section of the supply curve. The most important section of the supply curve is the upward-sloping section corresponding to the portion of the marginal cost curve above minimum average variable cost.

Figure 11.6 Firm and Industry Supply Curves

The relationship between the firm and industry supply curves is straightforward. The industry supply curve is obtained by adding horizontally the individual supply curves of the firms in the industry. This means that the industry quantity supplied at any given price level is the total quantity supplied by all the firms in the industry.

Since the individual firm supply curves are the same as the marginal cost curve above minimum average variable cost, the industry supply curve is the sum of these marginal cost curves. Below minimum average variable cost, the industry supply curve is vertical at an output of zero since this is the sum of firm supply curves in this price range. As in text Fig. 11.5, the upward-sloping section of the supply curve is most important and we usually ignore the vertical section.

Figure 11.13 Long-Run Price and Quantity

This figure illustrates three alternative relationships between price and quantity supplied in the long run. Starting in a long-run equilibrium, suppose there is an increase in demand. The question of interest here is: In the long run, does the price of the good rise, fall, or remain the same?

In the short run, as industry demand increases, the price will rise and profit maximizing firms will be induced to employ more variable inputs and increase output. Thus the industry short-run supply curve is positively sloped since it is the horizontal sum of positively sloped firm supply curves (firm *MC* curves). But the increase in price will cause profits to increase and thus new firms will be attracted into the industry. This will shift the industry supply curve to the right.

When long-run equilibrium is restored (zero economic profits), the question becomes: Is the intersection of the new demand and new supply curves at a price which is higher, lower, or equal to the original price?

In industries where costs increase as output increases (external diseconomies), the price will be higher. In industries where costs decrease as output increases (external economies), the price will be lower. And in industries where costs remain unchanged as output increases (no external economies or diseconomies), the price will remain unchanged.

Figure 11.16 Allocative Efficiency

Allocative efficiency is achieved when marginal social benefit equals marginal social cost. Marginal social benefit (*MSB*) and marginal social cost (*MSC*) curves are shown in this figure in an attempt to illustrate the concept of allocative efficiency. Additional output adds both to social benefit and social cost. If the addition to social benefit (*MSB*) is greater than the addition to social cost (*MSC*), the additional unit should be produced. If the marginal social benefit of an additional unit of output is less that the marginal social cost, it should not be produced. Thus, efficiency is achieved when *MSB* = *MSC*. For levels of output less than *Q**, in the figure, *MSB* > *MSC* so additional units should be produced. Allocative efficiency occurs at output *Q**. If there are no external costs or benefits, the perfectly competitive industry supply curve is the marginal social cost curve and the industry demand curve is the marginal social benefit curve. Thus the competitive market equilibrium will achieve allocative efficiency.

SELF-TEST

CONCEPT REVIEW

1. Perfect competition occurs in a market where

    -   There are _____ firms, each selling a(n) _____ product.
    -   There are _____ buyers.
    -   There are no restrictions on _____ into the industry.

2. A firm in a perfectly competitive market is said to be a price _____ since it cannot influence the price of the good it produces. Such a firm faces a demand curve that is perfectly _____.

3. We assume that the firm's single objective is to maximize its _____.

4. Total revenue divided by the total quantity sold is called _____ _____. The change in revenue resulting from a one-unit increase in the quantity sold is called _____ _____.

5. In the case of perfect competition average revenue and marginal revenue are both equal to _____.

6. An output at which total cost equals total revenue is called a _____ point. The point at which a firm's maximum profit (minimum loss) is the same regardless of whether the firm produces any output or not is called the _____ point.

7. Profit is maximized when marginal revenue equals _____ _____.

8. Market price is determined by _____ demand and _____ supply.

9. In the range of prices greater than the minimum average variable cost, a perfectly competitive firm's supply curve is the same as its _____ _____ curve. At prices below minimum average variable cost, the firm will produce _____ and make a loss equal to its _____ _____ _____.

10. New firms will enter a perfectly competitive industry if firms in the industry are making economic _____. As new firms enter the industry the price will _____. If economic _____ are being made, firms will tend to exit from the industry.

11. Long-run equilibrium occurs in a perfectly competitive industry when economic profits are _____. Each firm will also be producing at the _____ point of its long-run average cost curve.

12. Factors beyond the control of an individual firm that lower its cost as industry output increases are called _____ _____. Factors beyond the control of an individual firm that raise its costs as industry output increases are called _____ _____.

13. _____ _____ occurs when no one can be made better off without making someone else worse off.

14. Costs which are not borne by the producer but are borne by other members of society are called _____ _____. Benefits which accrue to people other than the buyer of a good are called _____ _____.

TRUE OR FALSE

____ 1. In a perfectly competitive industry, no single firm can exert a significant effect on the market price of a good.

____ 2. In a perfectly competitive industry there are no restrictions on entry into the industry.

____ 3. The demand curve facing a firm in a perfectly competitive industry is essentially perfectly inelastic.

____ 4. The industry demand curve in a perfectly competitive industry is horizontal.

____ 5. The objective of firms in a competitive industry is to maximize revenue.

____ 6. The average revenue curve and marginal revenue curve are the same as the firm's demand curve in a perfectly competitive industry.

____ 7. If marginal revenue is greater than marginal cost, a firm can increase profit by decreasing output.

____ 8. Firms can make losses in the long run but not the short run.

____ 9. A firm is breaking even if its economic profit is zero.

____10. If the price is below the minimum average variable cost, a firm will shut down.

____11. In the price range above minimum average variable cost, the perfectly competitive firm's supply curve is the same as the marginal revenue curve.

____12. The supply curve of a perfectly competitive firm gives the quantities of output supplied at alternative prices as long as the firm earns economic profits.

____13. All firms in a competitive market will be maximizing profit in short-run equilibrium.

____14. The short-run industry supply curve is obtained as the horizontal sum of the supply curves of the individual firms.

____15. In long-run equilibrium, each firm in a perfectly competitive industry will be making zero economic profit.

____16. The entry of new firms into an industry will increase the price and increase the profit of each firm.

____17. In long-run equilibrium, each firm in a perfectly competitive industry will choose the scale of plant associated with the minimum long-run average cost.

____18. If, in a competitive industry, there are external economies, the long-run industry supply curve will be positively sloped.

____19. New technology allows firms to produce at lower cost.

____20. Suppose a competitive industry is in long-run equilibrium when a new technology is invented. During the adjustment to a new long-run equilibrium, some firms will be making economic profits while others will be experiencing economic losses.

____21. Suppose a competitive industry is in long-run equilibrium when there is a substantial increase in total fixed costs. All firms will now be making economic losses and some firms will go out of business.

____22. If a firm is economically efficient, then it must be allocatively efficient.

____23. A firm is economically efficient if it is maximizing profit.

____24. When the quantity of a good bought by a consumer at a given price is a point on the demand curve, consumer efficiency has occurred.

____25. Allocative efficiency occurs when marginal social benefit is greater than marginal social cost.

____26. A perfectly competitive industry will achieve allocative efficiency if there are no external costs or external benefits.

MULTIPLE CHOICE

1. Which of the following is <u>NOT</u> a characteristic of a perfectly competitive market?
   a. There are many firms.
   b. Each firm produces a slightly different product.
   c. There are no restrictions on entry into the industry.
   d. Firms in the industry have no advantage over potential new entrants.

2. A price taker is a firm that
   a. must lower its price if it wants to sell more output.
   b. must accept the price set by a monopoly.
   c. cannot influence the price of its product.
   d. is experiencing economic losses.

3. If a firm faces a perfectly elastic demand for its product, then
   a. it is not a price taker.
   b. it will want to lower its price to increase sales.
   c. it will want to raise its price to increase total revenue.
   d. its marginal revenue curve is equal to the price of the product.

4. A perfectly competitive firm is maximizing profit if
   a. marginal cost equals price and price is above minimum average variable cost.
   b. marginal cost equals price and price is above minimum average fixed cost.
   c. total revenue is a maximum.
   d. average variable cost is a minimum.

5. If a competitive firm is producing an output at which price is equal to average total cost, the firm
   a. should shut down.
   b. is breaking even.
   c. is still making a positive *economic* profit.
   d. is experiencing economic losses.

6. If a profit-maximizing firm's marginal revenue is less than its marginal cost, the firm
   a. must be experiencing economic losses.
   b. must be making economic profits.
   c. should decrease its output.
   d. should increase its output.

7. In which of the following situations will a perfectly competitive firm earn economic profits?
   a. $MR > AVC$
   b. $MR > ATC$
   c. $ATC > MC$
   d. $ATC > AR$

8. The maximum loss a firm will experience
   in the short run is
   a. zero.
   b. its total costs.
   c. its total variable costs.
   d. its total fixed costs.

9. If, in the short run, the price falls below
   minimum average variable cost, a firm
   a. should produce no output.
   b. will be making a loss but should still
      continue producing in the short run.
   c. should produce the output for which
      marginal cost is equal to price.
   d. is not necessarily experiencing
      economic losses.

10. In the price range above minimum
    average variable cost, a perfectly
    competitive firm's supply curve is
    a. horizontal at the market price.
    b. vertical at zero output.
    c. the same as its marginal cost curve.
    d. the same as its average variable cost
       curve.

11. The short-run industry supply curve is
    a. constructed as the horizontal sum of
       the supply curves of the individual
       firms.
    b. constructed as the vertical sum of the
       supply curves of the individual firms.
    c. vertical at the total level of output
       being produced by all firms.
    d. horizontal at the current market price.

12. If a perfectly competitive firm in the short
    run is able to pay its variable costs and
    part, but not all, of its fixed costs, then it
    is operating in the range on its marginal
    cost curve that is
    a. below the breakeven point.
    b. above the shutdown point.
    c. below the shutdown point.
    d. between the shutdown and breakeven
       points.

13. If profits are being made by firms in a
    competitive industry, new firms will enter.
    This will shift the industry
    a. demand curve to the left causing
       market price to fall.
    b. demand curve to the right causing
       market price to rise.
    c. supply curve to the left causing market
       price to rise.
    d. supply curve to the right causing
       market price to fall.

14. The maximum loss a firm will experience
    in long-run equilibrium is
    a. zero.
    b. its total cost.
    c. its total variable cost.
    d. its average variable cost.

15. In a perfectly competitive industry, the
    market price is $10. An individual firm is
    producing the output at which $MC = ATC$
    $= \$15$. AVC at that output is $10. What
    should the firm do to maximize its short-
    run profits?
    a. Shut down.
    b. Expand output.
    c. Contract output.
    d. Leave output unchanged.

16. If a profit maximizing firm in perfect
    competition is earning economic profits,
    then it must be producing a level of
    output where
    a. price is greater than marginal cost.
    b. price is greater than marginal revenue.
    c. marginal cost is greater than marginal
       revenue.
    d. marginal cost is greater than average
       total cost.

17. A firm in a perfectly competitive industry is maximizing its short-run profits by producing 500 units of output. At 500 units of output, which of the following *must be false*?
    a. $MC < AVC$
    b. $MC < ATC$
    c. $MC > ATC$
    d. $AR < ATC$

18. Figure 11.1 illustrates the cost curves for a perfectly competitive firm. In the short run the price is $11 and the firm has the scale of plant associated with $SRAC_1$. How much will the firm produce in short-run equilibrium?
    a. 7 units.
    b. 9 units.
    c. 10 units.
    d. 17 units.

19. Figure 11.1 illustrates the cost curves for a perfectly competitive firm. Suppose the current price is $11 and that the firm has the scale of plant associated with $SRAC_1$. Over time, this firm will
    a. exit from the industry.
    b. increase its scale of plant and other firms will exit from the industry.
    c. retain its current scale of plant and other firms will enter the industry.
    d. increase its scale of plant and other firms will enter the industry.

20. Figure 11.1 illustrates the cost curves for a perfectly competitive firm. In long-run equilibrium, the market price will be
    a. $6.
    b. $8.
    c. $9.
    d. $11.

Figure 11.1

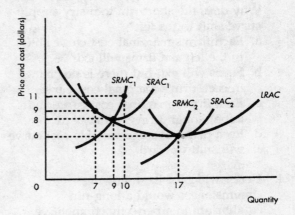

21. The long-run competitive industry supply curve will be positively sloped if
    a. there are external economies.
    b. there are external diseconomies.
    c. there are no external economies or diseconomies.
    d. the external economies equal the external diseconomies.

22. Which of the following is <u>NOT</u> true of a new long-run equilibrium resulting from a new technology in a perfectly competitive industry?
    a. Price will be lower.
    b. Industry output will be greater.
    c. Firm profits will be greater.
    d. All firms in the industry will be using the new technology.

23. A perfectly competitive industry is in long-run equilibrium when an increase in total fixed costs facing each firm occurs. Why does the short-run industry supply curve shift to the left?
    a. Each firm's marginal cost curve shifts to the left *and* firms will exit.
    b. Firms will exit but there is no change in each firm's marginal cost curve.
    c. Each firm's marginal cost curve shifts left although firms will *not* exit.
    d. Each firm's average variable cost curve will shift upward.

24. Under which of the following circumstances would a long-run equilibrium in a perfectly competitive industry <u>NOT</u> be allocatively efficient?
    a. Firms are price takers.
    b. There are new technologies developed.
    c. There are external economies or external diseconomies.
    d. There are external costs or external benefits.

25. Which of the following is an important obstacle to allocative efficiency?
    a. The existence of monopoly.
    b. The objective of firms to maximize profit.
    c. The invisible hand.
    d. Prices.

SHORT ANSWER

1. List the principal characteristics of a perfectly competitive market.

2. Why will a firm in a perfectly competitive industry choose *not* to charge a price either above or below the market price?

3. When will a firm shut down in the short-run?

4. Why is the perfectly competitive firm's supply curve the same as the marginal cost curve above the minimum average variable cost?

5. Why will economic profits be zero in long-run equilibrium in a perfectly competitive industry?

6. Suppose we observe a perfectly competitive industry in a long-run equilibrium when there is a permanent decrease in demand for the product produced by the industry. Assume that there are no external economies or diseconomies. How does the industry adjust to a new long-run equilibrium? What happens to price, industry quantity traded, firm profits, and the number of firms during the adjustment process?

7. What is meant by external diseconomies?

8. What is meant by allocative efficiency?

9. What is meant by external costs?

10. Suppose output is at a level such that marginal social benefit is greater than marginal social cost. Explain why this level of output is allocatively *inefficient*.

PROBLEMS

1. a) Table 11.1 gives the total cost structure for one of many identical firms in a perfectly competitive industry. Complete the table by computing total variable cost, average total cost, average variable cost, and marginal cost at each level of output. (Remember, as in the Chapter 10 problems in the *Study Guide*, marginal cost should be entered midway between rows.)

Table 11.1

Quantity (units per day)	Total cost ($)	Total variable cost ($)	Average total cost ($)	Average variable cost ($)	Marginal cost ($)
0	12				...
1	24				...
2	32				...
3	42				...
4	54				...
5	68				...
6	84				

b) Complete Table 11.2 by computing the profit (per day) for the firm at each level of output if the price of output is $9, $11, or $15.

Table 11.2

Quantity (units per day)	Profit if price = $9 ($)	Profit if price = $11 ($)	Profit if price = $15 ($)
0			
1			
2			
3			
4			
5			
6			

c) Consider the profit-maximizing output decision of the firm at alternative prices. How much will the firm produce if the price of output is $9? $11? $15? Explain each of your answers.

2. A firm will maximize profit if it produces every unit of output for which marginal revenue exceeds marginal cost. This is sometimes called the marginal approach to profit maximization. Using the marginal approach, determine the profit-maximizing level of output for the firm of Problem 1 when the price of output is $15. How does your answer here compare with your answer in 1(c)?

3. This problem concerns a hypothetical pottery manufacturing firm that produces ceramic mugs for sale in a purely competitive market. With a plant of given size, the firm can turn out the quantities

of ceramic mugs shown in Table 11.3, by varying the amount it uses of a single variable input, labor.

Suppose the firm can hire all the labor it would ever want at the going wage of $8 per labor-hour. The firm's total fixed costs are $64 per day.

a) Draw a table showing output, total variable cost (TVC), total cost (TC), average variable cost (AVC), average total cost (ATC), and marginal cost (MC). (Remember that marginal cost should be entered midway between rows of output.)

Table 11.3

Number of mugs	Labor-hours (per day)
20	6.50
40	11.50
60	14.50
80	17.50
100	20.50
120	23.75
140	27.50
160	32.00
180	37.50
200	44.50
220	53.50
240	65.00
260	79.50
280	97.50

b) On a graph with *Mugs (per day)* on the horizontal axis, draw the three "per-unit" cost curves, *AVC, ATC,* and *MC*. (Note that the marginal cost values from your table should be plotted on the graph *midway* between the corresponding units of output.)

c) Consider (separately) the following alternative market prices that the firm

might face: $P = \$3.20$, $P = \$2$, $P = \$1.65$, $P = \$1.40$. Assuming that the firm wants to maximize its profit, for *each* of the above prices, answer the following:

i) Approximately how many mugs per day would the firm produce? How do you know?

ii) Is the firm making a profit at that price? And if so, approximately how much?

d) Suppose that the ceramic pottery mug industry consists of 60 firms, each identical to the single firm discussed above. On another graph, draw the industry short-run supply curve.

e) The industry demand schedule is given in Table 11.4.

Table 11.4

Price (dollars)	Q_D
1.00	15,900
1.60	14,400
2.20	12,900
2.80	11,400
3.40	9,900
4.00	8,400
4.60	6,900
5.20	5,400
5.80	3,900
6.40	2,400
7.00	900

i) Plot the industry demand curve on the same graph as the industry supply curve of part (d).

ii) What is the short-run equilibrium price of ceramic pottery mugs?

iii) Is the ceramic pottery mug industry in long-run equilibrium? Explain your answer.

4. A perfectly competitive industry has 100 identical firms in the short run, each of which has the short-run cost structure given in Table 11.5.

   This short-run average total cost curve touches the long-run average cost curve at the minimum point on the long-run average cost curve as in text Fig. 11.10. The industry demand schedule in the long run and the short run is given by Table 11.6.

Table 11.5

Output (units)	Average total cost ($)	Average variable cost ($)	Marginal cost ($)
11	20.5	13.1	
			...12
12	19.8	13.0	
			...14
13	19.3	13.1	
			...16
14	19.1	13.3	
			...18
15	19.0	13.6	
			...20
16	19.1	14.0	
			...22
17	19.2	14.5	
			...24
18	19.5	15.0	
			...26
19	19.8	15.6	
			...28
20	20.3	16.2	
			...30
21	20.7	16.9	

a) What is the quantity of output corresponding to the firm's breakeven point? The shutdown point? Explain your answers.

b) What is the short-run equilibrium price in this market? Show how you found your answer.

c) What amount of profit or loss is being made by each firm at the short-run equilibrium price? Is this industry in long-run equilibrium at its present size? Why or why not?

d) Exactly how many firms will exist in this industry in the long run? Explain your answer. How much economic profit will each firm earn in the long run?

Table 11.6

Price ($)	Q_D
11	3200
13	3000
15	2800
17	2600
19	2400
21	2200
23	2000
25	1800
27	1600
29	1400
31	1200

5. Consider a perfectly competitive industry in long-run equilibrium. Suppose that all the firms in the industry face the same cost structure. Draw a two-part graph illustrating the long-run equilibrium for the industry (part (a) on the left—and the typical firm—part (b) on the right). Label the equilibrium price P_0, the equilibrium industry quantity traded Q_0, and the output of the firm q_0.

6. Now, suppose there is a decline in market demand. Using the graphs drawn in Problem 6,
    a) show what happens to market price, firm output, firm profits, and industry quantity traded in the short run. (Assume that the shutdown point is not reached.)
    b) show what happens to market price, firm output, firm profits, and industry quantity traded in the long run. (Assume that there are no external economies or diseconomies.) What has happened to the number of firms?

ANSWERS

CONCEPT REVIEW

1. many; identical; many; entry

2. taker; elastic

3. profit

4. average revenue; marginal revenue

5. price

6. breakeven; shutdown

7. marginal cost

8. industry; industry

9. marginal cost; nothing; total fixed cost

10. profits; fall; losses

11. zero; minimum

12. external economies; external diseconomies

13. Allocative efficiency

14. external costs; external benefits

TRUE OR FALSE

1. T	6. T	11. F	16. F	21. F
2. T	7. F	12. F	17. T	22. T
3. F	8. F	13. T	18. F	23. T
4. F	9. T	14. T	19. T	24. F
5. F	10. T	15. T	20. T	25. T

MULTIPLE CHOICE

1. b	6. c	11. a	16. d	21. b
2. c	7. b	12. d	17. a	22. c
3. d	8. d	13. d	18. c	23. b
4. a	9. a	14. a	19. d	24. d
5. b	10. c	15. c	20. a	25. a

SHORT ANSWER

1. The principal characteristics of a perfectly competitive market are:
    • There are many firms, each selling an identical product.
    • There are many buyers.
    • There are no restrictions on entry into the industry.
    • Firms in the industry have no advantage over potential new entrants.
    • Firms and buyers are completely informed about the prices of each firm in the industry.

2. If a firm in a perfectly competitive industry charged a price even slightly higher than the market price, it would lose all of its sales. Thus, it will not charge a price above the market price. Since it can sell all it wants at the market price, it would not be able to increase sales by lowering its price. Thus, it would not charge a price below the market price.

3. A firm will shut down when the price falls below minimum average variable

cost. The loss will be equal to total fixed cost. If the firm continued to produce at a price below minimum average variable cost, its losses would exceed total fixed cost.

4. A perfectly competitive firm will want to supply the quantity that will maximize profit. This is done by equating marginal revenue and marginal cost. For a perfectly competitive firm, marginal revenue is equal to price, so at any given price, the firm will produce the level of output at which price equals marginal cost. Since this is true for each price, the firm's supply curve is the same as its marginal cost curve.

5. In a perfectly competitive industry, the existence of positive economic profits will attract the entry of new firms, which will shift the industry supply curve to the right, causing the market price to fall and firm profits to decline. This tendency will exist so long as there are positive economic profits. Similarly, the existence of economic losses will cause firms to exit from the industry, which will shift the industry supply curve to the left, causing the market price to rise and firm profits to rise (losses to decline). This tendency will exist as long as losses are being made. Thus, the only point of rest in the long run (i.e., the only equilibrium) is one in which firm profits are zero.

6. The decrease in market demand will cause the market price to fall. Since, in the initial long-run equilibrium, each firm was earning zero economic profit, the fall in price means that profits will fall and so firms will now be making losses. Since the decrease in demand is permanent, these losses will induce some firms, to leave the industry. This will shift the industry supply curve to the left, causing an increase in market price. The

increasing price will cause profits to increase for the remaining firms which means that their losses will decline. The exit of firms will continue until the losses are eliminated. If there are no external economies or diseconomies, since costs have not been affected by the decrease in demand, the price must continue rising until it reaches its original level in the new long-run equilibrium. The output of each firm will also equal its original level but the quantity traded at the industry level will be less because the number of firms has declined.

7. External diseconomies are factors beyond the firm's control that raise its costs as industry output increases. This might occur, for example, if the prices of inputs increase as greater quantities of inputs are demanded to produce the increased industry output.

8. Allocative efficiency occurs when resources are allocated in such a way that no one can be made better off without making someone else worse off.

9. External costs are costs associated with production that are not borne by the producer but by other members of society. An example is pollution that is a by-product of the production of steel. Pollution is a cost associated with the production of steel that is not borne by the producer but is borne by those who live in the affected area.

10. A level of output at which marginal social benefit is greater than marginal social cost is allocatively inefficient, because some people can be made better off without making anyone worse off if more is produced. Since the production of an additional unit of output will add more to social benefit than to social cost, those who bear the additional costs can be

compensated out of the additional benefits (and thus be left no worse off) with some additional benefits left over (making those who receive the additional benefits better off).

PROBLEMS

1. a) Completed Table 11.1 is shown here as Table 11.1 Solution above.
   b) Completed Table 11.2 is given here at Table 11.2 Solution. The values for profit are computed as total revenue minus total cost, where total revenue is price times quantity and total cost is given in Table 11.1.

Table 11.2 Solution

Quantity (units per day)	Profit if price = $9 ($)	Profit if price = $11 ($)	Profit if price = $15 ($)
0	-12	-12	-12
1	-15	-13	-9
2	-14	-10	-2
3	-15	-9	3
4	-18	-10	6
5	-23	-13	7
6	-30	-18	6

Table 11.1 Solution

Quantity (units per day)	Total cost ($)	Total variable cost ($)	Average total cost ($)	Average variable cost ($)	Marginal cost ($)
0	12	0	—	—	
					...12
1	24	12	24.00	12.00	
					... 8
2	32	20	16.00	10.00	
					...10
3	42	30	14.00	10.00	
					...12
4	54	42	13.50	10.50	
					...14
5	68	56	13.60	11.20	
					...16
6	84	72	14.00	12.00	

c) If the price is $9, profit is maximized (actually loss is minimized) when the firm shuts down and produces zero units. If the firm chooses to produce, its loss will be at least $14, which is greater than the fixed cost loss of $12. Therefore the firm will minimize losses by shutting down. If the price is $11, the firm is still unable to make a positive economic profit. The loss is minimized (at $9) if the firm produces 3 units. At this price, all of variable cost and part of fixed cost can be recovered. At a price of $15, the firm will maximize profit (at $7) at an output of 5 units per day.

2. The marginal approach to profit maximization states that the firm should produce all units of output for which marginal revenue exceeds marginal cost. For a perfectly competitive firm, marginal revenue equals price, so the approach states (equivalently) that the firm should produce every unit for which price exceeds marginal cost. If the price of output is $15, we can see from Table 11.1 Solution that the firm should produce 5 units. Since the marginal cost of moving from the fourth to the fifth unit ($14) is less than price ($15), the fifth unit should be produced. The marginal cost of moving to the sixth unit ($16), however, is greater than price. It should not be produced. The answer obtained here is the same as the answer obtained in 1(c).

3. a) With only one variable input (labor), *TVC* (for any level of output) = (labor hours x wage rate). The requested table is Table 11.7.
   b) The graph appears in Fig. 11.2. It also illustrates the answers to part (c).

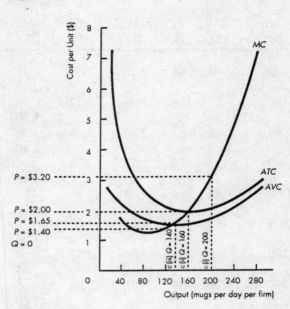

Figure 11.2

c) In every case, the output at which profit is a maximum is the output at which marginal revenue (which, for a price-taking firm in a perfectly competitive market, is the same as market price) is equal to marginal cost, provided that price is greater than average variable cost. Profit "per unit of output" is the difference between average revenue (price) and average total cost at the level of output. Total profit is "per unit profit" x number of units of output. Economic profit might be zero or negative (a loss) and still be the best the firm can attain in the short run. The calculations of total profit at each price appear in Table 11.8.

Table 11.7

Output (per day)	TVC ($)	TC ($)	AVC ($)	ATC ($)	MC ($)
0	0	64	–	–	
					...2.60
20	52	116	2.60	5.80	
					...1.80
40	88	152	2.20	3.80	
					...1.40
60	116	180	1.93	3.00	
					...1.20
80	140	204	1.75	2.55	
					...1.20
100	164	228	1.64	2.28	
					...1.30
120	190	254	1.58	2.12	
					...1.50
140	220	284	1.57	2.03	
					...1.80
160	256	320	1.60	2.00	
					...2.20
180	300	364	1.67	2.02	
					...2.80
200	356	420	1.78	2.10	
					...3.60
220	428	492	1.95	2.24	
					...4.60
240	520	584	2.17	2.43	
					...5.80
260	636	700	2.45	2.69	
					...7.20
280	780	844	2.79	3.01	

d) There are 60 identical price-taking firms. For every possible price (above minimum AVC of *approximately* about ($1.57), each firm will supply the quantity at which P = MC. We can derive (in Table 11.9) the industry supply schedule from the MC curve of an individual firm.

The graph of the industry supply curve appears in Fig. 11.3, along with the industry demand curve from part (e).

Table 11.8

Price ($)	Output chosen	Per unit profit ($)	Total profit ($)
3.20	200	1.10	220.00
2.00	160	0	0
1.65	140	-0.38	-53.20
1.40	0	0	-64.00

Note the following:
1. Marginal cost is $3.20 at approximately 200 units.
2. The per unit profit is P - ATC.
3. An output of 160 units is the "breakeven" level of output, where MC = minimum ATC and the firm is just covering all its opportunity costs.
4. At an output of 140 units, the firm continues to produce in the short run because it can more than cover its variable costs. If it produced zero units, its loss would be greater, $64, which is the amount of its fixed costs.
5. Any positive output increases losses when the price is below the shutdown price, which here is about $1.57. When price is less than minimum AVC, the firm not only loses its fixed costs, it would also lose additional money on every unit it produced.

Table 11.9

Quantity price ($)	Quantity supplied by 1 firm	Quantity supplied by 60 firms
1.57	134	8,040
1.80	150	9,000
2.20	170	10,200
2.80	190	11,400
3.60	210	12,600
4.60	230	13,800
5.80	250	15,000
7.20	270	16,200

Figure 11.3

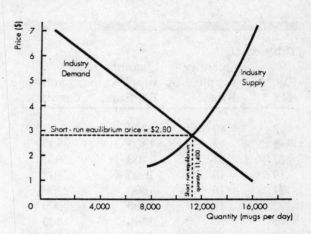

e) i) See Fig. 11.3.
   ii) The short-run equilibrium price is $2.80 (where a total of 11,400 mugs per day are supplied and sold; or 190 mugs per day supplied by each firm at MC of $2.80).
   iii) At a price of $2.80 and output of 190, for each firm, P > ATC where C = $2.06. So all existing firms are making economic profits after covering *all* opportunity costs including a "normal" profit. The industry will attract new entrants because it offers more than normal profits. Therefore, even though the industry is in short-run equilibrium, it is *not* in long-run equilibrium because the number of firms has not "stabilized." New firms will enter the industry, the industry supply curve will shift to the right, and price will fall until no firm is making economic profits.

4. a) The breakeven point occurs at 15 units of output. At this level of output, ATC is at its minimum ($19) and is equal to MC. Since the MC of moving from the fourteenth to the fifteenth unit is $18, and the MC of moving from the fifteenth to the sixteenth units is $20, we can interpolate the MC exactly at 15 units as a midway between $18 and $20, or as $19. The shutdown point occurs at 12 units of output. At this level of output, AVC is at its minimum ($13) and is equal to MC. The interpolated value of MC at exactly 12 units of output is midway between $12 and $14, or is $13.
   b) The short-run equilibrium price is $25. This is the price at which industry quantity supplied equals quantity demanded as shown in Table 11.10.
   c) At a price of $25, each firm produces 18 units of output. At 18 units, ATC is $19.50, so economic profits are being earned. The amount of profit is ($25 - $19.50) per unit = $5.50 per unit. Total economic profit per *firm* is $5.50/unit x 18 units = $99. This means that new

entrants will be attracted to the industry. We conclude that the industry is *not* in long-run equilibrium.

Table 11.10

P = MC ($)	Quantity supplied by 1 firm	Quantity supplied by 100 firms	Quantity demanded
13	12	1200	3000
15	13	1300	2800
17	14	1400	2600
19	15	1500	2400
21	16	1600	2200
23	17	1700	2000
25	**18**	**1800**	**1800**
27	19	1900	1600
29	20	2000	1400

5. A long-run equilibrium in a perfectly competitive industry is illustrated in Fig. 11.4 below. Part (a) illustrates industry equilibrium at the intersection of industry demand (D_0) and industry supply (S_0): point *a*. The equilibrium industry quantity traded is labeled Q_0 and the equilibrium market price is labeled P_0. Part (b) illustrates the situation for a single firm in long-run equilibrium. The firm is at point *a'*, the minimum point of the (long-run) average cost curve (*ATC*). The firm is producing the output labeled q_0 and earning zero economic profit.

Figure 11.4

(a) Industry

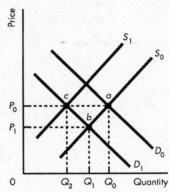

(b) Firm

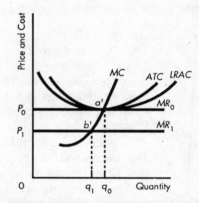

6. a) The new short-run equilibrium is illustrated in Fig. 11.4. The decrease in demand shifts the market demand curve to the left, from D_0 to D_1. The new market equilibrium is at point *b*. The price has fallen from P_0 to P_1 and the industry quantity traded has fallen from Q_0 to Q_1. The fall in price induces firms to reduce output as shown by the move from point *a'* to point *b'* on the *MC* curve in part (b). Since P_1 is less than minimum *ATC*, firms are making losses in the new short-run equilibrium.

b) The new long-run equilibrium is also illustrated in Fig. 11.4.   Since losses are experienced in short-run equilibrium, firms will exit from the industry in the long run. This will cause the industry supply curve to shift to the left causing the price to rise and thus reducing losses. Firms will continue to leave as long as losses continue; that is, until the industry supply curve has shifted enough to eliminate losses: from S_0 to S_1. This gives a new long-run industry equilibrium at point c and the price has returned to its initial level, P_o, but industry quantity traded has fallen to Q_2. As firms exit and the market price rises, remaining firms will increase their output and their losses will be reduced. When sufficient firms have left the industry, the price will have risen (returned) to P_0 and firms will have returned to point a' in part (b). At this point, each firm is again earning zero economic profit and firm output has returned to q_0. But, since there are now fewer firms, industry quantity traded is less.

12 MONOPOLY

CHAPTER IN PERSPECTIVE

The perfectly competitive firms of Chapter 11 are price takers. Each firm is so small relative to the size of the industry that its output decision cannot influence the product price. At the other extreme are industries in which there is a single firm, a monopoly. Unlike a perfectly competitive firm, a monopoly's output decision has a direct effect on price; it cannot sell more output unless it drops its price.

This chapter pursues the answers to numerous questions about monopoly: Why does monopoly exist? How does a monopoly choose how much to produce? What constraints on behavior does a monopoly face? How much profit will a monopoly make? When will a monopoly charge different prices to different customers for the same good or service? How does a monopoly compare with perfect competition in terms of efficiency? Is monopoly always "bad"?

LEARNING OBJECTIVES

After studying this chapter, you will be able to:

- Define monopoly

- Explain the conditions under which monopoly arises

- Distinguish between legal monopoly and natural monopoly

- Explain how a monopoly determines its price and output

- Define price discrimination

- Explain why price discrimination leads to a bigger profit

- Compare the performance of a competitive and monopolistic industry

- Define rent seeking and explain why it arises

- Explain the conditions under which monopoly is more efficient than competition

HELPFUL HINTS

1. As you first learn about monopoly it is useful to examine carefully the differences between a perfectly competitive firm and a monopoly. The exercise will increase your understanding of both. The first fundamental difference is that in a perfectly competitive industry there are many firms, while in the case of monopoly there is only one. A second fundamental difference is that there are barriers to entry in the case of monopoly but free entry for perfect competition. These differences in fundamental characteristics imply many other differences; for example, in the nature of the demand curve faced by each firm and in their respective profit possibilities in the short run and the long run. Try to understand how these and other differences follow from the fundamental differences between industry types.

2. Practice drawing the principle graphs used in this chapter to represent a monopoly.
   a) When identifying the profit-maximizing price for a single-price monopoly, be sure to find it on the demand curve, not the marginal revenue curve.
   b) Practice graphically identifying the profit made by a monopoly. Draw a monopoly breaking even and a monopoly making a loss.
   c) Learn to identify consumer surplus, producer surplus, and the deadweight loss as regions on a graph. Do this for a perfectly competitive industry, a single-price monopoly, a two-price price-discriminating monopoly, and a perfect price-discriminating monopoly.

3. There is an easy trick for drawing the marginal revenue curve corresponding to any linear demand curve. The price intercept (where Q = 0) is the same for the demand curve, and the quantity intercept (where P = 0) is exactly *half* of the output of the demand curve. The marginal revenue curve is, there-

fore, a downward-sloping straight line whose slope is twice as steep as the slope of the slope of the demand curve.

KEY FIGURES AND TABLES

Figure 12.1 Demand and Marginal Revenue for a Single-Price Monopoly

In a monopoly industry there is a single firm facing the industry (market) demand. Thus the firm has some control over the price it will charge. A single-price monopolist charges the same price to all customers. This figure illustrates the relationship between the demand and marginal revenue curves for a single-price monopolist using the example of Bobbie's Barbershop.

Because the firm faces a negatively sloped demand curve, if it wants to sell one more unit of output it must lower its price. This has two effects on revenue. First the sale of an additional unit will *increase* revenue by the amount of the price. However, since the firm must also drop the price on previous units, revenue will *decrease* on these. The net change in revenue, (i.e., the marginal revenue), will thus be less than price and the marginal revenue curve will lie below the demand curve.

Figure 12.2 A Single-Price Monopoly's Revenue Curves

This figure illustrates the relationship between a single-price monopolist's revenue curves and the elasticity of demand. Recall (from Chapter 5) that a straight-line demand curve is elastic (elasticity > 1) above its midpoint, unit elastic (elasticity = 1) at its midpoint, and inelastic (elasticity < 1) below its midpoint. Recall also, that in the elastic range of the demand curve, the sale of an additional unit by dropping the price will increase total revenue and so marginal revenue will be positive. When the demand curve is unit elastic, the sale of an additional unit by dropping the price will leave total revenue unchanged and so marginal revenue is zero.

In the inelastic range of the demand curve, the sale of an additional unit by dropping the price will decrease total revenue and so marginal revenue will be negative. These relationships are combined and shown graphically in part (a) of the figure. The corresponding ranges of increasing total revenue, maximum total revenue, and decreasing total revenue are shown in part (b).

Figure 12.3 A Monopoly's Output and Price
Since profit is the difference between total revenue and total cost, the determination of profit-maximizing output and price requires looking at cost as well as revenue. The table associated with this figure reports the revenues and costs for Bobbie's Barbershop. This information is used to illustrate how a single-price monopoly will choose the profit-maximizing output and price.

Part (a) of the figure shows the total revenue and total cost curves facing the firm. Profit is a maximum when the vertical amount by which total revenue exceeds total cost is a maximum. For Bobbie's Barbershop, this turns out to be 3 haircuts per hour.

Part (b) shows the total profit curve itself; it is derived from the figure in part (a) by taking the difference between total revenue and total cost at each level of output. Profit is maximized when this curve reaches its maximum.

Part (c) shows that profit is a maximum at the quantity where marginal revenue is equal to marginal cost. The price the monopoly will charge is the highest possible for this quantity; that is, the corresponding point on the demand curve. In the case of Bobbie's Barbershop, the profit-maximizing output is 3 haircuts per hour, the price is $14 per haircut, and total profit is $12 per hour. The diagram of marginal cost and marginal revenue in part (c) is the most important and useful of the three diagrams.

Figure 12.7 Monopoly and Competition Compared

This figure compares the price and quantity that will result in a monopoly industry with the price and quantity that would result if the same industry were competitive. Specifically, we imagine that a competitive industry with a large number of competitive firms is taken over by a single monopoly. Recall from Chapter 12 that a competitive industry will produce at the intersection of the industry supply and demand curves (labeled S and D in the figure). Thus, a competitive industry will produce the quantity given by C in the diagram and charge a price given by P_C. If the same industry became a monopoly, its marginal cost curve would be the supply curve of the competitive industry. (Recall that the competitive industry supply curve is just the horizontal sum of the competitive firm marginal cost curves.) A profit-maximizing single-price monopoly will produce the output level at which marginal revenue equals marginal cost. Thus the monopoly will produce the quantity given by M and charge a price of P_M. We note that monopoly output is lower than for a competitive industry and the monopoly price is higher than the competitive price.

SELF-TEST

CONCEPT REVIEW

1. A firm that is the single supplier of a good in an industry is called a(n) monopoly. The key feature of such an industry is the existence of barriers preventing the entry of new firms.

2. A monopoly that charges the same price for every unit of output it sells is called

a(n) <u>single</u> - <u>price</u> monopoly.

3. The demand curve facing a monopoly firm is the <u>industry</u> demand curve.

4. For a monopoly charging a single price, the average revenue curve is the <u>demand</u> curve and the marginal revenue curve is <u>below</u> the average revenue curve.

5. The output range over which total revenue is rising is the same as that over which marginal revenue is <u>positive</u>. This is the same range of input over which the (price) elasticity of demand is <u>greater</u> than 1. If elasticity of demand is exactly 1, marginal revenue is <u>zero</u>. This implies that a profit-maximizing monopoly will never produce an output in the <u>inelastic</u> range of its demand curve.

6. Unlike a perfectly competitive firm, a monopoly's decision to produce more or less of a good will affect the <u>price</u> of the good.

7. A profit-maximizing monopoly will want to produce less if, at the current level of output, marginal <u>cost</u> is greater than marginal <u>revenue</u>.

8. Unlike a perfectly competitive firm, a monopoly can be making positive economic <u>profits</u> in the long run.

9. The practice of charging some customers a higher price than others for exactly the same good is called <u>price</u> <u>descrimination</u>. This kind of a pricing policy can be seen as an attempt by the monopoly to capture all or part of the consumer <u>surplus</u>.

10. Charging different prices to different groups of customers will increase the profits of a monopoly only if the groups of customers have different <u>elasticities</u> of demand for the product. A monopoly that charges different prices to different groups of customers will produce <u>more</u> than would a monopoly that charges a single price.

11. If a perfectly competitive industry is taken over by a single monopoly firm, output will <u>decrease</u> and the price will <u>increase</u>. The reduction in consumer and producer surplus resulting from this new monopoly is called the <u>deadweight</u> loss.

12. The activity of creating monopoly is called <u>rent</u> <u>seeking</u>. If there are no barriers to such activity, the value of the resources used up in the process will, in equilibrium, be <u>equal</u> <u>to</u> the monopoly's profit.

13. A firm that has a decrease in average total cost when it increases the number of dif-

ferent goods it produces is said to have
economies of ___scope___ .

TRUE OR FALSE

____ 1. An essential difference between a
perfectly competitive firm and a
monopoly is that the monopolist's
output decisions can affect the price
of output.

____ 2. Natural monopoly can arise because
of economies of scale.

____ 3. For a single-price monopoly, average
revenue will always equal price.

____ 4. Over the output range where total
revenue is decreasing, marginal revenue is positive.

____ 5. The marginal revenue curve lies
below the demand curve for a single-
price monopoly because when the
price is lowered to sell one more
unit, it must also be lowered on
earlier units of output.

____ 6. A profit-maximizing single-price
monopoly will produce only in the
elastic range of its demand curve.

____ 7. The supply curve of a monopoly
firm is its marginal cost curve.

____ 8. If, at the current level of output,
marginal revenue exceeds marginal
cost, the production and sale of additional output will increase profits.

____ 9. For a single-price monopoly, price
will be less than marginal revenue at
the profit-maximizing output.

____ 10. A monopoly will always make economic profits.

____ 11. Price discrimination occurs when a
firm charges one group of customers
more than another or when a firm
gives "quantity discounts" (i.e., charges a lower price if larger quantities
are purchased.)

____ 12. A monopoly can acquire all of the
consumer surplus for itself if it practices perfect price discrimination.

____ 13. A price-discriminating monopolist
will charge a higher price to the
consumer group with the more elastic demand.

____ 14. Firms that give price discounts to
students or senior citizens could not
be maximizing profits.

____ 15. If a monopoly practices perfect price
discrimination, it will produce the
level of output at which the marginal
cost curve intersects the demand
curve.

____ 16. A perfectly price-discriminating monopolist achieves the same allocative
efficiency as perfect competition.

____ 17. Price discrimination only works for
goods that cannot be readily resold.

____ 18. The more perfectly a monopoly price
discriminates, the closer its output
gets to the competitive level of output.

____ 19. In moving from perfect competition
to single-price monopoly, all of the
surplus lost by consumers is captured by the monopoly.

_____20. In moving from perfect competition to single-price monopoly, part of the deadweight loss is due to a reduction in producer surplus.

_____21. No deadweight loss results from a perfect price discriminating monopoly because the monopoly gains everything the consumer loses.

_____22. Because of the existence of rent seeking, the social cost of monopoly is smaller than the deadweight loss.

_____23. Because of rent seeking, a monopoly can guarantee itself economic profits in the long run.

_____24. If there is no barrier to rent seeking, the resources used up in rent seeking equal the monopoly profits.

_____25. It is possible for a monopoly industry with large economies of scale and scope to produce more output and charge a lower price than would be the case if the industry were competitive.

MULTIPLE CHOICE

1. Which of the following is an example of a *natural* barrier to the entry of new firms in an industry?
   a. Licensing of professions
   b. Economies of scale
   c. Issuing a patent
   d. A public franchise

2. Which of the following is **NOT** true of a single-price monopoly?
   a. Since there is a single firm, the firm demand is the industry demand.
   b. Demand is inelastic since there are no good substitutes for the good.
   c. The average revenue curve is the demand curve.
   d. Marginal revenue is less than price.

3. In order to increase sales from seven units to eight units, a single-price monopolist must drop the price from $7/unit to $6/unit. What is marginal revenue in this range?
   a. $48
   b. $6.
   c. $1
   d. -$1

4. In order to sell an additional unit, a single-price monopoly must reduce the price, not only on the additional unit but on all units. This explains why
   a. marginal revenue is less than average revenue.
   b. a monopoly will never lower price.
   c. a monopoly will not be able to maximize profits.
   d. the marginal cost curve is positively sloped.

5. If marginal revenue is negative at a particular output, then
   a. price must be negative.
   b. a profit-maximizing monopoly should increase output.
   c. the elasticity of demand is less than one at that output.
   d. demand must be elastic at that output.

6. A single-price monopolist will maximize profits if it produces the output where
   a. price equals marginal cost.
   b. price equals marginal revenue.
   c. marginal revenue equals marginal cost.
   d. average revenue equals marginal cost.

7. A profit-maximizing monopoly will never produce at an output level
   a. at which it would make economic losses.
   b. where marginal revenue is less than price.
   c. at which average cost is greater than marginal cost.
   d. in the inelastic range of its demand curve.

8. If a profit-maximizing monopoly is producing at an output at which marginal cost exceeds marginal revenue, it
   a. should raise price and lower output.
   b. should lower price and raise output.
   c. is making losses.
   d. is maximizing profit.

9. A monopoly will go out of business in the short run if
   a. it is making an economic loss.
   b. it cannot maximize profit due to government regulation.
   c. price is less than average variable cost.
   d. the profit maximizing level of output is in the elastic range of the demand curve.

10. The supply curve for a monopoly
    a. is the marginal cost curve above average total cost.
    b. is the marginal cost curve above average variable cost.
    c. is the positively sloped portion of the marginal revenue curve.
    d. does not exist.

11. For the single-price monopoly depicted in Fig. 12.1, when profit is maximized, quantity is
    a. 3 and price will be $3.
    b. 3 and price will be $6.
    c. 4 and price will be $4.
    d. 4 and price will be $5.

Figure 12.1

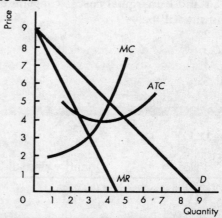

12. If the monopoly depicted in Figure 13.1 is maximizing profit, total profit will be
    a. $3.
    b. $4.
    c. $6.
    d. $9.

13. If a price discriminating monopoly charges a lower price to students, it is likely that the firm
    a. believes that student demand is relatively elastic.
    b. believes that student demand is relatively inelastic.
    c. wants to shift student demand.
    d. is primarily concerned about the well-being of students.

14. A perfect price-discriminating monopoly
    a. will maximize revenue.
    b. is assured of making a profit.
    c. will produce the quantity at which the marginal cost curve intersects the demand curve.
    d. will be allocatively inefficient.

15. If a perfect price discriminating monopoly faces the demand relation given in Table 12.1 and if marginal cost is constant at $4, output will be
    a. 2.
    b. 3.
    c. 4.
    d. 5.

Table 12.1

Price	Quantity demanded
$8	0
7	1
6	2
5	3
4	4
3	5
2	6
1	7

16. Table 12.1 gives the demand schedule faced by a monopoly. If the monopoly is a perfect price discriminator, the marginal revenue from the sale of the third unit of output is
    a. $2.
    b. $3.
    c. $4.
    d. $5.

17. Table 12.1 gives the demand schedule faced by a perfect price-discriminating monopoly. If 3 units are sold, total revenue is
    a. $15.
    b. $16.
    c. $17.
    d. $18.

18. The output of a (not perfect) price-discriminating monopoly will be
    a. less than a single-price monopoly.
    b. more than a single-price monopoly but less than a perfectly competitive industry.
    c. the same amount as a perfectly competitive industry.
    d. more than a perfectly competitive industry.

19. Table 12.2 lists marginal costs for the XYZ firm. If XYZ sells 3 units at a price of $6 each, what is its producer surplus?
    a. $2.
    b. $6.
    c. $9.
    d. $12.

Table 12.2

Quantity	Marginal cost
1	2
2	3
3	4
4	5

20. Consider the industry demand curve in Fig. 12.2. Which area in the diagram indicates the deadweight loss from a single-price monopoly?
    a. *eacf*
    b. *abd*
    c. *acd*
    d. The deadweight loss is zero.

Figure 12.2

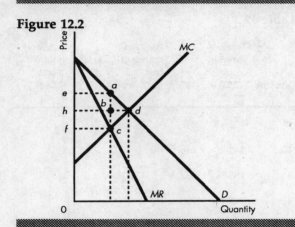

21. Consider the industry demand curve in Fig. 12.2. Which area in the diagram indicates the deadweight loss from a perfect price discriminating monopoly?
    a. *eacf*
    b. *abd*
    c. *acd*
    d. The deadweight loss is zero.

22. Why is the quantity of output produced by a single-price monopolist allocatively inefficient?
    a. Average social cost exceeds average social benefit.
    b. Marginal social cost exceeds marginal social benefit.
    c. Average social benefit exceeds average social cost.
    d. Marginal social benefit exceeds marginal social cost.

23. Activity with the purpose of creating monopoly is
    a. called rent seeking.
    b. illegal in the U.S.
    c. known as price discrimination.
    d. called legal monopoly.

24. A monopoly has economies of scope if
    a. average total cost declines as output increases.
    b. total profit declines as output increases.
    c. average total cost declines as the number of different goods produced increases.
    d. total profit declines as the number of different goods produced increases.

SHORT ANSWER

1. Why are barriers to entry a key feature of a monopoly industry?

2. Why is marginal revenue less than price for a single-price monopoly?

3. Why will marginal revenue be negative in an output range over which demand is inelastic?

4. Explain why the profit-maximizing level of output for a monopoly will be where marginal revenue is equal to marginal cost.

5. Does a single-price monopoly produce in the elastic or inelastic range of its demand curve? Why?

6. Explain why the output of a competitive industry will always be greater than the output of the *same* industry under single-price monopoly.

7. Firm *A* produces and sells wristwatches and firm *B* is a restaurant. Which firm is more likely to practice price discrimination? Why?

8. What is rent seeking? Why does it exist?

9. The price of the last unit sold and the quantity sold are exactly the same in an industry under perfect competition and

under a perfect price discriminating monopoly. Why do consumers prefer perfect competition?

10. Under what circumstances would a monopoly be more efficient than a large number of competitive firms? Illustrate graphically such a situation where a monopoly produces more and charges a lower price than would be the case if the industry consisted of a large number of perfectly competitive firms.

PROBLEMS

1. a) Skyhooks-R-Us, a single-price monopoly, is the only seller of skyhooks in the U.S. market. The firm's total fixed cost is $112 per day. Its total variable costs and total costs (both in dollars per day) are shown in Table 12.3. Complete the table by computing marginal cost, average variable cost, and average total cost. (Remember that marginal cost should be entered midway between rows of output.)

   b) The firm has determined that it faces the demand schedule given in Table 12.4. Table 12.4 also lists the total cost information from part (a). Complete the table by copying your values for marginal cost from Table 12.3 and by computing total revenue, marginal revenue, and profit. (Remember that marginal revenue, like marginal cost, should be entered midway between rows of output.)

Table 12.3

Quantity	Total variable cost (TVC)	Total cost (TC)	Average marginal cost (MC)	Variable cost (AVC)	Average total cost (ATC)
9	135	247			
10	144	256			
11	155	267			
12	168	280			
13	183	295			
14	200	312			
15	219	331			
16	240	352			
17	263	375			
18	288	400			
19	315	427			
20	344	456			
21	375	487			

What is the firm's profit-maximizing quantity of output? At what price will it sell skyhooks? What will be its total profit? Explain your answers.

   c) On the graph in Fig. 12.3, plot the demand curve and the MR, AVC, ATC, and MC curves corresponding to the data in parts (a) and (b). Show the equilibrium output and the *area* of profit on your diagram.

Table 12.4

Price (P)	Quantity demanded (Q)	Total revenue (TR)	Marginal revenue (MR)	Total cost (TC)	Marginal cost (MC)	Profit
57	9			247		
56	10			256		
55	11			267		
54	12			280		
53	13			295		
52	14			312		
51	15			331		
50	16			352		
49	17			375		
48	18			300		
47	19			427		
46	20			456		
45	21			487		

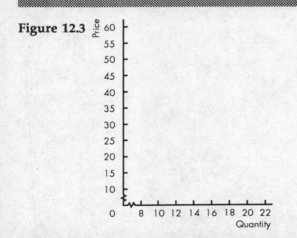

Figure 12.3

d) The firm's cost curves are unchanged, but now consumer demand shifts. The new demand schedule is given by Table 12.5. Table 12.5 also lists the total cost information from part (a). Complete the table by copying your values for marginal cost from Table 12.3, and by computing the new values for total revenue, marginal revenue, and profit.

Table 12.5

Price (P)	Quantity demanded (Q)	Total revenue (TR)	Marginal revenue (MR)	Total cost (TC)	Marginal cost (MC)	Profit
24.50	9			247		
24.00	10			256		
23.50	11			267		
23.00	12			280		
22.50	13			295		
22.00	14			312		
21.50	15			331		
21.00	16			352		
20.50	17			375		
20.00	18			400		
19.50	19			427		
19.00	20			256		
18.50	21			487		

What is the firm's new profit-maximizing quantity of output? At what price will it now sell skyhooks? What will be its total profit? Explain your answers.

e) On the graph in Fig. 12.4, plot the new demand curve and MR curve. Copy the AVC, ATC, and MC curves from Fig. 12.3. Show the new equilibrium output and the *area* of profit on your diagram.

Figure 12.4

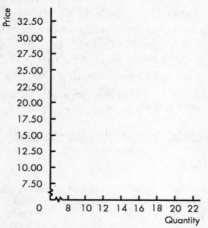

2. Keith's Lunch has two kinds of customers for lunch: stockbrokers and retired senior citizens. The demand schedules for lunches for the two groups is given in Table 12.6.

   Keith has decided to price discriminate between the two groups by treating each demand separately and charging the price that maximizes profit in each of the two sub-markets. Marginal cost and average total cost are equal and constant at $2 per lunch.

   a) Complete Table 12.6 by computing the total and marginal revenue associated with stock broker demand (TR_{SB} and MR_{SB}) as well as total and marginal revenue associated with senior citizen demand (TR_{SC} and MR_{SC}). (Remember that marginal revenue should be entered midway between rows.)

   b) What are the profit-maximizing output and price for stock brokers?

   c) What are the profit-maximizing output and price for senior citizens?

   d) What is total profit?

   e) Show that the total profit in part (d) is the maximum by comparing it with total profit if instead Keith served
      i) 1 additional lunch *each* to stockbrokers and senior citizens.
      ii) 1 less lunch *each* to stockbrokers and senior citizens.

3. Several computer manufacturers make their personal computers available to university students at significantly lower prices than are generally available from their dealers. Students buy the computer through a university-affiliated "store" and sign an agreement stating that they will not resell the personal computer for some specified period of time.

   a) Why do the computer companies offer personal computers to students at substantially reduced prices?

   b) What must these companies believe about the elasticity of student demand for personal computers compared to that of their other customers who must pay higher prices when buying from a dealer?

   c) Why do they require student purchasers to sign the agreement?

Table 12.6

	Stockbrokers			Senior Citizens		
Price (P)	Quantity demanded (Q_D)	Total revenue (TR_{SB})	Marginal revenue (MR_{SB})	Quantity demanded (Q_D)	Total revenue (TR_{SC})	Marginal revenue (MR_{SC})
8	0			0		
7	1			0		
6	2			0		
5	3			1		
4	4			2		
3	5			3		
2	6			4		
1	7			5		
0	8			6		

4. Figure 12.5 gives the demand, marginal revenue, and marginal cost curves for a certain industry. In this problem we consider how consumer and producer surplus are distributed under each of four ways of organizing the industry. In each case, redraw any relevant part of Fig. 12.5 and then (1) indicate the region of the graph corresponding to consumer surplus by drawing horizontal lines through it; (2) indicate the region corresponding to producer surplus by drawing vertical lines through it; and (3) indicate the region (if any) corresponding to deadweight loss by putting dots in the area.

a) The industry consists of many perfectly competitive firms.

b) The industry is a single-price monopoly.

c) The industry is a price-discriminating monopoly charging two prices: P_1 and P_3.

d) The industry is a perfect price-discriminating monopoly.

Figure 12.5

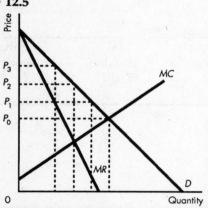

5. In New York City (and many other cities), in order to operate a taxi cab, one must own a taxi "medallion" issued by the city. Since the city has restricted the number of medallions it will issue, cabs in New York City with medallions have been granted a degree of legal monopoly power and thus can earn monopoly profit. Since the city is not issuing more medallions, if you want to operate a cab, you must buy a medallion from someone who has one and is willing to sell it. How much would such a medallion (a right to a future stream of profits) be worth on the open market? Suppose the expected profit from operating a cab is $10,000 per year every year into the indefinite future. Use your knowledge of present value (from Chapter 9) to determine the market value of a medallion if the market rate of interest is 10 percent.

SHORT ANSWER

1. Barriers to entry can either be legal (i.e., created by the government) or natural, but some such barrier must exist in order for a monopoly to continue as a monopoly. Since monopolies are likely to make positive economic profit, other firms would be attracted to the industry unless there are such barriers.

2. In order to sell an additional unit of output, a monopoly must drop the price. This has two effects on revenue: one positive and equal to price and the other negative. Marginal revenue is the net effect which must be less than price. First, the additional unit sold at the new lower price adds an amount equal to the price to revenue. But a single-price monopoly must also lower the price to "previous" customers who would have paid more. The net effect on marginal revenue is the price minus the loss of revenue from lowering the price to previous customers. This difference must necessarily be less than price.

3. If demand is inelastic, we know that a given percentage fall in price will cause quantity demanded to increase but by a smaller percentage amount. This is the reason that, in Chapter 6, we concluded that if demand is inelastic, total revenue declines when the price falls. This means that marginal revenue must be negative in this range since the increase in quantity sold (due to the price decrease) actually decreases total revenue.

4. If marginal revenue is greater than marginal cost, profits will increase by producing more. Since marginal revenue decreases and marginal cost increases as output increases, there is a tendency for the gap to close. Similarly, if marginal revenue is less than marginal cost, profits will increase by producing less, which will also tend to close the gap. Thus, if any deviation from the marginal revenue equals marginal cost condition implies that firms can increase profit by moving back, it must be the profit-maximizing level of output.

5. A single-price monopoly will always produce in the elastic range of the demand curve. The reason is straightforward. Marginal cost is always positive. Thus the profit maximizing condition that marginal cost equals marginal revenue, must be satisfied over the range of output for which marginal revenue is positive; that is, the elastic range.

6. A competitive industry will produce the level of output at which the industry marginal cost curve intersects the demand curve facing the industry. A single-price monopoly will produce at the level of output at which the industry marginal cost curve intersects the monopoly marginal revenue curve. Since the marginal revenue curve lies below the demand curve, this implies a lower level of output in the monopoly industry.

7. In order for price discrimination to work, it must be the case that the good cannot readily be resold. Thus firm *b* is more likely to practice price discrimination since a restaurant meal is virtually impossible to resell while a wristwatch is rather easily resold.

8. Rent seeking is any activity by economic agents designed to create monopoly. It exists because individuals are willing to expend resources to be able to earn monopoly profit.

9. While the quantity sold and the price charged to the last customer are the same

in the cases of perfect competition and a perfect price discriminator, the distribution of consumer surplus is not the same. Since a perfect price discriminator charges each customer the most he/she is willing to pay, they have no consumer surplus. Any consumer surplus that would have occurred under perfect competition now accrues to the monopoly. Obviously consumers would like to obtain more consumer surplus; that is, pay less for the same amount. Consequently, consumers prefer perfect competition.

10. A monopoly would be more efficient than perfect competition if the monopoly has sufficient economies of scale and/or scope. Those economies must be large enough that the monopoly produces more than the competitive industry and sells it at a lower price. Figure 12.6 illustrates such a situation. The important feature is that the marginal cost curve for the monopoly must not only be lower than the supply curve of the competitive industry, but it must be sufficiently lower so that it intersects the *MR* curve at an output greater than *C* (the competitive output). Such a situation could arise if there are extensive economies of scale and/or scope.

Figure 12.6

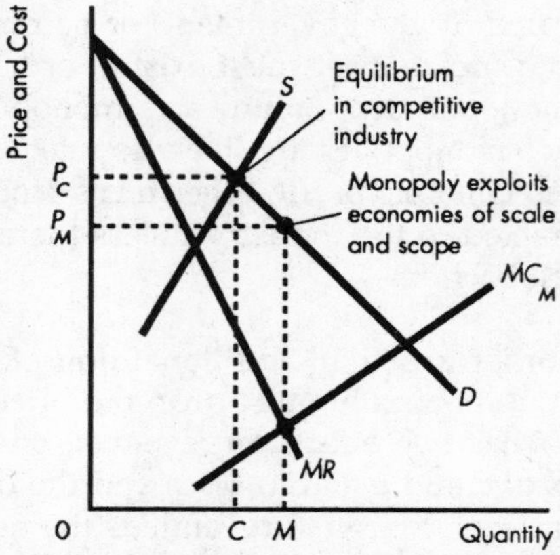

PROBLEMS

1. a) Completed Table 12.3 is given here as Table 12.3 Solution.
    b) Completed Table 12.4 is shown as Table 12.4 Solution.
       The profit-maximizing quantity of output occurs where marginal cost equals marginal revenue, at 19 units. The maximum price the firm can charge and still sell 19 units is $47. This combination of quantity and price yields a total profit of $466, which, as can be seen from the table, is the maximum possible profit.
    c) The requested diagram appears in Fig. 12.3 Solution.

Table 12.3 Solution

Quantity	Total variable cost (TVC)	Total cost (TC)	Average marginal cost (MC)	Variable cost (AVC)	Average total cost (ATC)
9	135	247		15.00	27.44
			... 9		
10	144	256		14.40	25.60
			...11		
11	155	267		14.09	24.27
			...13		
12	168	280		14.00	23.33
			...15		
13	183	295		14.08	22.69
			...17		
14	200	312		14.29	22.29
			...19		
15	219	331		14.60	22.07
			...21		
16	240	352		15.00	22.00
			...23		
17	263	375		15.47	22.06
			...25		
18	288	400		16.00	22.22
			...27		
19	315	427		16.58	22.47
			...29		
20	344	456		17.20	22.80
			...31		
21	375	487		17.86	23.19

Table 12.4 Solution

Price (P)	Quantity demanded (Q)	Total revenue (TR)	Marginal revenue (MR)	Total cost (TC)	Marginal cost (MC)	Profit
57	9	513		247		266
			... 47		... 9	
56	10	560		256		304
			... 45		... 11	
55	11	605		267		338
			... 43		... 13	
54	12	648		280		368
			... 41		... 15	
53	13	689		295		394
			... 39		... 17	
52	14	728		312		416
			... 37		... 19	
51	15	765		331		434
			... 35		... 21	
50	16	800		352		448
			... 33		... 23	
49	17	833		375		458
			... 31		... 25	
48	18	864		400		464
			... 29		... 27	
_47_	_19_	_893_		_427_		_466_
			... 27		... 29	
46	20	920		456		464
			... 25		... 31	
45	21	945		487		458

Equilibrium output occurs where MC = MR = 28, Q = 19, P = 47, profit = $466

Figure 12.3 Solution

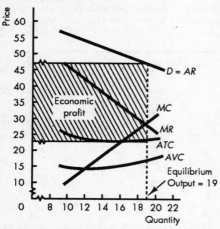

Table 12.5 Solution

Price (P)	Quantity demanded (Q)	Total revenue (TR)	Marginal revenue (MR)	Total cost (TC)	Marginal cost (MC)	Profit
24.50	9	220.50		247		-26.50
			...19.50		... 9	
24.00	10	240.00		256		-16.00
			...18.50		...11	
23.50	11	258.50		267		-8.50
			...17.50		...13	
23.00	12	276.00		280		-4.00
			...16.50		...15	
__22.50__	__13__	__292.50__		__295__		__-2.50__
			...15.50		...17	
22.00	14	308.00		312		-4.00
			...14.50		...19	
21.50	15	322.50		331		-8.50
			...13.50		...21	
21.00	16	336.00		352		-16.00
			...12.50		...23	
20.50	17	348.50		375		-26.50
			...11.50		.25	
20.00	18	360.00		400		-40.00
			...10.50		...27	
19.50	19	370.50		427		-56.50
			... 9.50		...29	
19.00	20	380.00		256		-76.00
			... 8.50		...31	
18.50	21	388.50		487		-98.50

Equilibrium output occurs where $MC = MR = 16$, $Q = 13$, $P = 22.50$, profit = -\$2.50.

d) Completed Table 12.5 is given here as Table 12.5 Solution.

   The profit-maximizing quantity of output occurs where marginal cost equals marginal revenue, now at 13 units. The maximum price the firm can charge and still sell 13 units is $22.50. This combination of quantity and price yields a total profit of -$2.50 (a loss). As can be seen from the table, this is the minimum possible loss. The firm will continue to produce in the short run because this loss is less than its shut-down loss, which would be $112, the amount of its fixed cost.

e) The requested diagram appears in Fig. 12.4 Solution.

Figure 12.4 Solution

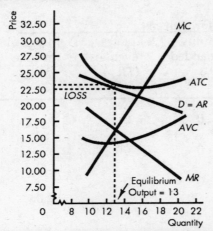

2. a) The completed table is given in Table 12.6 Solution.
   b) The profit-maximizing output for stock brokers occurs when $MC = \$2 = MR_{SB}$. This is at 3 lunches and the price is $5 per lunch to stockbrokers.
   c) The profit-maximizing output for senior citizens occurs when $MC = \$2 = MR_{SC}$. This occurs at 2 lunches and the price to senior citizens is $4 per lunch.
   d) Since average total cost is also $2 per lunch, the total cost is $2 x 5 lunches = $10. Total revenue is $15 from stockbrokers and $8 from senior citizens, or $23. Thus total profit is $13.
   e) i) If Keith served 1 additional lunch each to stockbrokers and senior citizens, that would make 4 lunches for stockbrokers (at $4/lunch) and 3 lunches for senior citizens (at $3/lunch). Since average total cost is $2 x 7 lunches = $14. Total revenue is $16 from stockbrokers and $9 from senior citizens, or $25. Thus total profit is $11, less than the $13 in part (d).
      ii) If Keith served 1 less lunch each to stockbrokers and senior citizens, that

would make 2 lunches for stockbrokers (at $6/lunch) and 1 lunch for senior citizens (at $5/lunch). Since average total cost is $2 x 3 lunches = $6. Total revenue is $12 from stockbrokers and $5 from senior citizens, or $17. Thus total profit is $11, less than the $13 in part (d).

3. a) There are no doubt several possible reasons, but it is likely that one of the reasons is that such price discrimination will increase profits of the computer manufacturers.
   b) The computer companies must believe that the elasticity of student demand is more elastic than the demand by other customers.
   c) We know that price discrimination will fail to increase profit if the good in question can readily be resold. Thus, students who purchase a personal computer at the lower price are required to promise not to resell.

4. a) Under perfect competition, price equals marginal cost. The amount of consumer surplus is given by the area under the demand curve but above the price (P_0) while the amount of producer surplus is given by the area above the MC curve but below the price. See Fig. 12.5 Solution (a).

Table 12.6 Solution

Price (P)	Stockbrokers Quantity demanded (Q_D)	Total revenue (TR_{SB})	Marginal revenue (MR_{SB})	Senior Citizens Quantity demanded (Q_D)	Total revenue (TR_{SC})	Marginal revenue (MR_{SC})
8	0	0		0	0	
			...7			...0
7	1	7		0	0	
			...5			...0
6	2	12		0	0	
			...3			...0
<u>5</u>	<u>3</u>	<u>15</u>		1	5	
			...1			...3
4	4	16		<u>2</u>	<u>8</u>	
			...-1			...1
3	5	15		3	9	
			...3			...-1
2	6	12		4	8	
			...-5			...-3
1	7	7		5	5	
			...-7			...-5
0	8	0		6	0	

For stock brokers, equilibrium output occurs where $MC = MR = 2$, $Q_{SB} = 3$, $P_{SB} = 5$.
For senior citizens equilibrium output occurs where $MC = MR = 2$, $Q_{SC} = 2$, $P_{SC} = 4$.

b) If the industry is a single-price monopoly, price will be greater than MC and output will be less than under competition. Consumer surplus is still given by the area under the demand curve but above the price (P_2), while producer surplus is given by the area above the MC curve but below the price *up to the monopoly level of output*. The remaining part of the large triangle is a deadweight loss since it is the amount of surplus under competition that is lost under a single-price monopoly. See Fig. 12.5 Solution (b).

c) Similar Similar reasoning allows us to establish regions in Fig. 12.5 Solution (c) corresponding to consumer surplus, producer surplus, and deadweight loss.

d) Under perfect price discrimination, all of the potential surplus is captured by the producer and there is no deadweight loss (or consumer surplus). See Fig. 12.5 Solution (d).

Figure 12.5 Solution

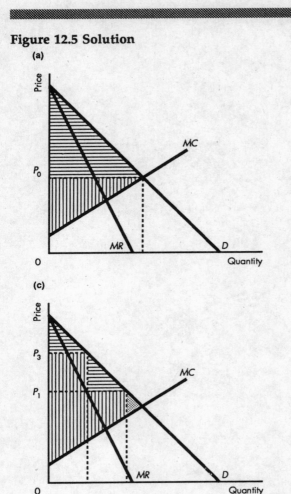

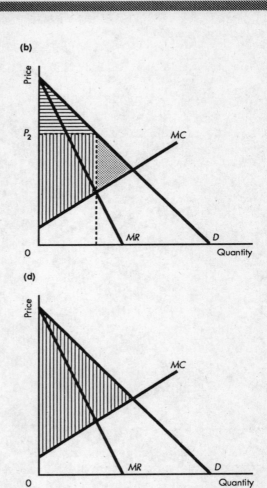

5. The market value of a taxi medallion will be the present value of the future expected profit. The present value of $10,000 per year every year into the indefinite future is the amount which, if invested today at the market rate of interest, would yield the same stream of income each year. Since the market rate of interest is 10 percent, an investment of $100,000 today will yield $10,000 per year. Thus the present value of the taxi medallion is $100,000.

13 MONOPOLISTIC COMPETITION AND OLIGOPOLY

CHAPTER IN PERSPECTIVE

In Chapter 11 we examined the output and price decisions facing firms in a perfectly competitive industry and in Chapter 12 we investigated the output and price decisions of a monopoly. A perfectly competitive industry is characterized by a large number of firms, each of which produces a homogeneous product and has no control over the price of the good they sell — they are price takers. Monopoly represents the other end of the market structure spectrum. A monopoly is the only firm in an industry with barriers to entry and it produces a good with no close substitutes. It faces a downward sloping demand curve and thus can choose its price.

Our analysis of the behavior of firms in these two extreme forms of market structure yielded some very useful principles. However, perfect competition and strict monopoly are actually quite rare. Most firms that we observe seem to lie somewhere between these two polar cases. In this chapter we explore the behavior of these in-between firms that populate the real world. We will discover that the tools of analysis developed in the previous two chapters will take us a long way.

LEARNING OBJECTIVES

After studying this chapter, you will be able to:

- **Describe and distinguish among market structures that lie between perfect competition and monopoly**

- **Define monopolistic competition and oligopoly**

- **Explain how price and output are determined in a monopolistically competitive industry**

- **Explain why the price may be sticky in an oligopoly industry**

- **Explain how price and output are determined when there is one dominant firm and several small firms in an industry**

- **Explain what game theory is**

- **Explain the prisoner's dilemma game**

- •   Explain duopoly and oligopoly as games that firms play

- •   Predict the price and output behavior of duopolists

- •   Make predictions about price wars and competition among small numbers of firms

HELPFUL HINTS

1. Most industries are neither perfectly competitive nor monopolies; they lie somewhere between these two extremes. This does not mean that the last two chapters have been wasted. Indeed, because we have spent the previous two chapters examining firms under these opposite market structures, we are able to spend a single chapter discussing the range of industries between them. It is important not only to know the different key characteristics of the alternative forms of market structure (see Table 13.2 in the text for a review) but to understand how these characteristics explain the differences in behavior.

2. We continue to assume that all firms are profit maximizers. In spite of this common objective, the equilibrium price and level of output will be different for each of the market structures. This is because of differences in the nature of constraints faced by firms in each of the four types of market structure. For example, except in the case of perfect competition, firms face downward sloping demand curves and thus have some control over the price of the good they sell. In these cases, profit maximizing firms will (typically) produce less than would have been produced in the competitive case and charge a price higher than the competitive price.

3. *Graphing hints*: Be sure that the various curves on a given graph are consistent. For example, in representing a monopolistic competitor in long-run equilibrium be sure that the ATC curve is tangent to the demand curve at the same level of output at which the MC

and MR curves intersect. Also, be sure that the MC curve intersects the ATC curve at its minimum point.

4. This chapter introduces the use of elementary game theory to help us understand oligopoly. Be sure to thoroughly understand the prisoner's dilemma game because it illustrates, simply, the most important game theory concepts (rule, strategies, payoffs), which are then used in more complex game theory models like those of repeated games.

Understand the incentives faced by the players and why the outcome is an equilibrium. The key to finding the equilibrium of a simple game is to carefully construct and examine the payoff matrix.

KEY FIGURES AND TABLES

Figure 13.3 Monopolistic Competition

This figure illustrates the output and pricing decisions of a monopolistically competitive firm. Such a firm is similar to monopoly since it faces a downward-sloping demand curve. It therefore maximizes profit by choosing to produce the level of output at which marginal revenue (MR) is equal to marginal cost (MC) and charges the highest possible price P_s, which is determined by the height of the demand curve at that quantity.

In the short run, the firm can make either a positive profit, as illustrated in part (a) of the figure, or a loss. A monopolistically competitive firm is like a competitive firm since there are many firms and there is free entry into the industry.

When firms are making profits, new firms will have an incentive to enter. Such entry will cause the demand curves of existing firms to shift to the left and thus prices to fall. This means that firm profits will fall. Entry will continue as long as profit opportunities remain. Similarly, if firms are making losses in the short run, some will leave the industry, which will increase prices and profits (i.e., reduce losses).

Thus, in long-run equilibrium, illustrated in part (b) of the figure, firms will be making zero profits and there will be no more tendency for firms to either exit or enter the industry.

Figure 13.6 Costs and Demand

If there are no barriers to entry, an industry will be characterized by duopoly if costs and industry demand are such that only two firms can survive in the long run. This figure illustrates such an industry using the example of the two firms: Trick and Gear.

The firms have identical costs, which are shown in part (a). Note that the minimum *ATC* of $6,000 occurs at the quantity of 3,000 switchgears per week. Since, at a price of $6,000, the total quantity demanded in the industry is only 6,000 switchgears per week, only two firms can survive in the long run.

Figure 13.7 Colluding to Make Monopoly Profits

The two firms of a duopoly industry can obtain maximum total profit by colluding. This is illustrated in this figure once again using the example of Trick and Gear.

In order to maximize total profit, the firms will, together, behave as a single monopolist by producing the output at which *industry* marginal cost is equal to *industry* marginal revenue.

The individual (identical) firm cost curves are given in part (a) of the figure. The industry marginal cost curve is the horizontal sum of the two firm marginal cost curves and

is given in part (b). The industry marginal revenue curve is also given there.

The firms will produce the quantity at which these curves intersect (4,000 units here) and charge the monopoly price obtained from the industry demand curve ($9,000). The firms then divide the production and the profits. As seen in part (a), each firm produces 2,000 switchgears per week and earns a profit of $2 million per week.

Figure 13.9 Both Firms Cheat

After the firms of a duopoly enter into a collusive agreement, each firm can either abide by the agreement or cheat by increasing output and reducing price.

Each firm has an incentive to cheat since it can increase its profit (at the expense of the noncheating firm) by doing so. The case of both firms cheating is illustrated for Trick and Gear in this figure. The limiting situation for each firm is shown in part (a) and the result for the industry is shown in part (b).

Once the collusive agreement has broken down by the cheating of the firms, successively lower prices will result until the price has fallen to the competitive level and both firms are making zero profit as seen in part (a). The industry output and price will be those associated with the competitive equilibrium, at the intersection of the industry marginal cost curve and the industry demand curve.

Table 13.2 Market Structure

This table summarizes the characteristics of the four market types that have been discussed in this and previous chapters. These are, from most competitive to least competitive: perfect competition, monopolistic competition, oligopoly, and monopoly. These are compared on the basis of the number of firms in the industry, the kind of product, the nature of any barriers to entry, the firm's control over price, and the concentration ratio. It also gives a couple of examples in each case. This table provides an excellent study tool.

Table 13.4 Duopoly Payoff Matrix

One way to analyze the interactive behavior of firms in an oligopoly is to use game theory in which a payoff matrix is constructed. A payoff matrix indicates the payoffs associated with the alternative strategy combinations of the "players" of the game. The payoff matrix for Trick and Gear is illustrated in this table.

These two firms of a duopoly industry have entered into a collusive agreement with the intent of maximizing total profit. Once the agreement has been established, each firm has two possible strategies: to cheat on the agreement or to comply. The payoff matrix indicates the profit for each firm which results from each of the four possible strategy pairs. Each firm then chooses its best strategy.

For example, Trick will consider his best strategy under each choice that Gear might make. If Gear cheats, Trick is better off by cheating (zero profit is better than a $1 million loss). If Gear complies, Trick is also better off by cheating (a $4.5 million profit is better than a $2 million profit). Thus Trick's dominant strategy is to cheat. The same analysis leads Gear to also decide to cheat. The result is a Nash equilibrium in which both firms cheat.

SELF-TEST

CONCEPT REVIEW

1. The most commonly used measure of concentration is called the four-firm _concentration ratio_. This is the percentage of _sales_ accounted for by the largest four firms in the industry.

2. The market structure characterized by a large number of firms that compete with each other by making similar but slightly different products is called _Monopolistic competition_. The market structure characterized by a small number of producers competing with each other is called _oligopoly_.

3. When profits are being made in a monopolistically competitive industry, firms will _enter_. If losses are being made, firms will _leave_. As a result, in a monopolistically competitive industry, in long-run equilibrium, firms will make a(n) _zero_ economic profit. In the long-run, each firm will have _excess_ capacity.

4. Suppose that when an oligopoly firm raises its price, no other firm will follow, while if the firm reduces its price, all other firms will follow. This firm faces a _kinked_ demand curve for its product.

5. The modern approach to understanding oligopoly uses _____ theory, a method of analyzing strategic interaction invented by John von Neumann. In such a theory all the possible actions of each player are called _____ and the score of each player is called the _____.

6. A market structure in which only two producers of a commodity compete with each other is called _____.

7. The table that shows the payoffs for every possible action by each player for every possible action by the other player is called a(n) _____ _____ .

8. The equilibrium of a game is called a(n) _____ equilibrium. A special case of such an equilibrium occurs when the best strategy for each player is the same regardless of the action taken by the other player. This is called a(n)

   _____ _____

   equilibrium.

9. A group of firms that has entered into a collusive agreement to restrict output and increase price and profits is called a(n) _____ . Each firm in the group can pursue one of two strategies: it can either comply or _____ .

10. In a repeated game, the strategy in which a player begins by cooperating and then cheats only if the other player cheated the previous time the game was played is called a(n) _____ - _____ - _____ strategy.

11. In a repeated game, the strategy in which a player cooperates if the other player cooperates, but plays the Nash equilibrium strategy forever thereafter if the other player cheats is called a

   _____ .

12. The equilibrium which results from each player responding rationally to a credible threat of a heavy penalty from the other player if the agreement is broken is called a(n) _____ equilibrium.

TRUE OR FALSE

____ 1. A low concentration ratio indicates a low degree of competition.

____ 2. A high concentration ratio guarantees a low degree of competition.

____ 3. In a monopolistically competitive industry, each firm faces a downward sloping demand curve.

____ 4. A critical difference between monopoly and monopolistic competition is that in the latter case there is free entry.

____ 5. We use game theory to analyze monopolistic competition because the behavior of any one firm will have a significant influence on other firms.

____ 6. If firms in a monopolistically competitive industry are making profits we can expect to see their demand curves shift to the left as new firms enter.

____ 7. In long-run equilibrium, a firm in monopolistic competition will produce more output than that associated with the minimum point on their average total cost curve.

____ 8. When a monopolistically competitive industry is in long-run equilibrium, economic profits are zero and price equals minimum average total cost.

____ 9. Advertising by monopolistic competitors will always be allocatively inefficient.

____10. An oligopolist will consider the reaction of other firms before it decides to cut its price.

____11. A profit maximizing dominant firm in an oligopoly will operate like a monopoly in setting market price and the small firms will take that price as given in making their output decisions.

____12. In the "prisoner's dilemma," the choices of confessing or denying which are available to each player are called strategies.

____13. The prisoner's dilemma does not have an equilibrium.

____14. If two players in a game face the same choices, there cannot be a dominant strategy equilibrium.

____15. If duopolists agree to collude, they can (jointly) make as much profit as a single monopoly.

____16. A member of a cartel could increase its profit if it increased its output and all other members of the cartel produced their agreed level of output.

____17. In the case of colluding duopolists in a nonrepeated game, the dominant strategy equilibrium is for both firms to cheat.

____18. More than one equilibrium is possible if the game described in question 17 is repeated indefinitely.

____19. In a cartel with several firms, if a single firm cuts its price, the best strategy for the other firms is to maintain the agreed upon price.

____20. A situation in which both firms cheat could not be a Nash equilibrium.

MULTIPLE CHOICE

1. The four-firm concentration ratio measures the share of the largest four firms in the total industry.
   a. Profit
   b. Sales
   c. Cost
   d. Capital

2. Which of the following is NOT a problem with concentration ratios as a measure of industry competitiveness?
   a. Concentration ratios are national measures, but firms in some industries operate in regional markets.
   b. Concentration ratios are national measures, but firms in some industries operate in international markets.
   c. Concentration ratios tell us nothing about the severity of barriers to entry in the industry.
   d. Concentration ratios tell us nothing about how cost varies among firms in the industry.

3. The following are all characteristics of a
    monopoly. Which of them is <u>NOT</u> also a
    characteristic of a monopolistically
    competitive industry?
    a. There are barriers to entry.
    b. The firm is a profit maximizer.
    c. The firm faces a downward-sloping
       demand curve.
    d. The product produced by the firm is
       different from products produced by
       other firms.

4. The following are all characteristics of a
    competitive industry. Which of them is
    <u>NOT</u> also a characteristic of monopolistic
    competition?
    a. There is a large number of firms in the
       industry.
    b. Products produced by firms in the
       industry are identical.
    c. Firms are profit maximizers.
    d. There is free entry.

5. Figure 13.1 represents a monopolistically
    competitive firm in short-run equilibrium.
    The firm's level of output will be
    a. Q_1.
    b. Q_2.
    c. Q_3.
    d. Q_4.

6. The price charged by the monopolistic
    competitor of Fig. 13.1 will be
    a. P_1.
    b. P_2.
    c. P_3.
    d. P_4.

Figure 13.1

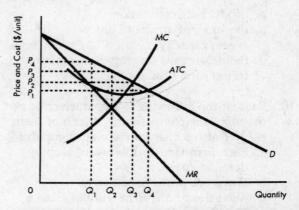

7. Refer again to the short-run situation
    illustrated in Fig. 13.1. We know that in
    the long run,
    a. there will be entry of new firms and
       each existing firm's demand will shift
       to the left.
    b. there will be entry of new firms and
       each existing firm's demand will shift
       to the right.
    c. existing firms will leave and each
       remaining firm's demand will shift to
       the left.
    d. existing firms will leave and each
       remaining firm's demand will shift to
       the right.

8. In the long run, a monopolistically
    competitive firm will produce the output
    at which price equals
    a. marginal cost.
    b. marginal revenue.
    c. average variable cost.
    d. average total cost.

9. Under monopolistic competition, long-run economic profits tend toward zero *because of*
   a. product differentiation.
   b. the lack of barriers to entry.
   c. excess capacity.
   d. the downward-sloping demand curve facing each firm.

10. Each of the following is a characteristic of monopolistic competition. Which of them is <u>NOT</u> also a characteristic of oligopoly?
    a. Each firm faces a downward-sloping demand curve.
    b. Firms are profit maximizers.
    c. The sales of one firm will not have a significant effect on other firms.
    d. There is more than one firm in the industry.

11. The kinked demand curve theory
    a. suggests that price will remain constant even with fluctuations in demand.
    b. suggests how the current price is determined.
    c. assumes that marginal revenue sometimes increases with output.
    d. assumes that competitors will match price cuts and ignore price increases.

12. The demand curve facing the dominant firm in a dominant firm oligopoly is
    a. kinked at the current price.
    b. the total market demand curve.
    c. the difference between total market quantity demanded and the quantity supplied by the rest of the market at each price.
    d. perfectly elastic.

13. Which of the following is <u>NOT</u> an aspect common to all games?
    a. Rules
    b. Collusion
    c. Strategies
    d. Score

14. In the "prisoner's dilemma," each "player" (prisoner) would be best off if
    a. he confesses and the other denies.
    b. he denies and the other confesses.
    c. both prisoners confess.
    d. both prisoners deny.

15. In the prisoner's dilemma, the dominant strategy equilibrium is
    a. both prisoners confess.
    b. neither prisoner confesses.
    c. one denies and the other confesses.
    d. indeterminate.

16. Consider a duopoly with collusion. If the duopoly maximizes profit,
    a. each firm will produce the same amount.
    b. each firm will produce its maximum output possible.
    c. industry marginal revenue will equal industry marginal cost at the level of total output.
    d. total output will be greater than before collusion.

17. Consider a cartel consisting of two firms in collusion to maximize profit. If this game is nonrepeated, the dominant strategy equilibrium is
    a. both firms cheat on the agreement.
    b. both firms adhere to the agreement.
    c. one firm cheats while the other adheres to the agreement.
    d. indeterminate.

18. Consider the same cartel consisting of two firms in collusion to maximize profit. Now, however, the game is repeated indefinitely and each player employs a tit-for-tat strategy. The equilibrium is
    a. both firms cheat on the agreement.
    b. both firms adhere to the agreement.
    c. one firm cheats while the other adheres to the agreement.
    d. indeterminate.

19. The equilibrium in Question 18 is called a
    a. credible strategy equilibrium.
    b. dominant player equilibrium.
    c. cooperative equilibrium.
    d. trigger strategy equilibrium.

20. Table 13.1 gives the payoff matrix in terms
    of profit for firms A and B when there are
    two strategies facing each firm: (1) charge
    a low price, or (2) charge a high price.
    The equilibrium in this game (played
    once) will be a dominant strategy
    equilibrium since
    a. firm B will reduce profit by more than
       A if both charge a lower price.
    b. firm B is the dominant firm.
    c. the best strategy for each firm does not
       depend on the strategy chosen by the
       other.
    d. there is no credible threat by either
       firm to "punish" the other if it breaks
       the agreement.

21. Refer again to the duopoly in Table 13.1.
    In equilibrium, firm A will make a profit
    of
    a. -$10.
    b. $2.
    c. $10.
    d. $20.

Table 13.1

		Firm B		
		Low price		High price
Firm A	Low Price	A:	$2	A: $20
		B:	$5	B: -$15
	High Price	A:	-$10	A: $10
		B:	$25	B: $20

22. It is difficult to maintain a cartel for a
    long period of time. Which of the
    following is the most important reason?
    a. Each firm has an incentive to cheat.
    b. Other firms will enter the industry.
    c. Firms in the cartel will want to drop
       out and stop colluding.
    d. Consumers will eventually decide not
       to buy the cartel's output.

SHORT ANSWER

1. Considering the geographical scope of
   markets, how might concentration ratios
   understate the degree of competitiveness in
   an industry? How might they *overstate*
   the degree of competitiveness in an
   industry?

2. How is the Herfindahl-Hirschman index
   calculated? What does a large value of
   the index mean?

3. Why will a firm in a monopolistically
   competitive industry always have excess
   capacity in long-run equilibrium?

4. Why might an oligopolist face a kinked
   demand curve? How might the existence
   of a kinked demand curve explain sticky
   prices and quantity if there are small
   changes in cost?

5. What is a dominant strategy equilibrium?

6. Consider a cartel in collusion to maximize
   total profit. If the cartel is already
   maximizing profit, why is there an
   incentive for each firm in the cartel to
   cheat?

7. Consider the case of two colluding
   duopolists. Why will both firms cheat on
   the agreement in equilibrium (assume a
   nonrepeated game)?

8. What is a tit-for-tat strategy in a repeated game?

9. Why will a tit-for-tat strategy lead to the monopoly equilibrium in the indefinitely repeated duopoly game?

10. How can a price war which eliminates profits be explained using game theory?

PROBLEMS

1. Graphically illustrate a firm in a monopolistically competitive industry in the short-run which is
   a) making a profit.
   b) making a loss sufficiently large that the firm will shut down in the short run.

2. We observe a monopolistically competitive industry in which the typical firm is making a loss but still produces.
   a) Draw a graph of the short-run situation for a typical firm.
   b) Explain what will happen in this industry. How will the graph you drew in part (a) be affected? (No new graph is required.)
   c) Draw the graph of a typical firm in long-run equilibrium.

3. Consider a monopolistically competitive industry in long-run equilibrium. Firm A in this industry decides to increase profits by advertising.
   a) Show graphically and briefly discuss what will happen in the short run as a result of the decision to advertise.
   b) If the firm is successful in raising profits in the short run, what will happen in the long run?

4. Suppose the volleyball industry is a dominant firm oligopoly consisting of one dominant firm, Big Ball, and several small firms. The profit-maximizing dominant firm sets the price and small firms take that price as given. Figure 13.2 gives the market demand curve for volleyballs, D, and the supply curve of the small price-taking firms all added together, S_R. The situation facing Big Ball is given in Fig. 13.3. As indicated there, we assume that Big Ball's marginal cost, MC, is constant at $20 per volleyball.
   a) In Fig. 13.3, draw the demand curve (label it XD) and the marginal revenue curve (label it MR) facing Big Ball.
   b) What price will Big Ball set and how many volleyballs will Big Ball supply?
   c) How many volleyballs will be supplied by the small firms together?

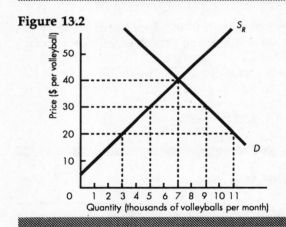

Figure 13.2

Figure 13.3

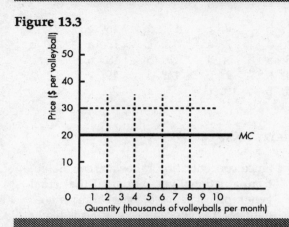

a) How much will each firm produce by the agreement and what price will they charge?
b) What is each firm's average total cost and profit?

Figure 13.4

(a)

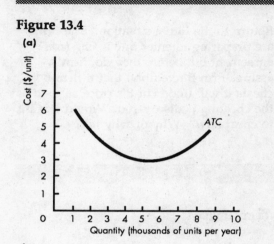

(b)

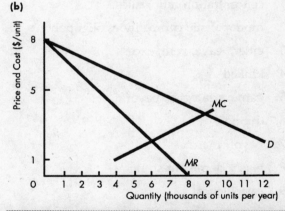

5. A duopoly industry with no collusion consists of firms A and B, which are essentially identical. Currently, neither firm is advertising and they are each making a profit of $5 million per year. If A advertises and B does not, A will make an annual profit of $12 million while B will make a *loss* of $5 million. On the other hand, if B advertises and A does not, B will make a $12 million profit and A will make a *loss* of $5 millon. If both advertise, each will make a zero profit.
   a) Represent this duopoly as a game by identifying the players, strategies, and possible outcomes.
   b) Construct the payoff matrix.
   c) What is the equilibrium outcome? Explain.

6. Use the graphs given in Fig. 13.4 to answer this and the next two questions. Figure 13.4 (a) gives the average total cost curve for each of two identical firms (call them A and B) in a duopoly. Figure 13.4 (b) gives the market demand curve and the firms' joint marginal cost curve. Suppose these firms collude to maximize profit and agree to divide output equally *for a single year*.

7. Now suppose that firm B convinces A that demand has decreased and they must reduce their price by $1 per unit in order to sell their agreed upon quantity. Of course, demand has *not* decreased but A produces its agreed amount and charges $1 less per unit. Firm B, the cheater, also charges $1 less than the original agreement price but increases output

sufficiently to satisfy the rest of demand at this price.
a) How much does B produce?
b) What is firm A's average total cost and profit?
c) What is firm B's average total cost and profit?

8. Return to the initial situation. The firms are preparing to enter into a *long-term* agreement but before they do, firm A assures firm B (credibly) that if firm B cheats it will undercut B's price as soon as the cheating is discovered. Would B want to cheat now? Why or why not?

ANSWERS

CONCEPT REVIEW

1. concentration ratio; sales
2. monopolistic competition; oligopoly
3. enter; leave; zero; excess
4. kinked
5. game; strategies; payoff
6. duopoly
7. payoff matrix
8. Nash; dominant strategy
9. cartel; cheat
10. tit-for-tat
11. trigger strategy
12. cooperative

TRUE OR FALSE

1. F	5. F	9. F	13. F	17. T
2. F	6. T	10. T	14. F	18. T
3. T	7. F	11. T	15. T	19. F
4. T	8. F	12. T	16. T	20. F

MULTIPLE CHOICE

1. b	6. c	11. d	16. c	21. b
2. d	7. a	12. c	17. a	22. a
3. a	8. d	13. b	18. b	
4. b	9. b	14. d	19. c	
5. b	10. c	15. a	20. c	

SHORT ANSWER

1. Since concentration ratios are calculated from a national perspective, if the actual geographical scope of the market is not national, the concentration ratio is likely to misstate the degree of competitiveness in an industry. For example, if the actual market is global, the concentration ratio will understate the degree of competitiveness (i.e., it will be too high). It is possible for a firm to have a concentration ratio of 100 (i.e., it is the only producer in the nation) but face a great deal of international competition. Similarly, when the scope of the market is regional, the degree of competitiveness is likely to be less than would be indicated by the simple concentration ratio.

2. The Herfindahl-Hirschman (H-H) index is calculated as the square of the market share (as a percent) of each firm summed over the largest 50 firms. If there are fewer than 50 firms, we sum over all the firms in the industry. A large value for this index indicates a high degree of concentration in that industry. This may reflect a low degree of competition.

3. Recall that a firm has excess capacity if it is producing in the negatively sloped portion of its average total cost curve. In long-run equilibrium, all firms in a monopolistically competitive industry will be earning zero profit. That is, at the long-run equilibrium level of output (sales), the average total cost curve will be

tangent to the demand curve. Since the demand curve of a monopolistic competitor is downward sloping, so is the average total cost curve at that level of output.

4. An oligopolist faces a kinked demand curve if other firms in the industry will not follow that firm's lead if it increased its price but will follow its lead if it decreased its price. This implies that, at prices above the current price, demand is relatively elastic since the firm will face a large decline in quantity demanded if it raised its price. On the other hand, the demand curve will be relatively inelastic at prices below the current price; the increase in quantity demanded will be small if the firm lowered its price since all other firms would do the same.

   The kink in the demand curve creates a break (a discontinuity) in the marginal revenue curve. As a result, small changes in marginal cost will not change the profit-maximizing output or price. Thus, prices will be sticky in the face of small changes in cost.

5. A player in a game has a dominant strategy if the best strategy is the same no matter what the other player does. A game has a dominant strategy equilibrium if each player has a dominant strategy.

6. Even though the cartel *as a whole* will maximize profit only if every firm keeps its agreement, *each individual* firm can increase its own profit by cheating (e.g., by lowering its price a little) if the other firms continue to follow the agreement.

7. Each firm will consider its best strategy is to cheat regardless of the strategy of the other firm. Call the firms A and B. Firm A knows that if firm B follows the collusive agreement, it can increase its profit by cheating. If firm B cheats, then

firm A knows that it must also cheat to minimize its loss of profit. Thus cheating is the dominant strategy for firm A. Accordingly, it is also the dominant strategy for firm B.

8. A tit-for-tat strategy is a strategy in which a player will cooperate as long as the other player cooperates. But if the other player cheats, the first player will respond by cheating in the next period.

9. The tit-for-tat strategy will lead to the monopoly equilibrium because it will pay both players to stick with the collusive agreement. The benefit of cheating (a short-term increase in profit) will almost surely be less than the cost (a long-term loss of profit).

10. The game theory explains price wars as the consequence of firms in a colluding industry responding to the cheating of a firm. If one firm cheats by cutting its price, then all other firms will cut their prices and a price war will ensue. Once the price has fallen sufficiently (perhaps to the zero profit level), the firms will again have a strong incentive to rebuild their collusion.

PROBLEMS

1. a) Figure 13.5 illustrates a monopolistically competitive firm making a profit in the short run. The important feature of the graph is that at the profit-maximizing output, price is greater than average total cost. Profit is shown by the shaded area in the graph.
   b) Figure 13.6 illustrates a firm that will shut down in the short run since price is less than average variable cost at the profit maximizing (loss minimizing) level of output.

Figure 13.5

(a)

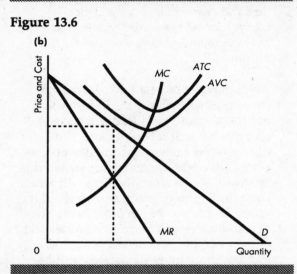

Figure 13.6

(b)

Figure 13.7

(c)

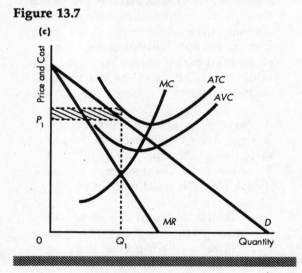

2. a) A typical firm making a loss but
       continuing to produce is illustrated in
       Fig. 13.7. The loss is indicated by the
       shaded area in the graph. Note that, at
       the profit maximizing output, price is
       less than *ATC* but greater than *AVC*.

    b) Since firms are typically experiencing a
       loss, firms will leave the industry. This
       means that the demand curves facing
       each of the remaining firms will begin
       to shift out as they each attract a part
       of the customers of the departing firms.
       As the firm demand curves shift out,
       losses are reduced. Firms will continue
       to have an incentive to leave until
       losses have been eliminated. Thus firm
       demand curves will continue to shift
       out until they are tangent to the *ATC*
       curve.

    c) Figure 13.8 illustrates a typical
       monopolistically competitive firm in
       long-run equilibrium. The key feature
       is that the demand curve facing the
       firm is tangent to the *ATC* curve at the
       profit-maximizing output. Thus, the
       firm is making a zero profit.

Figure 13.8

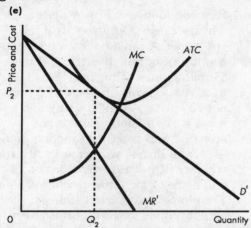

Figure 13.9

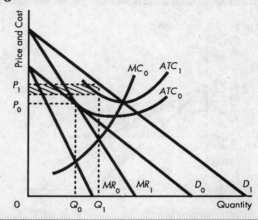

3. a) Advertising will increase firm A's cost but also increase demand (it hopes). If the increase in demand (i.e., revenue) is greater than the increase in cost, then firm A will have increased its profit. Figure 13.9 illustrates this situation. The initial curves are given by D_0, ATC_0, MR_0. Initially the firm is producing Q_0 and selling at price P_0 and making zero profit. Advertising raises the cost curves to ATC_1 and MC_1, but also increases the demand and marginal revenue curves to D_1 and MR_1, respectively. The shift in the demand curve is sufficiently great that there is now a positive profit at the new profit-maximizing level of output (Q_1). The profit is indicated by the shaded area of the graph.

   b) No doubt other firms will also begin to advertise in an attempt to increase their profit (or recover lost profit). As all other firms advertise, the demand curve for our firm will shift back to the left as it loses some of the customers it has gained. In the long run, once again, all firms will be making zero profit even after advertising.

4. a) The completed Fig. 13.3 is given in Fig. 13.3 Solution. The demand curve facing Big Ball (XD) is given by the excess demand arising from the rest of the market. The XD curve is obtained by taking the difference between market quantity demanded (given by D in Fig. 13.2) and quantity supplied by the small firms taken together (given by S_R) at each price. At a price of $40, for example, market quantity demanded and total quantity supplied by the small firms are both 7,000 volleyballs per month. Therefore, the excess demand at a price of $40 is zero. At a price of $30 per volleyball, the market of quantity demanded is 8,000 and the quantity supplied by the smaller firms is 6,000. Thus, the excess demand (quantity demanded faced by Big Ball) is 2,000 at a price of $30. The rest of the XD curve is constructed in a similar fashion. Since the XD curve is linear, the marginal revenue curve (MR) for Big Ball is drawn using Helpful Hint number 3 in Chapter 12: it is the straight line that is exactly half of the horizontal distance between the

vertical axis and the demand (*XD*) curve.

Figure 13.3 Solution

b) Big Ball will operate like a profit-maximizing monopoly in determining price and output. It will supply the level of output at which marginal revenue equals marginal cost and charge the highest price it can given by the height of *XD* curve. As we can see from Fig. 13.3 Solution, Big Ball will set the price at $30 and will supply 4,000 volleyballs per month.

c) Each small firm will take the price set by the dominant firm (Big Ball) as given and act like competitive firms. Thus, taken together, the small firms will supply the quantity of volleyballs given by the S_R curve at the price of $30: 5,000 volleyballs per month.

5. a) The players are firms A and B. Each firm has two strategies: to advertise or not to advertise. There are four possible outcomes: (1) both firms advertise, (2) firm A advertises but firm B does not, (3) firm B advertises but firm A does not, and (4) neither firm advertises.

   b) The payoff matrix is given in Table 13.2. The entries give the profit earned by firms A and B under each of the four possible outcomes.

   c) First consider how firm A decides which strategy to pursue. If B advertises, A can advertise and make zero profit or not advertise and make a $5 million loss. Thus firm A will want to advertise if firm B does. If B does not advertise, A can advertise and make a $12 million profit or not advertise and make a $5 million profit. Therefore firm A will want to advertise whether firm B advertises or not. B will come to the same conclusion. Therefore the dominant strategy equilibrium is that both firms advertise.

Table 13.2

		Firm B	
		Advertise	Not advertise
Firm A	Advertise	A: $0 B: $0	A: $12 million B: -$5 million
	Not advertise	A: -$5 million B: $12 million	A: $5 million B: $5 million

6. a) The firms will agree to produce 3,000 units each and sell at a price of $5 per unit. We determine this by noticing (Fig. 13.4) that the profit-maximizing (monopoly) output is 6,000 units for the industry (*MR* = *MC* at 6,000) at a price of $5. Since the firms have agreed to divide output equally, each will produce 3,000 units.

   b) From Fig. 13.2(a) we determine that, at 3,000 units, each firm's average total cost is $4 per unit. Since price is $5, profit will be $3,000 for each firm.

7. a) At the new price of $4 the total quantity demanded is 8,000 units.

Since A continues to produce 3,000 units this means that firm B will produce the remaining 5,000 units demanded.

b) Since firm A continues to produce 3,000 units, its average total cost continues to be $4 per unit. With the new price also at $4, firm A will make a zero profit.

c) Firm B has increased output to 5,000 units, which implies average total cost of $3 per unit. Thus, given a price of $4, firm B's profit will be $5,000.

8. Given that the agreement is long-term, firm B would almost surely not cheat. The reason is that, while firm B could increase short-term profit by cheating, it would lose much more future profit (in terms of present value) if firm A retaliates. The basic point to be understood is that firm B's behavior changes, not because cost or demand have changed, but rather because firm A's behavior is different. That is, the best strategy for any firm will depend on the behavior of other firms.

14 PRICING AND ALLOCATING FACTORS OF PRODUCTION

CHAPTER IN PERSPECTIVE

In Chapters 9 and 10 we examined the production choices that firms make. We explored the nature of costs and how firms bring together factors of production to produce output. For convenience and to allow us to focus directly on the issues at hand, we assumed there that the prices of the factors of production were given and constant. In this chapter we think more carefully about how those prices arise.

As with the prices of goods and services, the prices of productive resources are determined in markets - markets for factors of production. These markets have many of the same aspects as the markets for goods and services we have examined in Chapters 11 through 13. Here we take a broad first look at markets for factors of production, leaving more detailed discussion of specific markets to later chapters.

LEARNING OBJECTIVES

After studying this chapter, you will be able to:

- Explain how firms choose the quantities of labor, capital, and land to employ in their production activities

- Explain how households choose the quantities of labor, capital, and land to supply

- Explain how wages, interest, and land rent are determined in competitive factor markets

- Explain the concept of economic rent

- Distinguish between economic rent and transfer earnings

213

HELPFUL HINTS

1. The purpose of this chapter is to give a broad overview to the characteristics that are common to the markets for all factors of production. For example, the assumption that firms are profit maximizers implies that they will hire each factor of production up to the point where marginal revenue product is equal to the marginal cost of the factor, regardless of what factor of production we are interested in.

2. Be sure to carefully distinguish between the marginal revenue product of a factor of production and the marginal revenue of a unit of output. Similarly, be careful to distinguish between the marginal cost of a factor of production and the marginal cost of a unit of output.

3. As noted in the text, the marginal revenue product of a factor of production can be calculated by multiplying marginal revenue and marginal product (i.e., $MRP = MR \times MP$). We can think of this intuitively as follows: marginal product tells us how much more output we get from using more of a factor, and marginal revenue tells us how much more revenue we get from that additional output. Therefore $MP \times MR$ tells us how much more revenue we get from using more of the factor (the MRP). Though not mentioned in the text, the marginal cost of a factor of production can be calculated as by multiplying marginal cost and marginal product. The intuition is similar: marginal product tells us how much more output we get from using more of a factor, and marginal cost tells us how much cost increases by producing the additional output. Therefore $MP \times MC$ tells us the additional cost of using more of the factor (the marginal cost of the factor).

4. From Hint 3 we have another way to see that the following two profit-maximizing conditions are equivalent:

a) $MR = MC$

b) MRP = marginal cost of the factor (call this MFC)

Since $MRP = MR \times MP$ and $MFC = MC \times MP$, we see that the condition $MRP = MFC$ implies that $MR = MC$ and the condition $MR = MC$ implies that $MRP = MFC$.

KEY FIGURES AND TABLES

Figure 14.1 Demand and Supply in a Factor Market

Factor prices are determined in factor markets. The demand and supply curves for factors of production have the same properties as the demand and supply curves for goods. The quantity of a factor demanded decreases as the price of the factor increases and the quantity of a factor supplied increases as the price of the factor increases. The market for some factor of production is depicted in this figure. The equilibrium occurs at the intersection of the demand and supply curves. The amount of total factor income is given by the area of the blue rectangle; that is, the price of a unit of the factor times the quantity of factors hired.

Figure 14.4 The Demand for Labor at Max's Wash 'n' Wax

A firm's demand for labor curve is the same as the marginal revenue product curve of labor. This is illustrated in this figure using the example of Max's Wash 'n' Wax. Part (a) of the figure shows the average revenue product curve (ARP) and the corresponding marginal revenue product curve (MRP). For this example, these curves simply plot the values reported in Table 15.1. Part (b) constructs Max's demand for labor by asking how much labor Max would be willing to hire at alternative wage rates. Since Max is a profit maximizer, he will want to hire labor up to the point where the marginal revenue product of labor is equal to the wage rate. For example, if the wage rate is $10 per hour, Max will hire 3 workers since marginal revenue product is $10 when 3 workers are hired. Other points on the labor demand curve can be obtained in similar fashion. The result, as seen in part (b), is that the labor demand curve will be the same as the *MRP*.

Figure 14.8 Labor Market Equilibrium

This figure shows equilibrium in two different labor markets. Part (a) shows the labor market for news anchors. News anchors are portrayed as having very high marginal revenue product (as indicated by the height of the demand curve). The supply of news anchors is also rather low. Thus the equilibrium wage rate for news anchors is very high ($500 per hour in the example). Part (b) illustrates the labor market for babysitters. Babysitters have relatively low marginal revenue product and the supply is large. As a result, the wage rate for babysitters is quite low ($2 an hour in this example).

Figure 14.9 Capital Market Equilibrium

Two markets for capital are illustrated here. Part (a) gives the market for capital in the steel industry and part (b) gives the market for capital in the computer industry. In both cases we note that the quantity of capital demanded is inversely related to the interest rate. Also, in both industries, the long-run supply of capital is perfectly elastic at interest R. In the short run, however, the equilibrium interest rate earned by owners of capital in the steel industry is R_1 while the interest rate earned by owners of capital in the computer industry is R_2 which is greater than R_1. Since the return on capital is higher in the computer industry than in the steel industry there will be an incentive to transfer capital from the steel industry to the computer industry. This will reduce the supply of capital in the steel industry and increase the supply of capital in the computer industry. As a result, the inter-

est rate on capital in the steel industry will rise and the interest rate on capital in the computer industry will fall. This transfer of capital will continue until the interest rates in both capital markets are equal to R, which will then be a long-run equilibrium.

Figure 14.10 Land Market Equilibrium

This figure illustrates factors that determine whether equilibrium rent in specific land markets will be high or low. Part (a) illustrates a market in which the marginal revenue product of land is high but there is a very limited fixed supply (note that the quantity of land is measured in square feet). This market is for well-located urban land: Chicago's Magnificent Mile. The combination of high marginal revenue product (i.e., high demand) and low supply yields an equilibrium annual land rent which is very high: $10,000 per square foot. Part (b) illustrates a market in which the marginal revenue product of land is not so high and the fixed supply is large (note that the quantity of land is measured in acres). This is the market for Iowa farmland. The resulting equilibrium annual land rent is rather low: $1,000 per acre.

Figure 14.11 Economic Rent and Transfer Earnings

Total income received by the owner of a factor of production can be divided into two components: economic rent and transfer earnings. This figure illustrates this division. It shows the demand and supply curves for a factor of production. The total income received by owners of the factor is given by the price of the factor times the quantity of the factor hired; that is, by the area of the green and yellow rectangle in the figure. Transfer earnings are the part of income that is required to induce the supply of the factor. They are measured by the part of the income rectangle that lies below the supply curve; shown in yellow in the figure. Economic rent is the part of factor income that exceeds transfer earnings; shown in green in the figure.

Table 14.2 A Compact Glossary of Factor Market Terms

While this chapter discusses a variety of specific factor markets, there are some important terms that are used generally when discussing factor markets. These are conveniently reviewed here. Thus, this table provides a handy resource for reference and review.

Table 14.3 Two Conditions for Maximum Profit

Not only are output decisions guided by the firm's desire to maximize profit, but decisions regarding the use of inputs are guided by the same objective. In previous chapters we learned that a profit-maximizing firm will choose the level of output at which marginal revenue equals marginal cost ($MR = MC$). In this chapter, we have seen that a profit-maximizing firm will hire a factor up to the level at which marginal revenue product equals the price of the factor ($MRP = PF$). This table demonstrates that these two profit maximization conditions are equivalent. The key to discovering their equivalence is to recognize that MRP is the product of MR and MP (marginal product) while $MC = PF \div MP$.

Table 14.4 A Firm's Demand for Labor

This table summarizes the law of demand as it applies to labor: the quantity of labor demanded is negatively related to the price of labor (the wage rate). It also indicates factors that cause the demand for labor to change; that is, the demand curve for labor to shift.

SELF-TEST

CONCEPT REVIEW

1. Owners of factors of production receive income from firms for the use of those factors of production. The payment for labor is called __wages__, the payment for capital is called __interest__, and the payment for land is called __rent__.

2. An increase in the demand for a factor of production will __increase__ that factor's income. If the supply curve for a factor of production is very elastic, the resulting change in quantity traded will be __large__ and the change in price will be __small__.

3. The demand for a factor as an input in the productive process rather than for its own sake is called a(n) __derived__ demand.

4. The change in total revenue resulting from __hiring__ an additional unit of __labor__ is called the marginal revenue product of labor. If a profit-maximizing firm finds that the marginal revenue product of labor exceeds the wage, the firm should __increase__ the quantity of labor it hires.

5. The law of diminishing returns implies that the marginal revenue product curve will be __negatively__ sloped. A firm's demand for labor curve will be based on its __marginal__ __revenue__ __product__ curve.

6. If the price of the good produced by firm A increases, the demand curve for labor hired by firm A will shift to the

right. A technological change that increases the marginal product of labor will shift the demand curve for labor to the _right_.

7. Other things being equal, the higher the elasticity of demand for a product, the _higher_ is the elasticity of demand for the labor that produces it. The more readily capital can be substituted for labor in production, the _more_ elastic is the long-run elasticity of demand for labor.

8. The lowest wage for which a household will supply labor to the market is called its _reservation_ wage.

9. An increase in the wage will have two effects on the quantity of labor supplied by a household. The income effect will lead to a(n) _decrease_ in the quantity of labor supplied and the substitution effect will lead to a(n) _increase_ in the quantity of labor supplied.

10. The amount of saving by households will determine the supply of _capital_. Other things being equal, as the interest rate rises, households will _increase_ the amount they save.

11. The income received by the owner of a factor of production which exceeds the amount just necessary to induce the owner to offer the factor for use is called

economic rent. The income required to induce the supply of the factor is called _transfer_ earnings.

TRUE OR FALSE

____1. When the elasticity of demand for labor is greater than 1, an increase in the supply of labor will lead to a decrease in labor income.

____2. As long as the labor supply curve is positively sloped, an increase in the demand for labor will increase total labor income.

____3. A profit-maximizing firm will hire the quantity of a factor of production for which the marginal revenue product equals the marginal cost of the factor.

____4. Marginal revenue product can be calculated as marginal revenue times average product.

____5. The firm's demand curve for labor is the same as the average revenue product curve.

____6. When discussing the short-run demand for labor, labor is considered to be the only variable input.

____7. If the production of good *A* is labor intensive, the demand for labor used in the production of good *A* is likely to be rather inelastic.

____8. The steeper the marginal product curve for labor, the less elastic is the firm's demand for labor.

____9. The marginal revenue product of labor diminishes as more workers are hired because of the principle of diminishing marginal utility.

____10. If the wage rate increases, the substitution effect results in the household increasing the time spent in market activities and decreasing the time spent in nonmarket activities.

____11. A household supplies no labor at wage rates below its reservation wage.

____12. If the wage rate increases, the income effect results in the household increasing its demand for leisure.

____13. A backward-bending supply curve for labor will arise if the substitution effect dominates the income effect.

____14. If a household has current income that is low when compared with its expected future income, it will save very little.

____15. The household supply curve for capital shows the relationship between the interest rate and the quantity of capital supplied.

____16. The market supply curve of capital is likely to be quite inelastic.

____17. The market supply of a particular piece of land is perfectly elastic.

____18. In the long run, the equilibrium interest rate on capital will be the same in all industries.

____19. If the supply of a factor of production is perfectly inelastic, its entire income is transfer earnings.

____20. If Dan Rather would be willing to read the news for $100,000 per year and he is paid $2,100,000 per year to do so, he is earning economic rent of $2,000,000.

MULTIPLE CHOICE

1. The income received by owners of factors of production are wages paid for labor,
    a. profit paid for capital, and interest paid for money.
    b. dividends paid for capital, and interest paid for money.
    c. interest paid for capital, and rent paid for land.
    d. profit paid for capital, and rent paid for land.

2. Suppose that the supply of a factor of production is very elastic. Then an increase in the demand for that factor will result in
    a. a large increase in the quantity of the factor traded and a small increase in its price.
    b. a small increase in the quantity of the factor traded and a large increase in its price.
    c. a large increase in both the quantity of the factor traded and its price.
    d. a small increase in both the quantity of the factor traded and its price.

3. An increase in the supply of a factor of production will
   a. increase income of the factor of production if the elasticity of demand is less than 1.
   b. decrease income of the factor of production if the elasticity of demand is less than 1.
   c. always increase income of the factor.
   d. always decrease income of the factor.

4. An example of derived demand is the demand for
   a. sweaters derived by an economics student.
   b. sweaters produced by labor and capital.
   c. labor used in the production of sweaters.
   d. sweater brushes.

5. The change in total revenue resulting from employing an additional unit of capital is the
   a. marginal product of capital.
   b. marginal revenue of capital.
   c. marginal revenue cost of capital.
   d. marginal revenue product of capital.

6. When a firm is a price taker in the labor market, its marginal revenue product of labor curve is also its
   a. marginal cost curve for labor
   b. demand curve for labor.
   c. supply curve of labor.
   d. supply curve of output.

7. Which of the following will NOT be true in a profit-maximizing equilibrium?
   a. Marginal revenue equals marginal product.
   b. Marginal revenue equals marginal cost.
   c. Marginal revenue times marginal product of a factor equals marginal cost of the factor.
   d. Marginal revenue product of a factor equals marginal cost of the factor.

8. A profit-maximizing firm will continue to hire units of a variable factor of production until the
   a. marginal cost of the factor equals its marginal product.
   b. marginal cost of the factor equals its average revenue product.
   c. average cost of the factor equals its marginal revenue product.
   d. marginal cost of the factor equals its marginal revenue product.

9. Suppose a profit-maximizing firm hires labor in a competitive labor market. If the marginal revenue product of labor is — greater than the wage, the firm should
   a. increase the wage rate.
   b. decrease the wage rate.
   c. increase the quantity of labor it hires.
   d. decrease the quantity of labor it hires.

10. A change in which of the following will NOT shift the firm's demand curve for labor?
    a. The wage rate
    b. The price of the firm's output
    c. The price of other inputs
    d. A change in technology

11. An increase in the price of a firm's output will cause
    a. the supply of labor to increase.
    b. a decline in the quantity of inputs hired.
    c. an increase in marginal product.
    d. an increase in marginal revenue product.

12. A technological change that causes an increase in the marginal product of labor will shift
    a. the labor demand curve to the left.
    b. the labor demand curve to the right.
    c. the labor supply curve to the left.
    d. the labor supply curve to the right.

13. Other things being equal, the larger the proportion of total cost coming from labor,
    a. the more elastic is the demand for labor.
    b. the less elastic is the demand for labor.
    c. the more elastic is the supply of labor.
    d. the less elastic is the supply of labor.

14. If the wage rate increases, the *substitution* effect will give a household an incentive to
    a. raise its reservation wage.
    b. increase its nonmarket activity and decrease its market activity.
    c. increase its market activity and decrease its nonmarket activity.
    d. increase both market and nonmarket activity.

15. If the wage rate increases, the *income* effect will give a household an incentive to
    a. raise its reservation.
    b. increase the amount of leisure it consumes.
    c. decrease the amount of leisure it consumes.
    d. increase the amount of work it offers.

16. As the wage rate continues to rise, a household will have a backward-bending supply of labor curve if
    a. the income effect is in the same direction as the substitution effect.
    b. the wage rate rises above the reservation wage.
    c. the substitution effect dominates the income effect.
    d. the income effect dominates the substitution effect.

17. Household savings are larger when either current income is
    a. low compared with expected future income or interest rates are high.
    b. low compared with expected future income or interest rates are low.
    c. high compared with expected future income or interest rates are high.
    d. high compared with expected future income or interest rates are low.

18. Whether a household's current income is high or low *compared with expected future income* is influenced by
    a. the stage of the life cycle the household is in.
    b. whether the household is rich or poor.
    c. whether interest rates are high or low.
    d. whether saving is high or low.

19. In the short run, a firm faces a supply of capital that is
    a. perfectly elastic.
    b. perfectly inelastic.
    c. positively sloped.
    d. backward bending.

20. If the desire for leisure increased, the wage rate would
    a. rise and the quantity of labor hired would fall.
    b. rise and the quantity of labor hired would rise.
    c. fall and the quantity of labor hired would fall.
    d. fall and the quantity of labor hired would rise.

21. If the interest rate on capital in industry A is lower than the interest rate on capital in industry B, then, in the long run,
   a. the supply of capital in industry A will gradually decrease and the supply of capital in industry B will gradually increase until the interest rates are equal.
   b. the supply of capital in industry A will gradually increase and the supply of capital in industry B will gradually decrease until the interest rates are equal.
   c. the supply of capital in industry A must be more elastic than the supply of capital in industry B.
   d. the supply of capital in industry A must be less elastic than the supply of capital in industry B.

22. Economic rent is
   a. the price paid for the use of an acre of land.
   b. the price paid for the use of a unit of capital.
   c. the income required to induce a given quantity of a factor of production to be supplied.
   d. the income received that is above the amount required to induce a given quantity of a factor of production to be supplied.

23. Consider the supply schedule of a factor of production given in Table 14.1. If 4 units of the factor are supplied at a price of $8 per unit, transfer earnings are
   a. $8.
   b. $12.
   c. $20.
   d. $32.

Table 14.1

Price of a factor	Quantity of factor supplied
$ 2	1
4	2
6	3
8	4
10	5

24. Consider the supply schedule of a factor of production given in Table 14.1. If 4 units of the factor are supplied at a price of $8 per unit, economic rent is
   a. $8.
   b. $12.
   c. $20.
   d. $32.

SHORT ANSWER

1. Why will an increase in the supply of a factor of production result in an increase in income if the demand for the factor has elasticity greater than 1 and result in a decrease in income if the elasticity of demand for the factor is less than 1.

2. Define average revenue product and marginal revenue product.

3. Why is the demand for a factor of production given by its marginal revenue product curve?

4. What happens to the amount of income received by labor inputs if the marginal product of labor increases? Explain.

5. Which of the following industries is likely to have the larger long-run elasticity of demand for labor? Explain.
   a) Industry A manufactures goods. There are a number of alternative production technologies which allow most jobs to be done by either labor or machines.
   b) Industry B is the retail sales industry.

6. Discuss the substitution and income effects on the quantity of labor supplied if the wage rate *decreases*.

7. Why do young households tend to save less than older households?

8. Define economic rent.

PROBLEMS

1. Table 14.2 gives the total and marginal product schedules for a firm that sells its output in a competitive market and buys labor in a competitive market. Initially, the price at which the firm can sell any level of output is $5 per unit and the wage rate at which it can purchase any quantity of labor is $15 per unit.
   a) Complete the first two blank columns in Table 14.2 by computing the TR and MRP_L corresponding to a price output = $5.
   b) The text informs us that the values obtained for the marginal revenue product of labor (MRP_L) are the same when they are computed by either of the following formulas:
   $$MRP_L = \Delta TR/\Delta L$$
   $$MRP_L = MR \times MP_L$$
   where ΔTR = the change in total revenue, ΔL = the change in labor, MR = marginal revenue, and MP_L = marginal product of labor. Show that these two formulas are equivalent for the case when the quantity of labor changes from 1 to 2 units.

Table 14.2

Quantity labor (L)	Output (Q)	Marginal product (MP_L)	Total revenue (TR)	Marginal revenue product (MRP_L)	Total revenue (TR)	Marginal revenue product (MRP_L)
0	0					
		...12				
1	12					
		...10				
2	22					
		... 8				
3	30					
		... 6				
4	36					
		... 4				
5	40					
		... 2				
6	42					

c) If the firm maximizes profit, what quantity of labor will it hire? How much output will it produce?
d) If total fixed cost is $125, what is the amount of profit?
e) What is its profit if the firm hires one more unit of labor than the profit-maximizing quantity? One less unit of labor than the profit-maximizing quantity?
f) Draw a graph of the demand for labor and the supply of labor and illustrate labor market equilibrium.

2. Now, suppose that the market demand for the output of the firm in Problem 1 decreases, causing the price of output to decrease to $3 per unit. The total and marginal product schedules remain unchanged and MRP_L corresponding to price of output = $3.
   a) Complete the last two blank columns in Table 14.2 by computing the TR and MRP_L corresponding to price of output = $3.
   b) If the wage remains at $15 per unit of labor, what is the profit-maximizing quantity of labor that the firm will

hire? How much output will it produce?

c) Total fixed cost continues to be $125. What is the amount of profit?

d) Will the firm shut down in the short run? Explain.

e) Draw a new graph of the new labor market equilibrium.

3. The price of output for the firm in Problem 2 remains at $3 but the wage now rises to $21 per unit of labor. The total and marginal product schedules remain unchanged.
   a) What happens to the demand curve for labor (the *MRP* of labor) curve?
   b) Under these circumstances, what is the profit-maximizing quantity of labor that the firm will hire? How much output will it produce?
   c) Total fixed cost continues to be $125. What is the amount of profit?
   d) Draw a graph of the labor market equilibrium.

4. Table 14.3 gives the market labor demand and supply schedules.
   a) What is the equilibrium wage rate and the quantity of labor hired?
   b) What is the total amount of income received by labor in this market?
   c) Represent the market graphically. Identify the equilibrium wage and quantity of labor.
   d) How much of labor income constitutes transfer earnings? How much constitutes economic rent?

5. Now suppose that the demand for labor increases by 60 hours at each wage rate.
   a) What are the new equilibrium wage rate and quantity of labor?
   b) What is the new total amount of labor income?
   c) How much of this is transfer earnings? How much is economic rent?

Table 14.3

Wage rate (dollars per hour)	Quantity of labor supplied (hours)	Quantity of labor demanded (hours)
0	0	240
1	20	200
2	40	160
3	60	120
4	80	80
5	100	40
6	120	0

ANSWERS

CONCEPT REVIEW

1. wages; interest; rent

2. increase; large; small

3. derived

4. hiring; labor; increase

5. negatively; marginal revenue product

6. right; right

7. higher; more

8. reservation

9. decrease; increase

10. capital; increase

11. economic rent; transfer

TRUE OR FALSE

1. F	5. F	9. F	13. F	17. F
2. T	6. T	10. T	14. T	18. T
3. T	7. F	11. T	15. T	19. F
4. F	8. T	12. T	16. F	20. T

MULTIPLE CHOICE

1. c	6. b	11. d	16. d	21. a
2. a	7. a	12. b	17. c	22. d
3. b	8. d	13. a	18. a	23. c
4. c	9. c	14. c	19. b	24. b
5. d	10. a	15. b	20. a	

SHORT ANSWER

1. An increase in the supply of a factor of production will cause the price of the factor to decrease and the quantity of the factor hired to increase. Income received by the factor is just the product of the price of the factor and the quantity hired. If the percentage increase in the quantity hired is greater than the percentage decrease in price (i.e., if the elasticity of demand for the factor in greater than 1), income will increase. Similarly, if the percentage increase in the quantity hired is less than the percentage decrease in price (i.e., if the elasticity of demand for the factor is less than 1), income will decrease.

2. Average revenue product is total revenue divided by the quantity of the factor hired. Marginal revenue product is the change in total revenue resulting from the use of an additional unit of the factor.

3. The marginal revenue product curve for a factor of production gives its demand curve because firms are profit maximizers. As a consequence they will hire an additional unit of a factor of production until the marginal cost of the factor (its price) is equal to the additional revenue from its use (its MRP). Thus the quantity of the factor demanded at each price (the demand curve) is given by the MRP curve.

4. If the marginal product of labor increases, its demand curve will shift to the right.

Given the supply of labor curve, both the wage rate and the quantity of labor hired will increase, which implies that income received by labor inputs will increase.

5. Industry A is likely to have the larger long-run elasticity of demand for labor since labor and capital are highly substitutable. Thus, for example, an increase in the price of labor will cause firms to shift to production processes that use more capital and less labor. Thus the quantity of labor demanded in the long run will fall by a relatively large amount.

6. If the wage rate decreases, households will have a tendency to shift from work to leisure (the substitution effect), thus reducing the quantity of labor supplied. The lower wage also decreases the household's income and, thus, causes the household to reduce its demand for leisure and other normal goods (the income effect) thereby increasing the quantity of labor supplied.

7. Households will tend to save less when current income is low relative to expected future income and save more when current income is high relative to expected future income. Young households are largely in this first situation while older households are largely in the second.

8. Economic rent is income received by the owner of a factor of production which exceeds the amount just necessary to induce the owner to supply the factor.

PROBLEMS

1. a) The completed columns for TR and MRP_L corresponding to a price of output = $5 are shown in Table 14.2 Solution. The values for TR are obtained by multiplying the quantity of output by the price of output ($5). The values for MRP_L between any two quantities of labor are obtained by dividing the change in TR by the change in quantity of labor.

Table 14.2 Solution

Quantity labor (L)	Output (Q)	Marginal product (MP_L)	Total revenue (TR)	Marginal revenue product (MRP_L)	Total revenue (TR)	Marginal revenue product (MRP_L)
0	0		0		0	
		...12		...60		...36
1	12		60		36	
		...10		...50		...30
2	22		110		66	
		... 8		...40		...24
3	30		150		90	
		... 6		...30		...18
4	36		180		108	
		... 4		...20		...12
5	40		200		120	
		... 2		...10		... 6
6	42		210		126	

b) From part (a), the formula $MRP_L = \Delta TR/\Delta L$, yields a marginal revenue product of labor of 60 when the quantity of labor changes from 1 to 2 units. To confirm that the second formula ($MRP_L = MR \times MP_L$) gives the same answer when the quantity of labor changes from 1 to 2 units, substitute in the values for MR ($5, the price of an additional unit of output) and MP_L(12 units of output). This yields the same marginal revenue product of labor as above; $5 x 12 units = $60.

c) The firm maximizes profit by hiring labor up to the point where the MRP of labor is equal to the marginal cost of labor, (the wage rate). That point occurs at 5 units of labor. The MRP of moving from 4 to 5 units of labor is 20, and the MRP of moving from 5 to 6 units of labor is 10. Thus, by interpolation, the MRP at exactly 5 units of labor is 15 (midway between 20 and 10). So when 5 units of labor are hired, the MRP of labor is wqual to the wage rate ($15). Given that 5 units of labor are hired, the profit-maximizing output will be 40 units (from Table 14.2 Solution)

d) To calculate profit, we must first calculate total revenue and then subtract total cost. Total revenue is $200 (40 units of output times $5 per unit) and total cost is also $200—the sum of total variable (labor) cost of $75 (5 units of labor times $15 per unit) and total fixed cost of $125. Thus profit is zero.

e) If the firm hires one more unit of labor (6 units), total revenue will be $210 (42 units of output times the $5 price). Total cost will be the $125 fixed cost plus $90 in total variable cost (6 units of labor times the $15 wage rate) or $215. Thus profit will be a negative $5 (a $5 loss).

   If the firm hires one less unit of labor (4 units), total revenue will be $180 (36 units of output times the $5 price). Total cost will be the $125 fixed cost plus $60 in total variable cost (4 units of labor times the $15 wage rate) or $185. Thus profit will be a negative $5 (a $5 loss).

f) The graph of labor market equilibrium appears in Fig. 14.1. The demand for labor is given by the firm's MRP_L curve which is labelled D_0 (D_1 will be discussed in Problem 2).

   Notice that the values for MRP are plotted midway between the corresponding quantities of labor. For example, MRP of 60 is plotted midway between 1 and 2 units of labor.

Since the firm purchases labor in a perfectly competitive labor market, the supply of labor to the firm is perfectly elastic at the market wage rate. The labor supply curve is labelled $W = \$15$. The equilibrium is at the intersection of these curves, and corresponds to a wage rate of \$15 and a quantity of labor hired of 5 units.

Figure 14.1

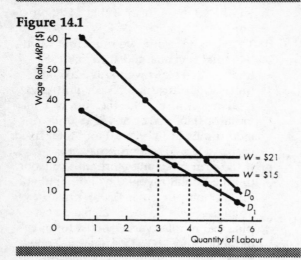

2. a) The completed columns for TR and MRP_L corresponding to price of output = \$3 are shown above in Table 14.2 Solution. The values for TR are obtained by multiplying the quantity of output by the price of output (\$3). The values for MRP_L between any two quantities of labor are obtained by dividing the change in TR by the change in quantity of labor.

    b) If the wage rate remains at \$15, the profit-maximizing quantity of labor will fall to 4 units since MRP_L equals the wage rate at 4 units of labor. The MRP of moving from 3 to 4 units of labor is 18, and the MRP of moving from 4 to 5 units of labor is 12. Thus, by interpolation, the MRP at exactly 4 units of labor is 15 (midway between

18 and 12). Given that 4 units of labor are employed, the profit-maximizing output will be 36 units (from Table 14.2 Solution).

  c) Profit equals total revenue minus total cost. Total revenue is \$108 (36 units of output times \$3 per unit) and total cost is \$185—the sum of total variable (labor) cost of \$60 (4 units of labor times \$15 per unit) and total fixed cost of \$125. Thus profit is -\$77, or a loss of \$77.

  d) The firm will not shut down since total revenue (\$108) is enough to cover total variable cost (\$60) and part of fixed cost. If the firm decided to shut down, it would lose the \$125 of fixed cost rather than just \$77.

  e) The graph of labor market equilibrium appears in Fig. 14.1. The new demand for labor is given by the firm's new MRP_L curve, which is labelled D_1. The supply of labor has not changed; it continues to be horzontal at \$15, the competitive market wage. The new equilibrium is at the intersection of these curves, and corresponds to a wage rate of \$15 and a quantity of labor hired of 4 units.

3. a) Since marginal revenue and the marginal product of labor are unaffected by a change in the wage rate, the demand curve for labor (the MRP of labor) will remain at D_1.

    b) If the wage rate rises to \$21, the profit-maximizing quantity of labor will fall to 3 units since MRP_L equals the wage rate at 3 units of labor. Given that 3 units of labor are employed, the profit-maximizing output will be 30 units (from Table 14.2 Solution).

    c) Profit equals total revenue minus total cost. Total revenue is \$90 (3 units of output times \$3 per unit) and total cost is \$188—the sum of total variable (labor) cost of \$63 (3 units of labor times \$21 per unit) and total fixed cost of $125. Thus profit is -$98, or a loss of $98.

d) See Fig. 14.1. The relevant demand for labor curve continues to be D_1, but the labor supply curve reflects the rise in the competitive wage rate; it is now horizontal at a wage rate of $21 (labelled $W = \$21$). The equilibrium is at the intersection of these curves and corresponds to a wage rate of $21 and a quantity of labor hired of 3 units.

4. a) The equilibrium wage rate is $4 per hour and the quantity of labor hired is 80 hours.

b) Total income is $4 per hour times 80 hours: $320.

c) See Fig. 14.2. The supply of labor is given by S and the initial demand for labor is represented by D. The equilibrium occurs at the intersection of these two curves. the equilibrium wage is seen to be $4 per hour and the quantity of labor is 80 hours.

d) Given that the supply of labor curve starts at the origin, half of income is transfer earnings (the area below the supply curve) and the other half is economic rent (the area above the supply curve). Since income is $320, each of these is $160.

Figure 14.2

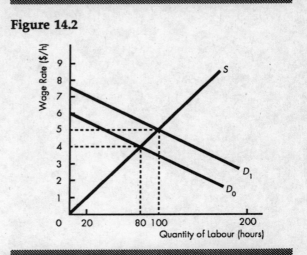

5. a) Each entry in the last column of Table 14.2 Solution will increase by 60 units. The new equilibrium wage rate is $5 per hour and the equilibrium quantity of labor is 100 hours. The new labor demand curve appears in Fig. 14.2 as D'.

b) Total income is now $500 (100 hours of labor times $5 an hour).

c) Transfer earnings and economic rent are each $250. Once again, the nature of the labor supply curve implies that in our case, income is split evenly between them.

15 LABOR MARKETS

CHAPTER IN PERSPECTIVE

Labor markets play a very important role in the economic well-being of almost every household since household income is largely determined by the operation of these markets. This chapter looks carefully at labor markets in an attempt to explain how wage rates and employment levels are determined. We investigate why some groups earn more than other groups: why skilled workers earn more than unskilled workers; why union workers earn more than nonunion workers; why, on average, men earn more than women and whites earn more than minorities.

LEARNING OBJECTIVES

After studying this chapter, you will be able to:

- **Explain why skilled workers earn more, on the average, than unskilled workers**

- **Explain why college graduates earn more, on the average, than high school graduates**

- **Explain why union workers earn higher wages than nonunion workers**

- **Explain why, on the average, men earn more than women and whites earn more than minorities**

- **Predict the effects of a comparable worth program**

HELPFUL HINTS

1. This chapter introduces the concept of a monopsonist, a firm which is the only *buyer* in a market (for labor, for example). The monopsonist faces an upward-sloping supply curve of labor and, as a result, its marginal cost of labor curve (MCL) is different from the labor supply curve.

There is a close parallel between a) the relationship between the labor supply curve and the MCL curve for the monopsonist and b) the already familiar relationship (Chapter 12) between the demand curve and the marginal revenue curve (MR) for the monopolist. Both sets of relationships stem from the assumption of a single price for labor or output in the relevant market.

The monopolist, as the only seller in an output market, faces a downward-sloping demand curve. The marginal revenue from the sale of an additional unit of output is *less* than the selling price because the monpolist must *lower* the price on all previous units as well. Thus, the MR curve lies *below* the demand curve for the monopolist.

For the monopsonist in a labor market, the marginal cost of hiring an additional unit of labor is *higher* than the wage because the monopsonist must *raise* the wage on all previous units of labor as well. Thus, the MCL curve lies *above* the supply of labor curve for the monopsonist.

2. This chapter also discusses wage differences between the sexes and the races. These are issues of considerable importance but popular discussion of them are frequently fraught with emotional and normative overtones. You will gain greater insight if you remember what we learned in Chapter 1: as a science, economics is positive rather than normative; it is concerned about what *is* and is silent about what *ought* to be.

KEY FIGURES AND TABLES

Figure 15.1 Skill Differentials
Different workers receive different wages depending on level of skill. This figure shows how that difference in wages can be explained using the model of competitive labor markets.

Part (a) of the figure shows that the demand for skilled labor is higher than the demand for unskilled labor because it has a higher marginal revenue product. The vertical distance between the two demand curves gives the difference in marginal revenue product; that is, the marginal revenue product of the skill.

Part (b) gives the supply curves for skilled and unskilled labor. It illustrates that the supply curve for skilled labor will lie above the supply curve for unskilled labor because skills are costly to obtain. As a result, skilled labor must receive a higher wage in order to induce workers to obtain the skill. The vertical distance between the two labor supply curves gives the required additional wage.

Part (c) puts the demand and supply curves from parts (a) and (b) together in order to look at the equilibrium wage rates for each type of labor. Not surprisingly, the equilibrium wage rate for skilled workers will be higher than for unskilled workers.

Figure 15.4 A Union in a Competitive Labor Market
This figure shows the consequences for the wage rate and quantity of labor employed when a union operates in a previously competitive labor market.

The competitive demand for labor and the competitive supply of labor are indicated by D_C and S_C, respectively. In the competitive market the equilibrium wage rate is $4 an hour and 100 hours of labor are employed.

The principal method by which a union causes the wage rate to rise is to restrict the supply of labor. Thus the union supply of labor is given by S_U. If this is all the union does, the wage rate will rise to $10 an hour and employment will fall to 62.5 hours. If, in addition to restricting supply, the union is also able to increase the demand for its labor, the union demand curve, D_U, will be to the right of the competitive demand curve. In this case, the wage rate will be even higher ($16 an hour in this example) and employment will rise to 75 hours.

Figure 15.8 Discrimination

This figure illustrates how discrimination will affect wage rates and employment. Part (a) shows that discrimination against a particular class of workers (in this case, black female investment advisors) will reduce wages and employment below what they would have been in the absence of discrimination. The reason is that the effective marginal revenue product under discrimination, MRP_{DA}, is lower than the marginal revenue product without discrimination, MRP, since employers are only willing to hire at a lower wage due to prejudice.

Part (b) shows that discrimination in favor of a particular group (in the example, white male investment advisors) will have the effect of raising the wage and the level of employment above what they would have been without discrimination.

Table 15.1 A Compact Glossary on Unions

This table conveniently brings together much of the terminology associated with labor unions. It offers definitions of terms used frequently in analyzing the operation of unions in the economy.

CONCEPT REVIEW

1. The demand curve for skilled labor lies _____ the demand curve for unskilled labor, because the marginal revenue product of skilled workers is _____ than that of unskilled workers. The supply curve for skilled labor lies_____ the supply curve for unskilled labor, because skills are costly to acquire.

2. Education and training can be viewed as investments in _____ capital. The value of that capital is the _____ _____ of the extra future earnings as a result of the increased education or training.

3. There are two main types of unions. A union that organizes workers with similar skills but who work for many different firms or industries is called a(n) _____ union. A(n) _____ union organizes workers with a variety of skills but who work for the same firm or industry.

4. A union work arrangement in which workers have the right to be employed without joining a union is called a(n) _____ shop. An arrangement in which a firm can hire nonunion workers,

but the workers must join the union to remain employed, is called a(n) _____ shop.

5. A market in which there is only one buyer is called _____. If there is only one firm which buys labor, the wage rate will be _____ than the marginal cost of labor. A situation in which a single seller of labor (e.g., a union) faces a single buyer of labor is called _____ monopoly.

6. Certain identifiable groups (e.g., white males) have higher earnings than other groups (e.g., black females). Three possible explanations of these differences are discussed in Chapter 15. The first explanation is discrimination. The second possible explanation is that the two groups have differences in _____ capital. The third possible explanation is that there are differences in the degree of _____ in market and nonmarket activities.

7. Paying the same wage for different jobs, but jobs which are judged to be comparable is called _____ _____.

TRUE OR FALSE

____ 1. The marginal revenue product of unskilled workers is higher than that of skilled workers.

____ 2. The vertical distance between the labor supply curves for skilled and unskilled workers is the compensation for the cost of acquiring the skill.

____ 3. The larger the marginal revenue product of a skill and the more costly it is to acquire, the smaller is the wage differential between skilled and unskilled workers.

____ 4. A closed shop refers to a firm that is not operating because its workers are on strike.

____ 5. A right-to-work law makes a union shop illegal.

____ 6. A lockout occurs when a firm refuses to employ its workers or operate its plant.

____ 7. Unions support minimum wage laws in part because they increase the cost of unskilled labor, a substitute for skilled union labor.

____ 8. A firm that is a monopsonist in the labor market must compete with other firms for the labor it hires.

____ 9. For a firm that is a monopsonist in the labor market, the supply curve of labor is the marginal cost of labor curve.

____ 10. The more elastic is labor supply, the less opportunity a monopsonist has to make an economic profit.

____ 11. In a monopsonistic labor market, the introduction of a minimum wage that is above the current wage will raise the wage but reduce employment.

____12. In the case of bilateral monopoly in a labor market, the wage is indeterminate; the wage depends on the bargaining strength of the two traders.

____13. The evidence suggests that, after allowing for the effects of skill differentials, union workers earn no more than nonunion workers.

____14. Economic theory tells us that discrimination in employment will result in wage differentials.

____15. If white males on average earn more than black females, we can conclude that there must be discrimination.

____16. Comparable worth means paying comparable salaries for the same job.

MULTIPLE CHOICE

1. Which of the following is NOT a reason why the wage of skilled workers exceeds the wage of unskilled workers?
   a. The market for skilled workers is more competitive than the market for unskilled labor.
   b. The marginal revenue product of skilled workers is greater than that of unskilled workers.
   c. The cost of training skilled workers is greater than the cost of training unskilled workers.
   d. Skilled workers have acquired more human capital than unskilled workers.

2. Other things remaining the same, if education costs rise substantially we would expect to see
   a. a decrease in the marginal revenue product of skilled workers.
   b. a decrease in the supply of unskilled workers.
   c. an increase in the wage received by skilled workers.
   d. an increase in the number of skilled workers employed.

3. The economic value of the increase in human capital due to additional education is
   a. the money cost of the additional education.
   b. the money cost of the additional education plus forgone earnings.
   c. the present value of all expected future earnings.
   d. the present value of all extra expected future earnings that are the result of the additional education.

4. A union working arrangement in which all workers must be members of the union before they can be hired by the firm is called
   a. an open shop.
   b. a closed shop.
   c. a union shop.
   d. a craft shop.

5. A union that organizes workers with a similar skill regardless of the firm or industry that employs them is
   a. an industrial union.
   b. a craft union.
   c. a local union.
   d. a national union.

6. Which of the following would unions be <u>LEAST</u> likely to support?
   a. An increase in the legal minimum wage
   b. Immigration restrictions
   c. Reducing barriers to imports
   d. Increasing demand for the goods their workers produce

7. The most important way in which unions increase wages is by
   a. increasing the marginal (physical) product of labor.
   b. increasing the marginal revenue product of labor.
   c. increasing the demand for labor.
   d. decreasing the supply for labor.

8. When compared to a competitive labor market with the same marginal revenue product and labor supply curves, a monopsonist labor market will pay a
   a. lower wage and employ fewer workers.
   b. lower wage and employ more workers.
   c. higher wage and employ fewer workers.
   d. higher wage and employ more workers.

9. Figure 15.1 illustrates a monopsonist in the labor market (*MCL* = marginal cost of labor). The profit maximizing wage rate and quantity of labor hired will be
   a. $4 per hour and 800 hours of labor.
   b. $4 per hour and 400 hours of labor.
   c. $7 per hour and 600 hours of labor.
   d. $9 per hour and 400 hours of labor.

10. If the labor market illustrated in Fig. 15.1 became competitive, the equilibrium wage rate and quantity of labor hired would be
    a. $4 per hour and 800 hours of labor.
    b. $4 per hour and 400 hours of labor.
    c. $7 per hour and 600 hours of labor.
    d. $9 per hour and 400 hours of labor.

Figure 15.1

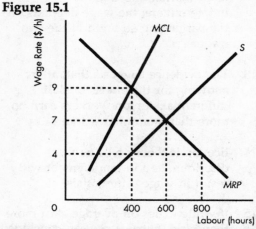

11. Consider two types of workers: types A and B. In competitive labor markets the wage paid to type A workers is substantially higher than the wage paid to type B workers. Suppose that a comparable worth law is enacted and type A and B workers are judged to be comparable. Furthermore, assume that to equalize wages, the wage rate for type B workers rises and the wage rate for type A workers falls. We can conclude that
    a. employment of type A worker will rise while employment of type B workers will fall.
    b. employment of type A workers will fall while employment of type B workers will rise.
    c. employment of both types of workers will rise.
    d. employment of both types of workers will fall.

12. If discrimination takes the form of restricting a group's access to education and training, the effect on this group of workers will be to shift the
    a. marginal revenue product curve to the right and increase the wage.
    b. marginal revenue product curve to the left and decrease the wage.
    c. supply of labor curve up and decrease the wage.
    d. supply of labor curve down and decrease the wage.

SHORT ANSWER

1. Why does the demand curve for skilled labor lie above the demand curve for unskilled labor?

2. Why does the supply curve of skilled labor lie above the supply curve for unskilled labor?

3. In a labor market without a union, the wage rate is determined by the intersection of the supply and demand curves for labor. How, in general, do unions cause wage rates to rise?

4. How are professional associations (e.g., the American Medical Association) like unions?

5. Members of labor unions earn wages well above the minimum wage. Even so, why is it in the interest of a union to support increases in the legal minimum wage?

6. Bob and Sue form a household. They have decided that Sue will fully specialize in market activity and Bob will pursue activities both in the job market and in the household. If most households are like Bob and Sue, why would the result be a difference between the earnings of men

and women, even if there is no discrimination?

PROBLEMS

1. Figure 15.2 shows the demand and supply of skilled and unskilled labor. S_U and S_S are the supply curves for unskilled and skilled workers respectively and D_U and D_S are the demand curves for unskilled and skilled workers respectively.
    a) What is the marginal revenue product of skill if 5,000 hours of each kind of labor are hired?
    b) What is the amount of extra compensation (per hour) required to induce the acquisition of skill at the same level of hiring ?
    c) What are the equilibrium wage and quantity of labor in the market for skilled labor?
    d) What are the equilibrium wage and quantity of labor in the market for unskilled labor?

Figure 15.2

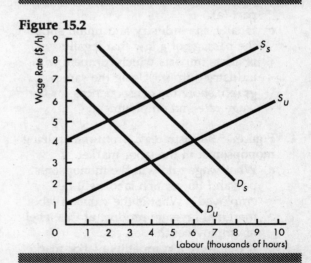

2. Jim has an opportunity to increase his human capital by taking a training course that will raise his income by $100 every year for the rest of his life. Assume that

there are no other benefits of the course. The cost of the course is $1200 and Jim's best alternative investment pays an interest rate of 10 percent. Should Jim pay the $1200 and take the course? Explain.

3. Initially we observe an industry facing a competitive labor market in which the supply of labor comes from two sources: domestic workers and foreign workers. All workers have similar skills. Also assume that the output of the industry competes with imported goods.
   a) Graphically represent the initial competitive labor market. Draw the labor demand and supply curves and identify the equilibrium wage rate and level of employment.
   b) Now suppose a union consisting of domestic workers is formed. Through its support a law is passed which prohibits firms from hiring foreign workers. What effect will this have on employment and the wage rate? Illustrate graphically using the graph in part (a).
   c) Finally, the industry and union support the passage of a law that legally restricts imports which compete with industry output. Using the same graph, show the consequences for the wage rate and employment.

4. Figure 15.3 illustrates a profit-maximizing monopsonist in the labor market.
   a) What wage rate will the monopsonist pay and how much labor will be employed? What is the value of labor's marginal revenue product at this level of employment?
   b) If this were a competitive labor market with the same marginal revenue product curve, what would the equilibrium wage rate and level of employment be?

c) Now, suppose the government imposes a minimum wage of $4 per hour. What wage rate will the monopsonist pay and how much labor will be employed now?

Figure 15.3

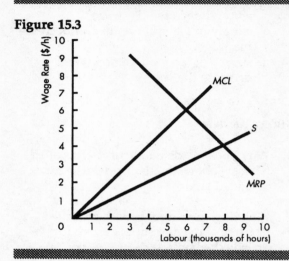

5. Figure 15.4 (a) illustrates the market for plumbers and Figure 15.4 (b) illustrates the market for secretaries. Both of these labor markets are competitive.
   a) What are the wage rates and employment levels for plumbers and secretaries?
   b) Suppose that under a legally enforced comparable worth program these two jobs are judged to be comparable and therefore must pay the same wage. Consider the following three possible ways of equalizing wages. In each case determine the amount of employment for plumbers and secretaries that will result. Also determine the amount of any excess supply of labor or excess demand for labor that will result.
      i) The wage rate for plumbers is reduced to $6 per hour and the wage rate for secretaries is increased to $6.

ii) The wage rate for secretaries is increased to $8.

iii) The wage rate for plumbers is reduced to $4.

Figure 15.4

(a)

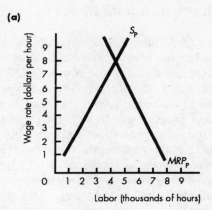

(b)

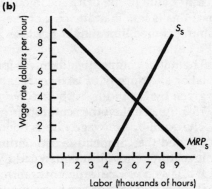

ANSWERS

ANSWERS

CONCEPT REVIEW

1. above; greater; above
2. human; present value
3. craft; industrial
4. open; union
5. monopsony; lower; bilateral
6. human; specialization
7. comparable worth;

TRUE OR FALSE

1. F	5. T	9. F	13. F
2. T	6. T	10. T	14. T
3. F	7. T	11. F	15. F
4. F	8. F	12. T	16. F

MULTIPLE CHOICE

1. a	4. b	7. d	10. c
2. c	5. b	8. a	11. d
3. d	6. c	9. b	12. d

SHORT ANSWER

1. The marginal revenue product of skilled workers is greater than that of unskilled workers. As a result, the demand curve for skilled labor will lie above the demand curve for unskilled labor.

2. It is costly to obtain skills (i.e., it requires training or education). The height of the labor supply curve reflects the cost of acquiring the relevant skill. Therefore the supply curve of skilled labor will lie above the supply curve of unskilled labor.

3. In general, unions cause wage rates to rise by restricting the supply of labor below its competitive level. Thus the increase in wage rates is at the expense of reduced employment.

4. Professional associations (like the AMA.) are like labor unions because they also restrict the supply of "labor" with which they must compete.

5. An increase in the minimum wage will increase the cost of hiring unskilled labor, which will tend to increase the demand for skilled labor (a substitute).

6. If Sue specializes in market activity while Bob is diversified, it is likely that Sue's earning ability will exceed Bob's due to the gains from her specialization. If most households followed this pattern of specialization, the income of women would exceed that of men even without discrimination.

PROBLEMS

1. a) The marginal revenue product of skill is the difference between the marginal revenue products of skilled versus unskilled labor; that is, the vertical distance between the demand curves for skilled and unskilled labor. In Fig. 15.2, the marginal revenue product of skill is $3 per hour when 5000 hours of each kind of labor are employed.

   b) Since labor supply curves give the minimum compensation workers are willing to accept in return for supplying a given quantity of labor, the extra compensation for skill is the vertical distance between the supply curves of skilled and unskilled labor. At 5,000 hours of employment for both kinds of labor, this is $3 per hour.

c) In equilibrium in the market for skilled labor, the wage rate will be $6 per hour and employment will be 4000 hours of labor. This occurs at the intersection of the D_S and S_S curves.

   d) In equilibrium in the market for unskilled labor, the wage rate will be $3 per hour and employment will be 4000 hours of labor. This occurs at the intersection of the D_U and S_U curves.

2. Jim should take the course only if the value of the course exceeds the cost of the course. The cost of the course is $1200 while the value of the course is the *present value* of the extra $100 in income Jim can expect to receive each year for the rest of his life. The present value of this income stream is the amount of money which, if invested today at 10 percent (Jim's best alternative return) would yield an equivalent stream of income. Thus the present value of the extra income is $1000. Since this is less than the cost of the training course, Jim should not take it.

3. a) The initial competitive demand for labor and supply of labor curves are given by D_C and S_C respectively in Fig. 15.5 (ignore the other curves for now). The equilibrium wage rate is denoted W_C and the competitive equilibrium level of employment is denoted Q_C.

   b) If a law is passed prohibiting firms from hiring foreign workers, the labor supply curve (now under a union) will shift to the left (to S_U in Fig. 15.5 above). This will have the effect of raising the wage rate (to W_1 in the figure) and decreasing the quantity of labor employed (to Q_1 in the figure).

   c) Restrictions on imports will increase the demand for the product produced in the industry and thus increase the derived demand (marginal revenue product) of labor in the industry. In Fig. 15.5 this is illustrated by a shift from D_C to D_U. The result will be a further increase in the wage rate (to W_2 in the diagram) and an increase in employment (to Q_2 in the diagram). Whether the quantity of labor hired now exceeds the initial competitive quantity depends on the magnitude of the shift in the labor demand curve.

Figure 15.5

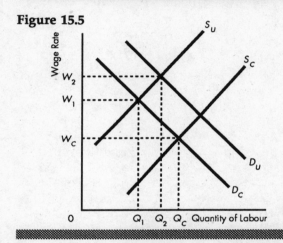

4. a) The profit-maximizing monopsonist will hire additional labor up to the point where the marginal cost of labor (*MCL*) equals the marginal revenue product of labor (*MRP*). Referring to Fig. 15.3, this means that the monopsonist illustrated there will hire 6000 hours of labor. The wage rate is given by the labor supply curve S and, for 6000 hours of labor, will be $3 per hour. This is less than the $6 per hour marginal revenue product of labor.
   b) In a competitive market, the wage rate would be $4 per hour and 8000 hours of labor would be employed.
   c) If the government establishes a minimum wage at $4 per hour, the marginal cost of labor to the monopsonist becomes constant at $4 per hour (up to 8000 hours of labor). Thus, equating the marginal cost of

labor and the marginal revenue product of labor leads to a wage rate of $4 and 8000 hours of labor employed.

5. a) In a competitive market, the wage rate for plumbers will be $8 per hour and 4000 plumber hours will be purchased. The wage rate for secretaries will be $4 per hour and 6000 secretary hours will be purchased.
   b) i) If the wage rate is equalized at $6 per hour:
      • Plumber employment will fall to 3000 hours.
      • Secretary employment will fall to 4000 hours.
      • There will be an excess demand for plumbers in the amount of 2000 hours.
      • There will be an excess supply of secretaries in the amount of 3000 hours.
      ii) If the wage rate is equalized at $8 per hour:
      • Plumber employment will remain at 4000 hours.
      • Secretary employment will fall to 2000 hours.
      • There will be no excess demand for plumbers.
      • The excess supply of secretaries will be 6000 hours.
      iii) If the wage rate is equalized at $4 per hour:
      • Plumber employment will fall to 2000 hours.
      • Secretary employment will remain at 6000 hours.
      • The excess demand for plumbers will be 4000 hours.
      • There will be no excess supply of secretaries.

16 CAPITAL AND NATURAL RESOURCE MARKETS

CHAPTER IN PERSPECTIVE

This chapter continues a more detailed examination of markets for specific factors of production. In Chapter 15 we looked closely at labor markets. Here we expand our understanding of capital and natural resource markets. What determines interest rates and stock prices? How are the prices of natural resources determined. Can we rely on natural market forces to regulate the use of exhaustible resources? These and related issues are discussed in this chapter.

LEARNING OBJECTIVES

After studying this chapter, you will be able to:

- Define and distinguish among financial and physical assets, capital, and investment

- Define and distinguish between saving and portfolio choice

- Describe the structure of capital markets in the United States today

- Explain how interest rates and stock prices are determined and why the stock market fluctuates

- Define natural resources and explain how their prices are determined

- Explain how markets regulate the pace at which we use exhaustible resources such as oil

HELPFUL HINTS

1. A profit-maximizing firm will hire an additional unit of a factor as long as its use adds more to revenue than to cost; in other word, as long as its marginal revenue product (MRP) is greater than its marginal cost (MC). Thus, the profit-maximizing quantity will be the quantity at which the marginal revenue product of a factor is just equal to its marginal cost. Since, in a competitive market, the marginal cost is the price of the factor (P_F), this profit-maximizing becomes $MRP = P_F$ in a competitive factor market. This implies that the demand curve for a factor is given by its MRP curve.

2. The profit-maximizing condition given in Hint 1 is straightforward to apply in the case of capital markets in which capital is rented. The profit-maximizing firm will rent capital up to the point at which the marginal revenue product per rental period is equal to the rental price.

If, however, a firm considers purchasing capital rather than renting it, we must be careful in applying the profit-maximizing condition. The reason is that capital is generally operated over more than one period and thus will generate marginal revenue products which are distributed over time. The purchase price, however, must be paid now. Therefore, in order to compare the purchase price (P_F) with the stream of marginal revenue products we must compute the present value of that stream.

Thus, in the case of capital which will be used over more than one period, the profit-maximizing condition becomes the present value of the stream of marginal revenue products is equal to the price of the unit of capital. Since the *net* present value is defined as the difference between the present value of the stream of marginal revenue products and the price of the unit of capital, an equivalent condition is the net present value of the last unit of capital is zero. (If you need to review

the concept of present value, return to Chapter 9.)

KEY FIGURES AND TABLES

Figure 16.1 Capital Market Flows
This diagram shows the major participants in capital markets and indicates the directions of interactions among them. Households purchase some capital directly (proprietorships and partnerships) and finance the purchase of other capital indirectly through the stock and bond markets and by making deposits in financial intermediaries. These financial intermediaries then use these deposited funds to make loans to households and firms. Financial intermediaries also buy and sell stocks and bonds. Firms finance capital purchases through direct purchase of capital by households, selling stocks and bonds, and by borrowing from financial intermediaries.

Figure 16.2 The Nation's Balance Sheet
The nation's balance sheet combines the balance sheets of households, financial intermediaries, firms, and governments. Financial assets (in blue) and liabilities (in red) for each of these are shown in the top part of the figure as well as the direction of the flow of funds (by green arrows). The bottom part of the figure shows capital (real asset) holdings by each of the four sectors.

Note that total financial asset holdings of households greatly exceed their financial liabilities. Thus, households are net suppliers of funds to the other sectors through deposits in financial intermediaries, savings in life insurance and pension funds, and holding of stocks and bonds. Financial intermediaries have both financial assets and liabilities while firms and governments have only financial liabilities.

Figure 16.6 Capital Market Equilibrium

Equilibrium in the capital market is achieved at the interest rate at which the quantity of capital demanded is equal to the quantity of capital supplied. For the example illustrated in this figure, the equilibrium interest rate is 6 percent and the equilibrium quantity of capital traded is $10 trillion.

Table 16.1 Balance Sheet of Rocky's Mountain Bikes

A balance sheet is a list of assets and liabilities. This table illustrates the concept of a balance sheet by reporting the assets and liabilities of Rocky's Mountain Bikes. The firm's assets (items owned by the firm) are listed on the left-hand side of the table, and the firm's liabilities (money the firm owes — to the bank and to Rocky) are listed on the right. Note that the two sides of the balance sheet balance because total assets equal total liabilities.

Table 16.2 Financial Assets and Physical Assets of Rocky's Mountain Bikes

This table uses the same information contained in the balance sheet of Table 16.1, but distinguishes between financial assets and physical assets. Some of the firm's assets and liabilities are financial and some of its assets are physical assets.

Thetop part of the table lists the firm's financial assets and liabilities, which consist of cash in the bank (an asset), a bank loan (a liability), and Rocky's equity (also a liability of the firm). Net financial assets are financial assets minus financial liabilities. For this firm, net financial assets are -$225,000 since financial liabilities exceed financial assets.

The bottom part of the table lists the firm's physical assets, which consist of its inventory of bikes and fixtures and fittings. Total capital is $225,000.

Table 16.5 Net Present Value of an Investment—Taxfile, Inc.

A firm will decide to purchase an additional unit of capital if the net present value of the investment is positive; that is, if the present value of the marginal revenue product of the investment is greater than the price of the unit of capital. The calculation of net present value is illustrated in this table using the example of Tina's decision to purchase a new computer for her firm, Taxfile, Inc.

Part (a) of the table reports the information necessary to compute the net present value of the investment: the price of the computer, the life of the computer, the marginal revenue product in each year, and the interest rate.

Part (b) uses this information to compute the present value of the marginal revenue product.

In part (c), the price of the computer is subtracted from the present value of the marginal revenue product of the computer to obtain the net present value of the investment. Since the net present value is positive, it pays Tina to buy the computer.

SELF-TEST

CONCEPT REVIEW

1. There are two broad classes of assets. Those which are paper claims against a household, firm or the government are _____ assets. Assets like buildings, factories, and machinery are _____ assets.

2. The choices by households regarding which assets to hold and what liabilities to have are called _____ choices. The purchase of new capital by a firm or a household is called _____.

3. Firms whose principal business is taking deposits, making loans, and buying securities are called financial _____.

4. A firm maximizes its net worth when the _____ _____ of the marginal revenue product of capital is equal to the price of capital. Thus an increase in the interest rate means that the quantity of capital demanded will _____.

5. The quantity of capital supplied depends on the _____ decisions of households. As the interest rate increases, the substitution effect causes a(n) _____ in the quantity of capital supplied by the household; the income effect causes a(n) _____ in the quantity of capital supplied if the household is a net borrower. If the proportion of young people in the population increases, we would expect to see the capital supply curve shift to the _____.

6. The ratio of the current price of a share of a stock to the most recent year's profit per share is called the _____-_____ ratio. This ratio will fall if future profits are expected to _____.

7. A takeover occurs when the stock market value of a firm is _____ than the present value of expected future profits from operating the firm. A merger occurs when the two firms involved think that by combining their assets, their combined stock market value will _____.

8. Natural resources that can only be used once and not replaced are called _____ natural resources. According to the Hotelling Principle, the market for the stock of such a resource will be in equilibrium when the price of the resource is expected to rise over time, at a rate equal to the _____ _____.

9. The price at which it no longer pays to use a natural resource is called its _____ price.

10. The higher the interest rate, the _____ will be the current price of a natural resource. The higher the marginal revenue product of a natural resource, the _____ will be its current price. The larger is the initial stock of a natural resource, the _____ will be its current price.

TRUE OR FALSE

____ 1. Net financial assets can be zero for a household but never negative.

____ 2. If we add depreciation to net investment, we get gross investment.

_____ 3. Depositing wealth in a financial intermediary is generally safer than buying stocks or bonds.

_____ 4. If the price of a unit of capital exceeds the present value of its marginal revenue product, a profit-maximizing firm should buy it.

_____ 5. If the net present value of an investment is positive, a profit-maximizing firm will buy the item.

_____ 6. A new machine that is expected to last one year and (at the end of the year) increase firm revenue by $1050 sells at a price of $1000. The firm should buy the machine if the interest rate is 6 percent.

_____ 7. As the average age of the population increases (other things remaining unchanged), the supply of capital is likely to increase.

_____ 8. If a household has positive net financial assets, the income effect of a *decrease* in the interest rate will be to increase its saving.

_____ 9. In equilibrium, if financial asset A is riskier than financial asset B, it will have a higher rate of interest.

_____10. To say that the price of a bond has risen is the same as saying that the yield on the bond has declined.

_____11. The current price of a stock is the present value of the firm's expected future profits.

_____12. When current profit is quite high relative to expected future profits, the price-earnings ratio of the firm will be high.

_____13. Large stock price changes with low volume of trading implies wide agreement that something fundamental has changed.

_____14. A takeover of firm A by firm B would occur if firm B believes that the stock market value of firm A is greater than the present value of expected potential future profits.

_____15. While markets may be good at efficiently allocating goods that can be replaced or reproduced, they cannot allocate exhaustible natural resources efficiently.

_____16. If a cheap substitute for oil is developed, we would expect to see the choke price for oil decline.

_____17. The higher the interest rate, the lower is the current price of a natural resource.

_____18. The economic model of exhaustible natural resources implies that the market will provide an automatic incentive to conserve as the resource gets closer to being depleted.

MULTIPLE CHOICE

1. Which of the following is a physical asset?
   a. A shovel
   b. IBM stock
   c. Money
   d. A General Motors bond

2. The decline in the value of capital resulting from its use over time is given by
   a. the level of saving.
   b. investment.
   c. net investment.
   d. gross investment minus net investment.

3. Household determination of how much to hold in various assets and how much to owe in various liabilities is called
   a. investment.
   b. balance sheet decision making.
   c. portfolio choice.
   d. the price-earnings problem.

4. Firms that are primarily engaged in taking deposits, making loans, and buying securities are called
   a. brokers.
   b. financial intermediaries.
   c. insurance companies.
   d. monopsonists.

5. A profit-maximizing firm will choose to buy an extra unit of capital whenever
   a. its net present value is greater than zero.
   b. its net marginal revenue product is greater than zero.
   c. the present value of expected future profit is greater than zero.
   d. the present value of expected future profit exceeds the market rate of interest.

6. The higher the rate of interest
   a. the higher the net present value of an investment.
   b. the lower the present value of the stream of marginal revenue products of an investment.
   c. the greater the quantity of capital demanded.
   d. the greater the marginal revenue product of capital.

7. If the interest rate increases, the
   a. substitution effect encourages more saving only if the household is a net borrower.
   b. substitution effect encourages more saving only if the household is a net lender.
   c. income effect encourages more saving only if the household is a net borrower.
   d. income effect encourages more saving only if the household is a net lender.

8. Which of the following would cause the supply of capital curve to shift to the right?
   a. An increase in the proportion of young households in the population.
   b. An increase in the interest rate.
   c. An increase in average household income.
   d. An increase in the marginal revenue product of capital.

9. A machine that costs $2000 will generate marginal revenue product of $1100 at the end of one year and the same amount at the end of two years. What is the net present value of the machine if the rate of interest is 10 percent?
   a. -$90.91
   b. -$49.90
   c. 0
   d. $90.91

10. The yield on a stock will rise if
    a. either the dividend increases or the share price of the stock increases.
    b. either the dividend increases or the share price of the stock decreases.
    c. either the dividend decreases or the share price of the stock increases.
    d. either the dividend decreases or the share price of the stock decreases.

11. Bond A is more risky than bond B. Then, in equilibrium,
    a. the interest rate on A must be higher than that on B.
    b. the interest rate on A must be lower than that on B.
    c. no one will want to buy bond A.
    d. only those who prefer risk will buy bond A.

12. A firm is expected to pay an $8 dividend per share of stock each year into the indefinite future. If the market rate of interest is 8 percent, the price of a share of stock in this firm will be
    a. $8.
    b. $64.
    c. $80.
    d. $100.

13. The price of a share of XYZ Corporation's stock is $80, and the current dividend payment is $4. The stock yield is
    a. 4 percent.
    b. 5 percent.
    c. 8 percent.
    d. 20 percent.

14. A newly issued bond promises to pay $100 at the end of one year plus a $10 interest payment. If the price of the bond today is $98, what is its yield?
    a. 2 percent
    b. 8 percent
    c. 11 percent
    d. 12 percent

15. An event occurs which almost everyone agrees will cause a decline in the future profit of the XYZ Corporation. Immediately after the event becomes known, what would we expect to observe with regard to XYZ stock?
    a. The stock price will fluctuate up and down with a high volume of trading.
    b. The stock price will fall gradually with a high volume of trading.
    c. The stock price will fall quickly with a low volume of trading.
    d. The stock price will fall quickly with a high volume of trading.

16. A *takeover* of a firm is likely to occur when
    a. the stock market value of the firm is higher than expected future profit from operating the firm.
    b. the stock market value of the firm is lower than expected future profit from operating the firm.
    c. current firm profit is higher than expected future profit from operating the firm.
    d. current firm profit is lower than expected future profit from operating the firm.

17. Which of the following is an exhaustible natural resource?
    a. Coal
    b. Land
    c. Water
    d. Trees

18. The yield on a stock of a natural resource is
    a. the rate of interest on the loan used to buy the resource.
    b. the marginal revenue product of the resource divided by its price.
    c. the marginal revenue product of the resource multiplied by the market interest rate.
    d. the rate of change in the price of the resource.

19. If the market for a stock of a natural resource is in equilibrium, then it must be that the price of the resource is
   a. expected to rise at a rate equal to the rate of interest.
   b. equal to the choke price of the resource.
   c. equal to the marginal revenue product of the resource.
   d. equal to the Hotelling price of the resource.

20. The *current* price of a natural resource is higher, the
   a. lower its marginal revenue product.
   b. larger is the stock of the resource remaining.
   c. lower the interest rate.
   d. lower the choke price.

SHORT ANSWER

1. Why does the quantity of capital demanded increase when the interest rate falls?

2. Explain the substitution effect of a decline in the interest rate on the level of saving.

3. Suppose the interest rate increases. Why is the income effect on saving negative if the household is a net borrower?

4. Explain why an increase in the price of an asset means that the yield on the asset has declined.

5. Suppose firms A and B earned the same amount of profit per share in the most recent year but that the price of a share of stock in firm A is higher than for firm B. What does this imply about the two firms' price-earnings ratios? What does this reflect about expected future profits of the two firms?

6. Exxoff Oil Company experiences a large and potentially very costly oil spill Sunday night. What can we infer about the degree of consensus among stock market participants' beliefs if on Monday
   a) the price of Exxoff stock declines significantly at the opening of the stock market and remains there.
   b) the price of Exxoff stock fluctuates narrowly all day with a large volume of trade.

7. When will a takeover occur?

8. Why will the market for the stock of an exhaustible natural resource be in equilibrium only if the price of the resource is expected to rise at a rate equal to the rate of interest?

9. What is meant by the choke price of a natural resource?

10. Why does a higher interest rate imply a lower current price of an exhaustible resource?

PROBLEMS

1. Larry's Lawn Care began the year with a stock of capital equal to $100,000. The value of that stock of capital depreciated by 12 percent during the year. Larry also bought $10,000 worth of new lawn care equipment during the year. What was Larry's gross investment during the year? Net investment?

2. Larry's Lawn Care is considering the purchase of additional lawn mowers. These lawn mowers have a life of two years and cost $120 each. Marginal revenue products for each year are given in Table 16.1.
   a) Complete Table 16.1 by computing net present values (*NPV*) if the interest rate

is 5 percent ($r = .05$), 10 percent ($r = .10$), or 15 percent ($r = .15$).

b) How many lawn mowers will Larry's purchase if the interest rate is 15 percent? 10 percent? 5 percent?

c) Construct an approximate lawn mower demand curve for Larry's by graphically representing the three points identified in part (b) and drawing a curve through them.

Table 16.1

Number of lawn mowers	MRP in first year ($)	MRP in second year ($)	NPV ($r = 0.05$)	NPV ($r = 0.10$)	NPV ($r = 0.15$)
1	100	80			
2	80	64			
3	72	62			

3. Suppose the price of a lawn mower rises to $130.

a) Compute the new net present values at each interest rate.

b) What has happened to Larry's demand curve for mowers?

4. The present value of expected future profits for Larry's Lawn Care is $400,000. There are 800 outstanding shares of stock in Larry's Lawn Care. The dividend paid in the current year was $7.50 a share.

a) What is the market price of a share of Larry's Lawn Care stock?

b) What is the stock yield?

5. The city of Metropolis (in which Larry's operates) initiates a "Yard Beautiful" award with a cash prize. As a result, the present value of expected future profits for Larry's Lawn Care increases to $600,000.

a) What is the market price of a share of Larry's Lawn Care stock now?

b) If the dividend remains at $7.50 a share, what is the stock yield?

6. Gunk is an exhaustible natural resource and we are running out of it. There are only 1215 barrels of gunk remaining. Table 16.2 gives the marginal revenue product schedule for gunk.

a) Draw a graph of the demand curve for gunk (as a flow).

b) What is the choke price of gunk?

Table 16.2

Barrels of gunk per year	Marginal revenue product (dollars)
0	14.64
133	13.31
254	12.10
364	11.00
464	10.00
555	9.09

7. Suppose that the interest rate is 10 percent.

a) What is the current equilibrium price of a barrel of gunk? How did you determine this?

b) If the current year is year 1, complete Table 16.3 below for each year until the stock of gunk is exhausted.

Table 16.3

Year	Price	Initial stock of gunk	Final stock of gunk
1			1215
2			
3			
4			
5			

ANSWERS

CONCEPT REVIEW

1. financial; physical

2. portfolio; investment

3. intermediaries

4. present value; decrease

5. savings; increase; decrease; left

6. price-earnings; fall

7. lower; increase

8. exhaustible; interest rate

9. choke

10. lower; higher; lower

TRUE OR FALSE

1. F	5. T	9. T	13. T	17. T
2. T	6. F	10. T	14. F	18. T
3. T	7. T	11. T	15. F	
4. F	8. F	12. F	16. T	

MULTIPLE CHOICE

1. a	5. a	9. a	13. b	17. a
2. d	6. b	10. b	14. d	18. d
3. c	7. d	11. a	15. c	19. a
4. b	8. c	12. d	16. b	20. c

SHORT ANSWER

1. Profit-maximizing firms will demand capital as long as the present value of the stream of future marginal revenue product from the new capital exceeds the price of the new capital (i.e., as long as its net present value is positive). Since a lower interest rate implies that the present value of any given future stream of marginal revenue product will be larger, the net present value will be positive for a larger number of additional capital and thus more capital will be purchased. Thus the quantity of capital demanded increases as the interest rate falls.

2. A decline in the interest rate implies that the amount of future consumption that can be had from saving today is reduced. Thus, the cost of current consumption in terms of future consumption given up is lower and thus current consumption will increase and saving will fall.

3. The income effect of an increase in the interest rate is negative if household income declines as a result. If the household tends to borrow more than it saves, the higher interest rate means that its interest expenses will increase by more than its interest income and thus the net effect on income left for spending on goods and services is negative.

4. The yield of an asset is computed as the earnings of the asset divided by its price. Since an increase in the price of the asset

increases the denominator of this ratio, the yield will decrease.

5. The price-earnings ratio is the current price of a share of stock divided by the most recent profits per share. Thus the price-earnings ratio of firm A's stock is greater than the price-earnings ratio of firm B's stock. This implies that, although the recent profits (per share) of the two firms may be the same, future profits (per share) for firm A are expected to be higher than for firm B.

6. a) A significant decline in the price of Exxoff stock with little volume of trade implies that there is wide consensus that the oil spill means a significant reduction in the present value of future Exxoff profits.

   b) If, on the other hand, there is a large volume of trade in Exxoff stock with little net price movement, it must be that there is little consensus about the implications of the oil spill for the future profitability of Exxoff.

7. A takeover will occur when the stock market value of a firm is less that the present value of expected future profits of the firm under new management.

8. The yield on the stock of an exhaustible resource is the percentage rate of change in the price of the resource. In order for the market for the stock of the resource to be in equilibrium there must be no incentive for movement into or out of the market. This will only be the case if the yield on the stock of the exhaustible resource is the same as the yield on other assets, which is given by the rate of interest.

9. The choke price of a natural resource is the price at which the resource will no longer be purchased.

10. In equilibrium, the current price of the resource will be the price which, if the price continues to increase at a rate equal to the interest rate, the choke price will be reached at the same time that the resource is depleted. A higher interest rate means that the price is expected to rise at a faster rate. Therefore, if it is to reach the choke price at the right time, it must start from a lower current price.

PROBLEMS

1. Gross investment is $10,000, the amount of the purchase of new capital. Net investment is -$2000, the amount of gross investment minus depreciation of $12,000.

2. a) Table 16.1 is completed as Table 16.1 Solution. *NPV* is calculated as the present value of the stream of marginal revenue products resulting from an investment minus the cost of the investment. For lawn mowers with a two-year life, the *NPV* is calculated using the following equation.

$$NPV = \frac{MRP_1}{1 + r} + \frac{MRP_2}{(1 + r)^2} - P_L$$

where MRP_1 and MRP_2 are the marginal revenue products in the first and second years, respectively, and P_L is the price of a lawnmower. The values of MRP_1 and MRP_2 are given in Table 16.1 for 1, 2, and 3 lawnmowers and P_L is given as $120. The values for *NPV* given in Table 16.1 Solution are obtained by substituting these values into the above equation and evaluating the expression for the alternative values of *r*, the interest rate.

Table 16.1 Solution

Number of lawn mowers	MRP in first year ($)	MRP in second year ($)	NPV (r=0.05)	NPV (r=0.10)	NPV (r=0.15)
1	100	80	47.80	37.02	27.45
2	80	64	14.24	5.62	-2.04
3	72	62	4.81	-3.31	-10.51

b) If the interest rate is 15 percent, only one additional lawn mower will be purchased since the second lawn mower has negative net present value. If the rate of interest is 10 percent, 2 lawn mowers will be purchased and if the rate of interest is 5 percent, 3 lawn mowers will be purchased.

c) The approximate lawn mower demand curve is illustrated in Fig. 16.1 below. The curve indicates that, at an interest of 15 percent, one lawnmower will be demanded. At an interest rate of 10 percent, two lawnmowers will be demanded, and, at an interest rate of 5 percent, three lawnmowers will be demanded.

Figure 16.1

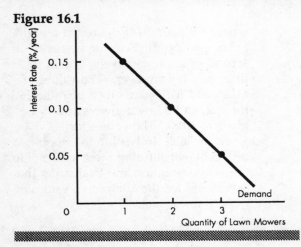

3. a) The new net present values are all $10 less than those given in the completed Table 16.1 above. These values are obtained by noting that P_L in equation (1) is now $130 instead of $120.
   b) The $10 increase in the price of a lawn mower means that the third lawn mower at an interest rate of 5 percent and the second lawn mower at an interest rate of 10 percent would not be purchased. Larry's demand curve for lawn mowers has shifted to the left.

4. a) The market price of a share of Larry's Lawn Care stock will be the present value of expected future profits for the firm divided by the number of shares outstanding: $50.
   b) The stock yield is 15 percent. This is the dividend ($7.50) as a percentage of the price of a share of stock ($50).

5. a) The price of a share of stock will increase to $75 (= $600,000/800).
   b) The stock yield will now be 10 percent. This is the dividend ($7.50) as a percentage of the new price of a share of stock ($75).

6. a) The demand curve for gunk is given by the marginal revenue product curve. It is illustrated below in Fig. 16.2.
   b) The choke price for gunk is $14.64. This is the price that is high enough that the resource will not be used at all.

Figure 16.2

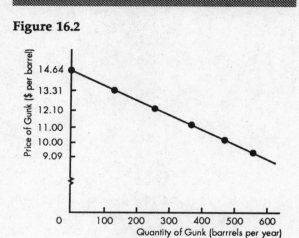

b) Using the procedure outlined in part (a), Table 16.3 can be completed as shown in Table 16.3 Solution.

Table 16.3 Solution

Year	Price	Initial stock of gunk	Final stock of gunk
1	10.00	1215	751
2	11.00	751	387
3	12.10	387	133
4	13.31	133	0
5	14.64	0	

7. a) If the interest rate is 10 percent, the current price of a barrel of gunk is $10. We know that the current (equilibrium) price must be such that if the price of gunk is increasing at a rate of 10 percent per year (equal to the rate of interest), the stock will be depleted just as the choke price is achieved. We can find the current price by noting that (1) the choke price is $14.64 and (2) the remaining stock is 1215 barrels and working backwards. Since the price of gunk is growing at the rate of 10 percent per year, the price in the year before the choke price is reached must be $14.64 (the choke price) divided by 1.10 (1 + the 10% growth rate of price) or $13.31. From Table 16.2 (and recognizing that gunk is just depleted as the $14.64 price is reached) we can infer that 133 barrels of gunk would be purchased in that year. Proceeding in a similar manner, working backward until all 1215 barrels of gunk have been purchased, we discover that the current equilibrium price must be $10.

17 UNCERTAINTY AND INFORMATION

CHAPTER IN PERSPECTIVE

To this point, we have assumed a world of certainty. We have assumed that individuals have complete and certain information about prices, their income, and other economic variables that are important when making economic decisions. In this chapter, we recognize that life is uncertain and that information is costly to obtain. How will economic decisions be made in this more realistic environment of uncertainty and risk? What kinds of problems arise because of uncertainty? What kinds of institutions and markets have arisen to reduce risk?

LEARNING OBJECTIVES

After studying this chapter, you will be able to:

p 459-63

- Explain how people make decisions when they are uncertain about the consequences

- Explain why people buy insurance and how insurance companies make a profit

- Explain why buyers search and sellers advertise

- Explain why private information can limit the gains from exchange and how markets attempt to overcome these problems with warranties and other devices

- Explain how people use financial markets to lower risk

HELPFUL HINT

1. When individuals are faced with uncertain outcomes, they will make decisions on the basis of *expected* wealth and *expected* utility. Expected wealth is the average wealth arising from all possible outcomes. It is computed as the weighted average of the wealth associated with different possible outcomes, where the weights are the probabilities of those possible outcomes. For example, suppose there are three possible outcomes yielding wealth of W_1, W_2, and W_3 and that the probabilities associated with these outcomes are p_1, p_2, and p_3, respectively. Expected wealth is then calculated as

$$(W_1 \times p_1) + (W_2 \times p_2) + (W_3 \times p_3).$$

Expected utility is calculated in the same way. If the utilities associated with each level of wealth are U_1, U_2, and U_3, respectively, then expected utility is calculated as

$$(U_1 \times p_1) + (U_2 \times p_2) + (U_3 \times p_3).$$

Consider the information in Table 17.1. The first column gives all possible outcomes for wealth, the second gives the utility of each of these levels of wealth, and the third column gives the probability of each outcome.

Table 17.1

Wealth ($)	Utility	Probability
100	50	0.2
200	80	0.5
300	90	0.3

Note that the sum of the probabilities of all outcomes is 1.0. This means that one of them *must* occur.

Expected wealth is $210: ($100 \times 0.2) + ($200 \times .5) + ($300 \times .3)$. Expected utility is 77: $(50 \times 0.2) + (80 \times 0.5) + (90 \times 0.3)$.

KEY FIGURES AND TABLES

Figure 17.1 The Utility of Wealth Curve
This figure illustrates the utility of wealth schedule and curve for Tania. Each row of the table associates a level of utility with each level of wealth and is represented by a point on the graph. As wealth increases, the utility of wealth increases but at a decreasing rate. This reflects the diminishing marginal utility of wealth. For example, when wealth increases by $3,000 from $3,000 to $6,000, utility increases by 20 units, However, when wealth increases by an additional $3,000 to $9,000, utility increases by only 10 units.

Figure 17.2 Choice in a Risky Situation
When faced with uncertainty, people make the choice that maximizes *expected* utility. This figure illustrates this by looking at Tania's choice between two jobs. Tania has the same utility of wealth curve as in Fig. 17.1. If she takes the first job, Tania will receive $5,000 with certainty and, as illustrated in part (a), this yields (expected) utility of 80 units. The value of the second risky job is shown in part (b). If Tania takes the second job, she will receive either $9,000 or $3,000 with equal probability. Her expected wealth will be $6,000, calculated as ($9,000 \times 0.5) + ($3,000 \times 0.5)$, but Tania will choose the job with higher expected utility. If she receives $9,000, her utility will be 95 units whereas, if she receives $3,000, her utility will be only 65 units. Thus, her expected utility will be the average utility over these two outcomes: $(95 \times 0.5) + (65 \times 0.5) = 80$. So, the second job yields the same expected utility as the first job and Tania is indifferent between them. Since expected wealth of $6,000 in the uncertain second job yields the same expected utility as the $5,000

from the no risk first job, the cost of risk is $1,000, the difference between them.

Figure 17.5 Insurance
This figure illustrates why insurance pays and why it is profitable by looking at the example of Dan and his car. Dan's car is his only wealth and it is worth $10,000. As we can see from his utility of wealth curve, this yields 100 units of utility for Dan. However, there is a ten percent chance (probability of 0.1) that Dan will have an accident within a year. An accident will leave Dan's car worthless. If Dan has an accident, his wealth and his utility will both be zero. Without insurance, Dan's expected wealth is $9,000 [calculated as ($0 × 0.1) + ($10,000 × 0.9)] and his expected utility is 90 [(0 × 0.1) + (100 × 0.9)].

Notice from the utility of wealth curve that a certain outcome of $7,000 also yields (expected) utility of 90 units. Thus, Dan is indifferent between the uncertain outcome without insurance and a certain outcome of $7,000. This means that Dan would be willing to pay up to $3,000 for insurance that would pay out $10,000 in the event of an accident. If, for example, Dan bought such an insurance policy for $2,000, he would have a certain outcome of $8,000 ($10,000 - $2,000) which yields more expected utility (95 units) than the uncertain situation without insurance (80 units).

If there are many people like Dan, an insurance company will pay out an average of $1,000 per policy since there is a 10 percent chance that any given car will be in an accident. So, assuming no operating costs, an insurance company would be willing to sell an insurance policy for anything over $1,000.

Figure 17.6 Optimal-Search Rule
This figure illustrates the optimal-search rule and shows how the buyer's reservation price is determined.The text uses an example of searching for the lowest price for a car (a Mazda Miata). Searching takes the form of visiting dealers in turn and learning each

one's price. The longer one searches, the better the chance of finding a lower price. But, search is costly. So, the optimal decision rule, as shown in this figure, is to search for a lower price until the expected marginal benefit of search is equal to the marginal cost of search.

The vertical axis measures the benefit and cost of search. The horizontal axis measures the quantity of search which is expressed in terms of the lowest price found. As we search more, the lowest price found declines. That is why the numbers on the horizontal axis decreases as we move to the right.

The marginal cost of search is constant at $C while the expected marginal benefit of search declines as we engage in more search (measured by the lowest price found). The price at which the expected marginal benefit of search equals the marginal cost of search is the buyer's reservation price; $8,000 in this case. This is the highest price the buyer would be willing to pay. The optimal-search rule is to search until the buyer finds a price at (or below) the reservation price and then buy at the lowest price found.

Figure 17.10 A Rational Expectation of Price
The rational expectation of a price is the best forecast that can be made using all available information. Since the actual price is determined when the quantity demanded and the quantity supplied are equal, the rational expectation of the price of a good is the price at which expected quantity demanded equals expected quantity supplied. As illustrated in this figure, this is given by the intersection of the expected demand and expected supply curves.

SELF-TEST

CONCEPT REVIEW

1. In economics, uncertainty with probabilities attached to each possible outcome is called _____.

2. Faced with uncertainty, people make decisions to maximize _____ _____. The amount by which expected wealth must be increased to give the same expected utility as a no risk situation is the _____ of _____.

3. Individuals who, other things equal, prefer situations with less risk are _____ _____.

4. A buyer is searching for information about the price of a good she wants to buy. The highest price she is willing to pay is the buyer's _____ _____. At this price, the expected marginal benefit of search is _____ _____ the marginal cost of search.

5. The fact that Brandon behaves less carefully after he buys insurance is an example of _____ _____. The fact that high risk people are more anxious to buy insurance is an example of _____ _____.

6. An individual can reduce the risk of holding financial assets by buying assets with uncorrelated returns. This is called _____.

7. Contracts for the future delivery of goods are exchanged in the _____ market.

8. A forecast which is the best that can be made based on available relevant information is called a(n) _____ expectation.

9. A market in which the actual price embodies all currently available relevant information is called a(n) _____ market. In such a market the actual price is _____ _____ the expected future price.

10. The volatility of actual stock prices in the stock market is due to fluctuations in _____ future stock prices.

TRUE OR FALSE

____ 1. Since everyone prefers less risk to more, other things being equal, the marginal utility of wealth increases as wealth increases.

____ 2. Faced with uncertainty, people will make decisions to maximize the average utility arising from all possible outcomes.

____ 3. Other things equal, the cost of risk is smaller for someone who is more risk averse.

Fact: Joan faces two options, A and B.
  A: receive a certain payment of $10
  B: an equal chance of receiving $5 or $15

____ 4. Refer to the *Fact* above. Joan will be indifferent between A and B if she is risk averse.

____ 5. Refer to the *Fact* above. Joan will be indifferent between A and B if she is risk neutral.

____ 6. Insurance reduces the risk of financial loss by pooling risk.

____ 7. Providing insurance would be unprofitable if every one were risk neutral.

____ 8. An individual will continue to acquire information as long as the additional information has any benefit.

____ 9. Other things being equal, an individual with a high marginal cost of search will have a low buyer's reservation price.

____ 10. If the lowest price a buyer has yet found is above that buyer's reservation price, he or she will continue searching.

____ 11. The fact that a salesperson has a tendency to be lazy when paid a fixed hourly wage regardless of sales is an example of moral hazard.

____ 12. The adverse selection problem concerns the behavior of an individual *after* an agreement is made.

____ 13. Moral hazard exists in the credit market because some individuals who have borrowed money will have an incentive to default.

____ 14. Diversification increases risk in financial markets since holding more assets with uncertain prices means more risk.

____ 15. The existence of futures markets allows farmers to reduce their risk arising from price variations.

____ 16. The rational expectation of price is the price at which expected demand equals expected supply.

____ 17. A forecast based on rational expectations will be correct.

____ 18. In order to form a rational expectation about the future price of corn one must forecast the future price of soybeans, a substitute for corn.

____ 19. Uncertainty about future household income implies uncertainty about the supply curve for peanut butter.

____ 20. In an efficient market, the actual price would only rarely be equal to the expected future price.

____ 21. Rational expectations about future prices are stable and thus will not change with every new piece of relevant information.

____ 22. If prices in an efficient market are volatile, it must be that expectations about future prices are volatile.

MULTIPLE CHOICE

1. In the face of uncertainty, people will maximize
    a. wealth.
    b. expected wealth.
    c. utility.
    d. expected utility.

2. To an individual facing uncertainty, the cost of risk is the amount by which
    a. expected utility must be *increased* to give the same expected wealth as a no-risk situation.
    b. expected utility must be *decreased* to give the same expected wealth as a no-risk situation.
    c. expected wealth must be *increased* to give the same expected utility as a no-risk situation.
    d. expected wealth must be *decreased* to give the same expected utility as a no-risk situation.

3. Clara faces two options, *A* and *B*. Option *A* pays either $5 or $15 with equal probability and option *B* pays either zero or $20 with equal probability. Then, the expected utility of *A* is _____ the expected utility of *B* if Clara is risk averse and the expected utility of *A* is _____ the expected utility of *B* if she is risk neutral.
    a. greater than; equal to
    b. less than; equal to
    c. equal to; greater than
    d. equal to; less than

4. As wealth increases, the marginal utility of wealth
    a. increases for someone who is risk averse but remains constant for someone who is risk neutral.
    b. decreases for someone who is risk averse but remains constant for someone who is risk neutral.
    c. decreases for someone who is risk averse but increases for someone who is risk neutral.
    d. decreases for someone who is risk averse as well as for someone who is risk neutral.

5. A buyer will acquire additional information until
    a. complete information is obtained.
    b. the expected marginal benefit from additional information is zero.
    c. the expected marginal benefit from additional information is equal to its marginal cost.
    d. additional information is no longer free.

6. The lowest price found that makes expected marginal benefit equal the marginal cost of further search is the
    a. buyer's reservation price.
    b. lowest available price.
    c. rationally expected price.
    d. futures market price.

7. A buyer will stop searching for a better price and buy when he or she has found a price that is
    a. greater than the buyer's reservation price.
    b. less than or equal to the buyer's reservation price.
    c. greater than the cost of risk.
    d. less than or equal to the cost of risk.

8. Advertising typically
   a. persuades in the case of search goods and typically informs in the case of experience goods.
   b. informs in the case of search goods and typically persuades in the case of experience goods.
   c. persuades for both search and experience goods.
   d. informs for both search and experience goods.

9. Which of the following is NOT a method used to limit the problems caused by private information?
   a. Warranties
   b. Loan limits
   c. Insurance deductibles
   d. Diversification

10. Which of the following is an example of moral hazard?
    a. A car dealer offers a warranty on a used car.
    b. There is a greater incentive for someone in poor health to buy health insurance.
    c. There is a greater incentive for someone with health insurance to be careless.
    d. The existence of efficient markets.

11. Which of the following is an example of adverse selection?
    a. A car dealer offers a warranty on a used car.
    b. There is a greater incentive for someone in poor health to buy health insurance.
    c. There is a greater incentive for someone with health insurance to be careless.
    d. The existence of efficient markets.

12. A: Moral hazard exists in a car market without warranties because sellers have an incentive to claim that lemons are good cars.
    B: Adverse selection exists in a car market without warranties because sellers have an incentive to sell only lemons.
    a. A and B are both true.
    b. A and B are both false.
    c. A is true and B is false.
    d. A is false and B is true.

13. Which of the following is NOT a method for reducing risk?
    a. Diversification
    b. Trading in forward markets
    c. Trading in futures markets
    d. Using the optimal-search rule

14. _____ are traded in futures markets.
    a. Forecasts of future prices
    b. Contracts for future delivery of goods
    c. Actual commodities
    d. Stocks and bonds

15. Which of the following would NOT cause uncertainty about the demand for peanut butter?
    a. Uncertainty about the prices of substitutes and complements for peanut butter
    b. Uncertainty about household income
    c. Uncertainty about the costs of producing peanut butter
    d. Uncertainty about consumer tastes

16. A rational expectation is best described as
    a. determining price by equating demand and supply curves.
    b. a rational explanation of current demand and supply curves.
    c. any estimates of future demand and supply.
    d. a forecast that uses all relevant available information and has the least possible error.

17. Refer to Fig. 17.1. The rational expectations forecast of demand and supply are denoted by ED and ES and the realized demand and supply curves are given by D and S. What is the forecast for price and quantity sold?
    a. Price = $10, quantity = 100
    b. Price = $10, quantity = 160
    c. Price = $18, quantity = 160
    d. Price = $18, quantity = 200

Figure 17.1

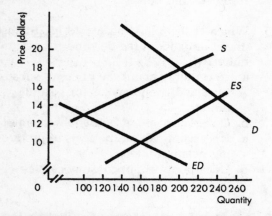

18. If the stock market is an efficient market, which of the following statements is NOT true?
    a. The current price is equal to the expected future price.
    b. The current price embodies all available information.
    c. No predictable profit opportunities exist.
    d. Prices are not volatile since holding stocks is holding inventories.

19. The best explanation for the volatility of stock market prices is that they
    a. result from frequently changing expectations due to new information.
    b. are due to the quantity smoothing effect of holding inventories.
    c. are due to the volatility in interest rates.
    d. are due to the manipulation of large investment institutions.

SHORT ANSWER

1. What is meant by the cost of risk?

2. Why are people willing to buy insurance and why are firms will to sell it?

3. How will a buyer decide how long to search for a lower price?

4. Distinguish between moral hazard and adverse selection.

5. Why will a used car dealer offer warranties on certain cars?

6. How does diversification reduce risk?

7. What is a rational expectation?

8. What is meant by an efficient market?

9. Explain why the current market price will always be equal to the expected future price in an efficient market.

10. Why are stock market prices so volatile?

PROBLEMS

1. Bart's utility of wealth schedule is given in Table 17.2.

Table 17.2

Wealth (thousands of $)	Utility
0	0
4	52
5	60
8	79
10	87
15	98
20	104

a) Suppose that Bart faces a project that will pay either $5,000 or $15,000 with equal probability.
   i) What is Bart's expected wealth from the project?
   ii) What is his expected utility?
   iii) What is Bart's cost of risk?
   iv) Would Bart be willing to undertake the project if it cost him $9,000? $7,000?

b) Suppose that Bart now faces a project that will pay either zero or $20,000 with equal probability.
   i) What is Bart's expected wealth from this project?
   ii) What is his expected utility?
   iii) What is Bart's cost of risk?
   iv) Would Bart be willing to undertake the project if it cost him $5,000?

2. Return to the situation in 1(b). Suppose there are many projects of the type described there and many individuals with the same utility of wealth schedule as Bart. Bart wants to buy insurance against the zero payment outcome (failure of the project).
a) What is the most Bart would be willing to pay for an insurance policy that pays him $20,000 if the project fails?
b) What is the least an insurance company would charge if its operating cost is $1,000 per policy?
c) Is there an opportunity for an insurance market in this situation?

3. Figure 17.2 illustrates the market for loans in which there are two kinds of borrowers. Part (a) gives the demand for loans by no-risk borrowers, D_n, and the supply of loans to no-risk borrowers, S_n. Part (b) gives the demand for loans by risky borrowers, D_r, and the supply of loans to risky borrowers, S_r. Loans are supplied by banks which cannot distinguish between no-risk and risky borrowers. The supply curves give the cost of supplying loans to each type of borrower.
a) Suppose banks charge an interest rate of two percent on loans to all borrowers and that they do not impose loan limits.
   i) How much will be borrowed by no-risk borrowers? By risky borrowers?
   ii) Will banks make a profit or a loss? How much?
b) Suppose banks charge an interest rate of six percent on loans to all borrowers and that they do not impose loan limits.
   i) How much will be borrowed by no-risk borrowers? By risky borrowers?
   ii) Will banks make a profit or a loss? How much? What incentives for entry into banking will exist?

c) Now suppose banks use signals (such as length of time in a job or ownership of a home) to discriminate among borrowers and that they limit the amount of loans. Suppose that the effect is to limit loans to no-risk borrowers to $6 million and to limit loans to risky borrowers to $2 million. Banks now charge an interest rate of three percent on all loans.

i) How much will be borrowed by no-risk borrowers? By risky borrowers?

ii) Will banks make a profit or a loss? How much? What incentives for entry or exit will now exist?

iii) What is the excess demand for loans by no-risk borrowers? By risky borrowers?

4. Lisa faces two risky projects, A and B, and has $1,000 to allocate between them. The projects have the same risk and return but are independent of each other. The price of a share in either project is $500. There is a 50 percent chance that project A will fail in which case each share of A will lose $100. There is a 50 percent chance that project A will succeed in which case each share of A will make $200. Project B is independent of project A but has the same probabilities of failure and success and the same promise of return per share. Lisa is risk averse.

a) Suppose Lisa "puts all her eggs in one basket" by spending her $1,000 to buy two shares of project A. What are the possible outcomes for Lisa and what is the probability (as a decimal) of each outcome? What is Lisa's expected return? Would expected return be different if she had decided to buy two shares of project B instead?

b) Suppose now that Lisa decides to diversify by buying one share of

project A and one share of project B. What are the possible outcomes for Lisa now and what is the probability of each? What is Lisa's expected return? Why is this situation better than buying two shares of either project A or project B?

Figure 17.2

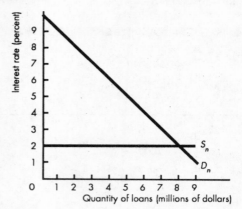

(a)

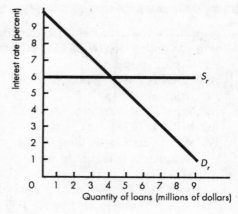

(b)

5. The expected demand and supply of wheat are given in Table 17.3.

a) If nothing happens to change expectations, what is the rational expectation of
   i) the price of a bushel of wheat?
   ii) the quantity of wheat traded?
b) Suppose that actual demand is exactly as expected but the weather turns out to be better than usual for growing wheat and actual wheat production is 40 million bushels greater than the quantity expected.
   i) What is the quantity of wheat actually traded?
   ii) What is the actual price of a bushel of wheat?
   iii) How much wheat would farmers have supplied if they were able to accurately forecast the price?

Table 17.3

Price (dollar per bushel)	Expected quantity demanded (millions of bushels per year)	Expected quantity supplied (millions of bushels per year)
4.00	140	350
3.50	180	320
3.00	220	290
2.50	260	260
2.00	300	230
1.50	340	200

ANSWERS

CONCEPT REVIEW

1. risk
2. expected; utility; cost; risk
3. risk; averse
4. reservation; price; equal to
5. moral; hazard; adverse; selection
6. diversification
7. futures
8. rational
9. efficient; equal to
10. expected

TRUE OR FALSE

1. F	6. T	11. T	16. T	21. F
2. T	7. T	12. F	17. F	22. T
3. F	8. F	13. T	18. T	
4. F	9. F	14. F	19. F	
5. T	10. T	15. T	20. F	

MULTIPLE CHOICE

1. d	5. c	9. d	13. d	17. b
2. c	6. a	10. c	14. b	18. d
3. a	7. b	11. b	15. c	19. a
4. b	8. b	12. a	16. d	

SHORT ANSWER

1. The cost of risk is the amount by which expected wealth must be increased to give the same expected utility as a certain (no risk) outcome.

2. People are willing to buy insurance because they are risk averse. Thus, they are willing to pay insurance premiums in

order to reduce the risk they face. An insurance company can pool risk by selling insurance policies to a large number of people. As a result, the insurance company has very little overall risk.

3. A buyer expects to benefit from additional search by finding a lower price, but search is also costly since the time and resources used have alternative uses. Thus, a buyer will search for a lower price until the expected marginal benefit of search equals the marginal cost of search. This is the optimal-search rule. The lowest price found that satisfies this rule is called the buyer's reservation price.

4. Moral hazard exists if one of the parties to a contract has an incentive, *after the agreement is made*, to change his or her behavior at the expense of the other party. It arises because it is too costly for the second party to obtain information about the behavior of the first party.

    Adverse selection occurs when there is a tendency for the people who enter into an agreement to be those with private information they plan to use to their own advantage and to the disadvantage of the other party.

5. In a car market without warranties, the problems of moral hazard and adverse selection will tend to imply that only lemons will be offered for sale. However, a car dealer can signal that a car is not a lemon by offering a warranty. Since the warranty implies that the car is not a lemon, the car dealer will be able to charge a higher price.

6. Diversification lowers risk by combining the returns on projects that are independent of each other and whose returns are uncorrelated.

7. A rational expectation is the best forecast that can be made on the basis of all available and relevant information.

8. An efficient market is one in which the actual price embodies all available relevant information. The price will thus be equal to the rational expectation of the future price and there will be no predictable profit opportunities.

9. The current market price will always be equal to the expected future price in an efficient market because any deviation would immediately be eliminated since it provides an expected profit opportunity. (See the discussion of the role of inventories in the answer to number 7 above.)

10. The stock market is an efficient market and so stock market prices are always equal to their expected future price. The volatility of stock prices, then, reflects the volatility of expected future stock prices. These expectations will change any time there is new information that is relevant for future stock prices. Such information becomes available frequently and so expectations are revised frequently. The consequence is frequent movements in stock market prices.

PROBLEMS

1. a) i)   Each of the two possible outcomes, $5,000 or $15,000, will occur with a probability of 0.5 (50 percent). Thus, by Helpful Hint 1, Bart's expected wealth is the average wealth over the two outcomes, $10,000: ($5,000 × 0.5) + ($15,000 × 0.5).
        ii) Bart's expected utility is 79: (60 × 0.5) + (98 × 0.5).
        iii) Bart's cost of risk is the amount by which expected wealth must be

increased to give the same utility as a no risk situation. Uncertain wealth of $5,000 or $15,000 implies expected wealth of $10,000 and expected utility of 79. From the table, we see that certain (no risk) wealth of $8,000 also yields utility of 79. Thus the cost of risk is $2,000, the amount by which expected wealth must be increased to give the same utility as the no risk situation ($10,000 - $8,000).

iv) The expected payoff of the risky project is $10,000. Nevertheless, Bart would not be willing to undertake the project if it cost him $9,000 since the foregone utility of the $9,000 (not given in the table but greater than 79) is greater than the expected utility of the risky project (79). On the other hand, the utility of $7,000 is less than expected utility of the risky project (79) so Bart would undertake the project at this price.

b) i) Each of the two possible outcomes, zero or $20,000, will occur with a probability of 0.5. Thus Bart's expected wealth is $10,000: ($0 × 0.5) + ($20,000 × 0.5).

ii) Bart's expected utility is now 52: (0 × 0.5) + (104 × 0.5).

iii) Uncertain wealth of $0 or $20,000 implies expected wealth of $10,000 and expected utility of 52. From the table, we see that certain (no risk) wealth of $4,000 also yields utility of 52. Thus the cost of risk is $6,000, the amount by which expected wealth must be increased to give the same utility as the no risk situation ($10,000 - $4,000).

iv) The expected payoff of the risky project is $10,000. Nevertheless, Bart would not be willing to undertake the project if it cost him $5,000 since the foregone utility of the $5,000 (60) is greater than the expected utility of the risky project (52).

2. a) Bart is willing to buy insurance as long as the utility from the certain outcome after buying insurance yields at least as much expected utility as the risky project. Since the expected utility of the risky project (52) is the same as a certain outcome of $4,000, Bart would be willing to pay up to $16,000 for an insurance policy that pays him $20,000 if the project fails. If he buys insurance, Bart will receive $20,000 whether the project succeeds or fails. An insurance premium of $16,000 leaves him with a certain net income of $4,000. Thus, at that price, Bart would be indifferent between purchasing insurance and bearing the risk. At any premium below $16,000 Bart would be better off with insurance since he will have a certain net income that exceeds $4,000 and thus will yield more than 52 units of utility.

b) The minimum premium that an insurance company would charge is just enough to cover its expected costs: the expected pay out per project plus its operating costs per policy. Since half the projects fail, the insurance company will pay out $20,000 on half the projects. This amounts to an average of $10,000 per project. Since the operating cost is $1,000, the least an insurance company would charge is $11,000 ($10,000 + $1,000).

c) Since the most individuals would be willing to pay is more than the least insurance companies must charge, there is an opportunity for an insurance market to exist. Both parties will gain at any premium between $11,000 and $16,000.

3. a) i)   At an interest rate of two percent, no-risk borrowers will borrow $8 million and risky borrowers will borrow $8 million. These amounts are obtained by finding the quantity demanded by no-risk and risky borrowers in parts (a) and (b) of Fig. 17.2.

    ii) Overall, banks will make a loss. They will make zero profit on loans made to no-risk borrowers but will make a loss on loans to risky borrowers. The loss occurs because the cost of providing loans to risky borrowers (including collection costs) is six percent of the loan as reflected by the S curve. This exceeds the two percent interest rate charged.

    b) i)   The amount borrowed by no-risk and risky borrowers at an interest rate of six percent is given by the respective demand curves in Fig. 17.2. No-risk and risky borrowers will both borrow $4 million.

    ii) Banks will now make a profit overall. They will make zero profit on loans to risky borrowers but will make a profit on loans to no-risk borrowers since the cost of providing those loans is only two percent which is less than the interest rate of six percent charged. These profits would likely attract new banking firms.

    c) i)   Borrowing by each of the two groups of borrowers will be the amount of their loan limits since these limits are less than the quantity of loans demanded at an interest rate of three percent. No-risk borrowers will borrow $6 million and risky borrowers will borrow $2 million.

    ii) Banks will make zero profit overall. Profits from loans to no-risk borrowers (one percent profit per loan times $6 million in loans) will just offset the losses from loans to risky borrowers (three percent loss per loan times $2 million in loans). The existence of zero profit implies no incentive for either entry into banking or exit from banking.

    iii) At an interest rate of three percent, no-risk borrowers would like to borrow $7 million but are limited to $6 million. Therefore, their excess demand for loans is $1 million. At three percent, risky borrowers would also like to borrow $7 million but the loan limit restricts borrowing to $2 million. The excess demand for loans by risky borrowers is, thus, $5 million.

4. a) If Lisa buys two shares of Project A, there are only two possible outcomes: the project will either succeed or fail. Table 17.4 lists these outcomes along with their respective returns and the probability of each outcome.

Table 17.4

Outcome	Return ($)	Probability (percent)
A succeeds	400	0.5
A fails	-200	0.5

Lisa's expected return is $100: ($400 × 0.5) + (-$200 × 0.5). This is a 10 percent expected rate of return on Lisa's original $1000.

The expected return for project B is exactly the same since it has the same consequences and the same risk.

    b) If Lisa diversifies by spending her $1000 to buy one share of Project A and one share of Project B, there are four possible outcomes. These, along with their associated probabilities are indicated in Table 17. 5.

Table 17.5

Outcome	Return ($)	Probability (percent)
Both A and B succeed	400	0.25
A succeeds, B fails	100	0.25
A fails, B succeeds	100	0.25
Both A and B fail	-200	0.25

Since projects A and B are independent, each of the four outcomes is equally likely; each has a probability of 0.25. Lisa's expected return is again $100: ($400 × 0.25) + ($100 × 0.25) + ($100 × 0.25) + (-$200 × 0.25). This is a 10 percent return on her original $1000.

Even though Lisa's expected return on a diversified portfolio is the same, she will prefer it because it is less risky than buying two shares of either Project A or Project B. With the diversified portfolio, there is a 50 percent chance that Lisa will receive a return of $100 and only a 25 percent chance of losing $200 (as opposed to a 50 percent chance of losing $200). Of course, the chance of receiving $400 is now 25 percent instead of 50 percent, but, because Lisa is risk averse, she will value the reduction in the probability of loss more than the reduction in the probability of large gain.

5. a) i) The rational expectation of the price of a bushel of wheat is $2.50 since, at that price, expected quantity demanded equals expected quantity supplied.
   ii) The rational expectation of the quantity of wheat traded is 260 million bushels.

   b) i) The actual quantity of wheat traded is 300 million bushels, 40 million bushels more than the 260 million expected (it is momentary supply that is relevant).
   ii) The actual price of a bushel of wheat is $2.00 per bushel.
   iii) If farmers had been accurately able to forecast the price of $2.00 per bushel, they would have produced 230 million bushels of wheat.

18 THE DISTRIBUTION OF INCOME AND WEALTH

CHAPTER IN PERSPECTIVE

Income is the payment by firms to owners of factors of production for the use of those resources. Individuals with more resources to sell or whose resources sell for a higher price will receive larger incomes. Thus the distribution of income depends on the distribution of ownership of resources used in production and the market prices of those resources. In the last three chapters we learned that the prices of factors of production are determined in markets and we studied the operation of those markets.

In this chapter, we discuss the distribution of income and wealth in the United States. We will discover that if one is not careful, it is easy to distort the degree of inequality. How unequally are income and wealth actually distributed in the United States? What accounts for this inequality? What are the consequences of government policies intended to redistribute income or wealth? What are the major ideas about what constitutes a "fair" distribution of income?

LEARNING OBJECTIVES

After studying this chapter, you will be able to:

- **Describe the distribution of income and wealth in the United States today**

- **Explain the effects of income redistribution policies**

- **Explain why the wealth distribution shows greater inequality than the income distribution**

- **Explain how the distribution of income arises from the prices of productive resources and the distribution of endowments**

- **Explain how the distribution of income and wealth is affected by individual choices**

- **Explain the different views about fairness in the distribution of income and wealth**

HELPFUL HINTS

1. The major tool used by economists to "picture" the degree of inequality in an economy is the Lorenz curve. It is important to understand how to interpret such a curve. See Key Fig. 18.2 below.

2. A major message of this chapter is that statistics used to construct Lorenz curves do not always give an accurate picture of inequality. It is important to understand why inaccurate pictures might arise.

For example, you should understand why the distribution of wealth, exclusive of the value of human capital, will give a distorted picture relative to the distribution of income. You should also understand why the distribution of annual (static) income will give a distorted picture relative to the distribution of lifetime (dynamic) income. Finally, you should understand why the distribution of before-tax, before-transfer income will give a distorted picture relative to the distribution of after-tax, after-transfer income.

3. The issue of fairness discussed in this chapter is a normative issue. Note, however, that the tradeoff between equity and economic efficiency (the so-called big tradeoff) is a positive issue.

KEY FIGURES AND TABLES

Figure 18.2 Lorenz Curves for Income and Wealth

A Lorenz curve is a useful way to represent the distribution of income or wealth. It plots the cumulative percentage of income earned by a given cumulative percentage of families. This figure gives Lorenz curves for the United States. The table gives the values of the cumulative percentage of income corresponding to various cumulative percentages of families.

For example, the table indicates that the lowest 20 percent of families earn 5 percent of the income in the United States. Also, the lowest 80 percent of families earn 57 percent of the income. This information is illustrated graphically in the Lorenz curves of the figure.

The farther a Lorenz curve is from the line of equality, the more unequal the distribution. It is readily seen that wealth is much less equally distributed than income.

Figure 18.4 Distribution of Income by Selected Family Characteristics in 1989

This figure indicates the importance of certain family characteristics in influencing the size of family income. For example, we can see very clearly that education makes a big difference. On average, those with four years or more of college have income of almost $50,000 per year while those with less than eight years of schooling have income of less than $13,000 per year. On average, males or females who are married with spouse present have incomes of almost $40,000 while single females have incomes below $14,000. The influence of size of household, age of householder, race, and region are also reported.

Figure 18.6 Comparing Current Income Maintenance Programs a Negative Income and Tax

This figure compares current income maintenance programs with a negative income tax. In both parts, the horizontal axis measures market income *before* taxes are paid and benefits received. The vertical axis measures household income *after* taxes are paid and benefits are received. At points on the 45° line, there is no redistribution since market income is equal to after redistribution income. At points above the 45° line, benefits exceed taxes so income after redistribution exceeds market income. At points below the 45° line, taxes exceed benefits so income after redistribution is less than market income.

Part (a) illustrates current income maintenance programs. If a household has zero market income, it will receive benefits of amount *g*. As market income increases to *a*, benefits are reduced sufficiently that income after redistribution falls below *g*. This creates the welfare trap noted in the figure. At market incomes between *a* and *c*, there is no redistribution. As market income increases beyond *c*, income tax rates rise and income after redistribution declines.

Part (b) compares the current system with a hypothetical negative income tax. Once again, a household with zero market income will receive benefits of amount *g*. But now, as market income increases, benefits are reduced at a regular income tax rate (much less that 100 percent). As a result, the household's after-redistribution income will increase as market income rises eliminating the welfare trap. At market income level *b*, the household breaks even. As income rises above *b*, households pay taxes so after-redistribution income is less than market income.

SELF-TEST

CONCEPT REVIEW

1. Of the three basic factors of production, _____ earns the largest share of total income.

2. The diagram used by economists to illustrate the cumulative percentage of households ranked from the poorest to the richest is called a(n) _____ _____. The straight line running through the middle of the diagram is called the line of _____.

3. The most important factor in determining whether a person receives a high income or a low income is _____.

4. An income tax system in which the marginal tax rate rises as income rises is called a(n) _____ income tax. A(n) _____ income tax is one in which the marginal tax rate falls with the level of income while for a(n) _____ income tax, the marginal tax rate is constant for all levels of income.

5. The reform proposal that gives every family a guaranteed annual income and decreases the families benefit at a specified rate as its market income increases is called a(n) _____ _____ tax.

6. A gift from one generation to the next is called a(n) _____.

7. The tendency for people to marry within their own socioeconomic class is called _____ _____. This tendency contributes to a(n) _____ in the unequal distribution of wealth.

8. Theories of distributive justice that emphasize the equality of the outcomes of economic activity are called _____-_____ theories while those emphasizing the equality of opportunity are called _____ theories.

9. The _____ theory states that the fairest outcome is the one that maximizes

the sum of the utilities of all individuals in society.

10. According to the _____ theory, the fairest distribution of income gives the poorest member of society the largest income possible.

TRUE OR FALSE

_____ 1. In the U.S., the wealthiest 1 percent of households own approximately one-third of total wealth.

_____ 2. In the U.S., income is more unequally distributed than wealth.

_____ 3. The farther the Lorenz curve is from the line of equality, the more equal the distribution of income.

_____ 4. The distribution of income has become more equal since 1967.

_____ 5. Under a proportional income tax, total taxes rise as income rises.

_____ 6. Under a proportional income tax, the marginal tax rate does not change as income rises.

_____ 7. A regressive income tax redistributes income from the rich to the poor.

_____ 8. A negative income tax would allow the poor to keep a larger share of any income they earned than under our current income maintenance programs.

_____ 9. Compared to the market distribution of income, government benefits and taxes reduce the inequality of income distribution.

_____ 10. Income is a stock and wealth is a flow.

_____ 11. The distribution of financial wealth ignores the distribution of human capital and thus is not a good measure of the distribution of economic resources.

_____ 12. Because it does not take into account the family's stage in the life cycle, the measured distribution of annual income will *understate* the degree of inequality.

_____ 13. Wealthier families tend to leave larger bequests.

_____ 14. The existence of assortative mating tends to increase the inequality of the distribution of wealth.

_____ 15. The belief that everyone should have the same income and wealth is an example of a process theory of distributive justice.

_____ 16. The utilitarian theory is an example of an end-state theory of distributive justice.

_____ 17. Robert Nozick argues that a theory of distributive justice must be based on the mechanisms through which the distribution of income and wealth arises.

_____ 18. In general, reducing income inequality by redistributing income from the rich to the poor will lead to greater production of goods and services.

MULTIPLE CHOICE

1. Which of the following statements is true?
   a. Labor earns the largest share of total income and that share has decreased slightly over the years.
   b. Labor earns the largest share of total income and that share has increased slightly over the years.
   c. Owners of capital earn the largest share of total income and that share has decreased slightly over the years.
   d. Owners of capital earn the largest share of total income and that share has increased slightly over the years.

2. For the most part, differences in the wage rates received by different individuals reflect differences in
   a. inherited wealth.
   b. holdings of financial wealth.
   c. marginal product of labor.
   d. the quantity of labor offered.

3. The inequality in the distribution of wealth is
   a. less than the inequality in the distribution of income.
   b. decreased by the existence of assortative mating.
   c. a better measure of the inequality in the distribution of economic resources than is the inequality in the distribution of income.
   d. less if we look at total lifetime wealth rather than wealth in a given year.

4. The wealthiest 10 percent of U.S. families own approximately
   a. 10 percent of the wealth.
   b. one-third of the wealth.
   c. two-thirds of the wealth.
   d. 95 percent of the wealth.

5. The single most important factor influencing the size of a family's income is
   a. region of residence.
   b. education.
   c. race.
   d. size of household.

6. Which diagram is used by economists to illustrate the distribution of income or wealth?
   a. Lorenz curve
   b. normal distribution
   c. Rawls curve
   d. Okun tradeoff curve

7. Consider the Lorenz curves in Fig. 18.1. Which Lorenz curve corresponds to the greatest income *inequality*?
   a. *A*
   b. *B*
   c. *C*
   d. *D*

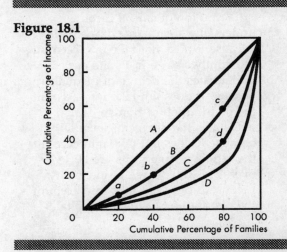

Figure 18.1

8. In Fig. 18.1, curve *A* (a straight line) is called the
   a. market distribution line.
   b. line of equality.
   c. fairness line.
   d. Okun trade-off curve.

9. Which point in Fig. 18.1 indicates that the richest 20 percent of families earn 40 percent of the income?
   a. *a*
   b. *b*
   c. *c*
   d. *d*

10. If the marginal tax rate increases as income increases, the income tax is
    a. progressive.
    b. proportional.
    c. negative.
    d. regressive.

11. A negative income tax does all of the following EXCEPT:
    a. It discourages work.
    b. It eliminates the "welfare trap."
    c. It provides a guaranteed minimum annual income for every family.
    d. It encourages lower income families to seek additional employment.

12. The distribution of *annual* income
    a. understates the degree of inequality because it does not take into account the family's stage in its life cycle.
    b. understates the degree of inequality because it does not take into account the distribution of human capital.
    c. overstates the degree of inequality because it does not take into account the family's stage in its life cycle.
    d. overstates the degree of inequality because it does not take into account the distribution of human capital.

13. The distribution of *wealth*
    a. understates the degree of inequality because it does not take into account the family's stage in its life cycle.
    b. understates the degree of inequality because it does not take into account the distribution of human capital.
    c. overstates the degree of inequality because it does not take into account the family's stage in its life cycle.
    d. overstates the degree of inequality because it does not take into account the distribution of human capital.

14. Suppose that if a family earns zero income, it receives a monthly transfer payment of $1,000 from the government. If the family earns $400 in a month, the government payment drops to $700. What is the marginal tax rate in this case?
    a. 10 percent
    b. 40 percent
    c. 50 percent
    d. 75 percent

15. Even if the distribution of wages is symmetric, the distribution of income will be skewed because
    a. abilities are distributed symmetrically.
    b. individuals tend to supply more labor at higher wages.
    c. more people will have incomes that are larger than average.
    d. many rich individuals are unwilling to work.

16. Which of the following *reduces* the inequality of income or wealth relative to the market distribution?
    a. Government payments to the poor
    b. A regressive income tax
    c. Large bequests
    d. Assortative mating

17. A theory of distributive justice that emphasizes the mechanism by which distribution takes place is
    a. a utilitarian theory.
    b. an end-state theory.
    c. a Rawlsian theory.
    d. a process theory.

18. According to the Rawlsian theory, income should be redistributed if the
    a. average person can be made better off.
    b. poorest person can be made better off.
    c. richest person can be made worse off.
    d. wage rate is not equal to the marginal product of labor.

19. Which of the following is an example of an end-state theory of distributive justice?
    a. Marginal product theory
    b. The theory of Robert Nozick
    c. The utilitarian theory
    d. The process theory

20. Redistribution of income from the rich to the poor will lead to a reduction in total output. This is known as
    a. market distribution.
    b. the process theory of distributive justice.
    c. the big tradeoff.
    d. the capitalist dilemma.

SHORT ANSWER

1. What is a Lorenz curve? What does it illustrate?

2. Why would a negative income tax be more successful at encouraging work than existing income maintenance programs?

3. Why is it that the *measured* distribution of wealth overstates the actual degree of inequality among individuals?

4. What are the two factors that determine a person's income? To what extent are these factors the result of forces beyond the control of the individual and to what extent are they the result of individual choice?

5. How does assortative mating enhance the concentration of wealth?

6. What is the principal characteristic of a process theory of distributive justice?

7. Why is the utilitarian theory an end-state theory of distributive justice?

8. Why is there a "big tradeoff" between fairness and efficiency?

PROBLEMS

1. Table 18.1 gives information regarding the distribution of income in an economy which generates $100 billion in total annual income.
   a) Complete Table 18.1 by computing the entries in the last three columns.
   b) Draw the Lorenz curve for income in this economy and label it *A*.

Table 18.1 Total Family Income

Percentage of families	Total income (billions of dollars)	Income share (percent)	Cumulative percentage of families	Cumulative percentage of income
Poorest 20%	5			
Second 20%	10			
Third 20%	15			
Fourth 20%	20			
Richest 20%	50			

2. Now suppose that a progressive income tax is levied on the economy. The distribution of after-tax income is given in Table 18.2. We have assumed that none of the revenue is redistributed to families in the economy. Note that total after-tax income is $71 billion.
   a) Complete Table 18.2.
   b) Draw the Lorenz curve for after-tax income on the same graph you used for problem 1 b) and label it B.
   c) What effect has the progressive income tax had on inequality?

Table 18.2 After-Tax Family Income

Percentage of families	After-tax income (billions of dollars)	After-tax income share (percent)	Cumulative percentage of families	Cumulative percentage of after-tax income
Poorest 20%	5			
Second 20%	9			
Third 20%	12			
Fourth 20%	15			
Richest 20%	30			

3. Finally, suppose that, in addition, the government redistributes all of the tax revenue so that the after-transfer (after-tax) income distribution is that given in Table 18.3. For example, those in the poorest group receive transfer income in the amount of $10 billion so that their after-transfer income becomes $15 billion.
   a) Complete Table 18.3.
   b) Draw the Lorenz curve for after-transfer income on the same graph you used for 1 (b) and 2 (b) and label it C.
   c) What effect has income redistribution through transfer payments had on inequality?

Table 18.3 After-Transfer Family Income

Percentage of families	After-transfer income (billions of dollars)	After-transfer income share (percent)	Cumulative percentage of families	Cumulative percentage of after-transfer income
Poorest 20%	15			
Second 20%	16			
Third 20%	18			
Fourth 20%	20			
Richest 20%	31			

4. Consider an economy consisting of 100 individuals who are identical in every way. They each live to be 80 years old and no older. Between birth and the age of 20 years they earn zero income; between the ages of 21 and 35 they each earn an annual income of $30,000; between the ages of 36 and 50 they each earn an annual income of $40,000; between 51 and 65 they each receive an annual income of $60,000; and between the ages of 66 and 80 they each receive an annual income of $20,000. At any given time there are 20 individuals in each of the 5 age groups. For simplicity, we assume that there are no bequests. This information is summarized in Table 18.4.
   a) Draw the Lorenz curve for *lifetime income* in this economy and label it A.
   b) Draw the Lorenz curve for *annual income* in this economy and label it B.
   c) Which of these is a better measure of the inequality among individuals in this economy? Why?

Table 18.4 Lifetime Income Patterns

Age group (years)	Number in age group	Individual annual income ($)
0-20	20	0
21-35	20	30,000
36-50	20	40,000
51-65	20	60,000
66-80	20	20,000

ANSWERS

CONCEPT REVIEW

1. labor

2. Lorenz curve; equality

3. education

4. progressive; regressive; proportional

5. negative income

6. bequest

7. assortative mating; increase

8. end-state; process

9. utilitarian

10. Rawlsian

TRUE OR FALSE

1. T	5. T	9. T	13. T	17. T
2. F	6. T	10. F	14. T	18. F
3. F	7. F	11. T	15. F	
4. F	8. T	12. F	16. T	

MULTIPLE CHOICE

1. b	5. a	9. c	13. d	17. d
2. c	6. a	10. a	14. d	18. b
3. d	7. d	11. a	15. b	19. c
4. c	8. b	12. c	16. a	20. c

SHORT ANSWER

1. The Lorenz curve gives a graphical representation of the distribution of income or wealth across some population.

   The horizontal axis measures the cumulative percentage of families ranked from the poorest to the richest. The cumulative percentages of income or wealth are measured on the vertical axis. The farther the Lorenz curve is from the line of equality, the more unequal the distribution of income or wealth.

2. Existing income maintenance programs create a disincentive for someone receiving benefits to find work because, up to a certain level, benefits will be reduced by more than the amount of market income they earn. Thus, the marginal tax rate is more than 100 percent on earnings from work. This eliminates any incentive to seek work and creates a welfare trap.

   A negative income tax guarantees each family a minimum annual income and decreases benefits by only a fraction of any market income. Since individuals are able to keep most of the market income they earn, they have an incentive to seek work even if it is low paid.

3. The problem is that the usual measures of wealth only include nonhuman wealth and omit human wealth. Human wealth, the value of human capital, is the amount an individual would have to invest today in order to receive interest income equal to the amount received as income from

his/her human capital. Since human wealth is much more equally distributed than nonhuman wealth, the truncated measure of wealth used in practice will overstate the degree of inequality.

4. A person's income is determined by the market prices for productive resource services and the quantity of resource services the person is able and willing to sell at those prices.

   These two factors depend on a number of things, some of which are (at least partially) under the control of the individual and some of which are not. The price of labor services, the wage rate, is determined in the market for labor. But, as we learned in Chapters 15 and 16, the wage rate will depend on the marginal product of labor which is affected by individual choices about training and education as well as personal inherent limits in ability.

   The quantity of labor services supplied will also depend on personal choices about how to spend one's time. The quantity of other resource services supplied will also depend on personal choices as well as the individual's endowment of the factor.

5. Assortative mating is the tendency for individuals to marry within their own socioeconomic class. This means that wealthy individuals tend to marry wealthy individuals. The result is that family wealth can become more concentrated.

6. A process theory of distributive justice focuses on the fairness of the process or mechanisms by which results are achieved instead of focusing on the results themselves.

7. The utilitarian theory suggests that the fairest system is one in which the sum of

the utilities in the society is a maximum. Since the theory focuses on the outcome or the ends, it is an end-state theory of distributive justice.

8. If greater fairness means increasing the equality of income it can only be achieved by income redistribution; the income of some must be taxed in order to make transfer payments to others. However, there are incentive effects which reduce the total amount of income available to be distributed.

   If productive activities (e.g., work) are taxed, there will be a tendency to reduce time spent in those activities.

   Furthermore, any redistribution program would require the use of resources to administer it and thus leave fewer resources for other productive activities. Thus we arrive at the insight: a more equally shared pie results in a smaller pie.

PROBLEMS

1. a) Table 18.1 is completed as Table 18.1 Solution. The income share for each group of families is the total income of that group as a percent of total income in the economy ($100 billion). The cumulative percentage of income (last column) is obtained by adding the percentage income share of the group (from the third column) to the total percentage income share of all poorer groups to families.

Table 18.1 Solution: Total Family Income

Percentage of families	Total income (billions of dollars)	Income share (percent)	Cumulative percentage of families	Cumulative percentage of income
Poorest 20%	5	5	20	5
Second 20%	10	10	40	15
Third 20%	15	15	60	30
Fourth 20%	20	20	80	50
Richest 20%	50	50	100	100

b) The curve labeled *A* in Fig. 18.2 is the Lorenz curve for total family income. This simply plots the values in the last two columns of Table 18.1 Solution.

Figure 18.2

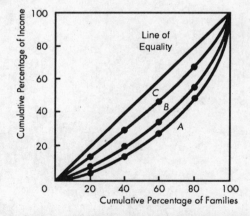

2. a) Table 18.2 is completed as Table 18.2 Solution.
   b) The curve labeled *B* in Fig. 18.2 is the Lorenz curve for after-tax family income.
   c) The progressive income tax has reduced inequality by taking a larger percentage of income from higher income groups.

Table 18.2 Solution: After-Tax Family Income

Percentage of families	After-tax income (billions of dollars)	After-tax income share (percent)	Cumulative percentage of families	Cumulative percentage of after-tax income
Poorest 20%	5	7	20	7
Second 20%	9	13	40	20
Third 20%	12	17	60	37
Fourth 20%	15	21	80	58
Richest 20%	30	42	100	100

3. a) Table 18.3 is completed as Table 18.3 Solution.
   b) The curve labeled *C* in Fig. 18.7 above is the Lorenz curve for (after-tax) after-transfer family income.
   c) Income redistribution through transfer payments has reduced inequality.

Table 18.3 Solution: After-Transfer Family Income

Percentage of families	After-transfer income (billions of dollars)	After-transfer income share (percent)	Cumulative percentage of families	Cumulative percentage of after-transfer income
Poorest 20%	15	15	20	15
Second 20%	16	16	40	31
Third 20%	18	18	60	49
Fourth 20%	20	20	80	69
Richest 20%	31	31	100	100

4. a) Since each individual in the economy earns exactly the same lifetime income, the Lorenz curve for lifetime income coincides with the line of equality and is labeled *A* in Fig. 18.3.
   b) The Lorenz curve for annual income is labeled *B* in Figure 18.3. It reflects the fact that the poorest 20 percent of the individuals (0–20 years) receive 0 percent of the annual income; the

second poorest 20 percent of the individuals (60–80 years) receive 13 percent of the annual income; the third poorest 20 percent of the individuals (21–35 years) receive 20 percent of the annual income; the fourth poorest 20 percent of the individuals (36–50 years) receive 27 percent of the annual income; and the richest 20 percent of the individuals (51–65 years) receive 40 percent of the income.

c) The distribution of lifetime income is a better measure of the degree of inequality. In this imaginary economy, all individuals are identical (equal), a fact that is reflected by equal lifetime incomes. The only reason annual income distribution in this economy is not equal is because the individuals are at different stages of identical life cycles.

Figure 18.3

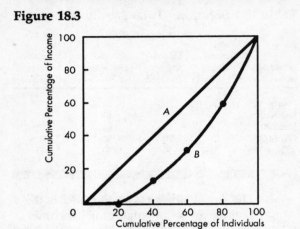

19 MARKET FAILURE

CHAPTER IN PERSPECTIVE

One of the conclusions of Chapter 11 is that competitive markets tend to be allocatively efficient. This fact suggests that when there are competitive markets there is no opportunity for the government to improve economic well-being through programs which reallocate resources. In Chapters 12 and 13, however, we noted that when markets are not competitive, allocative efficiency is not achieved. In the face of monopoly or oligopoly, are there things the government can do to improve efficiency? This question will be addressed in Chapter 21.

In this chapter we discover that there are circumstances in which even competitive markets fail to allocate goods and services efficiently. For example, if competitive markets are efficient, why is there so much pollution? As a result of such *market failure* to achieve efficiency, there may be additional opportunities for government to improve allocation. This chapter begins a discussion of how an "ideal" government might proceed to do so. In the next chapter we examine the behavior of actual governments.

LEARNING OBJECTIVES

After studying this chapter, you will be able to:

- **Describe the range of economic actions governments undertake**

- **Outline the structure of the government sector of the United States economy**

- **Distinguish between a normative and a positive analysis of government economic behavior**

- **Define market failure and explain how it might be overcome by government action**

- **Distinguish between private goods and public goods**

- **Explain the free-rider problem**

- **Explain how government provision of public goods avoids the free-rider problem**

Explain how property rights and taxes and subsidies may be used to achieve a more efficient allocation of resources when externalities are present

HELPFUL HINTS

1. The criterion economists use to judge the "success" of the market (or any other institution for that matter) is allocative efficiency. Allocative efficiency means that the economy is producing all goods and services up to the point at which the marginal cost is equal to the marginal benefit. In such a state, no one can be made better off without making someone else worse off.

When the market fails to achieve this "ideal" state of efficiency, we call it *market failure*. The market can fail by producing too little if the marginal benefit of the last unit exceeds the marginal cost. On the other hand, the market can fail by producing too much if the marginal cost of the last unit exceeds the marginal benefit.

2. Note that all goods provided by the government are not necessarily public goods. A public good is defined by the characteristics of nonrivalry and nonexcludability, not by whether or not it is publicly provided. For example, many cities and communities provide swimming pools and residential garbage pickup. Neither of these is a pure public good in spite of the fact that they may be provided by the government. Indeed, in many other communities the same services are provided by the private market.

3. It is important to understand why the properties of nonrivalry and nonexcludability associated with pure public goods imply that we obtain the marginal benefit curve for the economy as a whole differently than for private goods.

Since a private good is rival in consumption, to get the demand curve for the whole economy we sum the individual

marginal benefit (demand) curves horizontally. But, the economy's marginal benefit curve for a public good is obtained by summing the individual marginal benefit curves vertically. This is the relevant marginal benefit curve for evaluating the efficient provision level of the public good. See the discussion of Key Figure 19.1 below.

4. A competitive market will result in the quantity traded at which the marginal private cost is equal to the marginal private benefit. The efficient quantity is the quantity at which marginal social cost is equal to marginal social benefit. The difference between *marginal social* and *marginal private cost* is external cost and the difference between *marginal social benefit* and *marginal private benefit* is external benefit.

In most transactions, there are no affected third parties and so there are no external costs or benefits. This means that private and social costs and benefits coincide and competitive markets are efficient. However, when third parties are affected, there are external costs or benefits and competitive markets will not be efficient.

5. As indicated above, competitive markets with externalities are not efficient because some of the costs or benefits are *external*. If those costs or benefits could be *internalized* somehow, then the market would be efficient. There are two approaches to internalizing externalities that are discussed in this chapter.

The first of these is to clearly define and strictly enforce property rights. Then costs imposed on nonparticipants in a transaction can be recovered through the legal process and will thus be borne by those making the transaction decision, that is, the costs will become internal (private).

An alternative approach to internalizing externalities is to tax activities that generate external costs and subsidize activities that generate external benefits. By charging a tax equal to the external cost, the entire cost becomes internal. Similarly, by paying a subsidy in the amount of external benefits, all benefits become internal.

6. The production of steel also produces pollution, which will likely be an external cost. This means that the market will produce too much steel (and too much of the by-product, pollution). There are two important things to realize about the efficient level of steel production and thus the efficient level of pollution.

   a) If the production of steel is adjusted so that there is equality between marginal social cost and marginal benefit, *less* steel will be produced and will sell at a *higher* price.

   b) The external cost will not be so great that the efficient level of steel production is zero. This means that the efficient (optimal) level of pollution will not be zero.

KEY FIGURES AND TABLES

Figure 19.1 Benefits of a Public Good

An individual's marginal benefit curve for either a private good or a public good indicates willingness to pay. There is an important difference, however, in how we obtain the total *economy's* marginal benefit curve for private goods and public goods. This arises from the fact that private goods exhibit rivalry in consumption while public goods exhibit nonrivalry in consumption.

If one person consumes a unit of a private good, that unit cannot be consumed by anyone else. However, the consumption of a public good by one person does not reduce the amount available for others. This implies that the economy's marginal benefit curve

(demand curve) for a private good is obtained by summing the individual marginal benefit (demand) curves *horizontally* (see Chapter 7).

For a public good, however, the economy's marginal benefit curve is obtained by summing the individual marginal benefit curves *vertically*; that is, by adding up the individual marginal benefits at each quantity. This is illustrated in this figure by considering an economy in which there are two individuals, Lisa and Max, who receive benefits from antimissile lasers, a public good. Their total and marginal benefits are reported in the table. Their marginal benefit curves are given in parts (a) and (b) of the figure. The economy's marginal benefit curve is given in part (c) as the *vertical* sum of the marginal benefit curves of Max and Lisa.

Figure 19.2 The Efficient Scale of Provision of a Public Good

The efficient scale of provision of a public good is the amount that maximizes net benefit, which is total benefit minus total cost.

Part (a) of this figure graphs the total cost (*TC*) and total benefit (*TB*) curves. Net benefit is given by the vertical distance between the two curves. We find that this distance (net benefit) is a maximum at a quantity of two lasers. Thus two lasers is the efficient scale of provision.

Part (b) illustrates an alternative way to find the same result. The efficient scale of provision is achieved if lasers are produced up to the level at which marginal benefit equals marginal cost. The marginal benefit (*MB*) and marginal cost (*MC*) curves are shown in part (b). Marginal benefit equals marginal cost at a quantity of two lasers.

Figure 19.3 Taxing and Regulating an Externality

If the production of a good or service produces external costs, a competitive market will result in a quantity which exceeds the allocatively efficient level. This figure illustrates that taxing the production of that good or service can induce the allocatively efficient quantity. The example used here is that of transportation services, which produces external costs. The demand for transportation services is the same as marginal benefit. The marginal private cost (MPC) and marginal social cost (MSC) curves are not the same however. The MPC curve reflects the costs that directly accrue to the producer of transportation services. There are, however, other costs in the form of pollution and congestion that are imposed on others. The MSC curve reflects the marginal cost incurred by the producer as well as these external costs.

The allocatively efficient quantity of transportation services occurs at the intersection of the D (=MB) curve and the MSC curve; that is, Q_1. A competitive market, however, will result in the quantity at which the D and MPC curves intersect since producers will only take private costs into account; market price will be P_0 and quantity will be Q_0, which is greater than the allocatively efficient quantity.

If, however, a tax is levied on the producer in the amount of the external costs, the MSC curve becomes the new relevant marginal cost curve for producers. As a result the market price will rise to P_1 and the quantity will fall to Q_1, and allocative efficiency is achieved.

Figure 19.4 Subsidizing an External Benefit
In cases of external benefits, a competitive market will result in a quantity that is less than allocatively efficient. This is because the marginal social benefit associated with the good exceeds the marginal private benefit. In such a case, a subsidy can induce the market to achieve allocative efficiency.

This is illustrated in this figure using the example of education. The argument is similar to that of Fig. 19.3. In this case there is a divergence between the marginal private benefit (MPB) curve and the marginal social benefit (MSB) curve for education. The allocatively efficient quantity is Q_1. A

competitive market will result in a price of P_0 and quantity of Q_0, which is less than allocatively efficient. If the government subsidizes education so as to make it available for price P_1, the result will be the allocatively efficient quantity of Q_1.

CONCEPT REVIEW

1. If an unregulated market economy is unable to achieve allocative efficiency in all circumstances we have _____ _____.

2. There are two classes of economic theories of government behavior. The first of these, public _____ theories, predicts that government will pursue actions that will achieve allocative efficiency. Public _____ theories, however, study the behavior of government as the outcome of individual choices made by voters, politicians, and bureaucrats.

3. A good which, if consumed by one person, cannot be consumed by another is called a(n) _____ good. There are two important features of such a good. The fact that Bob's consumption of a good means that Sue cannot consume the same good illustrates the feature of _____. If Sue has purchased a good, she owns it

and can keep others from using it. This illustrates the feature of _____.

4. A good which, if consumed by one person, is necessarily also consumed by everyone else is called a(n) _____ _____ good.

5. Someone who consumes a good without paying for it is called a(n) _____ _____. When such individuals are prevalent in the consumption of a particular good, the amount of that good provided by the private market will be _____ than the allocatively efficient amount.

6. The maximum amount a person would be willing to pay for one more unit of a public good is the _____ _____ of that good to the individual.

7. A cost or a benefit arising from a transaction which affects someone other than the direct parties in the transaction is called a(n) _____. When a chemicals producing firm dumps its waste into the river, it kills a large number of fish downstream. This is an example of an external _____. When a neighbor plants flowers on the property line, you benefit. This is an example of an external _____.

8. A legally established title to the sole ownership of a resource is a(n)

_____ _____ _____.

9. The marginal cost borne directly by the producer of a good is called the marginal _____ cost. This marginal cost together with the marginal external cost is the marginal _____ cost.

10. If there are external costs in the production of steel (e.g., pollution), the output of steel produced by the market will be _____ than the allocatively efficient level.

TRUE OR FALSE

____ 1. The total government sector of the U.S. economy accounts for 35 percent of total spending.

____ 2. Since 1940, the U.S. government's total share of spending has remained about the same.

____ 3. Restriction of output by monopolies is an example of market failure.

____ 4. All redistribution of income or wealth by the government can be explained as motivated by notions of equity or distributive justice.

____ 5. The redistribution of income and wealth by the government arises partly from the rent-seeking activities of individuals in the economy.

____ 6. According to the public choice theory of government behavior, not only is there possibility of market failure, but there is also the possibility of "government failure."

____ 7. The existence of public goods gives rise to the free-rider problem.

____ 8. Any good made available by the government is a public good.

____ 9. The excludability feature of private goods will lead to free-riders.

____10. The economy's marginal benefit curve for a public good is obtained by adding the marginal benefits of each individual at each quantity of provision.

____11. The private market will produce much less than the efficient quantity of pure public goods.

____12. Net benefit is zero when the allocatively efficient level of output is obtained.

____13. Marginal social cost and external cost are the same thing.

____14. If the production of a good involves no external cost, then marginal social cost is equal to marginal private cost.

____15. If, at the current level of production of good A, marginal social benefit is less than marginal social cost, then output of good A should increase to achieve allocative efficiency.

____16. Externalities often arise from the absence of private property rights.

____17. The existence of external benefits means that marginal social cost is less than marginal private cost.

____18. When external costs are present, the private market will tend to produce more than the allocatively efficient level of output.

____19. Externalities exist because someone is willfully trying to harm others.

____20. The government can enhance allocative efficiency by subsidizing the production of goods that generate external benefits and taxing the production of goods that generate external costs.

MULTIPLE CHOICE

1. Which of the following is NOT a true statement about the U.S. government.
   a. Since 1940, the share of total government spending has risen from less than a fifth to over a third of all spending.
   b. The three levels of government are federal, state, and local.
   c. The department accounting for the largest share of federal expenditures is the Department of Defense.
   d. At all levels, government employs about one third of all workers.

2. Which of the following statements about theories of government is FALSE?
   a. Positive theories explain the reasons for and effects of government policies.
   b. Normative theories argue for the desirability of specific government policies.
   c. Public choice theories are positive theories.
   d. Public interest theories are normative theories.

3. If, in an unregulated economy, it is possible for someone to be made better off without making anyone worse off, then
   a. income is distributed unfairly.
   b. we have market failure.
   c. allocative efficiency has been achieved.
   d. net benefit is a maximum.

4. In the production of which of the following are we LEAST likely to experience market failure?
   a. Education
   b. National defense
   c. Bread
   d. Chemical fertilizer

5. Which of the following is <u>NOT</u> a source of which market failure?
   a. The existence of public goods
   b. The existence of monopolies
   c. Externalities
   d. An unequal distribution of income

6. When market failure occurs, the government will act to reduce the level of inefficiency. This is a prediction of
   a. an end-state theory of government behavior.
   b. a process theory of government behavior.
   c. a public interest theory of government behavior.
   d. a public choice theory of government behavior.

7. A good that exhibits both rivalry and excludability is a
   a. private good.
   b. public good.
   c. government good.
   d. mixed good.

8. Governments provide pure public goods like national defense because
   a. governments are more efficient than private firms at producing goods.
   b. of the free-rider problems, which results in underproduction by private markets.
   c. people do not value national defense very highly.
   d. of the potential that private firms will make excess profits.

9. Which of the following goods has the nonexcludability feature?
   a. A city bus
   b. A bridge that charges a toll
   c. A lighthouse
   d. An art museum

10. The market demand curve for a *private* good is obtained by
    a. summing the individual marginal cost curves horizontally.
    b. summing the individual marginal cost curves vertically.
    c. summing the individual marginal benefit curves horizontally.
    d. summing the individual marginal benefit curves vertically.

11. The economy's total demand curve for a *public* good is obtained by
    a. summing the individual marginal cost curves horizontally.
    b. summing the individual marginal cost curves vertically.
    c. summing the individual marginal benefit curves horizontally.
    d. summing the individual marginal benefit curves vertically.

12. The *total benefit* of a given level of provision of a public good can be obtained by
    a. adding the marginal benefit of each level of provision up to the given level.
    b. adding the marginal benefit of each level of provision and then subtracting the marginal cost of each level of provision.
    c. adding the net benefit of each level of provision up to the given level.
    d. multiplying net benefit by the quantity of the public good provided.

13. An externality is
   a. the effect of government regulation on market price and output.
   b. a cost or benefit that arises from a decision but is not borne by the decision maker.
   c. the amount by which price exceeds marginal cost.
   d. someone who consumes a good without paying for it.

14. Which of the following illustrates the concept of external cost?
   a. Bad weather reduces the size of the wheat crop.
   b. A reduction in the size of the wheat crop causes the income of wheat farmers to fall.
   c. Smoking harms the health of the smoker.
   d. Smoking harms the health of nonsmokers who are nearby.

15. Figure 19.1 depicts the demand for good A as well as the marginal private cost (MPC) and marginal social cost (MSC) associated with the production of good A. Production of the 6th unit of output generates an external
   a. cost of $3.
   b. cost of $6.
   c. benefit of $3.
   d. benefit of $6.

16. Refer to Fig. 19.1. How many units of good A will be produced in an unregulated market?
   a. 0 units
   b. 5 units
   c. 6 units
   d. 8 units

17. Refer to Fig. 19.1. What is the allocatively efficient quantity of good A?
   a. 0 units
   b. 5 units
   c. 6 units
   d. 8 units

Figure 19.1

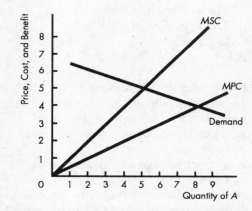

18. Figure 19.2 depicts the demand curve for good B as well as the marginal social benefit (MSB) and marginal cost (MC) curves. How many units of good B will be produced and consumed in an unregulated market?
   a. 0 units
   b. 3 units
   c. 5 units
   d. 7 units

19. Refer to Fig. 19.2. What is the allocatively efficient quantity of good B?
   a. 0 units
   b. 3 units
   c. 5 units
   d. 7 units

Figure 19.2

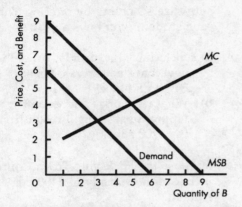

20. Refer to Fig. 19.2. Which of the following government policies would induce the market to achieve allocative efficiency?
    a. Tax the production of *B* in the amount of $3 per unit.
    b. Tax the production of *B* in the amount of $4 per unit.
    c. Subsidize the consumption of *B* in the amount of $3 per unit.
    d. Subsidize the consumption of *B* in the amount of $4 per unit.

SHORT ANSWER

1. What is meant by market failure?

2. Explain the *nonrival* and *nonexcludability* features of a pure public good?

3. What is the free-rider problem?

4. Governments provide education for free, or at least at a price (tuition) much less than cost. What is the economic argument that supports this policy?

5. Explain how a tax can be used to achieve efficiency in the face of external costs.

6. The production of steel also produces pollution and thus generates an external cost. Suppose the government attempts to solve the problem by imposing a tax on steel producers (who also produce pollution). At the after-tax level of output, we observe that the original marginal social cost curve is below the demand curve. Is the after-tax level of output efficient? If not, should steel production (and therefore pollution production) be increased or decreased?

PROBLEMS

1. Heritage Apartments has 100 residents who are concerned about security. Table 19.1 gives the total cost of hiring a 24-hour security guard service as well as the marginal benefit to each of the residents.
    a) Why is a security guard a public good for the residents of Heritage Apartments?
    b) Why will zero guards be hired if each of the residents must act individually?
    c) Complete the last column of Table 19.1 by computing the marginal benefit of security guards to the apartments; i.e., to all the residents together.

Table 19.1

Number of guards	Total cost per day (dollars)	Marginal benefit per resident (dollars)	Marginal benefit to all residents (dollars)
1	300	10	
2	600	4	
3	900	2	
4	1,200	1	

2. Now suppose that the residents form an Apartment Council which acts as a governing body in order to address the security issue.
   a) What is the optimal (allocatively efficient) number of guards? What is the net benefit at the optimal number of guards?
   b) Show that net benefit is less for either one less guard or for one more guard than the net benefit for the optimal number of guards.
   c) How can the Apartment Council pay for the optimal number of guards?

3. The first two columns of Table 19.2 give the demand schedule for education in Hicksville while the third column gives the marginal private cost. Since education generates external benefits, marginal social benefit, given in the last column, is greater than marginal private benefit.
   a) Represent the data in Table 19.2 graphically.
   b) What equilibrium price and quantity would result if the market for education is unregulated?
   c) What is the efficient quantity of students in Hicksville?

Table 19.2

Quantity (number of students)	Marginal private benefit (dollars)	Marginal private cost (dollars)	Marginal social benefit (dollars)
100	500	200	800
200	400	250	700
300	300	300	600
400	200	350	500
500	100	400	400
600	0	450	300

4. In an attempt to address the inefficient level of education in Hicksville the Town Council has decided to subsidize schooling by offering $200 to each student who buys a year of education.
   a) Including the subsidy, draw the new marginal private benefit curve and label it MPB_1.
   b) What new price and quantity (approximately) will result from the $200 subsidy?

5. Suppose the Hicksville Town Council increases the subsidy to $400 per student.
   a) Draw another marginal private benefit curve, which includes the subsidy, on your graph and label it MPB_2.
   b) What new price and quantity (approximately) will result from this $400 subsidy?
   c) What level of subsidy will achieve the efficient level of education?

ANSWERS

CONCEPT REVIEW

1. market failure
2. interest; choice
3. private; rivalry; excludability
4. pure public
5. free rider; less
6. marginal benefit
7. externality; cost; benefit
8. private property right
9. private; social
10. greater

TRUE OR FALSE

1. T	6. T	11. T	16. T
2. F	7. T	12. F	17. F
3. T	8. F	13. F	18. T
4. F	9. F	14. T	19. F
5. T	10. T	15. F	20. T

MULTIPLE CHOICE

1. c	6. c	11. d	16. d
2. d	7. a	12. a	17. b
3. b	8. b	13. b	18. b
4. c	9. c	14. d	19. c
5. d	10. c	15. a	20. c

SHORT ANSWER

1. Market failure occurs whenever the unregulated market fails to achieve allocative efficiency.

2. A good has the nonrivalry feature if its consumption by one person does not reduce the amount available for others. The nonexcludability feature means that if the good is produced and consumed by one person, others cannot be excluded from consuming it as well.

3. The free-rider problem is the fact that the unregulated market will produce too little of a pure public good since there will be little incentive for individuals to pay for the good. The reason is that the person's payment will likely have no perceptible effect on the amount the person will be able to consume.

4. Government subsidizes education heavily. The economic argument for this is that education generates external benefits. In particular, when individuals are educated, society at large receives benefits beyond the benefits that accrue to those choosing how much education to obtain.

5. The existence of external costs means that producers do not take into account all costs when deciding how much to produce. If a tax is levied that is exactly in the amount of the external cost, the cost will no longer be external. As a result, the producer will take it into account and thus be induced to produce the efficient quantity.

6. Since the marginal social cost curve is below the demand curve at the after-tax output, marginal social cost is less than marginal benefit. This means that the tax has been set too high; it has been set at a level in excess of the external cost. As a result, the after-tax level of steel production will be less than the efficient level. Thus, the level of steel production should be increased by decreasing the amount of the tax.

PROBLEMS

1. a) A security guard is a public good because, in this case, it has the features of nonrivalry and nonexcludability. It is nonrival because one resident's "consumption" of the security provided by a guard does not reduce the security of anyone else. The nonexcludability property is evidenced by the fact that once a security guard is in place, all residents enjoy the increased security; none can be excluded.
   b) If each resident must act individually in hiring a security guard none will be hired since each resident receives only $10 in benefit from the first guard which costs $300 per day.
   c) The entries in the last column of Table 19.1 are obtained by multiplying the marginal benefit per resident by the

number of residents, 100. This multiplication is the numerical equivalent of summing the individual marginal benefit curves *vertically* for each quantity of guards.

Table 19.1 Solution

Number of guards	Total cost per day (dollars)	Marginal benefit per resident (dollars)	Marginal benefit to all residents (dollars)
1	300	10	1,000
2	600	4	400
3	900	2	200
4	1,200	1	100

2. a) If the Apartment Council hires each guard for whom the marginal benefit exceeds the marginal cost, they will hire the optimal number of guards. The marginal cost of each additional guard is $300. The marginal benefit of the first guard is $1,000, so she will be hired. Similarly, the marginal benefit of the second guard is $400, and she will be hired. The marginal benefit of the third guard, however, is only $200 which is less than marginal cost. Therefore we conclude that the allocatively efficient (optimal) number of guards is two. For two guards, net benefit is $800: total benefit ($1,400) minus total cost ($600).
    b) For one guard, the net benefit is $700: total benefit ($1,000) minus total cost ($300). For three guards, the net benefit is also $700: total benefit ($1,600) minus total cost ($900). Thus, the net benefit of $800 is greater for two guards.
    c) The Apartment Council can achieve the optimal number of guards by collecting a "security fee" of $6 per day from each

of the 100 residents in order to hire two security guards.

3. a) Figure 19.3 is a graphical representation of the data in Table 19.2. The demand for education is given by the marginal private benefit curve (labeled *MPB*), the marginal private cost curve is labeled *MPC* and the marginal social benefit curve is labeled *MSB*.

Figure 19.3

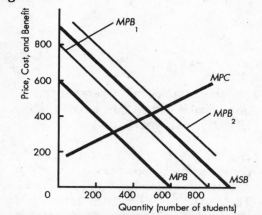

   b) In an unregulated market, equilibrium price and quantity are determined by the intersection of the *MPB* and *MPC* curves. Thus the equilibrium price would be $300 and the equilibrium quantity is 300 students.
   c) Since there are no external costs, the efficient quantity is determined by the intersection of the *MPC* and *MSB* curves. This implies that allocative efficiency is attained at 500 students.

4. a) The subsidy increases the marginal private benefit to each student by the amount of the subsidy, $200. The new *MPB* curve, labeled MPB_1, is included in Fig. 19.3.

b) The equilibrium after the $200 subsidy is at the intersection of the *MPC* and *MPB*₁ curves. The price of a unit of education will be approximately $370 ($366.67) and there will be approximately 430 (433.33) students.

5. a) With a subsidy of $400 per student, the *MPB* curve will shift to *MPB*₂ in Fig. 19.3.

b) With this subsidy the equilibrium will be at the intersection of the *MPC* and *MPB*₂ curves. The price of a unit of education will be approximately $430 ($433.33) and the number of students will be approximately 570 (566.67).
c) In order to achieve an efficient outcome, it must be that the subsidy makes the *MPB* curve coincide with the *MSB* curve. This requires a subsidy of $300 per student.

20 PUBLIC CHOICE

CHAPTER IN PERSPECTIVE

In Chapter 19, we learned that even when markets are competitive they are not always efficient. The existence of public goods and externalities implies an opportunity for government action to improve efficiency. For example, because of the free-rider problem, government must generally produce pure public goods in order for the efficient quantity to be produced. But, we observe the government providing goods and services that do not have the features of public goods; for example, garbage collection and mail service. Why? Even when a good provided by the government is a pure public good, will the quantity provided tend to maximize net benefit and thus be efficient?

In this chapter, our focus turns from the ideal to actual behavior of government. It presents the public choice theory, which recognizes that government actions are the consequences of interactions of participants in the *political marketplace*: voters, politicians, and bureaucrats. Just as in the markets for goods and services we have discussed to this point, participants in political markets pursue their own objectives. This powerful insight has significant implications for understanding the behavior of actual governments. We will discover why government actions are likely to fail to achieve efficiency.

LEARNING OBJECTIVES

After studying this chapter, you will be able to:

- Describe the components of the political marketplace

- Define a political equilibrium

- Explain how the main political parties choose an economic policy platform

- Explain how government bureaucracy interacts with politicians to determine the scale of provision of public goods and services

- Explain why we vote for redistributions of income and wealth

- Explain why we tax some goods at much higher rates than others

- Predict the effects of taxes on prices, quantities produced, and profits

- Explain why we subsidize the producers of some goods

- Predict the effects of subsidies on prices, quantities produced, and profits

HELPFUL HINTS

1. Public choice theory develops a theory of the political marketplace that parallels the economic theory of markets for goods and services we have developed to this point. It is very useful to think about the analogy between the operation of political markets and ordinary markets.

    a) In political markets the demanders are voters, while in ordinary markets the demanders are consumers. In both cases, demanders are concerned about costs and benefits they experience.

    b) The suppliers in political markets are politicians and bureaucrats, while in ordinary markets, goods and services are supplied by firms.

    c) In political markets, voters express their demands by means of votes, political contributions, and lobbying. This is because the suppliers (politicians) in this market are motivated by a desire to retain political office. In ordinary markets, consumers express their demands by means of dollars since suppliers are motivated by a desire to maximize profit.

    d) In both markets, equilibrium is a state of rest; that is, a state in which there is no tendency for change since no participant can become better off by making a different choice or engaging in an additional transaction.

2. Understand the logic behind the median voter theorem. Politicians want to be elected and then remain in office. To do so they must receive a majority of votes; that is, they must get at least one more than 50 percent of the votes. Since all politicians realize this, the median voter, the "middle" voter, becomes the key voter. A politician who offers a platform that deviates from the preferences of the median voter will lose to a politician who offers a platform closer to those preferences.

3. Well-informed special interest groups are able to induce the government to conduct programs that do not maximize net benefits because most voters are *rationally* ignorant. For most voters, it does not pay to be well informed about any particular issue. As a result, a small well-informed interest group will be able to have an influence on government programs that greatly exceeds their size relative to all voters.

4. From previous chapters we know that unregulated markets frequently fail to achieve allocative efficiency. In this chapter (and in the next) we learn that governments also frequently fail to achieve allocative efficiency. Since both markets and government fail, the relevant question in each case is: Which fails less?

KEY FIGURES AND TABLES

Figure 20.1 Provision of a Public Good in a Political System

    If voters are well informed and able to evaluate the benefits from alternative proposals, competition for votes among political parties will result in a political outcome that maximizes the net benefit of voters and is, therefore, allocatively efficient.   This is illustrated in this figure, which continues the example of antimissile lasers used in Chapter 19. These lasers are national defense public goods. The figure gives the total cost (TC) and total benefit (TB) curves (see Fig. 19.2a). Net benefit is maximized when two lasers are provided.

    There are two political parties, the Hawks and the Doves, with platforms that are identical in every way except their proposals regarding the number of lasers to install. If the Hawks propose to install 4 lasers and the doves propose to install 1 laser, the Doves will win the election since net benefits are $15 billion if 1 laser is installed but zero if 4 are installed.

If, on the other hand, the Hawks propose 2 lasers, they will win the election because the net benefit for 2 lasers is $20 billion. The only way the Doves can then avoid losing the election is to also propose 2 lasers.

Thus, if voters are in general agreement about the benefits and can readily calculate them, competition for voters between (among) political parties will produce the efficient scale of production of a public good.

Figure 20.2 The Principle of Minimum Differentiation

There is a tendency for individual competitors to minimize the differences between themselves and other competitors in order to maximize their appeal to customers or voters. This is the principle of minimum differentiation and is illustrated in this figure by examining two competing ice cream vendors on a one-mile stretch of beach (from A to B in the figure).

Assuming that sunbathers are evenly distributed along the beach, the first vendor will locate at C, halfway between A and B, so that no potential customer is more than half a mile away. The interesting question is: Assuming that ice cream customers will buy from the nearest stand, where will a second vendor locate?

This figure helps us understand that the second vendor will want to locate right next to the first. At this location, the second vendor can expect to attract half of the ice cream customers on the beach. This is the best he can do. At any other location (consider point D, for example), he will attract *less* than half the customers.

Figure 20.3 The Median Voter Theorem

The median voter theorem says that politicians will propose policies that maximize the net benefit of the median voter. This figure helps us clearly see the logic of the median voter theorem.

On any given political issue, there will be a range of views across voters. For example, in this figure, we consider the issue of what tax rate to charge polluters. If we arrange voters according to the tax rate they favor, the median voter is the one in the middle; that is, half the voters prefer a lower tax rate and half prefer a higher tax rate.

In the figure, we see that the median voter prefers a tax rate of 30 percent. Since politicians want to be elected and then stay in office they must obtain at least one more than 50 percent of the votes. As a result, a politician who proposes a tax rate of 30 percent will win against a politician who proposes any other tax rate.

If, for example, the second politician proposes any tax rate above 30 percent, the first politician will obtain the votes of the median voter (who prefers a 30 percent rate) as well as the half of voters who prefer tax rates less than 30 percent and thus win the election.

Similarly, if the second politician proposes any tax rate below that preferred by the median voter, the first politician will again win the election. Thus, the second politician cannot hope to win unless he too proposes the tax rate preferred by the median voter.

Figure 20.4 Bureaucratic Overprovision

This figure gives the same total benefit and cost curves depicted in Fig. 20.1. In the earlier figure, it was shown that the efficient scale of provision is two antimissile lasers and that if voters are well informed, the efficient scale would be achieved through the competitive political process. This will occur in spite of the fact that it is in the interest of the defense bureaucracy to increase expenditure of lasers as much as possible.

However, if some voters are rationally ignorant, the defense bureaucracy may be able to increase its budget and the number of lasers above the level that maximizes the net benefit of voters.

Figure 20.5 An Excise Tax

The effect of an excise tax on price and quantity traded is illustrated in this figure, using the market for gasoline as an example. We note that, before the tax is imposed, the price of gasoline is 60¢ a gallon and 400 million gallons a day are traded.

Then a tax of 60¢ a gallon is imposed. This causes the supply curve of gasoline to shift up by a vertical distance equal to the amount of the tax; i. e., the supply curve shifts from S to S + tax. The equilibrium price increases to $1.10 and the equilibrium quantity traded falls to 300 million gallons a day.

Note that even though the tax is 60¢ a gallon, the equilibrium price rises by only 50¢ a gallon. Thus, only 50¢ of the tax is borne by consumers and 10¢ is borne by the producer.

Figure 20.8 Subsidies
The effects of a subsidy are just opposite those of an excise tax. Subsidizing the production of a good will lower the price of the good and increase the quantity traded. This is illustrated in this figure, using the market for wheat.

In the wheat market without a subsidy, the equilibrium price of wheat is $3.50 a bushel and 2 billion bushels a year are traded. A government subsidy of $1.00 a bushel will cause the supply curve for wheat to shift down by a vertical distance equal to the amount of the subsidy; that is, the supply curve shifts from S to S-subsidy. This implies that the equilibrium price will fall to $3.00 a bushel and the quantity traded will rise to 3 billion bushels a year.

Wheat farmers receive just enough revenue (from the market price of $3 together with the subsidy of $1 per bushel) to cover their costs ($4 per bushel) of producing 3 billion bushels.

Figure 20.9 Subsidies with Quotas
This figure is a continuation of the wheat market example of Fig. 20.8. It shows the effects of the government imposing a quota on the production of wheat in addition to paying a subsidy. As in the previous figure, we note

that, without government involvement, the equilibrium price is $3.50 a bushel and 2 billion bushels of wheat a year are traded. Once again, the government introduces a subsidy of $1.00 a bushel, but now the government also introduces a quota of 2 billion bushels of wheat a year. With the quota of 2 billion bushels a year, the market price and quantity will not change from their values before the subsidy and quota are implemented. Thus, the producer receives $3.50 per bushel from consumers plus $1.00 per bushel from the government subsidy for a total of $4.50 per bushel. Since, at the quota amount, marginal cost is only $3.50, the extra dollar is like monopoly profit.

SELF-TEST

CONCEPT REVIEW

1. The theory that analyzes the "political market" using an approach similar to the economic analysis of ordinary markets is called _____ _____ theory.

2. In this theory, there are three key groups of players. The _____ are the consumers of the political process, while _____ are elected officials. Finally, _____ are appointed officials who work in the many departments and agencies of government.

3. Just as firms in ordinary markets seek dollars, politicians seek _____. The objective of a(n) _____ is to be elected and to remain in office.

4. If all voters have the same views and are able to correctly evaluate alternative government programs, political parties will produce platforms that _____ the net benefit of the _____.

5. The tendency for competitors (e.g., political parties) to make themselves almost identical in order to appeal to the maximum number of voters is called the principle of _____ _____. There is also a tendency for political parties to choose platforms that appeal to the _____ voter.

6. The theory of the behavior of bureaucracy discussed in the text assumes that bureaucrats try to maximize the _____ of the agency in which they work. Since all bureaucrats in all agencies have this objective, there is general _____ pressure on government spending across the board.

7. Since information is costly to obtain and voters are rational, only voters with a large direct interest in a political program will be well informed. As a result, the political equilibrium that emerges will tend to provide public goods on a scale that is _____ than the scale that maximizes net benefit.

8. A new tax will shift the _____ curve upward by the amount of the tax. The new equilibrium will be at a _____ price and a _____ quantity traded.

9. The loss of consumer surplus plus the loss of producer surplus associated with a tax is called the _____ loss of the tax. This loss is _____ the more inelastic the demand for the good being taxed.

10. A subsidy shifts the _____ curve of the subsidized good downward. Thus the market price of the good will _____ and the quantity traded will _____. If the subsidy is combined with a quota, the amount of the subsidy increases _____ surplus.

TRUE OR FALSE

_____ 1. The public choice theory of government behavior assumes that politicians and bureaucrats make decisions that are motivated only by concern for the public interest.

_____ 2. The only way voters can "express" their demands to politicians is through the votes they cast.

_____ 3. James Buchanan was awarded the Nobel Prize in economics for his contributions as one of the principal architects of public choice theory.

_____ 4. Public choice theory assumes that voters will support policies that they believe will make them better off and oppose policies that they believe will make them worse off.

_____ 5. Political parties will tend to propose fundamentally different policies in order to give voters a clearer choice.

_____ 6. In order to be elected, a politician will tend to choose a platform that will appeal to the median voter.

_____ 7. The income redistribution plan that has the greatest chance of being accepted by voters is the one that maximizes the income of the median voter.

_____ 8. According to William Niskanen's theory of bureaucracy, the objective of bureaucrats is to maximize the net benefit of voters.

_____ 9. The ability of bureaucrats to increase the size of their agency's budget is constrained by the ability of politicians to collect sufficient taxes.

_____ 10. If voters are all well informed, there will be a tendency for government policies to be those which maximize net benefit.

_____ 11. It is irrational for voters to be uninformed about an issue as important as national defense.

_____ 12. When many voters are not well informed about the costs and benefits of a public good, there will be a tendency for less of that good to be produced than the quantity that maximizes net benefit.

_____ 13. An excise tax that is set as a fixed percentage of the value of the commodity is called a specific tax.

_____ 14. The deadweight loss arising from a tax is equal to the loss of consumer surplus minus the loss of producer surplus due to the increase in price.

_____ 15. Imposing a sales tax on a monopoly industry will raise price but the quantity traded will remain unchanged.

_____ 16. Vote-seeking politicians will tend to impose heavier excise taxes on goods for which the demand is inelastic.

_____ 17. Subsidies to agriculture, especially when combined with quotas, are beneficial to consumers.

_____ 18. Subsidies combined with quotas generate an increase in producer surplus.

MULTIPLE CHOICE

1. Public choice theory
   a. argues that government has a tendency to conduct policies that help the economy toward allocative efficiency.
   b. argues that politicians and bureaucrats tend to be more concerned about the public interest than individuals in the private sector.
   c. applies the economic tools used to analyze markets to the analysis of government behavior.
   d. applies the tools of political analysis to the analysis of economic markets.

2. According to public choice theory, a voter will favor a candidate whose political program is
   a. perceived by the voter to offer the greatest personal benefit.
   b. best for the majority of the people.
   c. closest to allocative efficiency.
   d. favored by the median voter.

3. Who was awarded the Nobel Prize in economics for his fundamental contributions to public choice theory?
   a. Anthony Downs
   b. James Buchanan
   c. William Niskanen
   d. Milton Friedman

4. Public choice theory assumes that those involved in the political process are generally motivated by
   a. self-interest.
   b. the desire to achieve allocative efficiency.
   c. dishonesty.
   d. public spirit.

5. If voters have similar views and are well informed, the quantity of national defense provided by the government will tend to be
   a. greater than the allocatively efficient quantity.
   b. less than the allocatively efficient quantity.
   c. the least costly quantity.
   d. the quantity that maximizes net benefit.

6. Competition between two political parties will cause those parties to propose policies
   a. that are quite different.
   b. that are quite similar.
   c. of rational ignorance.
   d. that reduce the well-being of middle income families and increase the well-being of the rich and the poor.

7. On any given spending issue subject to a vote, the median voter is the one who favors
   a. the least spending.
   b. the most spending.
   c. the efficient level of spending.
   d. spending more than the amount favored by half the voters and less than the amount favored by half the voters.

8. Voters are asked to vote for either proposition A or proposition B. Proposition A will win if it
   a. is closer to allocative efficiency.
   b. is supported by bureaucrats.
   c. is preferred by the median voter.
   d. generates greater social benefit than social cost.

9. The tendency for redistribution policies to be stable for long periods of time is best explained by
   a. the trade-off between redistribution and the average level of income.
   b. the range of differences among voters.
   c. the principle of minimum differentiation.
   d. lobbying.

10. The claim that bureaucrats will attempt to maximize the budget of their agency follows from the assumption that bureaucrats
    a. have a superior understanding of the public interest.
    b. have an inferior understanding of the public interest.
    c. are motivated by the same forces of self-interest that motivate individuals in the private sector.
    d. are less honest than individuals in the private sector.

11. The budget of a government bureau is likely to increase beyond the quantity that maximizes net benefit of the economy if
    a. voters are well informed.
    b. there is rational voter ignorance combined with special interest lobbying.
    c. it is allocatively efficient to do so.
    d. bureaucrats are rationally ignorant.

12. According to public choice theory, a voter will tend to be well informed if the issue in question
    a. is complicated and difficult to understand.
    b. affects everyone a little.
    c. is of special interest to a small group to which the voter does not belong.
    d. has a large direct effect on the voter.

13. A sales tax that collects 5 percent of the amount of a purchase is an example of
    a. a specific tax.
    b. a proportional income tax.
    c. a flat tax.
    d. an *ad valorem* tax.

14. In general, a tax of $3 per unit of good A will
    a. shift the supply curve for *A* up by $3 and increase the price of *A* by $3.
    b. shift the supply curve for *A* up by $3 and increase the price of *A* by less than $3.
    c. shift the supply curve for *A* up by more than $3 and increase the price of *A* by $3.
    d. shift the supply curve for *A* up by less than $3 and increase the price of *A* by less than $3.

15. The deadweight loss due to a price increase resulting from a tax is
    a. the loss of consumer surplus.
    b. the loss of producer surplus.
    c. the loss of consumer surplus plus the loss of producer surplus.
    d. the loss of consumer surplus minus the loss of producer surplus.

16. The deadweight loss created by a new tax is zero if
    a. the supply curve is perfectly inelastic.
    b. the supply curve is perfectly elastic.
    c. the demand curve is more elastic than the supply curve.
    d. the demand curve is less elastic than the supply curve.

17. Figure 20.1 gives the demand and supply for imported cheese. Suppose that the government imposes a $3 tax per pound of imported cheese. What will happen to the price?
    a. It will increase by $3 to $7.
    b. It will increase by $3 to $6.
    c. It will increase by $2 to $6.
    d. It will increase by $2 to $5.

Figure 20.1

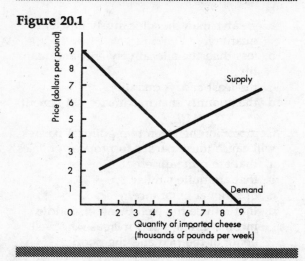

18. If the government subsidizes the production of a good, the
    a. supply curve will shift downward, price will fall, and quantity traded will increase.
    b. supply curve will shift upward, price will rise, and quantity traded will increase.
    c. demand curve will shift upward, price will rise, and quantity traded will increase.
    d. demand curve will shift downward, price will fall, and quantity traded will decrease.

SHORT ANSWER

1. How do voters express their demands in the "political market?"

2. Briefly compare an equilibrium in a political market to an equilibrium in a market for goods and services.

3. Why are the platforms of the two major political parties in the U.S. so similar?

4. The median voter theorem states that political candidates and parties will try to appeal to the median voter. Explain why the theorem holds.

5. Explain why it is rational for voters to be ignorant.

6. The fundamental assumption of the theory of public choice is that individuals involved in government activity are motivated by self-interest just as individuals involved in market activity. How does the assumption that bureaucrats aim to maximize the budget of the agency in which they work follow from this?

7. Why does the imposition of an excise tax cause the supply curve of the taxed good to shift upward?

8. How would public choice theory explain the existence of the current system of agricultural subsidies and quotas in the U.S.?

PROBLEMS

1. Two candidates are competing in an election for president of the Economics Club. The only issue dividing them is how much will be spent on the annual Economics Club party. It is well known that the 7 voting members of the club (A through G) have preferences as shown in Table 20.1.

Table 20.1

Voting member	Proposed amount (dollars)
A	10
B	20
C	30
D	40
E	50
F	60
G	70

These are strongly held preferences regarding exactly how much should be spent on the party.
a) How much will each candidate propose to be spent?
b) To demonstrate that your answer to (a) is correct, consider the outcome of the following two contests.

i) Candidate 1 proposes the amount you gave in part (a) and candidate 2 proposes $1 less. Which candidate will win? Why?

ii) Candidate 1 proposes the amount you gave in part (a) and candidate 2 proposes $1 more. Which candidate will win? Why?

c) Suppose that the Sociology Club is also electing a president and that the same single issue prevails. It is well known that the seven voting members of the Sociology Club have the strongly held preferences regarding exactly how much should be spent on their party given in Table 20.2.

Table 20.2

Voting member	Proposed amount (dollars)
T	0
U	0
V	0
W	40
X	41
Y	42
Z	43

How much will each of the two candidates propose in this case?

2. Table 20.3 gives three alternative income distributions for five individuals, A through E. Currently income is distributed according to distribution 1 (given in the second column of the table). Consider alternative proposed distributions 2 and 3 one at a time.

a) If distribution 2 is proposed as an alternative to distribution 1, will it have majority support? Why or why not?

b) If distribution 3 is proposed as an alternative to distribution 1, will it have majority support? Why or why not?

c) Suppose that distribution 2 is proposed with the following change. C is appointed the chief redistribution bureaucrat. This means that he will be paid $100 to oversee the collection of revenue from C, D, and E as well as make the payments to A and B. This arrangement, of course, leaves $100 less to be distributed to A and B, so suppose that their after-transfer incomes are $150 and $250, respectively. Call the new distribution 2a. If distribution 2a is proposed as an alternative to distribution 1, will it have majority support? Why or why not?

Table 20.3

Individual	Distribution 1 (dollars)	Distribution 2 (dollars)	Distribution 3 (dollars)
A	0	200	150
B	200	300	250
C	400	350	450
D	700	600	600
E	1,000	850	850

3. Figure 20.2 gives the supply and demand for movie tickets in Ourtown. The market is initially in equilibrium (point *a*) with a price of $5 per ticket and 5,000 tickets sold per week. Suppose that the town government establishes a new tax of $2 per movie ticket.

a) Illustrate the effect of the new tax graphically. What will the new equilibrium price and quantity traded be?

b) How much tax revenue will be collected each week?

c) How much consumer surplus will be lost due to the tax? How much producer surplus will be lost? What is the deadweight loss of the tax?

Figure 20.2

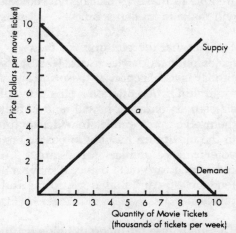

4. The supply and demand for Belgian endive (a leafy salad vegetable) are given in Fig. 20.3. Since this is a competitive market, the supply curve is the same as the industry marginal cost curve (the horizontal sum of the marginal cost curves for each producer). The competitive equilibrium price and quantity traded are $5 per pound and 5 million pounds per year respectively. There are 1000 Belgian endive farmers who are identical in every relevant way. Suppose that their congressman successfully establishes a government subsidy for Belgian endive in the amount of $2 per pound.
   a) Illustrate the effect of the subsidy graphically. What will the new equilibrium price and quantity traded be?
   b) What is the total amount of the subsidy paid? How much is received by each farmer? If there are 100 million

taxpayers, how much of the subsidy will each pay on average?
   c) Is price equal to the (after-subsidy) marginal cost?
   d) Does producer surplus increase or decrease with the subsidy? By how much?

Figure 20.3

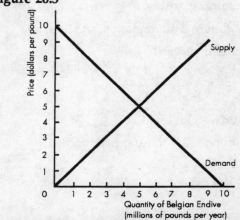

5. Now suppose that in addition to the subsidy of $2 per pound, a quota of 5 million pounds of Belgian endive per year is established.
   a) What are the resulting equilibrium price and quantity traded?
   b) What is the total amount of the subsidy paid?
   c) Is price equal to the (after-subsidy) marginal cost?
   d) Does producer surplus increase or decrease with the addition of the quota? By how much?

6. Suppose the Belgian endive farmers are able to choose the level of the government imposed quota while retaining the $2 per pound subsidy. What quota level would they choose? Why? (Hint: How would a cartel choose a restricted level of output?)

ANSWERS

CONCEPT REVIEW

1. public choice
2. voters; politicians; bureaucrats
3. votes; politician
4. maximize; voters
5. minimum differentiation; median
6. budget; upward
7. greater
8. supply; higher; lower
9. deadweight; less
10. supply; fall; increase; producer

TRUE OR FALSE

1. F	5. F	9. T	13. F	17. F
2. F	6. T	10. T	14. F	18. T
3. T	7. T	11. F	15. F	
4. T	8. F	12. F	16. T	

MULTIPLE CHOICE

1. c	5. d	9. a	13. d	17. c
2. a	6. b	10. c	14. b	18. a
3. b	7. d	11. b	15. c	
4. a	8. c	12. d	16. a	

SHORT ANSWER

1. Voters express their demands in the political marketplace by votes, by campaign contributions, and by lobbying.

2. In both cases, the equilibrium is a state of rest in the sense that no group has an incentive to change their choices. In the case of equilibrium in an ordinary market for goods and services, neither demanders nor suppliers are able to make an exchange that will make them better off. Similarly, when a political market is in equilibrium, neither demanders (voters) nor suppliers (politicians and bureaucrats) are able to make an alternative choice that will make them better off.

3. The fact that the platforms of the two major political parties in the U. S. are so similar is a reflection of the principle of minimum differentiation. This principle states that competitors will tend to make themselves very similar in order to appeal to the maximum number of customers or voters. Since political parties are competing for votes, they will have a tendency toward similar platforms and policies.

4. The median voter theorem holds because the objective of politicians is to be elected and then reelected to political office. In order to do so they must capture at least one more than 50 percent of the votes. Since all politicians are aware of this fact, the voter that can just put them over 50 percent becomes the key voter. That voter is the median voter. Politicians must choose a platform that appeals to the median voter in order to be elected.

5. Most issues have only a small and indirect effect on most voters. In such cases it would be irrational for a voter to spend much time and effort to become well informed since the additional cost would quickly exceed any additional benefit. Only if the voter is significantly and directly affected by an issue will it pay to become well informed. As a result most voters will be rationally ignorant regarding any given issue.

6. In general, maximizing the budget of the agency also promotes the self-interest of all the bureaucrats in the agency. The agency administrators obtain greater prestige and power as the agency's budget and the number of agency employees increases. For those who are not the top administrators, opportunities for promotion increase as the agency grows. Thus the self-interest of all agency members is served by maximizing its budget.

7. When an excise tax is imposed on a supplier, it raises the minimum price the supplier must receive in order to be willing to offer any given quantity for sale. This is nothing more than an upward shift in the supply curve. It is useful to think of a new excise tax as an increase in the cost of production.

8. Public choice theory would explain the existence of the current system of agricultural subsidies and quotas as the expected and inefficient consequence of rational voter ignorance and well-informed special interest groups. The costs borne by each of the great majority of voters is small so they will not be well informed or well organized.

On the other hand, the beneficiaries of these programs are much fewer in number and will each benefit significantly. Thus, they will tend to be well informed and well organized and will have a significant political impact. The resulting system will benefit producers at the expense of consumers.

PROBLEMS

1. a) Each candidate will propose spending $40 since that is the preference of the median voter (voter D).
   b) i) Candidate 1 will win because D, E, F, and G will vote for her since $40

comes closer to matching their preferences than the $39 proposed by candidate 2. Only A, B, and C will vote for candidate 2.
   ii) Candidate 1 will win because A, B, C, and D will vote for her while only E, F, and G will vote for candidate 2.
   c) Once again, the candidates will both propose spending $40 on the party since that is the preference of the median voter. Note that in this case, the median voter's view is not "average."

2. a) Only A and B are better off under distribution 2. Distribution 2 will receive the support of only A and B with C, D, and E opposed. Note particularly that the median voter (C) is worse off under distribution 2.
   b) Distribution 3 will receive majority support since it makes the median voter better off. It will be supported by A, B, and C and opposed by D and E.
   c) Under distribution 2a, C will now receive $450 (including the $100 payment as chief redistribution bureaucrat) while A and B will receive $150 and $250, respectively. Note that this is the same as distribution 3 except that C must now incur the costs of performing his new job. Assuming that these costs are small, C will prefer 2a to distribution 1 and it will thus have majority support.

3. a) The new tax shifts the supply curve for movie tickets up by $2, the amount of the tax. In Fig. 20.2 Solution the new curve is labeled S_1. The new equilibrium (point b) price and quantity traded are $6 per ticket and 4000 tickets per week respectively.

Figure 20.2 Solution

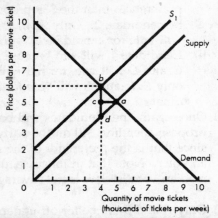

b) Total tax revenue will be $8,000 per week: $2 per ticket times 4000 tickets sold.

c) The loss of consumer surplus is given by the area of the triangle given by *abc* in Fig. 20.2 Solution and is equal to $500 (1/2 x base x height). Similarly, the loss of producer surplus is given by the area of the triangle given by *cda* and is equal to $500. Thus the deadweight loss is $1,000, the sum of consumer and producer surplus.

4. a) The subsidy shifts the supply curve for Belgian endive down by $2, the amount of the subsidy. The new supply curve is labeled S_1 in Fig. 20.3 Solution. The new equilibrium price is $4 per pound and the quantity traded is 6 million pounds per year.

b) The total subsidy paid is $12 million: $2 per pound times 6 million pounds of Belgian endive. This amounts to $12,000 received by each farmer but the 100 million taxpayers will pay an average of only 12 cents each.

c) Yes, price is equal to the after-subsidy marginal cost.

d) Producer surplus increases by $3.5 million; from $12.5 million before the

subsidy to $16 million after the subsidy. Recall that producer surplus is the amount by which revenue exceeds the opportunity cost of production (see Chapter 12). Graphically, it is given by the area below the price and above the relevant marginal cost curve. The producer surplus before the subsidy is given by the area in the triangle *0ab* ($12.5 million), while the producer surplus after the subsidy is given by the area in the trapezoid *0acf* ($16 million).

Figure 20.3 Solution

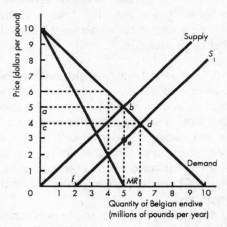

5. a) If a quota is established at 5 million pounds per year, the price will be $5 a pound and the quantity traded will be 5 million pounds.

b) The total amount of the subsidy is $10 million: $2 per pound times 5 million pounds.

c) Under the quota, price is $5 a pound but marginal cost (given by S_1) is only $3 a pound so price exceeds marginal cost (as in the case of monopoly).

d) The producer surplus increases by $4.5 million dollars to $20.5 million. Graphically, the producer surplus after the quota is given by the area of the 5-sided figure *0abef* in Fig. 20.3 Solution which is $20.5 million.

6. If the Belgian endive producers can choose the quota, they will set it so as to maximize industry profit. This level of output occurs when marginal revenue is equal to marginal cost for the industry.

The marginal revenue curve is labeled *MR* in Fig. 20.3 Solution and S_1 is the industry marginal cost curve given the subsidy. The profit maximizing output, and thus the quota that would be chosen by the farmers, is 4000 pounds per year.

In the situation described here, Belgian endive farmers will have, with the necessary help of the government, formed a cartel in which the government will enforce the output restrictions.

21 REGULATION AND ANTITRUST LAW

CHAPTER IN PERSPECTIVE

In Chapter 11, we found that as long as there are no externalities, unregulated competitive markets will tend to be efficient. In Chapter 12, we learned that profit-maximizing monopoly industries will produce less than the allocatively efficient quantity and charge a price that is higher than marginal cost. Similarly, from Chapter 13, we know that oligopoly industries can also behave like monopolies if the firms in the industry collude by forming an effective cartel. In this chapter, we examine government regulation of noncompetitive industries. We learn that there are government policies that can induce noncompetitive industries to come closer to allocative efficiency. If we have learned the lesson of the previous chapter, however, we will not be surprised to know that regulation does not always serve the public interest.

This is the last of three chapters on the allocative role of government. The existence of market failure provides opportunities for government to improve economic outcomes. However, it is important to remember that the political process involves people interacting; indeed it involves the same people who interact in markets for goods and services. This fact implies that the political process is also subject to failure to achieve allocative efficiency.

LEARNING OBJECTIVES

After studying this chapter, you will be able to:

- Define regulation

- Describe the main elements of antitrust law

- Distinguish between the public interest and capture theories of regulation

- State which parts of the economy are subject to regulation

- Describe the main trends in regulation and deregulation

- Explain how regulation of natural monopolies affects prices, outputs, profits, and the distribution of the gains from trade between consumers and producers

- Explain how the regulation of cartels affects prices, outputs, profits, and the distribution of the gains from trade between consumers and producers

- Explain how antitrust law has been applied in a number of landmark cases

HELPFUL HINTS

1. Consider Fig. 21.1, which depicts revenue and marginal cost curves for an industry. Using this figure, it is helpful to think of regulation as the determination of how the potential total surplus, represented by the area of the triangle *abc*, is divided among consumer surplus, producer surplus, and deadweight loss.

Figure 21.1

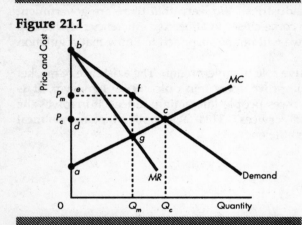

If the industry is perfectly competitive, then the quantity traded will be Q_c and the market price will be P_c. Total surplus is maximized and is given by the area of the triangle *abc*. Total surplus is equal to the sum of consumer surplus (given by the area of the triangle *dbc*) and producer surplus (given by the area of the triangle *adc*). There is no deadweight loss.

If the industry is a profit-maximizing monopoly, output will be Q_m, and the price will be P_m. In this case, total surplus is represented by the area of the trapezoid *abfg*. Because of monopoly restriction of output, total surplus under monopoly is less than under competition. The difference is the deadweight loss from monopoly, the amount of total surplus that is lost when we go from competition to monopoly. The deadweight loss is given by the area of the triangle *gfc*. Total surplus can

be divided into consumer surplus (given by the area of the triangle *ebf*) and producer surplus (given by the area of the trapezoid *aefg*). Consumer surplus is quite small but producer surplus is a maximum.

Of course, actual output may be between these bounds. As output moves from Q_c to Q_m, consumer surplus decreases while producer surplus and the deadweight loss both increase. If this industry is regulated, the public theory of regulation predicts that the result will be a level of output close to Q_c, while the capture theory of regulation predicts a level of output closer to Q_m.

KEY FIGURES AND TABLES

Figure 21.1 Natural Monopoly: Marginal Cost Pricing

Natural monopolies are heavily regulated. A natural monopoly has decreasing average total cost (*ATC*) over the entire range of market demand. Thus marginal cost (*MC*) is less than *ATC*. This figure illustrates a marginal cost pricing rule as applied to a natural monopoly.

The specific example of a natural monopoly examined here is that of a subway train system. Note the fact that the *ATC* curve is always decreasing. In this example, marginal cost is constant at 20¢ a ride. Setting the price at marginal cost maximizes total surplus and results in 8,000 rides an hour. The consumer surplus is indicated by the area of the green triangle. The producer will make a loss on each ride equal to the difference between ATC at 8,000 rides and the price of 20¢.

Figure 21.2 Natural Monopoly: Average Cost Pricing

This figure uses the same subway system as Fig. 21.1 to illustrate an average cost pricing rule as applied to a natural monopoly. The price is set equal to average total cost—at the intersection of the *ATC* curve and the demand curve.

Average cost pricing gives a price of 40¢ a ride and results in 6,000 rides an hour. The subway is now breaking even, but consumer surplus is less than under marginal cost pricing and there is a deadweight loss generated as indicated by the area of the gray triangle. This is the outcome predicted by the public interest theory of regulation.

Figure 21.3 Natural Monopoly: Profit Maximization

If the subway company is able to maximize profit, it will equate marginal cost (*MC*) and marginal revenue (*MR*). From the figure, we see that the price, given by the demand curve, will be 60¢ a ride and 4,000 rides an hour will be sold.

Since the price is above average total cost, the firm will now be making a profit as indicated by the area of the blue rectangle in the figure. Consumer surplus (the area of the green triangle) has declined even further, and the deadweight loss has increased (to the area of the gray triangle). This is the outcome predicted by the capture theory of regulation.

Figure 21.5 Collusive Oligopoly

From Chapter 13, we know that an oligopoly industry can make monopoly profits if the firms in the industry form a cartel and enter into a collusive agreement. Because each firm has an incentive to cheat, however, it is difficult to enforce the cartel agreement. As a result, an oligopoly may "demand" regulation which has the effect of having the government regulatory agency enforce the collusive agreement that generates monopoly profits for the industry. This is illustrated in this figure using the example of a ten-firm industry (trucking tomatoes from the San Joaquin valley to Los Angeles).

Under competition, the *MC* curve is the industry supply curve and the price will be $20 per trip and 300 trips per week will be made. However, the industry can maximize

profit if it can obtain regulation that restricts output to the level at which industry marginal cost is equal to industry marginal revenue and sets the price accordingly. In this example, industry output will be restricted to 200 trips per week and the price will be set at $30 per trip.

Table 21.1 Regulation at Its Peak in 1977

This table lists U. S. federal regulatory agencies at the peak of regulation in 1977. It also gives the year each agency was established and indicates the activities that it controlled and regulated.

Table 21.5 Antitrust Laws

The five most important U. S. antitrust laws are summarized in this table. Each of these laws is listed with the year it was enacted, and activities that are prohibited by the law.

Table 21.6 Landmark Antitrust Cases

The changing interpretation of antitrust law is indicated by this table summarizing the ten most important antitrust court cases in the United States. Each court case is listed and the year of the decision as well as the verdict and its consequences are indicated.

SELF-TEST

CONCEPT REVIEW

1. There are two principal ways that government intervenes in monopolistic and oligopolistic markets. The first of these is _____, which consists of rules administered by a government agency and intended to restrict the behavior of firms. The second is _____ _____, which legally prohibits certain kinds of monopoly practice.

2. The difference between the most that consumers are willing to pay and the amount they actually pay is called _____ _____. The difference between the revenue received by a producer and the opportunity cost of production is called _____ _____. The sum of these is _____ _____.

3. Allocative efficiency is achieved when total surplus is _____.

4. The larger the consumer surplus per buyer resulting from regulation, the _____ is the demand for regulation by buyers. The larger the producer surplus per seller resulting from regulation, the _____ is the demand for regulation by sellers.

5. The _____ _____ theory of regulation claims that regulations are supplied in order to attain allocative efficiency. The _____ theory of regulation states that regulations are intended to maximize producer surplus.

6. The first federal regulatory agency, established in 1887, is the _____ _____ Commission.

7. The pricing rule that maximizes total surplus and achieves allocative efficiency is the _____ _____ pricing rule.

8. When a regulatory agency sets the price of a regulated natural monopolist so that the regulated firm is able to earn a specified target percent return on its capital, it is using _____ _____ _____ regulation. If the target rate of return is a normal rate of return, this form of regulation gives the same result as the _____ _____ pricing rule.

9. The first antitrust law, passed in 1890, is the _____ Act.

10. The merger of two or more firms operating at different stages of the production process of a single good is called _____ integration. The merger of two or more firms providing essentially the same good is called _____ integration.

TRUE OR FALSE

_____ 1. Regulation and integration are the two main ways that the government intervenes in the operation of monopolistic and oligopolistic markets.

_____ 2. The first regulatory agency established in the U.S. is the Interstate Commerce Commission.

_____ 3. At the peak of regulation, in the late 1970s, almost a quarter of the nation's output was produced by regulated industries.

_____ 4. The first antitrust law was the Federal Trade Commission Act of 1914.

_____ 5. In a monopoly industry, producer surplus is maximized at the profit-maximizing level of output.

_____ 6. In a monopoly industry, total surplus is maximized at the profit-maximizing level of output.

_____ 7. For a given consumer surplus, the smaller the number of households who share that surplus, the smaller is the demand for the regulation that creates it.

_____ 8. Regulation is supplied by politicians and bureaucrats.

_____ 9. According to the public interest theory of regulation, all government regulation will move the economy closer to allocative efficiency.

_____ 10. According to the capture theory, government regulatory agencies eventually capture the profits of the industries they regulate.

_____ 11. A natural monopoly will always produce on the downward-sloping portion of its average total cost curve.

_____ 12. For a natural monopoly, marginal cost will always be less than average total cost.

_____ 13. An average cost pricing rule will achieve allocative efficiency.

_____ 14. In practice, rate of return regulation is equivalent to marginal cost pricing.

_____ 15. Under rate of return regulation, firms can get closer to maximizing producer surplus if they inflate their costs.

_____ 16. If, after deregulation of an industry, its prices and profits fall, we can reasonably conclude that the regulation was serving the interest of consumers.

_____ 17. According to the public interest theory of regulation, regulators will regulate a cartel to make sure that firms do not "cheat" on the collusive cartel agreement to restrict output.

_____ 18. The so-called rule of reason coming out of the American Tobacco Company and Standard Oil Company cases of 1911 softened the force of the Sherman Act.

_____ 19. The merger of Chrysler Corporation and American Motors Corporation, both of whom manufacture automobiles, is an example of a vertical merger.

_____ 20. The courts have interpreted the same antitrust laws differently at different periods of time.

MULTIPLE CHOICE

1. Which of the following industries has
    NOT been the object of significant deregu-
    lation in recent years?
    a. Airlines
    b. Telephones
    c. Postal service
    d. Banks and financial services

2. The difference between the maximum
    amount consumers are willing to pay and
    the amount they actually do pay for a
    given quantity of a good is called
    a. government surplus.
    b. consumer surplus.
    c. producer surplus.
    d. total surplus.

3. Total surplus is given by the sum of
    a. the gain from trade accruing to con-
        sumers and the gain from trade accru-
        ing to producers.
    b. the gain from regulation and the gain
        from antitrust laws.
    c. revenues received by firms and govern-
        ment subsidies.
    d. consumer payments and producer
        profit.

4. Total surplus is maximized when
    a. marginal revenue equals marginal cost.
    b. marginal cost equals average total cost.
    c. price equals marginal cost.
    d. price equals average total cost.

5. In a monopoly industry, producer surplus
    is maximized when
    a. marginal revenue equals marginal cost.
    b. marginal cost equals average total cost.
    c. price equals marginal cost.
    d. price equals average total cost.

6. Which of the following situations will
    generate a large demand for regulation by
    producers? Regulation results in
    a. small consumer surplus per buyer.
    b. large consumer surplus per buyer.
    c. small producer surplus per seller.
    d. large producer surplus per seller.

7. In a political equilibrium,
    a. allocative efficiency must be achieved.
    b. no one wants to change their proposals.
    c. firms will be making zero economic
        profit.
    d. all parties will agree that the appropri-
        ate level of regulation has been
        achieved.

8. Which of the following is consistent with
    the public interest theory of regulation?
    a. Regulation of a natural monopolist by
        setting price equal to marginal cost.
    b. Regulation of a competitive industry in
        order to increase output.
    c. Regulation of the airline industry by
        establishing minimum airfares.
    d. Regulation of agriculture by establish-
        ing barriers to exit from the industry.

9. Which of the following is consistent with
    the capture theory of regulation?
    a. Regulation of a natural monopolist by
        setting price equal to marginal cost.
    b. Regulation of a competitive industry in
        order to increase output.
    c. Regulation of the airline industry by
        establishing minimum airfares.
    d. Regulation of agriculture by establish-
        ing barriers to exit from the industry.

10. Which of the following is LEAST likely to
    be a *natural monopoly*?
    a. Local subway services
    b. Local electric utilities
    c. Local water and sewer services
    d. Local taxi cab service

11. Figure 21.2 gives the revenue and cost curves for an industry. This industry will become a natural monopoly because
    a. one firm can supply the entire market at a lower price than two or more firms could.
    b. the *MC* curve is negatively sloped when it intersects the demand curve.
    c. there are diseconomies of scale over the entire range of demand.
    d. even a single firm will be unable to earn a positive profit in this industry.

Figure 21.2

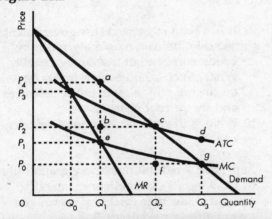

12. Consider the natural monopoly depicted in Fig. 21.2. Total surplus is a maximum when
    a. quantity is Q_1 and price is P_3.
    b. quantity is Q_1 and price is P_4.
    c. quantity is Q_2 and price is P_2.
    d. quantity is Q_3 and price is P_1.

13. Consider the natural monopoly depicted in Fig. 21.2. Producer surplus is a maximum when
    a. quantity is Q_1 and price is P_3.
    b. quantity is Q_1 and price is P_4.
    c. quantity is Q_2 and price is P_2.
    d. quantity is Q_3 and price is P_1.

14. Consider the natural monopoly depicted in Fig. 21.2. If a regulator uses a marginal cost pricing rule, what line segment gives the amount of subsidy (per unit of output) that will be required to assure that the monopolist will remain in business?
    a. *ba*
    b. *ea*
    c. *fc*
    d. *gd*

15. Consider the natural monopoly depicted in Fig. 21.2. What region in the graph represents the deadweight loss arising from an average cost pricing rule?
    a. *abc*
    b. *cdg*
    c. *cfg*
    d. *aeg*

16. A monopolist under rate of return regulation has an incentive to
    a. inflate costs.
    b. produce more than the efficient quantity of output.
    c. charge a price equal to marginal cost.
    d. maximize consumer surplus.

17. Which of the following is an example of horizontal integration?
    a. A steel company buys a fast food restaurant chain.
    b. An oil refining company buys an oil drilling company.
    c. A large television manufacturing firm buys a smaller television manufacturing firm.
    d. The accounting and marketing departments of a large firm are merged.

18. Which of the following best characterizes the interpretation of antitrust law in the U.S. since the Sherman Act?
    a. These laws have almost always been interpreted in favor of consumers.
    b. These laws have generally been interpreted in favor of producers.
    c. These laws have sometimes been interpreted in favor of producers and sometimes in favor of consumers.
    d. These laws have been interpreted as calling for deregulation of oligopoly industries.

SHORT ANSWER

1. Regulation of monopoly is necessary because of the tension between the public interest and the producer's interest. Explain.

2. In 1938, the Civil Aeronautics Board (CAB) was established to regulate the airline industry since it was an oligopoly industry.
   a) Consider the capture theory of regulation. What kind of price and output would be predicted by this theory? What kind of regulations about entry into the industry would be predicted?
   b) Consider the public interest theory of regulation. What kind of price and output would be predicted by this theory? What kind of regulations about entry into the industry would be predicted?
   c) Suppose you discovered that between 1938 and 1978 (when the industry was deregulated) the CAB did not grant even one long-distance route to a new airline even though more than 150 requests were made. With which of these theories is this fact consistent?

3. In the regulation of a natural monopoly, when would an average cost pricing rule

be better than a marginal cost pricing rule?

4. Why is rate of return regulation equivalent to average cost pricing?

5. What, if anything, can the behavior of prices and profits following deregulation of an industry tell us about whether regulation favored consumers or producers?

6. How did the "rule of reason" soften the effect of the Sherman Act?

PROBLEMS

1. a) It has been suggested that government should eliminate monopoly profit by taxing each unit of monopoly output. What effect would such a policy have on the quantity a monopolist produces and the price it charges?
   b) What is the effect on economic efficiency?

2. Represent a natural monopoly graphically by drawing its demand curve, marginal cost curve, average total cost curve, and marginal revenue curve.
   a) Indicate the quantity produced and the price charged if there is no regulation. Denote them Q_1 and P_1 respectively.
   b) Indicate the quantity produced and the price charged under a marginal cost pricing role. Denote them Q_2 and P_2 respectively.
   c) Indicate the quantity produced and the price charged under an average cost pricing rule. Denote them Q_3 and P_3 respectively.

3. Table 21.1 gives the demand for Aero-disks, a disk made from a unique material that flies a considerable distance when thrown. The Aerodisk Company, which makes them, is a natural monopoly. The firm's total fixed cost is $700 and the marginal cost is constant at $2 per disk. (Note that this implies that average variable cost is also constant at $2 per disk.) Suppose that the Aerodisk Company is not regulated.
    a) What will be the price of an Aerodisk and how many will be sold?
    b) How much is total profit or loss?
    c) How much is producer surplus?
    d) How much is consumer surplus?
    e) How much is total surplus?

Table 21.1 Demand for Aerodisks

Price (dollars)	Quantity demanded per year
10	0
9	100
8	200
7	300
6	400
5	500
4	600
3	700
2	800
1	900
0	1000

4. Now suppose that the Aerodisk Company becomes regulated and that the regulator uses a marginal cost pricing rule.
    a) What will be the price of an Aerodisk and how many will be sold?
    b) How much is total profit or loss?
    c) How much is producer surplus?
    d) How much is consumer surplus?
    e) How much is total surplus?

5. Suppose that the regulator of the Aerodisk Company uses an average cost pricing rule.
    a) What will be the price of an Aerodisk and how many will be sold?
    b) How much is total profit or loss?
    c) How much is producer surplus?
    d) How much is consumer surplus?
    e) How much is total surplus?

6. Since the Aerodisk company will make a loss under marginal cost pricing, the government must subsidize the production of Aerodisks in order for the firm to be willing to produce.
    a) What is the total subsidy necessary under a marginal cost pricing rule to leave the firm with a zero profit?
    b) What is the amount of the deadweight loss associated with an average cost pricing rule?
    c) In order to pay the necessary subsidy under the marginal cost rule, the government must raise tax revenue in the amount of the subsidy. If the deadweight loss associated with the tax is $100, which pricing rule is superior?

7. Figure 21.3 illustrates the industry demand, marginal revenue (MR), and marginal cost (MC) curves in an oligopoly industry. The industry is regulated.
    a) What price and quantity will be predicted by the public interest theory of regulation? Why?
    b) What price and quantity will be predicted by the capture theory of regulation? Why?
    c) Can you explain why the firms in this industry might be demanders of regulation?

Figure 21.3

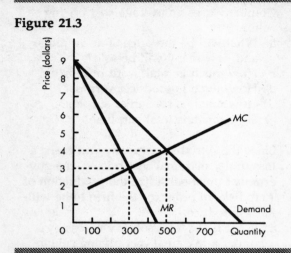

TRUE OR FALSE

1. F	5. T	9. T	13. F	17. F
2. T	6. F	10. F	14. F	18. T
3. T	7. F	11. T	15. T	19. F
4. F	8. T	12. T	16. F	20. T

MULTIPLE CHOICE

1. c	5. a	9. c	13. b	17. c
2. b	6. d	10. d	14. d	18. c
3. a	7. b	11. a	15. c	
4. c	8. a	12. d	16. a	

ANSWERS

CONCEPT REVIEW

1. regulation; antitrust law
2. consumer surplus; producer surplus; total surplus
3. maximized
4. larger; larger
5. public interest; capture
6. Interstate Commerce
7. marginal cost
8. rate of return; average cost
9. Sherman
10. vertical; horizontal

SHORT ANSWER

1. It is in the public interest to achieve allocative efficiency; that is, to expand output to the level that maximizes total surplus. On the other hand, it is in the interest of the monopoly producer to restrict output in order to maximize producer surplus and thus, monopoly profit. Since these interests are not the same, monopoly must be regulated in order to achieve allocative efficiency. The public interest theory of regulation suggests that this is the principle that guides regulation of monopoly industries.

2. a) The capture theory of regulation would predict that the market outcome would be closer to maximizing producer surplus than to maximizing total surplus. Thus we would expect industry output to be restricted and prices to be "high." This theory would also predict that there would be restrictions on the entry of new firms. Ideally (from the perspective of the capturing firms) all entry would be prohibited.
   b) The public interest theory of regulation would predict that regulation of the airlines will lead to the maximization of total surplus. This implies that

output will be expanded to the level at which marginal cost equals marginal revenue and price will be equal to marginal cost. Entry of new firms will certainly be allowed since the increase in competition will help to achieve efficiency.

c) The fact that the CAB did not grant a single long-distance route to a new airline (although requests were made) is quite consistent with the capture theory and quite inconsistent with the public interest theory.

3. An average cost pricing rule will create a deadweight loss but so will a marginal cost pricing rule, through the need to impose a tax.

   Since, for a natural monopoly, marginal cost is less than average total cost, regulation by use of a marginal cost pricing rule requires the government to pay a subsidy in order for the firm to be willing to produce at all.

   In order to pay that subsidy the government must levy a tax which will impose a deadweight loss on the economy. If the deadweight loss associated with the tax (i.e., the deadweight loss of the marginal cost pricing rule with its attendant subsidy) is greater than the deadweight loss of an average cost pricing rule, the average cost pricing rule is superior.

4. The key here is to recall that economic cost includes a normal rate of return. Thus, since rate of return regulation sets a price that allows the firm to achieve a normal rate of return, it is setting the price equal to average total cost.

5. If, after deregulation of an industry, prices and profits fall, we can conclude that the regulation must have favored producers.

6. The Sherman Act prohibits monopoly practices. In 1911, however, the Supreme Court enunciated the "rule of reason," which states that monopoly arising from mergers or agreements may not be illegal. This softened the effect of the Sherman Act, since such monopoly practices were said to be illegal only if they involve "unreasonable" restraint of trade.

PROBLEMS

1. a) Imposing a tax on each unit sold by a monopolist will increase marginal cost. As a consequence the profit-maximizing monopolist will raise the price and reduce the quantity produced.

   b) The tax will certainly reduce the profit of the monopolist and may even eliminate it, but the consequence will be to make the inefficiency due to monopoly even worse. This is illustrated in Fig. 21.4 below. The *MC* curve is the marginal cost curve before the tax. An unregulated monopolist will produce amount Q_2, while the economically efficient output is Q_3. The tax, however, causes the monopolist to *reduce* output from Q_1 to Q_2 which moves the market outcome farther away from efficiency.

2. Figure 21.5 illustrates a natural monopoly (note the economies of scale). Note the price and quantity outcomes under
   a) no regulation (Q_1, P_1).
   b) marginal cost pricing (Q_2, P_2).
   c) average cost pricing (Q_3, P_3).

Figure 21.4

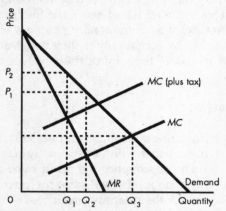

Figure 21.5

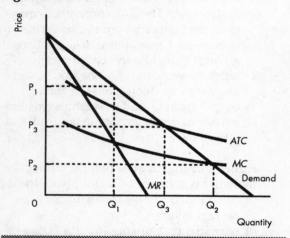

3. Figure 21.6 will be helpful in answering questions about the Aerodisk market. It gives the relevant revenue and cost curves for the aerodisk Company.

a) In an unregulated market, the Aerodisk company will choose output so as to maximize profit; i.e., where $MR = MC$. This means that the price of an Aerodisk will be $6 and 400 will be produced and sold.

b) To determine total profit we first determine average total cost (ATC) when output (Q) is 400 units.

$$ATC = AFC + AVC = (TFC/Q) + AVC$$
$$= (\$700/400) + \$2 = \$3.75$$

Therefore total profit is the difference between price (average revenue) and ATC times the quantity sold. This is equal to $90 and is represented in Fig. 21.6 by the region *fbcg*.

c) Producer surplus is the difference between the producers revenue and the opportunity cost of production. Total revenue is $2400 ($6 x 400 units) and total opportunity cost is $800 ($2 x 400 units) so producer surplus is $1600. Graphically, producer surplus is the area of the rectangle *abde* in Fig. 21.6

d) Consumer surplus is readily obtained graphically as the area in the triangle denoted *bcd* in Fig. 21.6. The area of that triangle is $800.

e) Total surplus is $2400, the sum of producer and consumer surplus.

Figure 21.6

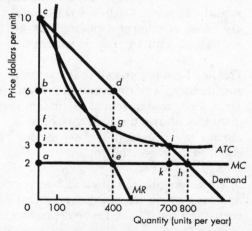

4. a) Under a marginal cost pricing rule, the price of an Aerodisk will be $2 and 800 will be sold.

   b) To determine the amount of profit or loss, we must first determine ATC when output is 800. Using the procedure in the previous problem we find that at $Q = 800$, ATC is $2.875 which is greater than price by $.875 (87.5¢). Therefore, the Aerodisk Company will make a loss in the amount of $700 (.875 x 800). (Alternatively, since MC is constant, if the price is set equal to MC which is equal to AVC, the total loss will be just TFC or $700.)

   c) Producer surplus is zero.

   d) Consumer surplus is given by the area of the triangle *ach* in Fig. 21.5 which is $3200.

   e) Total surplus is $3200 (a maximum).

5. a) Computation of ATC at various levels of output allows us to determine that the ATC curve crosses the demand curve when $Q = 700$ and $ATC = \$3$. Thus, under an average cost pricing rule, the price of an Aerodisk will be $3 and 700 units will be sold.

   b) Since price is equal to average total cost, profit is zero.

   c) Producer surplus is $700, the area of the rectangle *aijh* in Fig. 21.6.

   d) Consumer surplus is $2450, the area of the triangle *ijc* in Fig. 21.6.

   e) Total surplus is $3150.

6. a) The total subsidy is equal to the loss under marginal cost pricing. In Problem 4(b) we computed this to be $700.

   b) The deadweight loss associated with the average cost pricing rule is the loss of total surplus relative to the marginal cost pricing rule. We have computed the total surplus under marginal cost pricing ($3200) in Problem 4(e) and the total surplus under average cost pricing ($3150) in Problem 5(e). The deadweight loss is the difference: $50.

   c) The average cost pricing rule is superior since it has the smaller deadweight loss.

7. a) The public interest theory predicts that regulators will set price and quantity so as to maximize total surplus. This means that they will choose quantity (and price) where MC is equal to demand. This corresponds to a quantity of 500 units and a price of $4 per unit.

   b) The capture theory predicts that the regulator will choose quantity and price so as to maximize the profit of the industry. This is the quantity that would be chosen by a profit-maximizing monopolist, 300 units, where $MC = MR$. The highest price that could be charged and still sell that quantity can be read from the demand curve: $6 per unit.

   c) Firms in the industry would be demanders of regulation if the regulation had the effect of increasing profit to the industry. As we discovered in Chapter 14, cartels are unstable because there is always an incentive to cheat on output restriction agreements and it is very difficult to enforce the agreements. If, however, the firms in an industry can get the government, through regulation, to enforce a cartel agreement, they will want to do it.

22 TRADING WITH THE WORLD

CHAPTER IN PERSPECTIVE

Over the past two decades in the U.S., the volume of imports and exports as a percent of GDP has doubled. As the U.S. has become more dependent on international trade, issues associated with international trade have become more prominent in public discussion. Today, much is said and some is even done about our relationships with key trading partners and there seems to be much support among some political leaders for protectionist policies.

We first address the basic issue of why nations trade. What is the nature of the gains that make trade worthwhile? What determines which goods a country will import and which it will export? We then turn to more difficult issues such as: If there are significant gains to free trade, why do countries frequently restrict imports? What are the effects of a tariff or a quota or some other trade restriction?

These are timely issues which are not widely understood and which will likely become increasingly important.

LEARNING OBJECTIVES

After studying this chapter, you will be able to:

- **Describe the patterns and trends in international trade**

- **Explain comparative advantage**

- **Explain why all countries can gain from international trade**

- **Explain how prices adjust to bring about balanced trade**

- **Explain how economies of scale and diversity of taste lead to gains from international trade**

- **Explain why trade restrictions lower the volume of imports and exports and lower our consumption possibilities**

- **Explain why we have trade restrictions even though they lower our consumption possibilities**

HELPFUL HINTS

1.   It is useful to recall the discussion of opportunity cost, comparative advantage, and gains from trade in Chapter 3. The current chapter applies the fundamental concepts of opportunity cost and comparative advantage to the problem of trade between nations. The basic principles are the same whether we are talking about trade between individuals in the same country or between individuals in different countries.

Many students (and others involved in debates about trade) seem confused by the concept of comparative advantage, partially because they implicitly conceive of *absolute advantage* as the sole reason for trade. A country has an absolute advantage if it can produce all goods using less inputs than another country. However, such a country can still gain from trade.

To see this, consider comparing California to North Dakota. California has better weather and in combination with widespread irrigation has an absolute advantage in the production of all agricultural products— indeed, California frequently has more than one harvest a year! This would seem to imply that California has no need to trade with North Dakota. However, North Dakota has a *comparative advantage* in the production of wheat. Therefore, California will specialize in fruits and trade them for wheat. California could easily grow its own wheat, but to do so would have too high an opportunity cost—the lost fruit crops. By specializing and trading, both California and North Dakota can gain.

2.   In addition to the gains from trade, this chapter also discusses the economic effects of trade restrictions. One of the important things we learn is that the economic effects of a tariff and a quota are the same. We note that a voluntary export restraint (VER) is also a quota but a quota imposed by the exporting country rather than the importing country.

All these trade restrictions raise the domestic price of the imported good, reduce the volume of and value of imports. They will also reduce the value of exports by the same amount as the reduction in the value of imports. The increase in price that results from each of these trade restrictions produces a gap between the domestic price of the imported good and the foreign supply price of the good.

The difference between the alternative trade restrictions lies in which party captures this excess. In the case of a tariff, the government receives the tariff revenue. In the case of a quota imposed by the importing country, domestic importers who have been awarded a license to import capture this excess through increased profit. When a VER is imposed, the excess is captured by foreign exporters who have been awarded licenses to export by their government.

3.   The major point of this chapter is that gains from free trade can be considerable. Why then do countries have such a strong tendency to impose trade restrictions? The key is that while free trade creates overall benefits to the economy as a whole, there are both winners and losers. The winners gain more in total than the losers lose, but the latter tend to be concentrated in a few industries.

It is therefore not surprising that free trade will be resisted by some acting on the basis of rational self-interest. Even though only a small minority benefit from any given trade restriction, while the overwhelming majority will be hurt, it is not surprising to see trade restrictions implemented. The reason is that the cost of a given trade restriction to each of the many is individually quite small, while the benefit to each of the few will be individually large. Thus, the few will have a significant incentive to see that restriction takes place, while the many will have little incentive to expend time and energy in resisting trade restriction.

KEY FIGURES

Figure 22.2 Opportunity Cost in Pioneerland
This figure shows the production possibility frontier for the imaginary country of Pioneerland. Currently it is producing and consuming 15 billion bushels of grain and 8 million cars a year at point *a* on the production possibility frontier. Opportunity cost is measured as the slope of the production possibility frontier at this point. At point *a*, 1 car costs 9,000 bushels of grain, or 9,000 bushels cost 1 car.

Figure 22.3 Opportunity Cost in Magic Empire
This figure shows the production possibility frontier for the imaginary country of Magic Empire. Currently it is producing and consuming 18 billion bushels of grain and 4 million cars a year at point *a* on the production possibility frontier. Opportunity cost is measured as the slope of the production possibility frontier at this point. At point *a*, 1 car costs 1,000 bushels of grain, or 1,000 bushels cost 1 car.

Figure 22.4 International Trade in Cars
The price at which a good trades internationally and the quantity traded are determined by the international market for the good. This figure illustrates a hypothetical international market for cars using the example of Pioneerland and Magic Empire.

Magic Empire has a comparative advantage in the production of cars and so supplies cars to the world market. At higher prices, Magic Empire is willing to supply more cars although it must receive at least 1 thousand bushels of grain (its opportunity cost of a car) to be willing to produce.

The supply curve in the figure gives Magic Empire's export supply of cars. Similarly, the demand curve in the figure gives Pioneerland's import demand for cars. It shows that as the price of a car falls, the quantity of cars that Pioneerland wants to import increases

although it will not buy any cars at a price above 9 thousand bushels of grain (its opportunity cost of a car). The equilibrium price when trade takes place is at the intersection of these two curves. The price of a car (under free trade) is 3 thousand bushels of grain and 4 million cars per year are imported by Pioneerland from Magic Empire.

Figure 22.5 Expanding Consumption Possibilities
This figure clearly illustrates the gains from trade experienced by Pioneerland and Magic Empire. Without trade, each country consumes what it produces. Its consumption is constrained by the production possibility frontier. The gain from trade for each country is that, with trade, while production is constrained by the production possibility frontier, consumption can exceed that frontier. Consumption is only constrained by the consumption possibility curve which (except for a single point) lies beyond the production possibility curve.

Part (a) of the figure shows the situation for Pioneerland. Without trade, Pioneerland produces and consumes at point *a*: 8 million cars and 15 billion bushels of grain. With trade (at 1 car trading for 3 thousand bushels of grain), Pioneerland produces at point *b*: 5 million cars and 30 bushels of grain.

But, because of trade, consumption can be different. Indeed, with trade, Pioneerland consumes at point *c*: 9 million cars and 18 billion bushels of grain. This is 1 million more cars and 3 billion more bushels of grain than were consumed without trade (at point *a*). This additional consumption is the gain from trade for Pioneerland. A similar analysis in part (b) illustrates that Magic Empire also gains from trade.

Figure 22.7 The Effects of a Tariff
The effects of a tariff on the price of a good and the quantity traded are shown in this figure by using the Pioneerland and Magic Empire example of trade in cars. Pioneer-

land imposes a tariff of $4,000 per car on cars imported from Magic Empire. This shifts the export supply curve upward by $4,000 since Magic Empire must also be able to cover the tariff. Thus the price of a car in Pioneerland increases from $3,000 to $6,000 and the quantity of cars traded falls to 2 million per year. The total revenue from the tariff (which is received by the government of Pioneerland) is $8 billion: $4,000 per car times 2 million cars. Although this figure does not show it directly, Pioneerland's grain exports will also decrease because Magic Empire's income from export of cars has fallen.

Figure 22.8 The Effects of a Quota

This figure illustrates the effects of a quota on domestic price and quantity traded again using the Pioneerland and Magic Empire example. Pioneerland imposes a quota of 2 million cars per year. This restriction is indicated in the graph by a vertical line at 2 million cars. This becomes the effective supply curve for the purpose of determining the price, which turns out to be $6,000. The quantity traded, of course, is 2 million cars per year, the quota limit. At 2 million cars, Magic Empire is willing to supply cars for $2,000 each. This $4,000 per car difference between the selling price and the price received by the exporter is captured by the importer.

SELF-TEST

CONCEPT REVIEW

1. The goods and services purchased from people in foreign countries are called _____. The goods and services sold to people in foreign countries are called _____. The value of exports minus the value of imports is called the _____ of _____.

2. A country is said to have a(n) _____ _____ in the production of a good if it can produce that good at a lower opportunity cost than any other country. A country is said to have a(n) _____ _____ if for all goods its output per unit of inputs is higher than any other country.

3. The restriction of international trade is called _____. A tax imposed by the importing country on an imported good is called a(n) _____. The result of imposing such a tax is to _____ the price that consumers in the importing country pay and _____ the quantity traded. When such a tax is imposed the tax revenue is received by the _____.

4. The international agreement negotiated after World War II and designed to limit government restriction of international trade is called the _____ _____ on _____ and _____.

5. A restriction that specifies a limit on the quantity of a particular good that can be imported is called a(n) _____. The result of such a limit is to _____ the price that consumers in the importing country pay. The extra

revenue from such a limit is received by the _____.

6. An agreement between two governments in which the government of the exporting country agrees to restrict the quantity of its exports to the importing country is called a(n) _____ _____ _____. Such an agreement will _____ the price that consumers in the importing country pay for the good.

7. When a good is sold in a foreign market at a lower price than in a domestic market or for a price that is lower than the cost of production it is called _____.

8. A tariff that enables domestic producers to compete with subsidized foreign producers is called a _____ _____.

TRUE OR FALSE

____ 1. The United States imports more manufactured goods than it exports.

____ 2. The United States is a net exporter of agricultural products.

____ 3. When a U.S. citizen stays in a hotel in France, the U.S. is exporting a service.

____ 4. In the U.S., international trade has become less important as a percent of GDP since 1950.

____ 5. If there are two countries, A and B, and two goods, X and Y, and country A has a comparative advantage in the production of X, then country B must have a comparative advantage in the production of Y.

____ 6. If country A must give up 3 units of Y to produce 1 unit of X and B must give up 4 units of Y to produce 1 unit of X, then A has a comparative advantage in the production of X.

____ 7. If countries specialize in goods for which they have a comparative advantage, then some countries will gain and others will lose but the gains will be larger than the losses.

____ 8. Trading according to comparative advantage allows all trading countries to consume outside their production possibility frontier.

____ 9. If a country has an absolute advantage, it will not benefit from trade.

____10. Countries may exchange similar goods for each other due to economies of scale in the face of diversified tastes.

____11. When governments impose tariffs, they are increasing their country's gain from trade.

____12. Tariffs in the U.S. are much higher than they were before World War II.

____13. The General Agreement on Tariffs and Trade (GATT) has successfully reduced trade restrictions in the world.

____14. A tariff on a good will raise its price and reduce the quantity traded.

____15. A tariff not only reduces the total value of imports but it reduces the total value of exports as well.

____16. A quota will cause the price of the imported good to fall.

____17. The government will raise no revenue from a quota.

____18. The "excess revenue" created by a voluntary export restraint is captured by the exporter.

____19. Japan is dumping steel if it sells it in Japan at a lower price than it sells it in the U.S.

____20. Elected governments are likely to be slow to reduce trade restrictions even though the gains would be much larger than the losses because there would be many fewer losers than gainers.

MULTIPLE CHOICE

1. The U.S. is a
   a. net exporter of manufactured goods and net importer of agricultural products.
   b. net exporter of manufactured goods and net exporter of agricultural products.
   c. net importer of manufactured goods and net importer of agricultural products.
   d. net importer of manufactured goods and net exporter of agricultural products.

2. Which of the following is a U.S. export of a service?
   a. A U.S. citizen buys a restaurant meal while traveling in Switzerland.
   b. A Swiss citizen buys a restaurant meal while traveling in the U.S.
   c. A U.S. citizen buys a clock made in Switzerland.
   d. A Swiss citizen buys a computer made in the U.S.

3. The country with which the U.S. has the largest international trade deficit is
   a. Canada.
   b. Japan.
   c. Mexico.
   d. the European Economic Community.

4. Suppose there are two countries, A and B, producing two goods, X and Y. Country A has a comparative advantage in the production of good X if less
   a. of good Y must be given up to produce one unit of X than in country B.
   b. labor is required to produce one unit of X than in country B.
   c. capital is required to produce one unit of X than in country B.
   d. labor and capital are required to produce one unit of X than in country B.

5. Suppose there are two countries, A and B, producing two goods, X and Y and that country A has a comparative advantage in the production of X. If the countries trade, the price of X in terms of Y will be
   a. greater than the opportunity cost of X in country A and less than the opportunity cost of X in country B.
   b. less than the opportunity cost of X in country A and greater than the opportunity cost of X in country B.
   c. greater than the opportunity cost of X in both countries.
   d. less than the opportunity cost of X in both countries.

6. Compared to a no-trade situation, international trade according to comparative advantage allows each country to consume
   a. more of the goods it exports but less of the goods it imports.
   b. more of the goods it imports but less of the goods it exports.
   c. more of both goods it exports and goods it imports.
   d. less of both goods it exports and goods it imports.

7. In country A, it requires one unit of capital and one unit of labor to produce a unit of X and it requires two units of capital and two units of labor to produce a unit of Y. What is the opportunity cost of good X?
   a. The price of a unit of capital plus the price of a unit of labor.
   b. One unit of capital and one unit of labor.
   c. Two units of capital and two units of labor.
   d. One half unit of Y.

8. If country A has an absolute advantage in the production of everything,
   a. no trade will take place because country A will have a comparative advantage in everything.
   b. no trade will take place because no country will have a comparative advantage in anything.
   c. trade will probably take place and all countries will gain.
   d. trade will probably take place but country A will not gain.

9. The imposition of a tariff on imported goods will increase the price consumers pay for imported goods and
   a. reduce the volume of imports and the volume of exports.
   b. reduce the volume of imports and increase the volume of exports.
   c. reduce the volume of imports and leave the volume of exports unchanged.
   d. will not affect either the volume of imports or the volume of exports.

10. Who benefits from a tariff on good X?
    a. Domestic consumers of good X.
    b. Domestic producers of good X.
    c. Foreign consumers of good X.
    d. Foreign producers of good X.

11. Which of the following is responsible for significant reduction in trade restrictions since World War II?
    a. The Smoot-Hawley Act.
    b. The voluntary exports restraint agreement between the U.S. and Japan.
    c. The United Nations.
    d. The General Agreement on Tariffs and Trade.

12. A tariff on good X which is imported by country A will cause
    a. the demand curve for X in country A to shift upward.
    b. the demand curve for X in country A to shift downward.
    c. the supply curve of X in country A to shift upward.
    d. the supply curve of X in country A to shift downward.

13. Country A and country B are currently engaging in free trade. Country A imports good X from country B and exports Y to B. If country A imposes a *tariff* on X, country A's X producing industry will
    a. expand and its Y producing industry will contract.
    b. expand and its Y producing industry will expand.
    c. contract and its Y producing industry will contract.
    d. contract and its Y producing industry will expand.

14. Country A and country B are currently engaging in free trade. Country A imports good X from country B and exports Y to B. If country A imposes a *quota* on X, country A's X producing industry will
    a. expand and its Y producing industry will contract.
    b. expand and its Y producing industry will expand.
    c. contract and its Y producing industry will contract.
    d. contract and its Y producing industry will expand.

15. When a *tariff* is imposed, the gap between the domestic price and the export price is captured by
    a. consumers in the importing country.
    b. the person with the right to import the good.
    c. the government of the importing country.
    d. foreign exporters.

16. When a *quota* is imposed, the gap between the domestic price and the export price is captured by
    a. consumers in the importing country.
    b. the person with the right to import the good.
    c. the government of the importing country.
    d. foreign exporters.

17. When a voluntary export restraint agreement is reached, the gap between the domestic price and the export price is captured by
    a. consumers in the importing country.
    b. the person with the right to import the good.
    c. the government of the importing country.
    d. foreign exporters.

18. Country A imports good X from country B and exports Y to B. Which of the following is a reason why country A might prefer arranging a voluntary export restraint rather than a quota on X?
    a. So as NOT to reduce the volume of its own exports of Y.
    b. To prevent country B from retaliating by restricting country A's exports.
    c. To keep the domestic price of X low.
    d. To increase government revenue.

SHORT ANSWER

1. What is meant by comparative advantage?

2. How is it that *both* parties involved in trade can gain?

3. Why do countries exchange similar manufactured goods with each other?

4. How does a tariff on a particular imported good affect the domestic price of the good, the export price, the quantity imported,

and the quantity of the good produced domestically?

5. How does a tariff on imports affect the exports of the country?

6. How does a quota on a particular imported good affect the domestic price of the good, the export price, the quantity imported, and the quantity of the good produced domestically?

7. How does a voluntary export restraint (by the foreign exporting country) on a particular imported good affect the domestic price of the good, the export price, the quantity imported, and the quantity of the good produced domestically?

8. Why might a government prefer a quota to a tariff?

9. Why might an importing country prefer to arrange a voluntary export restraint than to impose a quota or a tariff?

10. Who benefits and who loses if the U.S. obtains a "voluntary" export restraint on Japanese cars? Why might the United Auto Workers (a union) lobby strongly for such a trade restriction?

PROBLEMS

1. Consider a simple world in which there are two countries, Atlantis and Beltran, each producing two goods, food and cloth. The production possibility frontier for each country is given in Table 22.1 below.
   a) Assuming a constant opportunity cost in each country, complete the table.
   b) What is the opportunity cost of food in Atlantis? Of cloth?
   c) What is the opportunity cost of food in Beltran? Of cloth?

d) Draw the production possibility frontiers on separate graphs.

Table 22.1

Atlantis		Beltran	
Food (units)	Cloth (units)	Food (units)	Cloth (units)
0	500	0	800
200	400	100	600
400		200	
600		300	
800		400	
1,000		--	--

2. Suppose that Atlantis and Beltran engage in trade.
   a) In which good will each country specialize?
   b) If 1 unit of food trades for 1 unit of cloth, what will happen to the production of each good in each country?
   c) If 1 unit of food trades for 1 unit of cloth, draw the consumption possibility frontiers for each country on the corresponding graph from Problem 1 (a).
   d) Before trade, if Atlantis consumed 600 units of food, the most cloth it could consume was 200 units. After trade, how many units of cloth can be consumed if 600 units of food are consumed?

3. Continue the analysis of Atlantis and Beltran trading at the rate of 1 unit of food for 1 unit of cloth.
   a) If Atlantis consumes 600 units of food and 400 units of cloth how much food and cloth will be consumed by Beltran?
   b) Given the consumption quantities and the production quantities from problem 2 (b), how much food and cloth will

Atlantis and Beltran import and export?

4. Figure 22.1 gives the import demand curve for shirts for country A, labeled D, and the export supply curve of shifts for country B, labeled S.
    a) What is the price of a shirt under free trade?
    b) How many shirts will be imported by country A?

Figure 22.1

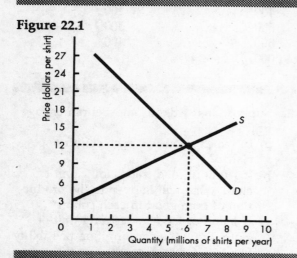

Quantity (millions of shirts per year)

5. Suppose the shirtmakers in country A of Problem 4 are concerned about foreign competition and so the government of country A imposes a tariff of $9 per shirt. Using Fig. 22.1, answer the following questions.
    a) What will happen to the price of a shirt in country A?
    b) What is the price the exporter will actually receive?
    c) How many shirts will be imported by country A?
    d) What is the revenue from the tariff? Who captures it?

6. Suppose that instead of a tariff, country A imposes a quota of 4 million shirts per

year. Again, use Fig. 22.1 to answer the following questions.
    a) What will be the price of a shirt in country A?
    b) What price will the exporter actually receive?
    c) How many shirts will be imported by country A?
    d) What is the difference between the total amount paid by consumers and the total amount received by exporters—the "excess profit?" Who captures it?

7. Finally, suppose that instead of a tariff or a quota, country A induces country B to impose a voluntary export restraint (VER) of 4 million shirts per year.
    a) What will be the price of a shirt in country A?
    b) How many shirts will be imported by country A?
    c) Is there any "excess" profit here? If so, how much is it and who captures it?

CONCEPT REVIEW

1. imports; exports; balance; trade
2. comparative advantage; absolute advantage
3. protectionism; tariff; increase; decrease; government
4. General Agreement; Tariffs; Trade
5. quota; raise; importer
6. voluntary export restraint; raise
7. dumping
8. countervailing duty

TRUE OR FALSE

1. T	6. T	11. F	16. F
2. T	7. F	12. F	17. T
3. F	8. T	13. T	18. T
4. F	9. F	14. T	19. F
5. T	10. T	15. T	20. T

MULTIPLE CHOICE

1. d	6. c	11. d	16. b
2. b	7. d	12. c	17. d
3. b	8. c	13. a	18. b
4. a	9. a	14. a	
5. a	10. b	15. c	

SHORT ANSWER

1. Comparative advantage simply means lowest opportunity cost. A country is said to have a comparative advantage in the production of some good if it can produce that good at a lower opportunity cost than any other country.

2. In order for two potential trading partners to be willing to trade, they must have different comparative advantages; that is, different opportunity costs. If they do, then they will trade and both parties will gain. If the parties do not trade, they will each face their own opportunity costs. A price at which trade takes place must be somewhere between the opportunity costs of the two traders. This means that the party with the lower opportunity cost of the good in question will gain because it will receive a price above its opportunity cost. Similarly, the party with the higher opportunity cost will gain because it will pay a price below its opportunity cost.

3. The exchange of similar manufactured goods is the result of economies of scale in the face of diversified tastes. With international trade, each manufacturer faces the entire world market. Thus they can specialize very narrowly to satisfy a particular taste and still take advantage of economies of scale.

4. A tariff on an imported good will *raise its price to domestic consumers* as the export supply curve shifts upward. The export price is determined by the original export supply curve. As the domestic price of the good rises, the quantity of the good demanded falls and thus the relevant point on the original export supply curve is at a lower quantity and a *lower export price*. This lower quantity means that the *quantity imported falls*. The rise in the domestic price will also lead to an *increase in the quantity of the good supplied domestically*.

5. When country A imposes a tariff on its imports of good X, not only does the volume of imports shrink but the volume of exports of Y to country B will shrink by the same amount. Thus a balance of trade is maintained. As indicated in the answer to Short Answer Question 4, the export price of good X falls when a tariff is imposed. This fall in the price received by the exporter means that the price of imports in the foreign country has risen; i.e., if the amount of Y that country B gets for an X has fallen, the quantity of X that must be given up to obtain a Y has increased. This implies that the quantity of Y (A's export) demanded by country B will fall and thus A's exports decline.

6. The effect of a quota on the domestic price of the good, the export price, the quantity imported, and the quantity of the good produced domestically are exactly the same as the effects of a tariff discussed in the answer to Short Answer 4. The only difference is that the increase in the domestic price is here not the result of a

vertical shift in the export supply curve but the result of the fact that the quota forces a vertical effective export supply curve at the quota amount.

7. The effect of a voluntary export restraint (VER) is exactly the same as that of a quota. Indeed a VER is a quota. The only difference is that the government of the exporting country is able to distribute the excess revenue from the quota rather than the government of the importing country.

8. The effects of tariffs and quotas on prices and quantities (see the answers to Questions 4 and 6 above). The difference is that the excess revenue raised by a tariff is captured by the government whereas the excess revenue raised by a quota is captured by those persons who have been given the right to import by the government. In either case the government is in a position to benefit. It may prefer to use quotas in order to reward political supporters by giving them rights to import and thus allowing them to capture large profits. Second, quotas give the government more precise control over the quantity of imports. Also, it is politically easier to impose a quota than a tariff.

9. The only difference between a quota and a voluntary export restraint (VER) is which government has the ability to reward its political supporters. As discussed in the answer to Short Answer 8, under a quota, the importing country's government can take advantage of the quota to reward its political supporters. Under a VER, it is the exporting country's government that has this ability. An importing country may prefer a VER in order to avoid a tariff or quota war with the exporting country.

10. If the U.S. arranges a voluntary export restraint (VER) on Japanese cars, U.S.

producers of cars and their input suppliers benefit because the price of cars is higher. U.S. car buyers (a much larger group), however, lose because they must pay higher prices for cars. In addition, U.S. industries that would have exported to Japan (e.g., agricultural products, timber, and services) will lose because the demand for their products will fall (see the answer to Short Answer 5, which is applicable here). Since the United Auto Workers represent an important input in the U.S. car industry, they would lobby strongly for trade restrictions in order to at least temporarily retain jobs in the industry.

PROBLEMS

1. a) Completed Table 22.1 is shown here as Table 22.1 Solution. The values in the table are calculated using the opportunity cost of each good in each country. See parts (b) and (c) below.

Table 22.1 Solution

| Atlantis | | Beltran | |
Food (units)	Cloth (units)	Food (units)	Cloth (units)
0	500	0	800
200	400	100	600
400	300	200	400
600	200	300	200
800	100	400	0
1,000	0	--	--

b) In order to increase the output (consumption) of food by 200 units, cloth production (consumption) falls by 100 units in Atlantis. Thus the opportunity cost of a unit of food is 1/2 unit of cloth. This opportunity cost is constant as are all others in this problem, for simplicity. Similarly, the opportunity cost of clothing in Atlantis is 2 units of food.

c) In Beltran a 100 unit increase in the production (consumption) of food requires a reduction in the output (consumption) of cloth of 200 units. Thus the opportunity cost of food is 2 units of cloth. Similarly the opportunity cost of cloth in Beltran is 1/2 units of food.

d) Figure 22.2 parts (a) and (b) illustrate the production possibility frontiers for Atlantis and Beltran, respectively labeled PPF_A and PPF_B. The rest of the diagram is discussed in the solution to Problems 2 and 3.

2. a) We see from the solutions to Problems 1 (b) and (c) that Atlantis has lower opportunity cost (1/2 unit of cloth) in the production of food, Atlantis will specialize in the production of food. Beltran, with the lower opportunity cost for cloth (1/2 unit of food) will specialize in cloth.

b) Each country will want to produce every unit of the good in which they specialize as long as the amount they receive in trade exceeds their opportunity cost. For Atlantis, the opportunity cost of a unit of food is 1/2 unit of cloth but it can obtain 1 unit of cloth in trade. Since the opportunity cost is constant (in this simple example), Atlantis will totally specialize by producing all of the food it can: 1000 units per year (point b in Fig. 22.2(a). Similarly, in Beltran, the opportunity cost of a unit of cloth is 1/2 unit of food but a unit of cloth will trade for 1 unit of food. Since the opportunity cost is constant, Beltran

Figure 22.2

(a)

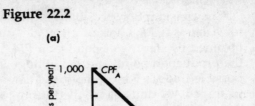
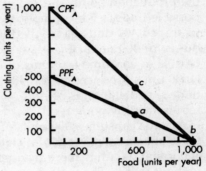

(b)

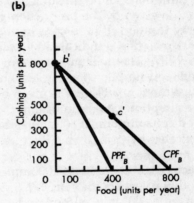

will totally specialize in the production of cloth and will produce 800 units per year (point b' in Fig. 22.2(b)).

c) The consumption possibility frontiers for Atlantis and Beltran (labeled CPF_A and CPF_B) are illustrated in Fig. 22.2, parts (a) and (b), respectively. These frontiers are straight lines that indicate all the combinations of food and cloth that can be consumed with trade. The position and slope of the consumption possibility frontier for an economy depend on the terms of trade between the goods and the production point of the economy.

The consumption possibility frontier for Atlantis (CPF_A), for example, is obtained by starting at point b on PPF_A, the production point, and examining possible trades. For example, if Atlantis traded 400 units of the food it produces for 400 units of cloth, it would be able to consume 600 units of food (1000 units produced minus 400 units traded) and 400 units of cloth, which is represented by point c.

d) If Atlantis consumes 600 units of food, trade allows consumption of cloth to be 400 units, 200 units more than possible without trade. The maximum amount of cloth that can be consumed *without trade* is given by the production possibility frontier. If food consumption is 600 units, this is indicated by point a on PPF_A. The maximum amount of cloth consumption for any level of food consumption *with trade* is given by the consumption possibility frontier. If food consumption is 600 units, this is indicated by point c on CPF_A.

3. a) Since Atlantis produces 1000 units of food per year (point b on PPF_A), to consume 600 units of food and 400 units of cloth (point c on CPF_A) it must trade 400 units of food for 400 units of cloth. This means that Beltran has traded 400 units of cloth for 400 units of food. Since Beltran produces 800 units of cloth, this implies that Beltran must consume 400 units of food and 400 units of cloth (point c' on CPF_B).

b) Atlantis exports 400 units of food per year and imports 400 units of cloth. Beltran exports 400 units of cloth per year and imports 400 units of food.

4. a) The price of a shirt under free trade will occur at the intersection of country A's import demand curve for shirts and country B's export supply curve of shirts. This occurs at a price of $12 per shirt.

b) Country A will import 6 million shirts per year.

5. a) The effect of the $9 per shirt tariff is to shift the export supply curve (S) upward by $9. This is shown as a shift from S to S' in Fig. 22.1 Solution. The price is now determined by the intersection of the D curve (which is unaffected by the tariff) and the S' curve. The new price of a shirt is $18.

b) Of this $18, $9 is the tariff, so the exporter only receives the remaining $9.

c) Country A will now import only 4 million shirts per year.

d) The tariff revenue is $9 (the tariff per shirt) times 4 million (the number of shirts imported), which is $36 million. This money is received by the government of country A.

Figure 22.1 Solution

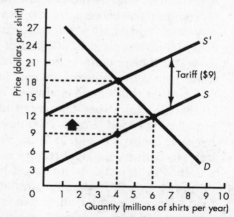

6. a) The quota restricts the quantity that can be imported to 4 million shirts per

year regardless of the price and is represented by a vertical line in Fig. 22.3 (which corresponds to Fig. 22.1). The market for shirts will thus clear at a price of $18 per shirt.

b) This $18 price is received by the people who are given the right to import shirts under the quota. The amount received by the exporter is $9, given by the height of the S curve at a quantity of 4 million shirts per year.

c) Country A will import 4 million shirts per year, the quota limit.

d) The "excess profit" is $9 per shirt (the $18 received by the importer minus the $9 received by the exporter) times 4 million shirts, which is $36 million. This is captured by the importers who have been rewarded by the government of country A since they have been given the right to import under the quota. This is essentially a right to make an "excess profit."

7. a) The effect of a VER of 4 million shirts per year will be the same as a quota of 4 million shirts per year. Indeed, a VER *is* a quota but one which is imposed by the government of the exporting country rather than the government of the importing country. Thus the situation under a VER is illustrated by Fig. 22.3. The price of a shirt will be $18.

b) Country A will import 4 million shirts per year, the VER limit.

c) The "excess profit" is the same as under a quota (Problem 6 (d)), $36 million. The only difference is that it is captured by those persons in the exporting country which have been given the right to export (at the higher price) under the VER.

Figure 22.3

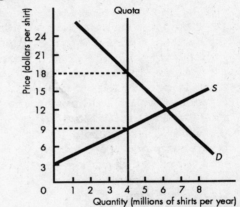

23 ECONOMIC SYSTEMS IN TRANSITION

CHAPTER IN PERSPECTIVE

Through the first 37 chapters of the text we have looked to capitalist economies in general and the U.S. economy in particular both as the object of description and as a source of examples. However, capitalism is not the only system that has been used to solve the fundamental problem of scarcity. Much of the world's population lives in countries with economic systems that have not been capitalist. The first major objective of this chapter is to briefly examine these alternative economic systems. A main focus is on the Soviet-style system of central planning.

Many formerly socialist countries are currently undergoing transitions from centrally planned economies to market economies. This chapter looks at these transitions in progress in the former Soviet Union, in several of the countries of Eastern Europe, and in China. The chapter also briefly discusses alternative strategies for making such a transition.

LEARNING OBJECTIVES

After studying this chapter, you will be able to:

- Describe the fundamental economic problem that confronts all nations

- Describe the alternative systems that have bee used to solve the economic problem

- Describe the Soviet style system of central planning

- Describe the economic problems confronting the former Soviet Union

- Describe the economic problems of other Eastern European countries

- Describe the process of economic change in China

- Describe and evaluate the alternative strategies for making the transition from a centrally planned economy to a market economy

HELPFUL HINTS

1.   It is appropriate that the textbook ends where it began, emphasizing the universal problems that face any economy regardless of the kind of economic system that organizes its economic activity. Foremost among these is the fundamental and universal problem of scarcity, which makes choice necessary. No economic system can eliminate scarcity. Each simply confronts the problem in a different way and thus induces a different incentive structure.

An additional underlying notion that is relevant under any economic system is the postulate of the rationality of economic agents that has been maintained throughout the text. In particular, we have assumed that individuals will pursue their own best interest as they understand it. This is a postulate about basic human attributes and is independent of economic environment. It is the case, however, that the specific way in which that pursuit of self-interest will be manifest will be different under different economic systems since alternative systems provide different incentive structures.   Socialism does not change the desire to pursue one's interest as indicated by the fact that managers of socialist enterprises receive bonuses if they achieve certain targets.

2.   The topic of this chapter is of great current practical interest and likely will continue to be for some time. Much of the socialist world is in a process of reform. In addition to the ongoing economic reforms in China rapid and fundamental changes are also taking place in the republics of the former Soviet Union as well as in other formerly socialist countries of Eastern Europe. It will be interesting for you to examine these changes as they progress using the principles taught here.

KEY FIGURES AND TABLES

Figure 23.1 The Fundamental Economic Problem

The fundamental economic problem is scarcity—households want to consume more goods and services than the available resources allow. Households have preferences about the goods and services they consume and the use of factors of production they control. Factors of production are combined using a technology to produce goods and services. Any economic system must decide *what* goods and services to produce, *how* to produce them (i.e., what technologies to use), and *for whom* to produce them (i.e., how the goods and services will be distributed among households).

Figure 23.2 Alternative Economic Systems

Alternative economic systems differ along two dimensions: (1) the nature of ownership of capital and land, and (2) the type of incentive structure. This figure creates a diagram in these two dimensions in order to easily compare the economic systems of different countries.

On the horizontal scale, the range of capital and land ownership patterns is given with all capital and land owned by individuals at the left and all capital and land owned by the state at the right. On the vertical scale, the range of incentive structures is given with an incentive system bases solely on market prices at the top and an incentive system based on administered prices or sanctions at the bottom. Using these two scales we can place a country in the figure according to its actual system.

The upper-left corner of the space corresponds to capitalism since all capital and land are owned by individuals and the incentive system is based on market prices. Similarly, the lower-right corner corresponds to socialism, the lower-left corner corresponds to welfare state capitalism, and the upper-right corner corresponds to market socialism.

It is useful to note that no country is located exactly at a corner. This reflects the fact that all countries have elements of both capitalism and socialism but differ in degree.

Figure 23.3 Capitalism's Solution to the Economic Problem

Under capitalism, factors of production are privately owned by and under the control of households. The allocation of these factors of production, as well as goods and services produced by firms using them, takes place in response to market incentives without any central planning. Under capitalism, household preferences paramount.

Households plan to sell factors of production in order to buy goods and services; that is., households supply factors of production and demand goods and services. Firms, on the other hand, plan to buy factors of production in order to produce goods and services by some technology chosen by the firm. Firms plan to sell these goods and services to households. Thus, firms demand factors of production and supply goods and services. The plans of households and firms are brought into balance through the operation of factor markets and goods markets. In each of these markets, market prices are determined which equate quantity demanded with quantity supplied.

Changes in market prices have important incentive effects for both households and firms. For example, if the price of labor rises, households have an incentive to increase the quantity of labor they supply and firms have an incentive to reduces the quantity they demand. Under capitalism, the choices of *what*, *how*, and *for whom* are made by the interaction of households and firms in markets.

Figure 23.4 Socialism's Solution to the Economic Problem

Under socialism, as under capitalism, households have preferences about goods and services they consume and about the use of their labor, the only factor of production over which they have any control. However, unlike capitalism, under socialism, capital and land are controlled by central planners who determine *what* goods and services will be produced by state enterprises, *how* they will be produced, and *for whom*. As a result, planners preferences play the predominant role in determining what goods will be available even though households can decide, on the basis of their own preferences, whether or not to buy the goods produced.

Prices are also set by the planners, but not at levels that equate quantity demanded and quantity supplied. As a result, socialist economies experience chronic shortages and surpluses. Rather than price incentives, firms respond to rewards and penalties imposed by superiors.

Table 23.1 A Compact Summary of Key Periods in the Economic History of the Soviet Union

In order to understand the nature and consequences of Soviet socialism, it is important to have a knowledge of the economic history of the Soviet Union since the Bolshevik revolution. The key aspects of that history are summarized here. As a consequence of the Bolshevik revolution under Lenin, the Soviet economic system began to change but the fundamental changes took place under Stalin during the 1930s. The Soviet-style system of planning described in this chapter was largely put in place by Stalin. This compact summary ends with the breakup of the Soviet Union in 1991 and the creation of the Commonwealth of Independent States in 1992.

Table 23.3 A Compact Summary of Key Periods in the Economic History of the People's Republic of China

The People's Republic of China was established in 1949. Since then, the Chinese economic system has undergone several changes. Although at first Mao Zedong followed the Soviet model of socialism, in 1958, he initiated the Great Leap Forward, which was a significant economic reform. It was an economic failure. During the cultural revolution, real GDP actually fell. Since the reforms of 1978 initiated by Deng Xiaoping, however, China has experienced a very rapid rate of growth. These reforms introduced many elements of capitalism into the Chinese economy.

SELF-TEST

CONCEPT REVIEW

1. The universal fundamental economic problem of _____ cannot be abolished by any economic system.

2. A set of arrangements that induce people to take certain actions is a(n) _____ _____.

3. _____ is a system based on private ownership of capital and land and on an incentive system based on market prices. _____ is a system based on state ownership of capital and land and on an incentive system based on administered prices arising from a central economic plan.

4. _____ _____ is an economic system that combines state ownership of capital and land with incentives based on a mixture of market and administered prices. _____ _____ is a system that combines the private ownership of capital and land with state intervention in

markets that change the price signals people respond to.

5. The _____ _____ _____, initiated by Mao Zedong in China, was an economic plan based on small-scale, labor-intensive production.

6. An industry owned and operated by a publicly owned authority directly responsible to the government is called a(n) _____ industry. The process of selling state-owned enterprises is called _____.

TRUE OR FALSE

____ 1. Scarcity is a greater problem for capitalist economies than for socialist economies.

____ 2. Under capitalism all capital is owned by the state.

____ 3. Capitalism has an incentive system based on market prices.

____ 4. Under socialism resources are allocated by freely functioning markets.

____ 5. Under market socialism there is decentralized planning.

____ 6. Under capitalism, household preferences carry the most weight.

____ 7. Great Britain is an example of a pure capitalist economy.

____8. The architect of the economic management system that was used by the Soviet Union beginning in the 1930s was Vladimir Lenin.

____9. A key element of Soviet-style central planning is the iterative nature of the planning process.

____10. During the 1980s, private plots constituted about 25 percent of the agricultural land of the Soviet Union but produced less than 3 percent of total agricultural output.

____11. Money played a very important role in transactions between state enterprise in the Soviet Union.

____12. The central planning system of the Soviet Union could not cope with the transition from an investment to a consumption economy.

____13. Of all the formerly planned economies of Eastern Europe, the transition to a market has been the most dramatic and complete in East Germany.

____14. The Great Leap Forward initiated by Mao Zedong in China in 1958 was one of the significant economic successes in modern China.

____15. Economic growth rates in China have increased considerably since the market-oriented economic reforms initiated by Deng Xiaoping in 1978.

____16. The most rapidly growing sector of the Chinese economy during the 1980s was non-state industrial firms.

____17. The scale of government is larger in Japan than in most other capitalist countries.

____18. In Japan, government economic intervention through the Ministry of Trade and Industry has been pro-business.

____19. In recent years, European welfare states have increasingly been selling state-owned enterprises to private groups.

____20. The fact that the socialist economy is a complete organism supports the case for gradual transition to a market economy.

MULTIPLE CHOICE

1. Which economic system is characterized by private ownership of capital and considerable state intervention in markets?
a. Capitalism.
b. Socialism.
c. Market socialism.
d. Welfare state capitalism.

2. Which economic system is characterized by private ownership of capital and reliance on market prices to allocate resources?
a. Capitalism.
b. Socialism.
c. Market socialism.
d. Welfare state capitalism.

3. Which economic system is characterized by state ownership of capital and reliance on market prices to allocate resources?
a. Capitalism.
b. Socialism.
c. Market socialism.
d. Welfare state capitalism.

4. Which economic system is characterized by state ownership of capital and central planning?
   a. Capitalism.
   b. Socialism.
   c. Market socialism.
   d. Welfare state capitalism.

5. In a socialist economy, prices are set to
   a. achieve equality between demand and supply.
   b. achieve social objectives.
   c. achieve household preferences.
   d. avoid shortages.

6. Which of the following has had a predominantly socialist economic system?
   a. China.
   b. Great Britain.
   c. Japan.
   d. Sweden.

7. The Soviet Union was founded in 1917 following the Bolshevik revolution led by
   a. Boris Yeltsin.
   b. Mikhail Gorbachev.
   c. Joseph Stalin.
   d. Vladimir Ilyich Lenin.

8. The Soviet Union collapsed in 1991 and was replaced by
   a. the Commonwealth of Independent States.
   b. Belorussia.
   c. GOSPLAN.
   d. the Supreme Soviet.

9. Which of the following did NOT exist in the former Soviet Union?
   a. Money.
   b. State enterprises.
   c. Resource markets.
   d. A central planning committee.

10. Which of the following is NOT a key element of Soviet style economic planning and control?
    a. Iterative planning process.
    b. Exchange of money between state enterprises.
    c. Administrative hierarchy.
    d. Taut and inflexible plans.

11. An important reason for the much slower growth rates experienced by the Soviet Union during the 1980s is
    a. the transition from an investment to a consumption economy.
    b. rising oil prices.
    c. high income tax rates.
    d. flexible prices.

12. Which of the following is NOT a major problem confronting the republics of the former Soviet Union as they make the transition to the capitalist economic system?
    a. Collapse of traditional trade flows.
    b. Value and legal systems alien to capitalism.
    c. Fiscal crisis.
    d. Deflation.

13. Which of the formerly planned Eastern European economies has made the transition to a market economy most readily?
    a. Poland.
    b. Czechoslovakia.
    c. East Germany.
    d. Hungary.

14. The People's Republic of China dates from
    a. 1917.
    b. 1927.
    c. 1936.
    d. 1949.

15. During the Great Leap Forward in China under Mao Zedong,
    a. there was a dramatic increase in agricultural production but not industrial production.
    b. the application of new technologies resulted in a significant general increase in production.
    c. China experienced very slow economic growth.
    d. China became a major exporter of grains and cotton.

16. The economic reforms of 1978 under Deng Xiaoping
    a. moved China off the "capitalist road" it had been on under Mao Zedong.
    b. abolished collectivized agriculture.
    c. have resulted in slower economic growth in China.
    d. have made China more dependent on food imports.

17. Which of the following is <u>NOT</u> a feature of China's economic reforms that have resulted in a high rate of economic growth?
    a. Elimination of inflation.
    b. An efficient taxation system.
    c. Gradual price deregulation.
    d. Massive entry of new non-state firms.

18. Which of the following is <u>NOT</u> a feature of the Japanese economy that appears to be responsible for its dramatic economic success?
    a. Reliance on free-market, capitalist methods.
    b. An abundance of natural resources.
    c. Small scale of government.
    d. Pro-business government intervention by the Ministry of Trade and Industry.

19. Which of the following countries has an economic system closest to market socialism?
    a. Japan.
    b. The former Soviet Union.
    c. Yugoslavia.
    d. Great Britain.

20. Which of the following countries has an economic system closest to welfare state capitalism?
    a. Japan.
    b. The former Soviet Union.
    c. Yugoslavia.
    d. Great Britain.

SHORT ANSWER

1. Distinguish between a capitalist economic system and a welfare state capitalist system.

2. Distinguish between a socialist economic system and a market socialist system.

3. Why did the economic growth rate in the Soviet Union decline significantly during the 1970s and 1980s?

4. Why did the Soviet Union experience a high rate of inflation in 1991?

5. Briefly describe the economic reforms proclaimed by Deng Xiaoping in China in 1978. What has been their effect?

6. What choices must be made in the transition from socialism to a market economy?

7. How has the fact that the Japanese government is the smallest (relative to income) in the capitalist world contributed to its rapid growth?

8. What is meant by privatization?

PROBLEMS

1. New Commonwealth (N.C.) is a capitalist country in which markets operate freely and consumers and producers respond to price incentives. Table 23.1 gives the demand and supply schedules for shoes in terms of collars, the currency of N.C.

Table 23.1

Price per pair of shoes (dollars)	Quantity of shoes demanded (millions of pairs)	Quantity of shoes supplied (millions of pairs)
2	4	2
4	3	3
6	2	4
8	1	5

   a) Illustrate the market for shoes in N.C. graphically.
   b) What is the price of a pair of shoes? How many pairs of shoes are produced in N.C.? How many do consumers want to buy?

2. Now, suppose that the demand for shoes in N.C. increases. Quantity demanded increases by 2 million pairs at each price.
   a) Illustrate the change in the shoe market on the same graph you constructed for Problem 1.
   b) What happens to the price of shoes? How does this affect the quantity supplied? The quantity demanded?

3. Bulmania is a socialist country in which the Central Planning Committee (CPC) sets prices and output targets for all goods. Table 23.2 gives the demand schedule for shoes in terms of cubles, the currency of Bulmania. The CPC sets the price at 4 cubles per pair of shoes and the output target at 3 million pairs of shoes.

Table 23.2

Price per pair of shoes (cubles)	Quantity of shoes demanded (millions of pairs)
2	4
4	3
6	2
8	1

   a) Illustrate the market for shoes in Bulmania graphically if the target output of shoes is achieved. How many pairs of shoes are produced and how many do consumers want to buy?
   b) Using the same graph, illustrate the market for shoes if the target level of output is not achieved: Only 2 million pairs of shoes are produced. Why are the quantity supplied and the quantity demanded not brought into equality?

4. Now, suppose that the demand for shoes in Bulmania increases: Quantity demanded increases by 2 million pairs at each price. On a new graph, illustrate the new shoe market in Bulmania if the target output of shoes is achieved. How many pairs of shoes are produced and how many do consumers want to buy? Why are these not brought into equality?

ANSWERS

CONCEPT REVIEW

1. scarcity

2. incentive structure

3. Capitalism; Socialism

4. Market socialism; Welfare state capitalism

5. Great Leap Forward

6. nationalized; privatization

TRUE OR FALSE

1. F	5. T	9. T	13. T	17. F
2. F	6. T	10. F	14. F	18. T
3. T	7. F	11. F	15. T	19. T
4. F	8. F	12. T	16. T	20. F

MULTIPLE CHOICE

1. d	5. b	9. c	13. c	17. a
2. a	6. a	10. b	14. d	18. b
3. c	7. d	11. a	15. c	19. c
4. b	8. a	12. d	16. b	20. d

SHORT ANSWER

1. Both capitalism and welfare state capitalism are characterized by private ownership of capital and land. They differ with regard to incentive structure. Capitalism has an incentive system based on market prices while welfare state capitalism is characterized by considerable state intervention in markets.

2. Both socialism and market socialism are characterized by state ownership of capital and labor. They differ with regard to incentive structure. Under socialism, incentives are based on administered prices or sanctions arising from a central economic plan. Under market socialism, incentives are based on a mixture of market and administered prices.

3. The three major factors contributing to the slow growth of the Soviet economy are: transition from an investment to a consumption economy, external shocks, and taut and inflexible plans.

   It is much easier for a centrally planned economy to accommodate expansion of the capital stock than to handle the complexities of producing a large variety of types, sizes, colors, designs, and styles of consumer goods. As the orientation of the Soviet economy changed in the 1960s to a consumption economy, central planning hindered growth.

   Much of the previous economic growth in the Soviet Union was a result of the rising price of oil and trade with its Eastern European allies. During the 1980s, however, the price of oil fell and the Soviet Union's traditional trading partners initiated economic reforms and began to look west for trading opportunities.

   The inflexibility of central planning did not allow the Soviet Union to adjust to its changing circumstances.

4. During the heyday of central planning, the Soviet government was able to acquire the revenue it needed to finance its expenditures from the profits of state enterprises. With the collapse of central planning, however, this source of revenue was greatly diminished. With no change in spending, the government was forced to run large deficits which it financed by printing money. The result was rapid inflation.

5. In 1978 Deng Xiaoping abolished collective agriculture (state-owned and state-operated farms) and raised prices paid to farmers for many crops. Agricultural land

was leased to farmers for the payment of a fixed tax and a commitment to sell part of its output to the state. The main thing is that individual farmers were free to decide what to plant and how to produce.

Since farmers now were able to profit from their productivity, there were new incentives for efficiency. The effects have been striking. The production of agricultural products increased dramatically with the output of some products (those for which the set price was increased the most) increasing by many times their previous level. China went from being the world's largest importer of agricultural products to being an exporter of these products. The overall growth rate in the economy increased to 7 percent per year.

6. When a country decides to abandon socialism and move toward a market economy it must make three important choices. First, it must decide the style of market economy to adopt. Should it choose U.S. style capitalism, Japanese style capitalism, or some style of welfare state capitalism? Second, it must choose the sequencing of reforms. For example, should prices be deregulated before or after a system of private ownership of capital and land is established? Third, it must decide the speed of reform. Should the transition be undertaken gradually or in a "big bang?"

7. The small scale of the Japanese government, less than one fifth of the economy, means not only that the level of government spending is low but, more important, taxes are low. Thus it is likely that taxes provide less of a disincentive for work and productivity. Lower taxes also usually mean higher saving and therefore more rapid capital accumulation.

8. Privatization is the process of selling state-owned enterprises to private groups. In

recent years, privatization of previously nationalized industries has been increasingly pursued by the Western European welfare state capitalist governments as well as by formerly centrally planned economies of Eastern Europe.

PROBLEMS

1. a) The market for shoes in N.C. is illustrated in Fig. 23.1. The demand curve is given by D_0 and the supply curve by S.

Figure 23.1

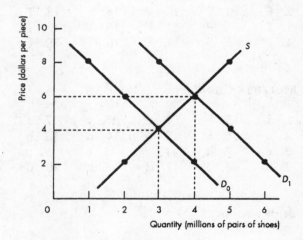

b) From Table 23.1 and Fig. 23.1 we see that the equilibrium market price of a pair of shoes is 4 collars. At this price, the quantity of shoes produced and the quantity desired by consumers are equal at 3 million pairs. In a free market, of course, the price always adjusts so that these quantities are equal.

2. a) The new demand curve is D_1 in Fig.
       23.1. It lies to the right of D_0 by 2
       million pairs of shoes.
    b) The increase in demand creates excess
       demand (a shortage) at the original
       price. This puts upward pressure on
       the price and the excess demand is
       eliminated by the resulting increase in
       quantity supplied and decrease in
       quantity demanded. The new market
       price for a pair of shoes is 6 collars.
       The rise in the price of shoes induces
       producers to increase quantity supplied
       from 3 million to 4 million pairs of
       shoes. It also induces consumers to
       reduce quantity demand from 5 million
       to 4 million pairs of shoes.

3. a) The demand and supply curves in the
       Bulmania shoe market are illustrated in
       Fig. 23.2. The demand curve is given
       by D_0. Because producers do not re-
       spond to prices, the supply curve will
       be vertical at the existing level of out-
       put. Since the target level of output is
       achieved, the supply curve is vertical at
       3 million pairs of shoes and is denoted
       S_0.
           There are 3 million pairs of shoes
       produced. This is independent of the
       price. At the set price of 4 cubles per
       pair, consumers want to buy 3 million
       pairs.

    b) If only 2 million pairs of shoes are
       produced, the supply curve is vertical
       at 2 million as represented by S_1 in Fig.
       23.2. Quantity supplied has fallen to 2
       million pairs of shoes but, at the set
       price of 4 cubles per pair, quantity
       demanded remains at 3 million pairs.
       Thus, there is a shortage of 1 million
       pairs of shoes. Since the price is set by
       the CPC it will not adjust to equate
       quantity supplied and quantity
       demanded.

Figure 23.2

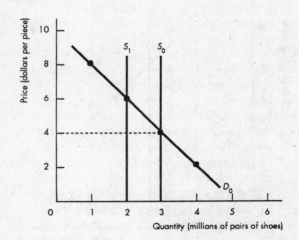

4. The shoe market in Bulmania after the
    increase in demand is given in Fig. 23.3.
    The new demand curve is D_1 and the
    supply curve, S_0, is vertical at 3 million
    pairs of shoes, the target output. While 3
    million pairs of shoes are produced, at the
    CPC administered price of 4 cubles per
    pair, consumers want to buy 5 million
    pairs. Thus, there is a shortage of 2
    million pairs of shoes. As in Problem 3.b),
    the price cannot adjust to bring quantity
    supplied and quantity demanded into
    equality and eliminate the shortage.

Figure 23.3

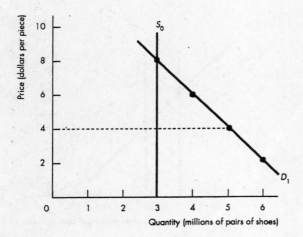